JIMMY
THE KING

JIMMY THE KING

MURDER, VICE, AND THE REIGN OF A DIRTY COP

GUS GARCIA-ROBERTS

PUBLICAFFAIRS
New York

PublicAffairs
Hachette Book Group
1290 Avenue of the Americas, New York, NY 10104
www.publicaffairsbooks.com
@Public_Affairs

Printed in the United States of America

Originally published in hardcover and ebook by PublicAffairs in May 2022
First Trade Paperback Edition: May 2024

Published by PublicAffairs, an imprint of Hachette Book Group, Inc. The PublicAffairs name and logo is a registered trademark of the Hachette Book Group.

The Hachette Speakers Bureau provides a wide range of authors for speaking events. To find out more, go to hachettespeakersbureau.com or email HachetteSpeakers@hbgusa.com.

PublicAffairs books may be purchased in bulk for business, educational, or promotional use. For more information, please contact your local bookseller or the Hachette Book Group Special Markets Department at special.markets@hbgusa.com.

The publisher is not responsible for websites (or their content) that are not owned by the publisher.

Print book interior design by Jeff Williams.

The Library of Congress has cataloged the hardcover as follows:
Names: Garcia-Roberts, Gus, author.
Title: Jimmy the king: murder, vice, and the reign of a dirty cop / Gus Garcia-Roberts.
Description: New York, NY: PublicAffairs, [2022] | Includes bibliographical references.
Identifiers: LCCN 2021056833 | ISBN 9781541730397 (hardcover) |
    ISBN 9781541730380 (ebook)
Subjects: LCSH: Police corruption—New York (State)—New York. |
    Criminal investigation—Corrupt practices—New York (State)—New York. |
    Burke, James Charles.
Classification: LCC HV7936.C85 G37 2022 | DDC 364.1/32309747—dc23/
    eng/20220104

LC record available at https://lccn.loc.gov/2021056833

ISBNs: 9781541730397 (hardcover), 9781541730380 (ebook), 9781541730403 (paperback)

LSC-C

Printing 1, 2024

For Jenny and Frankie

The kids Ed ran with all became hoodlums or cops. The ones that became cops were the ones that the Church got a hook into, the ones that cooked a little bit from guilt. But they all like the same things. They all like to butt heads and loosen people's teeth.

— TOM WOLFE,
BONFIRE OF THE VANITIES

Older teenage boys in packs are like dogs. Fine alone. But when they travel in packs, they feed on each other. And there's always a leader, and it's very difficult for them not to go along.

—EXCLUDED POTENTIAL JUROR
IN JOHN PIUS MURDER RETRIAL, 1989

He taught me if you're dealing with a drunk, keep the whiskey away from him; if you're dealing with a gambler, keep the money away from him; if you're dealing with people who have weaknesses, try to keep them away from the weakness; but there's nothing, nothing in the world you can do to solve the problems of a liar.

— WILLIAM ROSENBERG,
TIME TO MAKE THE DONUTS

CONTENTS

CONTENTS

PART III: THE DUFFEL BAG

A photo section appears after page 238

A NOTE ON SOURCES

This book is a work of nonfiction based on interviews with dozens of subjects and the review of tens of thousands of pages of records, as well as other materials. It includes descriptions of scenes and dialogue that I did not witness firsthand. Those descriptions were credibly drawn from witnesses who were privy to those events, via interviews, court testimony and filings, wiretap logs, and similar sources. Particularly in the final third of the book, the dialogue draws heavily from the testimony and filings of a sprawling federal trial in late 2019, which resulted in conviction by jury, and had one of the central players as its chief witness. In some instances depicted in this book, there were conflicting versions of an event or its dialogue. I sought in every case to portray the most accurate version of events to the best of my ability with the information available to me, which included corroboration through other sources and attempts to reach the people depicted, if they were still alive. More information on the sourcing of specific information is provided in the notes at the end of this book. The names of two individuals, whom I refer to as Doug and Michelle, have been changed because their story includes disputed allegations of domestic violence. The name of another individual, an aide to a public official, was withheld because he was alleged to be the victim of a blackmail scheme involving his sexuality, though he denies that allegation. With the exception of a major character pivotal to the story, I also chose not to name James Burke's girlfriends in order to protect their personal privacy.

CAST OF CHARACTERS

THE INNER CIRCLE

James "Jimmy" Burke—Chief of Department, Suffolk County Police Department

Thomas Spota—Suffolk County District Attorney

Chris McPartland—Chief, Government Corruption Bureau of the Suffolk County DA's office

James Hickey—Commanding Officer, SCPD Criminal Intelligence Bureau

William Madigan—Chief of Detectives, SCPD

JIMMY BURKE'S FAMILY, FRIENDS—AND LOWRITA

George Burke—father

Frances Burke—mother

Michael Burke—younger brother

John Toal—stepfather

John Toal Jr.—half-brother via same mother

George "Junie" Burke—half-brother via same father

Anthony D'Orazio—childhood friend

Dennis Sullivan—sector car partner

Sanjiv "Sammy" Panchal—tech consultant

John Rodriguez—SCPD detective and Burke loyalist

Lowrita Rickenbacker—lover

CAST OF CHARACTERS

THE PIUS CASE

John "Johnny" Pius—thirteen-year-old homicide victim, 1979

John Pius Jr. and Barbara Pius—Johnny's parents

Tony Cannone—Johnny's cousin

Anthony Palumbo, Thomas Gill, Richard Reck, Gary Leonard, Richard Jensen, Jack Miller—homicide detectives who worked Pius case

Robert V. Burke, Eddie Pembroke, Michael O'Neill, John Sparling, Raymond St. Denis—Pius suspects

Michael Quartararo, Peter Quartararo, Robert Brensic, Thomas Ryan—Pius defendants

Jimmy Burke, Michael Burke, Danny Culotta, John McCort, David O'Brien, George Heiselmann—teenage witnesses in Pius trials

Thomas Spota, William Keahon, Timothy Mazzei—Pius prosecutors, along with Spota

THE SUFFOLK COUNTY MILIEU

Stuart Namm—whistleblowing judge

Dennis Rafferty, James McCready, August Stahl—homicide detectives who helped secure false convictions

Gerald Sullivan—Spota's longtime legal partner

Martin Tankleff—teenager wrongfully convicted of murdering parents

Bruce Barket—Tankleff's attorney

Lindsay Henry—DA, 1947–53

Henry O'Brien—DA, 1975–77

Eugene Kelley—SCPD Commissioner who warred with O'Brien

Patrick Henry—DA, 1978–90

James Catterson—DA, 1990–2001

Steve Levy—County Executive, 2004–11

Richard Dormer—SCPD Commissioner 2004–11

Steve Bellone—County Executive, 2012–

Edward Webber—SCPD Commissioner, 2012–2015

Richard Schaffer—Democratic Party chairman

Frank MacKay—Independence Party chairman

Edward Walsh Jr.—Conservative Party chairman

THE LOEB CASE

Christopher Loeb—heroin addict and petty criminal

Gabe Miguelez—Loeb's partner in crime

Kenneth Bombace, Tony Leto, Michael Malone—Burke's "palace guard" detectives

Frank Catalina, Brian Draiss, Mike Kelly, Francine Ruggiero, Chris Nealis, Kenneth Regensburg, Keith Sinclair—Fourth Precinct police and probation officers

Spiros Moustakas—Government Corruption Bureau attorney who initially prosecuted Loeb

Peter Crusco—Special prosecutor assigned to case from Queens DA's office

Jeremy Bell, Ryan Carey—Manhattan-based FBI special agents

April Brooks—Bell and Carey's FBI boss

Joe Conway—Jimmy Burke's attorney

Russ McCormack, Noel DiGerolamo, Billy Plant, Lou Tutone, Timmy Morris—SCPD union officials

Loretta Lynch, Nicole Boeckmann, Bill Hessle, Ray Tierney, Lara Treinis Gatz—law enforcement officials, Eastern District of New York

JIMMY BURKE'S ENEMIES

John Oliva, Robert Trotta—SCPD detectives removed from federal task force

Tania Lopez—*Newsday* reporter

Patrick Cuff—Internal Affairs Bureau official who became assistant chief

Vincent DeMarco—Suffolk County Sheriff

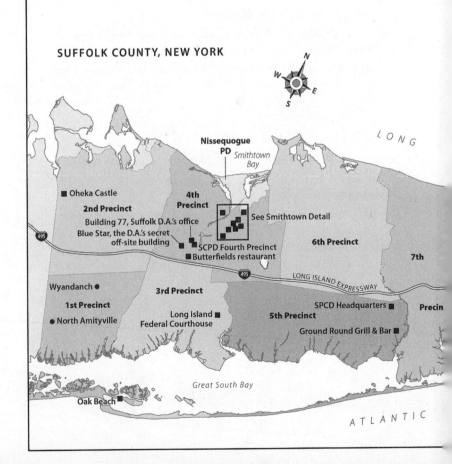

SUFFOLK COUNTY, NEW YORK

N
W · E
S

Nissequogue
PD
*Smithtown
Bay*

LONG

■ Oheka Castle

2nd Precinct

**4th
Precinct**

Building 77, Suffolk D.A.'s office

Blue Star, the D.A.'s secret
off-site building

■ See Smithtown Detail

6th Precinct

■ SCPD Fourth Precinct
■ Butterfields restaurant

7th

495

LONG ISLAND EXPRESSWAY

Wyandanch ●

3rd Precinct

1st Precinct

495

● North Amityville

Long Island ■
Federal Courthouse

SPCD Headquarters ■

Precin

5th Precinct

Ground Round Grill & Bar ■

Great South Bay

Oak Beach ●

ATLANTIC

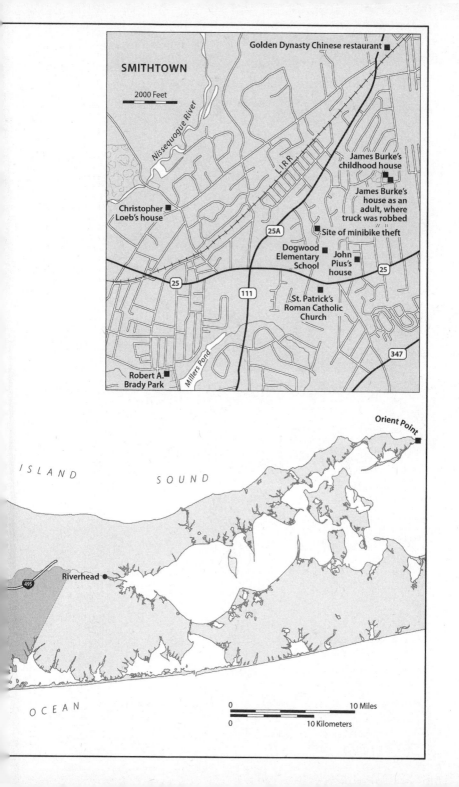

SMITHTOWN

2000 Feet

Golden Dynasty Chinese restaurant

Nissequogue River

L.I.R.R.

Christopher Loeb's house

James Burke's childhood house

James Burke's house as an adult, where truck was robbed

Site of minibike theft

25A

Dogwood Elementary School

John Pius's house

25

25

111

St. Patrick's Roman Catholic Church

347

Robert A. Brady Park

Millers Pond

Orient Point

I S L A N D   S O U N D

495

Riverhead

O C E A N

0   10 Miles

0   10 Kilometers

JIMMY
THE KING

SMITHTOWN

December 14, 2012

The moment Christopher Loeb suspected he had broken into a cop's SUV—finding a bolted-down box in the boot that he was pretty sure contained a gun—he probably should have gingerly closed the door of the black GMC Yukon and scurried down the street. But if you're out at four in the morning, tramping along snow-covered sidewalks in Polo sneakers with your sweatshirt sleeve wrapped around your hand, looking for unlocked vehicles and making off with other people's parking meter change and GPS devices, discretion may not be your first priority.

"Jigging whips" was Chris's term of art for this activity. In the estimation of Gabriel Miguelez, the accomplice who waited behind the steering wheel in the heated cab of a battered red Dodge pickup truck, Chris's methods were utter amateurism. Gabe was older—thirty-six to Chris's twenty-six, and something of a criminal mentor. He had taught Chris how to shatter a car window quietly, without leaving prints, just by throwing a handful of pebbles at it. But Chris was a purist of sorts. He was determined to stick to door jiggling, the least sophisticated entry in the criminal syllabus.

Gabe watched Chris hustle back from the Yukon, which was parked in the driveway of a two-level home, adorned with white vinyl siding and pinkish brick, on the corner of Fifty Acre Road and Sammis Street in suburban Suffolk County. Chris's black sweatpants drooped from his emaciated ass. When Chris was clean, he had an athletic build, along with a frenetic sense of humor that paired with his hazel eyes and a sideways smile. But now he looked like he was in the grips of a famine: scabbed skin, sunken cheeks, a dull gaze, and a gaunt frame. He weighed in at much less than the 150 pounds listed on his arrest records for addiction-fueled petty crimes, like tonight's.

Gabe had a hulking build and green eyes that often seemed to flash with hurt feelings, typically spelling bad news for the person who had offended him. When he was a kid, his father, a Uruguayan jeweler in Manhattan, followed the upwardly mobile New Yorker's handbook and moved his family to Lindenhurst, Long Island. There, Gabe learned that classmates would quit calling you spic and beaner after you attacked one of them with a hammer. He had served time upstate for setting fire to a bar to settle a beef with a bouncer.

Gabe and Chris had little in common besides heroin and a related chronic cash shortage. Hopefully whatever Chris had found in the Yukon and the rest of the cars that night would help with that. Chris tossed his haul—a black duffel bag with a Police Athletic League logo—in the back of the pickup, adorned with bumper stickers announcing Gabe's particular worldview: "Obama-Biden 2012"; "Unions: The Anti-Theft Device for Working People"; and "I ♥ Class Warfare."

April 20, 1979

Robert Brensic, a seventeen-year-old paperboy, was enamored.

His crush was a sky-blue motorized minibike. Or at least it had been a motorized minibike before it lost its engine, seat, brakes, and handlebar grips. What was left, stashed by the garbage cans outside of somebody's newly constructed split-level home, was a curved metal frame, rusted at the ends and joints, sitting on knobby tires low on air.

When he first spotted it on his afternoon route, Rob saw not the neglected remains of some kid's long-ago birthday present but a miniature chopper with a sissy bar—or tall backrest—like Peter Fonda's bike in *Easy Rider*. And its model name was painted on a front metal placard in badass flaming script: "Blue Blazer."

Rob's two central passions were smoking weed and restoring small, feral machinery. His black-fingered skills with bike engines had earned him the mostly derisive nickname Motorhead from his peers at Smithtown High School East. He already had a minibike, which he had jury-rigged with a fishing line for a throttle, but now he envisioned restoring the Blue Blazer to new, noisy glory and giving it to his buddy Mike Quartararo so that they could irritate their neighbors together.

At dusk on the Friday of Easter break, Rob made the case to the three other teenage occupants of a bright yellow Mercury Capri that acquiring the minibike was worthy of the time that could otherwise be spent pounding Miller miniatures in the woods. Sitting shotgun, Rob had directed the Capri's driver, Thomas Ryan, to the under-development cul-de-sac where he had seen the minibike. Tom rebutted Rob's enthusiasm with an intriguing counterpoint: the minibike wasn't theirs to take.

Rob Brensic and Tom Ryan were both seventeen-year-old products of the same sheltered, lily-white suburb, but they were an odd pair. Whereas Rob delivered copies of *Newsday* with a water bong lashed to his bike, Tom, at seventeen, was "the old man of the group," as his girlfriend put it, treating his job bussing tables at the local kosher deli as seriously as any white-collar position with a pension.

Whatever earnings Tom didn't sock away he poured into the Capri, making it perhaps the loudest privately owned vehicle in Smithtown. He had lifted the car on thick tires outfitted with shiny new rims, and he'd redone the carburetor, camshaft, and muffler and exhaust system with a racing setup that could drown out conversation while idling.

Tom couldn't understand why Rob, rather than spending his time coveting somebody else's busted minibike frame, didn't busy himself with more adult matters like buying a car and making it obscenely loud, or scouting for a girlfriend, or trying to get into a college that didn't have "Technical" in its title. The only interest Tom and Rob shared, the only reason they were in the same car, was pot. Rob had some, and Tom had a new pipe for them to christen later.

Rob spoke in a stoner's lilt, slurred sentences that petered out into self-conscious chuckles. "It's in a frickin' garbage pile," he argued. But he still wasn't about to just knock on the door at Wheelright Way and ask if he could have the minibike.

Mike and Peter Quartararo were bystanders to the debate, squeezed into the car's back seat with their sneakers mashing a bed of discarded burger wrappers. Peter, the older Quartararo brother, was Tom's best friend. Pete was as straitlaced as Tom, but in a more childlike way. He was almost sixteen years old and still collecting Boy Scout patches. Fourteen-year-old Mike would later be termed this crew's "hard case," though there is little evidence that before that night this crew had a reputation for being very hard at all. The brothers' parents had divorced, roughly four years earlier. The split seemed to play a role in turning Mike from a sharp kid dutifully reciting the Catechism at Sunday school to a smirking truant who hid his baby-fat face behind shaggy hair.

After Tom made it clear that there was no way he would let Rob just toss the minibike in the trunk of his extremely recognizable vehicle, the spirit of compromise prevailed. Tom drove to the end of the cul-de-sac, silenced the Capri's engine, and waited for dark. Then Rob walked back up the street, grabbed the minibike, and started to run while pushing it back to the car.

There was a ghost town vibe to the cul-de-sac. The house with the minibike was one of the few finished homes in a tract development called Point of Woods. Ten years before, Suffolk County was mostly potato fields and country roads. But developers were busy turning the eastern end of Long Island into a Shangri-la of split-level ranches as far as the eye could see, catering to hundreds of thousands of white, middle-class families from the outer boroughs of New York City forty miles to the west. For a low four-figure down payment, parents could buy safety and better futures for their children. Their aspirations were right there on the street signs, which bore the names of colleges Smithtown-raised children were expected to attend: Baylor, Dartmouth, Penn, Hofstra, Rutgers.

As Rob pushed the minibike, three little kids on skateboards appeared out of nowhere and spooked Tom, who brought the Capri to life and roared out of the cul-de-sac. That left Rob to push the minibike through a little trail in some woods up a small hill to the parking lot behind the Dogwood Elementary School, where he knew by ear that the Capri was waiting. Once in the parking lot, Rob hopped on the bike, grabbed hold of the car, and yelled to Tom to gun it.

At that moment, another group of boys walked through the parking lot. They were headed to Point of Woods to drink beers in a vacant house. They beheld the sight of Rob Brensic straddling a stripped minibike as it clunked along on flat tires. Rob steered the bike with his left hand as he used his right to grip a door handle of the little yellow pony car badly in need of a muffler. The tow didn't work as planned, and Rob yelled for Tom to stop before his arm got yanked from its socket. Rob threw the minibike in the Capri's trunk and hopped inside. Then they disappeared from view.

It was just before 8:30 p.m. Whether Rob, as he was loading the minibike in the trunk, saw at that moment another boy ride past them on the school grounds would be a point of contention for decades of court proceedings. But for now, *The Incredible Hulk* was on TV, and the boys in the Capri were on schedule to get to Mike and Peter's house in time to catch Lou Ferrigno turn green with rage.

2012

Chris and Gabe drove for roughly six minutes along silent suburban streets past sizable homes and snow-covered yards before the neighborhood got more rugged and woodsy. They turned down the long driveway of a grubby, 1960s-era four-bedroom home sheathed in frayed brown shingles and overgrown ivy.

This was Chris's mom's house, which, through no fault of her own, had become a hub for his increasingly feverish criminal schemes. The living room featured a brick wall charred messily by its fireplace, a mushy gray couch in front of a coffee table on top of a drab rug, and a tank that was home to a turtle named Gus.

Strewn among this decor: an Infiniti-branded car first aid kit, an assemblage of used baseball gloves, and a duffel bag stuffed with random items that included the cookbook *365 Ways to Cook Chicken*. This was only part of Chris's collection of boosted stuff. In his small bedroom off the living room, contraband was piled up and mixed in with the typical accessories of heroin use—used hypodermic needles, cotton balls, and rubber bands that had once tied up bundles.

Gabe was so skilled at fencing stolen loot online that he earned the nickname "Craigslist Guy." But his partner had an unusual trait for an addict: Chris refused to sell stolen goods at too steep of a discount, resulting in him hoarding other people's things: Torn-open Christmas presents that would never see the underside of a tree. A Mac laptop containing a doctor's life's work of cancer research. Golf clubs pilfered from a social worker's Prius. A Yankee Candle; a Leatherman knife; somebody's prescription glasses; and a small collection of driver's licenses, credit cards, and gift cards to Starbucks, Macy's, and Vera Bradley. Enough GPS devices to fill an aisle at Radio Shack.

The bag marked with PAL, logo of the Police Athletic League, tossed on Chris's sheetless, cigarette-scorched bed was the latest acquisition. Chris pulled out a gun belt. It didn't include a gun, though it did have two clips of ammunition, a canister of mace spray, a flashlight, and a whistle. The potential for trouble was obvious. "Why'd you even take this?" Gabe demanded. But his concern didn't stop him from grabbing the belt, trying it on, and doing some high-noon pantomiming.

Chris further rifled through the bag. Inside was a box of cigars and a miniature humidor. Then Chris reached into a side pocket of the gym bag, and there he felt something he didn't expect: slime.

April 28, 1979

"So it all starts over a minibike," the detective remarked to the weepy kid in his rearview mirror. "That fucking minibike, huh?"

Anthony Palumbo, a highly animated detective with big ears and thick eyebrows adorning a doughy cranium, wasn't supposed to be on this case. He had the case of a shot-to-death bank robber, folded into the trunk of a Pontiac in North Babylon, to solve. But a thirteen-year-old churchgoing Caucasian boy had been found slaughtered in the woods over a week ago. That sort of suburban existential crisis required all hands on deck, including one of the homicide squad's top confession-getters.

In Suffolk County, homicide detectives rarely if ever closed a case with forensics. No pinkie ring–wearing, Drakkar-doused homicide bull was going to wait on a lab technician to tell them what blood type was gleaned from the spittle on a discarded cigarette butt found near a corpse. The preferred way to solve a murder in Suffolk County was to first divine who did it, a skill requiring a seasoned detective's uncanny and unteachable intuition. The second, even more pivotal step was to get the person who did it in a room and not allow them out until they admitted it, preferably with a signed confession and no visible bruises. Because everybody knew innocent people didn't confess to murder.

The kid in the back seat was slightly big for his age—five-foot-eight and 140 pounds in the tenth grade, with straight black hair parted in the middle. He had never previously been within sniffing distance of any trouble. He was a Boy Scout. He built models. Like Rob, he delivered *Newsday*. He planned on joining the Navy. Peter Quartararo wasn't the only Smithtown boy that week, or even that day, who the homicide squad had yanked off the street and pressed for a confession to the murder in the woods. But he was the first one to oblige them.

"Where should I start, when we picked up the minibike?" Peter asked. Palumbo and his partner snuck a look at each other, hoping the tape recorder below the driver's seat was picking this up.

2012

Coated in lube, along with the sex toys and porn, were a handful of driver's license–sized plastic cards. They read "Suffolk Detective Association" over an icon of a badge. Under the badge, in white capital letters: "Chief of Department." The cards drove home the predicament the two thieves faced. Possessing the stolen gun belt was a felony charge. The sleazy stuff in the bag was embarrassing enough to motivate the rightful owner to retaliate. And the cards confirmed that the rightful owner wasn't just a cop but the top cop in Suffolk County's massive police department.

There was only one logical next step: bring the bag and gun belt back to the Yukon and stash it where they found it before the chief ever realized his party bag had been stolen. Instead, Chris and Gabe shot up heroin. Afterward, while Gabe gathered pilfered center-console change and went to 7-Eleven for Marlboros, Chris passed out on a futon. At around 10:00 a.m., he awoke to the smell of batter sizzling on the griddle.

In a just world, Jane Loeb would've had a squeaky-clean, sitcom-style family. She had lived here on Landing Avenue in Smithtown for five decades, worked for the town legal department for more than four of them, and was a knitting enthusiast. Instead she had a heavy-drinking husband and two drug users, Chris and his older brother, Frank, for sons. But Jane Loeb still babied Chris. If there was a silver lining to your son being too strung out to hold a job, it was this: he was always home in the morning for pancakes.

Just as Chris was about to sit down for some flapjacks, he spotted a blue Ford Taurus turning into the drive. One benefit of a very long driveway, Chris already knew, was it gave you some lead time. As he sprinted for the back door, he yelled for Gabe to hide the gun belt. He ran into the woods behind the house just as the air filled with the crackle of cops shouting logistics into their radios.

Careening around the house and into the woods after him was a barrel-chested probation officer with a blond buzz cut and goatee who was almost immediately out of breath by the pursuit. This guy was Special Operations for probation, which meant raids were his forte though he wasn't used to, as his colleague later described that terrain, a "hilly backyard" with "trees . . . leaves and stuff."

Special Ops kept losing things from his belt, and as he scrambled to find his flashlight and continue up the hill, Chris tried to use his home-field advantage to elude him. He buried himself with sticks and leaves on the floor of the woods just before Teapot Lane. Listening to the wheezing probation officer stomp by looking for him, Chris fell asleep. He was jarred awake when the big cop mashed his face into the soil, cuffed him, and lifted him out of his bed of leaves and sticks.

* * *

"This isn't *Law & Order*," spat Tony Leto, his thick hands gripping the trachea of the shackled prisoner who had just asked him for a lawyer.

Tony was a muscular detective with a shaved head, dark eyes, and leering, arched eyebrows. It had been Chris Loeb's poor luck that morning that the probation department had planned a search of his house on the same day he happened to have contraband from the chief's truck in his bedroom. Tony leaned into his ear and cooed in a laconic cadence about how Chris's mother was going to be arrested for the stolen shit in her house, and get raped in jail.

Tony Leto and two fellow detectives, Kenneth Bombace and Michael Malone, were working on Chris in Interview Room Number 3 of the Suffolk County Police Department's Fourth Precinct in Hauppauge. It was the height of corporate gulag decor. The room consisted of scuffed linoleum floors, white-painted cinder block walls, a white noise machine to drown out shouting, and no recording equipment of any kind. Seated in a metal chair, Loeb was handcuffed to a circular ring in the floor by a thick chain. The three cops were dressed in plain clothes and dad jeans.

Kenny and Mike took their own turns slapping Loeb around. This was an exciting moment for the guys of the Criminal Intelligence Unit, but not because of the caliber of the criminal before them. To them, Loeb was nothing more than a minor societal leech, an opioid goblin who filled his bedroom in his mom's house with the pilfered belongings of taxpayers. The Intel guys were an elite squad who typically dabbled in more high-profile and, frankly, cooler matters such as gangs, guns, and terrorism. But all that mattered was whose car this junkie had been caught stealing from that morning.

They were always eager to prove their loyalty to the chief. Typically such opportunities involved surveillance, like spying on the county executive, or putting a GPS on the deputy police commissioner's car, or tailing the stepson of the chief's girlfriend, hoping to catch him driving drunk. Now they actually had some excitement along with their two grand in combined daily pay—plus accruing pensions—in trying to slap a confession out of a door jiggler. But they were increasingly frustrated by this junkie, who cursed, spat, ranted about "nasty porn," and even dozed off instead of copping to the theft.

Loeb, drifting in and out of consciousness, was not aware that he had worn the detectives down, and he was barely aware that they had even left the room. After a few minutes, they returned to Interview Room Number 3 with a fourth cop joining the interrogation. The man was beefy and middle-aged, with neatly parted salt-and-pepper hair and a mustache shaved down to its bristles. This, it was clear, was the boss.

Jimmy Burke's usually pasty skin had burned red during a sunny three-week vacation to Turks and Caicos. He was dressed in a civilian suit. It was holiday party season, but the chief had heard what was happening and decided—against all police protocol and anything resembling good judgment—to drop by the Fourth to see for himself.

No way he was going to miss this. It was just like the good old days.

PART I

MURDER

James Burke, Smithtown High
School East yearbook, 1982

CHAPTER 1

HE WAS GONE

On an afternoon in March 1965, a young Queens couple, John and Barbara Pius, and their infant nephew Tony, were driving along Cross Bay Boulevard when a vehicle being pursued by police smashed into their rear going a hundred miles per hour. The fugitives in the other car were ejected from their vehicle and one of them died in the street. The Pius car overturned and burst into flames.

Somehow the Piuses and baby Tony survived, and so did the fetus in nineteen-year-old Barbara's belly. She was confined to a bed for the remainder of her pregnancy, and doctors told her that the baby, her first, would be the only one she could bear.

On August 1, 1965, John Anthony Pius was born. His parents nicknamed him Johnny, or John Boy, to differentiate him from his father and grandfather, who were both also named John. The turbulent pregnancy served to make Johnny particularly precious to Barbara.

Within a year, the new parents had resolved to move from Ridgewood to Smithtown. They chose a pink-and-red brick house with a picture window in front, a pool in the backyard, and a basement they planned to convert into an apartment for Johnny's grandparents. But Barbara had one last requirement before they dropped the down payment on the $17,000 home. She went door-to-door to the nearly identical houses surrounding it on Franklin Drive, vetting the neighbors. The potential neighbors that Barbara would've met were middle-class strivers of every stripe, though only one color.

The county's population had boomed from 276,000 in 1950 to more than 1.1 million twenty years later, and Smithtown was the epicenter of that transformation. Its population had grown exponentially from roughly 14,000 residents to nearly 115,000. More than 98 percent of those Smithtown residents were white—Manifest Destiny meets *Leave It to Beaver*.

Leaving the brown people behind was a principal driver of the boom in Smithtown, as it was in nearly every other suburb on Long Island. Nassau County, between Suffolk and the city boroughs of Queens and Brooklyn, was the home of the model modern suburb of Levittown, where the leases had stated that the home could "not be used or occupied by any person other than members of the Caucasian race." Suffolk County was even more hostile, a onetime Ku Klux Klan stronghold that included an enclave of Nazi sympathizers who had named streets after Adolf Hitler and Joseph Goebbels and where, until 2017, residents of the enclave were required to be of Germanic extraction.

One precept of the white flight into Nassau and Suffolk was that crime didn't take the Long Island Expressway. The Piuses' new neighbors kept the doors to their homes and cars unlocked. They allowed their children to bike, skate, and stroll unsupervised, and they even tolerated teenage hitchhiking. One of Johnny Pius's classmates recalled the collective parenting style as "free-range kids."

By Easter vacation in 1979, Johnny, thirteen, appeared to be leading the kind of wholesome, active childhood his parents had sought for him when they brought him to Smithtown as an infant: biking, camping, fishing, lacrosse, football, karate, and cartoons. His favorites were *The Flintstones*, *Jonny Quest*, and *Scooby-Doo*. His older cousin Tony, who was partially raised by the Piuses, says that Johnny dressed up as a fireman for Halloween and some days seemed likely to pursue that as a career. "But he also wanted to be a wrestler too, one week," Tony said of Johnny, whose idol was the headdress-wearing Chief Jay Strongbow.

Johnny spent Friday, April 20, 1979, fishing with a friend on a pier over an inlet of the Long Island Sound, six miles north of his house. On his bicycle ride back, he stopped to play some basketball.

He then realized he had a flat tire, and so his dad came to pick him up from a friend's house.

Early that evening, Johnny and his best friend Eddie Pembroke, who lived a few houses away, chatted as they tossed a lacrosse ball back and forth. The two kids were engaged in a mild conspiracy. Most nights, they went in the cover of darkness to steal scrap lumber from Point of Woods, an under-construction cul-de-sac a few minutes by bike from their houses. They were using the lumber to build a treehouse in the woods behind a nearby elementary school. They had worked on the treehouse the two nights before and had loose plans to do it again that night. Johnny told Eddie he'd call, but then never did. His friend thought nothing of it.

* * *

The next afternoon, seemingly all of the neighborhood had descended on the area behind the Dogwood Elementary School. Family, friends, and neighbors had been searching for Johnny Pius since that morning. Among the searchers were the elder John Piuses, Johnny's father and grandfather. They were there because they finally had some kind of news: a kid had found Johnny's wallet at the edge of the woods behind the school.

Dogwood was a squat, low-slung brick building in the shape of the letter T. Behind it was a play area, patchy with sand and grass, with a couple of nets for soccer, metal slides and monkey bars, and a mangy baseball diamond. The grass throughout the play area was marked with the curlicues of tire tracks, likely the work of bored teenagers doing donuts. The woods sloped downward for several hundred yards until they ended at the Jericho Turnpike, an artery cutting through Smithtown.

Johnny's father, a muscular man in his late thirties, had trudged down the hill nearly all the way to the turnpike when he heard shouting from those closer to the school: "They found him! They found him!"

Pius ran back and met his own father, standing at the crest of the hill. The older man tried to stop his son. "It's the worst," Johnny's grandfather shouted.

"Where is he?" Johnny's father demanded. He ran to where his neighbor, Joe Sabina, had covered something on the ground with his blue jacket.

"He's gone," Sabina said.

"I want to see him," John Pius demanded. "Take your jacket off of him."

Sabina relented. Pius looked and then ran to his car, screaming. He sped the half-mile home to the pink-and-red brick house with the picture window. "Johnny is dead," he told Barbara, and then punched a hole in a closet door.

* * *

It appeared at first glance like somebody had forgotten their windbreaker on the sparse forest floor. But then you saw a flash of white, the pale small of a boy's back, and with it the vague form of a body buried in leaves.

Detective Thomas Gill asked the uniformed cop on the scene to remove the jacket. That exposed the left side of a boy's face, turned up from the woods floor in the style of a swimmer getting air. He had delicate, sulking features, with plentiful dark hair, thin black eyebrows, big eyelashes over closed eyes, and swollen blue lips, all dusted with bits of leaves.

The boy's blue sweatshirt had ridden up his back nearly to his shoulder blades, with the hood partly pulled up over the back of his head. His lower back was red in places, and showed vertical scratch marks, perhaps from being dragged. He wore blue jeans smudged through with dirt. He was covered in a thin layer of leaves and had a log placed perpendicularly over his legs, suggesting somebody had done a poor job of trying to hide him.

Closer to the school, and near where the wallet had been found, the boy's bicycle was leaning against a tree. It was a brown-and-white Huffy Santa Fe. There were apparent drag marks leading from the area where the wallet had been found to the site of the boy's body.

Gill was a short, well-built man with blue eyes and red hair turning sandy with age. Under his dress shirt he had "USN" tattooed on his right upper arm and "Singapore" tattooed on the left, reminders of the six years he had spent in the Navy in the 1950s. Gill fit the very distinct mold of a Suffolk County homicide bull: masculine, well-paid, and unscientific, a studier less of crime scenes than of the criminal mind, which he was cocky about his ability to identify and crack.

This particular crime scene had been heavily trampled. Young baseball players in uniform, housewives in jogging suits, and children with bicycles milled about nearby, their footprints mingling with the possible drag marks. It looked like somebody had pulled police rope through a Norman Rockwell tableau, murder interrupting an early spring Saturday afternoon in the American suburbs.

Gill barked at the rubberneckers to back up and ordered a uniformed cop to cordon off more of the perimeter. Joe Sabina told Gill that he had removed a second log from across Johnny's torso.

Wheels crunched to a stop near the crime scene, the car tagged with a license plate reading "FORENSIC." This was the unsubtle ride of forensic serologist Ira DuBey, a big, puffed-chested man with neatly parted black hair. The Suffolk homicide squad appreciated DuBey for girding, not guiding, their investigations. He backed up their suspicions with confidently stated science, and juries believed him thanks to his recitation of intimidating academic credentials.

There was a play-acting quality to DuBey's vanity plates, and to the way he bent over the crime scene and bagged about ten cigarette butts around the body, as if he was going to test them. Testing the butts, even in the days before DNA analysis, could've revealed the blood type of the smoker, but DuBey didn't actually do it. Though it was Johnny's killer who had presumably placed the logs on his body, DuBey also didn't collect them to inspect for possible fibers or other evidence.

Gill wasn't exactly a by-the-manual adherent to the rules of physical evidence himself. In fact, he had never read the manual. Gill had been a homicide detective for more than a dozen years, making him the most senior member of the unit. But that seniority wasn't necessarily a desirable thing. Cops are transferred upon promotion, and Gill had twice during his homicide tenure taken the sergeant's exam. Both times, he hadn't fared well enough to earn the bump.

Gill had no homicide training. The only special training Gill received at all upon being promoted to the rank of detective in 1967 was a course sponsored by Diebold, the manufacturer of safes and vaults. It was perhaps unlikely that his knowledge of that company's drill-proof armor and bolts was going to help him figure out who deposited this dead kid in these woods. In fact, an absence of homicide training was the norm among the Suffolk squad. Even Gill's boss—the commander of the homicide squad—didn't have any specialized homicide training at the time. Which is not to say Gill couldn't read a clue, particularly when it had been stomped into his victim's face.

A police photographer took shots of the scene, including of the Huffy leaning against the tree. Then they flipped the boy's body, exposing for the first time the entirety of Johnny's face—scraped, battered, swollen, and caked with coagulated blood. On his right jaw, there was a clear imprint of a small diamond cut through by two intersecting lines. A sneaker print.

* * *

Johnny had something in his mouth: a rock, about the size of a marble, secreted under his tongue. Later that evening, when the boy was on a slab in the medical examiner's office in Hauppauge, a coroner noted the constellations of trauma on the nude 116-pound corpse. There were contusions and hemorrhages stretching from his right ear down through that side of his jaw, neck, shoulder, and chest. The most shocking visible damage appeared to be concentrated around Johnny's neck, jaw, and upper torso. The severity of the trauma inflicted on him had left his skin there an angry, volcanic red, laced through with lines of his natural hue like marbling on a steak.

And then there was that sneaker sole imprint, which the coroner described as resembling a "Greek cross." Johnny's eyes were shot through with blood, a possible indication of suffocation. But there is a bone in the neck that often breaks during strangulation, and Johnny's was intact, so it wasn't immediately clear what had caused him to suffocate. Then the coroner x-rayed his head and throat.

He later handed his colleague DuBey a vial. Inside were six small, smooth rocks the coroner had scrubbed clean after fishing them out of Johnny's mouth and upper larynx, where somebody had jammed them.

* * *

At the time, the Suffolk County homicide squad's de facto policy concerning record keeping was to do as little of it as possible. The detectives avoided taking notes when at a crime scene or interviewing a witness or suspect, because those notes could then become ammunition for the defense. Instead, their practice was to lean back in a chair at Homicide HQ and dictate their recollections to their female secretaries to type up. But even those resulting supplemental reports were carefully rationed, so as not to memorialize abandoned leads and alternative suspects that a defense lawyer might use to infuse a jury with doubt.

Detective Gill was a devoted adherent to these practices. Defense attorneys attempting to exercise their right of access to records in their clients' cases had to first endure Gill's brand of police report three-card monte. In the Pius case, Gill first said under oath that he didn't take any notes at the crime scene or in ensuing interviews. In later proceedings, he clarified that he took "mental notes." He then said he did take notes, but he destroyed them when he dictated supplemental reports. He initially said he produced fifteen supplemental reports, but then he said he was wrong, and had only made five or six of them.

Gill's attitude toward written statements from witnesses was just as arbitrary. When he finally produced his casework, the reports and the written statements often contradicted each other and weren't consistent with his later court testimony. It all served to muddy a case so badly that a defense attorney could make little sense of it.

One of the supplemental reports that Gill did turn over concerned his investigation on the day that he responded to the Pius murder scene. The report had the date of the next day, April 22, but Gill later stated that was an error. In the report, he noted a few of the bystanders that he spoke to at the scene, including a paper boy on his bicycle route, named Robert Brensic.

Gill and his partner, Detective Richard Reck, afterward drove the half-mile route that prosecutors and defense attorneys would spend the next two-plus decades scrutinizing. It was three turns in quick succession from the Dogwood school to the Pius home on Franklin Drive.

When the detectives arrived, John Pius was comforting his wife. The couple was so distressed over the murder of their only child that they had earlier been taken to a local hospital for tranquilizing shots. Johnny Pius's grandfather and his wife were also there, but there's no indication the detectives interviewed them. Gill recalled that they conducted the interview in the home's finished basement.

Gill later said that because of Barbara's condition, they allowed her to leave and spoke only to the husband. But in his report, Gill wrote that he "spoke to John Pius Sr. and Barbara Pius," who said that their son was last seen in the garage of their home between 8:15 and 8:30 p.m. the previous evening. Johnny was working on his bicycle, according to the report, and at around 8:30 p.m., the father went to the garage and "found that his son and his son's bike were gone from the garage."

The report stated that the father spent the next hour and a half checking "the area of their residence several times" before calling the police to report Johnny missing at 10:00 p.m. Reck's own report, which was even lighter on details than that of his partner, had a similar account of the interview, stating: "Subject was last seen at his home in the garage area repairing his bicycle."

But the written statement Gill took from the father that day, penned by the detective and signed by Pius, told the story quite differently. In the statement, Pius said that around 8:15, his son "asked me if he could take his bike for a test ride. He said he was going to ride up to the Dogwood school and see if Eddie Pembroke was there." Pius continued that he told his son that was fine, "but that I wanted him home no later than 8:30 pm as it was dark." He said he called police at 10:00 p.m. and was told to give the boy some time to return. He called again an hour later, the statement said, and a police officer came over to take a report.

"I remained home until about 7:30 am," Pius's statement read. That part of his story also changed, as Pius later testified that he searched for Johnny all night, including having his son's friend Eddie Pembroke join him to scour the area behind the Dogwood school.

The first Newsday article on the murder added a bit of clarity, as well as more confusion. The story paraphrased the parents' version of events: that at around 9:00 p.m., Johnny told his father that he planned to take the bike for a test run. "Some time thereafter," the story said, Pius returned to the garage to find the boy gone and his toolbox put away. When Johnny hadn't returned by 11:30 p.m., "his worried parents called police," the article read. The times were markedly later than Pius's account as recorded in the police reports, and the shelved toolbox disappeared from the father's later testimony concerning his son's disappearance. The *Newsday* story also included the detail that the father and Eddie Pembroke had searched the woods by flashlight at around 1:00 a.m.

Suffolk homicide detectives may have eschewed records, but the same wasn't true for everyday patrolmen of the sort who take missing persons reports. Police Officer Paul Fuhrmann jotted down a field report when he arrived at the Pius house after the father said his son was missing. That report further muddied the timeline and circumstances of the boy's disappearance.

According to that document, and Fuhrmann's later court testimony, Pius actually called to report his son's disappearance at around 12:20 on Saturday morning. That was roughly two hours later than reported in the statement Gill wrote for John Pius to sign and Gill's own report. A supplemental report stemming from Fuhrmann's visit memorialized yet another version of Johnny's disappearance. According to that report, at around ten o'clock on Friday night, father and son were working in the garage when the father went inside for half an hour. "When he returned to the garage [Johnny] was gone and so was his bicycle," Pius said, according to the police report. "He possibly went fishing at Stony Brook Harbor."

It was a collision of conflicting accounts all from the same bereaved father. The boy had either gone missing around 8:15 p.m., nine o'clock, or after ten. He had either asked his dad if he could test ride his bike, or he just disappeared. The dad had suspected he was at the school around the corner, or miles away fishing at Stony Brook Harbor. He had placed a call to the police reporting the boy missing at times ranging from nine o'clock to after midnight. And the dad had either stayed at home all night, or he had spent it searching for his boy, including in the very spot where the body was found the next morning.

It was a hell of a tangle on which to base an investigation. One might expect the detectives to probe the dad's shifting story, particularly after information they got from Johnny's school the next week.

The principal of Nesaquake Middle School told Gill and Reck that in the previous year, Johnny had suffered numerous injuries causing him to be absent from school. The detectives learned that Johnny had various bone fractures due to accidents while skiing, riding his minibike, and practicing judo. All the accidents were in the company of his father. It wasn't clear if the detectives learned the details of the injuries from Johnny's doctors or his dad. If they did bother to speak to the doctors, the detectives didn't record it in a report.

Perhaps the clearest sign that Gill and Reck were disinterested in any line of inquiry involving the father was the matter of his shoes. They requested from Pius only the shoes he had worn the afternoon he found his son's body. They were Florsheim dress shoes, clearly not of the type that had left the imprint on Johnny's face, but the detectives weren't requesting them in order to check him as a suspect. The father was among those who had stepped around his son's body that afternoon, and the detectives sought to exclude his shoe prints from others in the crime scene dirt. They never even asked John Pius, a martial artist, if he owned a pair of sneakers.

Gill, like many of his colleagues in the homicide squad, was prone to pursuing and ruling out leads based on nothing but his gut. The detective later said that by the end of the thirty-five-minute interview with John Pius on the day of the body's discovery, before basic facts of the case had emerged or an autopsy was completed, he had ruled out the dad as a suspect. "Absolutely not," Gill said when asked whether he even considered the possibility that Johnny's father had anything to do with his son's death.

On April 23, a few days after his interview with detectives, John Pius stood on his front lawn and spoke to a New York City television news crew about the tragedy. A karate teacher at the local YMCA and Elks Club, Pius was handsome in a hard way. During the interview, all of his internal turmoil seemed to be squeezing against his red skin as if trying to seep out. His veins pulsed in his neck, and he spoke in a sleep-deprived rasp. He wore sunglasses and a white dress shirt with a large collar, and his thinning brown hair was mussed.

"This is always something that happens to someone else," Pius told the news crew. "And this apparently isn't so because it happened to me, and it's a nightmare and something that you would never put in your mind."

Pius again suggested that his son had left without warning. "He was gone," Pius said. "Apparently he had taken his bike out for a test run, because if he had been going anyplace he would have told me. He was that type of a boy."

In the news segment featuring the interview with Pius, WCBS-TV anchor Carol Martin described the victim as a "thirteen-year-old boy from the all-American community of Smithtown, where things like this just don't happen, but now it has."

There was a collective amnesia by Long Island residents, and parachuting city journalists, as to the suburbs' capacity for the grisly and macabre. Suffolk County had seen its share of gruesome, senseless, and terrifying acts of violence. A particularly notorious example of the genre had rocked the nearby fishing village of Amityville in 1974, when an unbalanced young man used a hunting rifle to execute six members of his family.

It made for better TV and newspaper copy to act as if horror had never before touched these perfect communities, complete with descriptions and B-rolls of manicured lawns and boats bobbing in backyard docks. *Newsday*'s explanation for why the Pius murder so terrified residents was telling: "John Pius' murder stunned Smithtown," read a feature story in the paper entitled "Suburban Tragedy," because it "was not a crime rooted in racial, ethnic or economic tensions." The implication seemed to be that in a community with few poor people and even fewer minorities, the murder of a child should not be possible.

But Johnny Pius wasn't the first kid to be found dead in a patch of woods in Smithtown.

* * *

On a Thursday afternoon in November 1951, a couple of miles south of the potato field that would become Dogwood Elementary, an off-duty mailman was preparing to hunt some ducks at Miller's Pond. As he approached the slender fishing hole, he stumbled on something that prompted him to sprint back to his truck to get the police.

The dead girl he found lying in the woods had black eyes, scratches and bruises along her body, and, a coroner found, a ruptured kidney. She was determined to have been strangled with her own gray silk scarf. The schoolbooks found near her body identified her as twelve-year-old Lyde Kitchner.

There was not yet a countywide police department. The investigation of her homicide was handled by officials from three agencies: the Smithtown police, state troopers, and the district attorney's office. Their blunders, and those of the news reporters covering the sensational crime, began immediately.

Investigators declared Lyde's attack had been sexual in nature. That the coroner then found no physical evidence of sexual assault didn't stop newspapers around the state from erroneously reporting that the murdered girl had been raped. "Hunt Sex Slayer of LI Schoolgirl," read one of the headlines the next morning.

The investigators' best clue was the account of a schoolteacher and her friend who said they had spotted Lyde strolling down a nearby street with a blond boy or man shortly before her body was discovered. The usual tramps and sex offenders were rounded up and grilled to no avail. At one point detectives thought they had a strong lead when they learned of an Air Force sergeant who had walked into a Long Island church a couple of days after the murder to confess to a minister that he had "committed a great sin." But by the time investigators tracked down the sergeant, he had drowned himself. He was posthumously ruled out as a suspect.

Nearly a hundred days passed with no arrest, until a so-called breakthrough gave detectives their purported killer. Harold Lorentson, thirteen and blond, was among the boys who the eyewitness teacher had previously ruled out as the mystery male accompanying Lyde shortly before her murder. In fact, the teacher had twice told detectives that Harold wasn't the person she had seen. But then the teacher happened to encounter Harold at a village candy store. When Harold "blanched and furtively fled" at the sight of her, police said, the teacher changed her mind and decided he was in fact the boy.

Harold was a "superior student," according to his school, and had never been in trouble. But later on the day that the teacher implicated him, detectives extracted a confession from him. They said the boy initially denied his guilt but came clean after they pointed out discrepancies in his story. The "stoically calm" boy then led them on a "tour of the murder route" while recounting his crime, according to the detectives. The police said that he signed a statement in which he confessed that he and Lyde had walked around Miller's Pond, chatting about "school and things like that," when their stroll suddenly turned violent.

"When we got on the path I tried to kiss her," read Harold's purported statement as quoted in *Newsday* the next morning. "She slapped me and I threw her to the ground. We wrestled for a while and then Lyde was still. I called to her and shook her but she didn't move. I was scared so I ran."

The investigators told reporters they "are convinced the boy is telling the truth because he told us details heretofore and still withheld by police."

Newsday, a daily tabloid, which since its founding in 1940 has held an outsized sway on Long Island, ran a close-up of the pubescent perp on its front page. Harold appeared to be glaring out from sleepy eyes at the photographer. SCHOOLBOY SLAYER read the headline under the photo. The copy described the boy as "dry-eyed and sullen after confessing to the garrot murder" of his female classmate. The newspaper even had a midconfession action shot, showing Harold seemingly pointing out some element of the crime scene while a Smithtown lieutenant looked on.

The glory of a solved mystery was soon buried by an avalanche of mistakes. The day after the DA announced plans to charge the kid with first-degree murder, he realized that Harold's age precluded him from being charged with anything but juvenile delinquency in children's court.

Through his lawyer, Harold said from his jail cell that he had been coerced into confessing only after a ten-hour interrogation during which he was separated from his parents and his attorney. "They said I could see my parents if I admitted killing Lyde," Harold said. It also turned out that, contrary to what the police said, Harold had not signed a written confession.

During Harold's trial in children's court later that month, the two female witnesses—including the teacher who first initiated the prosecution against him—reversed themselves in court, each saying they couldn't be sure he was who they had seen. And two laborers who also said they had seen Lyde and the mystery person shortly before her death testified as well that they didn't recognize Harold.

A classmate's mother gave Harold a solid alibi, saying that he was riding a horse with her son at the time of Lyde's murder. And even that photo of Harold confessing at the crime scene turned out to be a sham, as testimony drew out that a police photographer had made the kid pose for it.

A judge ultimately found that the evidence against Harold couldn't support a finding of delinquency. *Newsday*, in an apparent fit of regret for having chronicled every twist and turn of Harold's case even though by law as a juvenile his identity should have been kept confidential, made amends by buying the child a farm animal.

Harold's horse, Lucky, who he was said to have been riding at the time of Lyde's killing, had died in the month he had spent in custody. So the newspaper gifted him a palomino named Candy. Under a photo spread of Harold riding the gift horse for the first time, *Newsday* explained that Candy's task was "erasing man-made scars from a youngster's memory."

And then the newspaper determined never to write about the debacle again, ending the horse article with an editor's note reading: "This as far as we are concerned is the end of the story of Harold Lorentson. He should be left alone."

The murder of twelve-year-old Lyde Kitchner was—unsurprisingly, given the hayseed tomfoolery that marked its investigation—never solved. And *Newsday* kept its word to cease mention of the case until Harold Lorentson died at age twenty-five, in 1964, when his well-drilling machine hit a power line.

In 1960, eight years after Lyde's murder, a countywide police department was chartered. Its homicide unit was billed as the antidote to the twenty-seven village and town police departments whose bumbling constables were so notorious for botching homicide investigations that *Newsday* had declared Suffolk County "the only place in the country where you can commit an imperfect murder and get away with it."

Policing in Suffolk County had previously been the purview of town officials who controlled the distribution of badges and guns, and in turn decided who got arrested. By the time of the Pius murder, the legacy of this system still ruled the consolidated department. Funneling all those town departments into one countywide force only served to concentrate, not dilute, the power of what those few cops inclined to speak out called the "old-boy network." A police lieutenant later testified that if you were from certain parts of the county, you not only had a better shot of getting hired by the Suffolk police but also of dodging discipline and rising to a position of power in the department. "The old Smithtown hierarchy, the Amityville hierarchy," the lieutenant testified in 1987, ticking off some of the chosen townships. "I think the mentality still prevails that prevailed then."

Despite the similarity and proximity of the two murders in Smithtown woods, albeit separated by almost three decades, the Kitchner case was never mentioned in court, news coverage, or any police report concerning the Pius investigation. That was partly thanks to *Newsday's* remorseful omertà concerning the case. But a more basic reason was that the vast majority of residents in Smithtown in 1979 simply hadn't been there in 1952.

* * *

On April 24, three days after Johnny's body was found, one of Gill's colleagues in Homicide boarded a waiting police helicopter in Hauppauge, the dull corporate center of office parks and county buildings. The Suffolk County Police Department chopper briefly flew south, where the detective directed a photographer to take aerial shots of the suburban environs where Johnny Pius lived and died.

The main drag of Jericho Turnpike hummed with light traffic heading east and west. But down Franklin Drive and the connecting warren of small side streets, filled with squat homes on winter-faded lawns, there were few cars about on a Tuesday mid-morning. The resulting glossy photos, developed in a police darkroom, captured Smithtown in a phase of awkward adolescence. Tightly packed tracts of lived-in homes bordered empty lots, bare fields, and doomed little patches of untouched woods. The chopper had lingered over the site where Johnny was found dead, a couple of acres of woods sloping from behind the school down to the Jericho Turnpike. If there was a name for these woods, the cops didn't know it, referring to it only as the "Wooded Area." The trees were still bald from winter, with fallen leaves giving the ground a rusty color.

With no foliage, the cops overhead could clearly spot two foot-paths in the woods. The path started as one, in the parking lot of the Power Test gas station at the intersection of Jericho and Franklin. The trails quickly forked like a T-bone in a steak. One path ran parallel to Franklin and headed to the little enclave of homes where Johnny had lived. The other path cut a jagged, indirect diagonal in the direction of Dogwood Elementary. It was that path heading to the school that the detectives were most interested in, tracing it on the photo with an orange grease pencil.

It took a kid being found dead there for the average adult resident of Smithtown to actually notice these woods. But for the teenagers who lived nearby, and whose main interests were inhaling from water bongs and blasting Ted Nugent, it was Narnia.

The grease pencil trail was its own teenage turnpike directly to Smithtown Beer & Soda. At that store across the street from the gas station, a high schooler could nearly always find somebody over eighteen in the parking lot willing to buy them beer. Elsewhere in the woods, the trail made a sharp turn to the "burn house," a pre-suburban construction that had been torched but still bore a basement where kids smoked weed and drank beers. In between both trails, closer to the streets surrounding the Pius home, was the half-finished treehouse Johnny and Eddie had been working on.

On the last night of Johnny's life, a temperate Friday after a week off school, the ecosystem of Smithtown adolescence had been in full swing. The detectives would find that the grease pencil trail was particularly busy. They focused on a couple of hours of juvenile activity there because they were operating on a few central assumptions.

The first assumption was their belief as to when the kid disappeared. The detectives appeared to have based the crucial question of when Johnny went missing solely on their interview with the father.

They decided Johnny had disappeared between 8:15 and 9:00 p.m. The coroner, unfortunately, provided little help in narrowing down the time of death. All he determined was that, based on the condition of the body, the boy had died between 4:00 p.m. on Friday and 7:00 a.m. on Saturday. The coroner had not analyzed the digestion of the boy's stomach contents, a routine step that could have narrowed that window further.

The second assumption was that the boy had been killed behind the school, and not dumped there from elsewhere, which was the opinion of the coroner.

The third assumption, and the one that would direct the investigation, was driven by the sneaker imprint on Johnny's face. Kids wore sneakers. And thus, seemingly from the first moment, Detective Gill had decided kids killed Johnny Pius.

So the cops, having boxed themselves into these parameters of Johnny's death, had to figure out how in forty-five minutes at the height of busy teenage activity in the woods, a boy was beaten and buried under sticks and leaves with six stones stuffed down his windpipe, by one or more of his schoolmates.

* * *

In the years following Pius's murder, no outsider got as acquainted with those woods and the kids who hung out there as magazine journalist Jesse Kornbluth. In 1982, he authored a two-part series in *New York* magazine about the flaws he found in the investigation and prosecution of the case. His reporting refuted the easy characterization favored by other journalists that Johnny Pius was a perfect kid raised in a perfect family. Kornbluth found that rifts in that facade had been exposed a couple of weeks before Johnny's death. Johnny's father had abruptly quit teaching karate, citing "family business." According to Kornbluth, two of Johnny's best friends said he told them he was considering running away because he heard his parents talking about divorce.

Kornbluth also grew intrigued by the whereabouts of Barbara Pius the night her son went missing. He interviewed Barbara and wrote that she initially told him she was home all night before it became clear that wasn't true. The police officer who visited the Pius home at

12:30 a.m. later testified that only John was there. It nagged at Korn-bluth. "Where was she?" he wrote of Barbara. "When, exactly, did she come home? Barbara wouldn't tell me."

Indeed, the Pius case would become one of the most extensive legal sagas in New York State history, producing tens of thousands of pages of reports and transcripts. But Barbara Pius's version of events that night is conspicuously absent. And perhaps the only cop who did take her story was never asked about it.

* * *

Police Officer Adam Gromacki's colleagues poked fun at his post in the Fourth Precinct as a "country club." The excitement usually topped out at catching a kid stealing letters from a mailbox. But during his 8:00 a.m. to 4:00 p.m. tour, cop-speak for a workday, on April 21, 1979, Gromacki dealt with a mother who was increasingly apoplectic that the police seemed to be doing nothing to find her missing son.

Barbara Pius first called at 9:00 a.m., demanding to know what type of investigation was being carried out concerning the boy her husband had reported missing the night prior. Gromacki told her to contact Juvenile Services. But three and a half hours later, Barbara called again, now begging Gromacki for something to be done to find the boy.

In these calls, Barbara gave Gromacki an account of Johnny's disappearance that was at odds with any story that was ever made public. Said Gromacki: "She said him and his father were working on a bike out in the garage and they had an argument, and the father went into the house and the son took off." The cop explicitly recalled Barbara saying her husband had argued with her son, because it informed his assumption that the kid had probably just temporarily run away. He guessed that was also the reason his colleagues weren't actively hunting for the kid. "I was going to fluff it off as, 'Look, your thirteen-year-old kid had a fight with his father and took off, that's why they're not doing anything,'" Gromacki said.

But because Barbara was so upset, Gromacki kept her on the line while he attempted to track down the status of the report. Gromacki called the missing persons desk. He learned that the police officer who took John Pius's missing persons report had failed to file it. Gromacki filed a report himself, and over the course of the next hour Barbara continued to call to update him on developments in the search. She told him her son's wallet had been found, and then that her husband was on his way to the school. Shortly afterward, Gromacki heard about the body being discovered.

That the boy may have argued with his dad before his disappearance was surely important information. But somehow Gromacki's story slipped through the cracks for more than four decades. He ultimately retired in 2000, and said he was never interviewed about that day by a detective, prosecutor, defense attorney, or until now, a journalist. Asked how he could've been so overlooked, Gromacki responded: "I didn't understand that either."

CHAPTER 2

PRIME SUSPECTS

When Eddie Pembroke and a gaggle of siblings moved onto Franklin Drive, he was in kindergarten and his new neighbor Johnny Pius was three years old. But the age difference didn't matter to the boys, who soon did nearly everything together. They swam in Johnny's pool, camped in tents in his backyard, took up lacrosse and football, and one summer started smoking cigarettes before deciding in tandem they didn't like it. They even tried pot a few times, though Eddie closely guarded this secret.

After Eddie got Puma-brand sneakers, popular with Smithtown jocks, Johnny convinced his parents to buy him a pair too. When Johnny was found dead a couple of weeks later, he was wearing his Pumas, and the imprint on his face was from the same brand of shoe.

On the day Johnny's body was found, Detectives Gill and Reck went to the Pembroke house and asked Eddie's mother if the boy might bring them to the treehouse that he and Johnny had been building. After she agreed, they instead took Eddie to Homicide HQ and interrogated him for five hours. Eddie was their first suspect.

The detectives noticed the sneakers, and after the interrogation they got permission from his mother to seize them. It's unclear what if anything they learned from those shoes. The soles had a pattern matching the imprint on Johnny's face, but so did all Puma sneakers. The sneakers were returned to Eddie a month later unaltered.

The net result of the marathon interview of Eddie was reduced by Reck to a couple hundred words in one of his minimalist supplemental reports. Eddie told them, according to the report, that he had seen Johnny at around five o'clock the night before, and then "sometime in the early evening hours," when he saw his friend working in his garage. Pembroke said he then went to Smithtown High School East. "There was no one there," the report read. "He returned home and spent the rest of the evening watching television."

Either the report was intentionally reductive, or Eddie's story changed. He later testified that John Pius showed up at his house at 11:00 p.m. looking for his son. (In John Pius's own account, he said he visited Eddie at 9:15 that night, yet another discrepancy in timing.) The father then stopped by again at 4:00 a.m. and asked Eddie to take him to his and Johnny's treehouse. The pair searched the area where Johnny's body, bicycle, and wallet were later found, but saw nothing. Eddie then returned home while John Pius went to the town dumps to look for his son there.

Kornbluth, the magazine journalist, interviewed Eddie Pembroke on three occasions. Eddie acknowledged that his first response to his best friend going missing was assuming that he had run away: "That's what I thought, that he either ran away or had gone over to one of his other friends' house." Eddie also suggested that the reason John Pius's story was so inconsistent was because, unlike his own, the father hadn't had it drilled into him during an interrogation.

"I don't think Mr. Pius remembered everything so good," Eddie told Kornbluth. "But I was questioned. That's how I remember everything so clearly, because they did it over and over. I don't think I'll ever forget anything that happened."

Suffolk County homicide cops exalted, to an obsessive extent, the concept of white hats and black hats. If a subject they encountered during an investigation wore the white hat, it meant that person had earned their way into the detectives' good graces. Typically, it was by doing their part, honestly or not, to help along the official theory of the crime. Wearing the black hat, on the other hand, meant the crime had landed on you, and the detectives were prepared to use any trick at their disposal to prove it.

Later that night, neighborhood kid Michael O'Neill went to check out the crime scene, which was still roped off and surrounded by cops and onlookers. A detective at the scene asked O'Neill his name. The detective then showed him a piece of paper, marked at the top with the header "Prime Suspects." Below that was a list of names of neighborhood kids, including O'Neill's.

As the detectives started picking up those kids one by one, starting with O'Neill the next day, the assumption was that Eddie Pembroke had provided the list, and in doing so had snagged himself a white hat.

* * *

Very late on the night following the discovery of Johnny's body, Mike O'Neill sat exhausted in a Hauppauge interrogation room, ready to give the detectives what they wanted so he could just go home. He was sixteen years old, had bright red hair, and was known for drinking and getting in a few fights. About five hours earlier, the detectives had intercepted him on the street, tossed his bicycle in their trunk, and hustled him off to this room in the Fourth Precinct, which was in the same complex as Homicide.

They caught him in a lie early on. O'Neill said he hadn't been to the area behind the school that Friday night. But the detectives had interviewed two girls who bought ice cream at Smithtown Beer & Soda right before its eight o'clock closing time. The girls said that they had seen O'Neill and a couple of friends, John Sparling and Raymond St. Denis, walking toward the woods' path with some bottles of beer.

It didn't take much in the Pius case to move one of the many prime suspects to the very top of the list. "At this point in time, it is the belief of the investigating officers that perhaps O'Neill, Sparling and St. Denis are the murderers of John Pius," read a line in one of Gill's reports. The detectives' new working theory of the murder was that the O'Neill crew had killed Pius in a botched attempt to rob him of his bicycle.

For hours, the detectives barred O'Neill from calling his parents, having anything to eat or drink, or even getting up from his chair. They lied to him, saying that his friends had already pinned the killing on O'Neill. The detectives vowed that he would never eat a home-cooked meal again or see his parents "without bars between them" unless he signed a confession, which was the only way he was leaving this room.

So O'Neill decided to give them what they wanted. Just as he was about to recite the details of a confession, one of the detectives tried another tack: "We know the word on the street is not to talk to cops."

"What are you talking about?" O'Neill said. "My father is a cop."

The detectives were stunned to learn that O'Neill's dad was in the NYPD. The entire tenor of the encounter changed. The cops were no longer interested in him as a suspect, and they even apologized.

Earlier in the night, his dad, John O'Neill, had searched through the woods with a flashlight, fearing the worst about his disappeared son. He was filing a missing persons report for the boy with a Suffolk officer when he learned that his son had in fact been in police custody, and the detectives would be bringing him home. He seethed to the patrolman: "Why don't you stick around and watch a New York City cop assault a detective from Suffolk County?"

When the detectives arrived with his son, they said that the boy "had been very cooperative, and that he was no longer a suspect, but maybe a witness." Despite his anger, John agreed to help facilitate a more fruitful conversation between the detectives and Mike's friend John Sparling. The O'Neill crew's story became that the three boys had walked down the path on their way to Point of Woods, the under-construction development where Johnny had sometimes pilfered lumber. They spent several hours in a half-built house there smoking weed, drinking beer, and listening to music. Then they hitchhiked to Setauket, nine miles northeast, to watch a midnight movie about the music festival at Woodstock.

The detectives later maintained, in attempting to excuse their actions concerning the next set of suspects, that O'Neill was still their prime suspect. If so, they seemed oddly disinterested in vetting his alibi. The boys didn't provide their movie stubs from that night, and the detectives didn't document any attempt to find witnesses to corroborate their story. The detectives didn't collect any sneakers from O'Neill, accepting his explanation that he only had "work shoes."

It would later become clear that O'Neill's friend John Sparling was still being dishonest, and Sparling would even later lie about elements of his story to a grand jury, but the detectives had by then focused on other suspects. Mike O'Neill had given the cops the tidbit of information that led them to those next suspects. The cop's son and his friends seemed to have gotten their own white hats via birthright, but now the supply was running low.

* * *

The little lie that kicked off the trouble came, by all accounts, from Rob Brensic. He was a small and wiry kid, ruled by impulse dating back to his toddler days. At age two, he had disappeared on his tricycle and a search party found him in an under-construction house. At twelve, he pulled off the pubescent version of that stunt, leading cops on a chase around the town dump on his dirt bike.

On the Wednesday afternoon following Johnny's murder, Detectives Gill and Reck approached Brensic, Tom Ryan, and the Quartararo brothers as they walked home from school. The cops asked where the boys had been the previous Friday.

Rob's impulse was to make something up. He said they were watching a baseball game up at the high school. Tom Ryan said he attempted to correct him, but the cops barked at him not to interrupt. The detectives then returned to their car. As the boys continued their walk home, their consensus was that Brensic was an idiot for covering up their theft of a minibike that was out in the garbage. But nobody thought his lie would amount to anything.

Immediately after speaking to the kids, Gill called up Smithtown High School East to inquire whether there was a game at the ballfield that Friday. He already had a hunch as to the answer.

* * *

To Suffolk County patrolman Joseph Bores, it seemed like every teenage boy who lived within a two-block radius in Smithtown had just evaporated. On the evening of April 28, the Saturday one week after Johnny's body was found, Officer Bores was at a house on Marquette Drive in Smithtown. Three sets of parents were at the home, distraught over their missing sons.

The well-appointed home belonged to Bernard and Elaine Ryan. Two of their neighbors, Carolyn Quartararo and Audrey Brensic, were also over. The Ryans told Bores that after working on his dad's boat all morning, their son Tom had gone to a nearby deli to pick up a couple of sandwiches for their lunch. But he had not come back or showed up for his shift at Cousins II, the eatery where he worked and was never late. Carolyn said that her son Peter had been with Ryan on his sandwich trip, his errand being that he needed to exchange some coins from his newspaper route for bills. He also had never returned, and his supervisor on the paper route was irate. And Audrey Brensic said that her son Robert had missed supper without explanation.

Bores dutifully went through the protocol. He put out an all-points bulletin for Ryan's yellow Capri and checked for hospitalizations or car accidents. Because the parents told him that another neighborhood boy, Mike O'Neill, had been subject to an extended interrogation a few days earlier, Bores called in to ask whether the detectives had picked up any of the boys. Bores was told the boys weren't in police custody. The parents began to wonder if their sons were the latest victims of a Smithtown serial killer.

The patrolman headed back to the Fourth Precinct to file paper-work. Once there, he asked a teletype officer to put through a report about the missing boys. The officer, with a knowing look, suggested he give it a few minutes.

Officer Bores realized then that every one of his colleagues with whom he had spoken that evening had lied to him. In fact, Bores learned that the yellow Capri, one of the most recognizable cars in town, was parked in the lot outside. No doubt it had been noticed by numerous cops who had gotten his bulletin for the car, but they said nothing.

Bores got pretty hot about it. He confronted the supervisor who he had spoken to on the phone, and who had told him the boys weren't there. "This is a homicide investigation," the detective-sergeant scolded Bores, who was only a beat cop. "Not just a case of stolen hubcaps."

* * *

The conversation in the boiler room under the homicide offices in Hauppauge centered on white hats and black hats. It was a concept Tom Ryan had never previously heard, but this Saturday afternoon he must have had it breathed into his face eighteen times. A de-tective's mug was so close to his that he could see every trimmed bristle of his well-groomed mustache. "Wear the white hat," the detective tried again, his tone becoming impatient. "Don't wear the black hat."

The detective was dapper: three-piece suit, hair greased back disco-style. Ryan's stomach was painfully empty, and as he smelled the cop's sweet cologne mixed with hot breath, the kid's thoughts turned to the roast beef subs baking on a seat of his Capri in the police parking lot.

"I'm going to be sick," Tom announced, scrambling away to lean over a drain in the floor.

That afternoon, Tom and Peter had been running the errands described by their parents when two sedans, horns going crazy, pulled a spy movie maneuver to box in Tom's car on the side of the road. Four men who didn't bother flashing badges threw Peter headfirst into the back seat of one of the cars and ordered Tom into the other. Tom protested that he didn't want to leave his car with its doors flung open and $40 worth of music tapes inside. He then watched in astonishment as one of the men got behind the wheel of the Capri and started driving it.

Tom protested that his and his father's lunch was in the car. He said that he had a work shift that afternoon. The man riding shotgun in the car grew impatient. Tom said he grabbed him, hurled him against the back of the seat, and barked: "Shut up, punk."

The detectives learned that Rob Brensic was on his paper route and scooped him up as well, tossing his bike and newspapers into the open trunk of a sedan. Tom recognized the Fourth Precinct building they were taken to from having toured it ten years earlier with his Cub Scout troop. The dimly lit boiler room he was trapped in with the well-dressed detective had not featured on that tour.

After Tom dry heaved over the floor drain, the detective brought him back upstairs for more interrogation. The detective told him: "You're going to take a big fall because all your friends are all turning against you."

But Tom heard what he recognized as Brensic screaming in another room: "I didn't do it! I didn't do it! Why are you doing this to me?"

Tom, noting that Brensic didn't appear to be capitulating, retorted to the detective: "It doesn't sound that way."

* * *

After a full week of failing to pierce the teenage code of silence, the Suffolk detectives and their bosses were determined to close the Pius matter. The two detectives on the case were joined by six others. They included Tony Palumbo, who was told to put on ice his investigation of the body found in the Pontiac. Palumbo was accompanied by his partner, Gary Leonard, a novice on the homicide squad, his role being to watch the Palumbo show and provide supporting dialogue.

Palumbo entered the Fourth Precinct's Juvenile Aid Room studying a piece of paper with a look of deep consternation. "Those Irish bastards are blaming you and your brother for the killing of John Pius," he informed Peter Quartararo, one aggrieved Italian to another.

He explained that the document in his hand was a statement written by Tom Ryan putting it all on Peter. He said Rob Brensic was preparing a similar document as they spoke. Palumbo pleaded: "Why, why, why don't you just tell us what happened?"

The detective assured Peter that since he and his brother were the youngest of the four boys, they would avoid jail time if they confessed and implicated the rest. Palumbo grew tempestuous: "You guinea bastards are going to hang and spend twenty-five years to life in jail," Peter later testified that Palumbo boomed, finger in the boy's face: "You're never going to see your parents again."

Then, according to Peter, Palumbo started kicking his legs. "What the hell are you doing that for?" Peter demanded.

"Because you are not telling the truth," he said Palumbo explained between kicks. "And I want you to tell the truth."

At one point, Peter said he picked up the phone to call his mother, and Palumbo slapped the receiver out of his hand. "You're not calling anybody," he said the detective told him. "You're not leaving here until you tell us what you did."

A story started to come into shape. Peter had already admitted that the boys had stolen the minibike. Now Peter said that Rob and Tom, in order to prevent Johnny from telling anybody he saw them stealing the minibike, chased the boy down and killed him while the Quartararo brothers watched.

At that point, the cops said they were going to get in their car and go on a rainy night field trip. As they drove, Peter said the detectives told him: "Now we're going to tell you what Ryan and Brensic said, and you're going to tell us the same thing later."

Peter could think only about his mom and dad and his home. His father had been an auxiliary Suffolk cop. Like most kids in Smithtown, Peter had been raised to trust cops innately. The ones in the front seat were saying all he had to do was say some words and he could go home. He also began to consider that if he was going to implicate his two friends, it was only right to say he and his brother Mike were also involved.

The detective's car bounced around the grassy area behind the elementary school, Peter later said, and Palumbo narrated: *This is where Brensic and Ryan said they saw Pius while loading the minibike into the car. This is where they said he dropped his wallet. This is where they said they dragged his body.*

The car stopped. Palumbo muttered about gas in the tank. They were parked along the side of Dogwood Drive. It was a five-minute dash through the rain to his mom, if only the detectives would let him go. He started at the beginning and told a story that wasn't perfect, but it satisfied the cops.

When he was done, he was given a burger, the kid's first meal after seven hours of interrogation. The detectives took him not home, but back to the precinct. Palumbo got on an office phone, dialed up the Quartararo house, and told Peter's mom to come join them.

When Carolyn asked what was happening, Palumbo barked: "Please, lady, not on the phone. Just get down here."

He told her to bring Mike too.

* * *

Bedlam was the word witnesses used to describe what had occurred at the precinct while Peter was being driven around the Dogwood school. Elaine Ryan, still in the dark as to her son Tommy's whereabouts, had decided to go with a handful of neighbors to the precinct. At around 7:30 p.m. this neighborhood contingent arrived and spotted both Tom's yellow car and another car with Rob's bicycle and newspapers visible in an open trunk. Elaine, now certain the boys were inside, banged on the windows, demanding to see her son. The desk cops continued the ruse that he wasn't there. A lieutenant passing by to use a coffee machine got fed up, took Elaine aside, and mouthed something to her. One of the neighbors watched the mom start screaming while slowly sinking to the floor. "What did you tell her?" the neighbor demanded of the lieutenant.

"I told her we arrested her son for homicide," he responded. At that point, it was a cruel lie, as nobody had yet been arrested. The lieutenant added: "Now get out."

* * *

Roughly thirty minutes later, Tom Spota, chief of the Major Offense Bureau of the DA's office, pulled up outside the Stony Brook railroad station. His number two, Billy Keahon, hustled through the rain and got into the shotgun seat. It was a twenty-minute drive to the Fourth.

At the precinct, they made a war room of a dingy downstairs cafeteria. They huddled with homicide commander Richard Jensen and his detectives Gill and Reck. Jensen gave them the rundown: three boys in custody, confession on tape.

Spota said he needed to listen to it. The audiocassette was scrawled on one side with the words "Body in Trunk," a notation about Palumbo's other homicide case. The tape recorder belonged to Palumbo's kids, but clearly he was growing attached to it.

While Peter was talking in the car, Palumbo had been secretly tinkering with the recorder. With his left hand he had fast-forwarded through the body in trunk recordings, ejected the tape, and flipped it to the blank other side. He then pressed record, dropped the device to the floorboard of the driver's seat, and booted it backward to better pick up Peter's voice. Leonard watched his partner out of the corner of his eye and tried to keep the boy going.

Spota strained to hear. The interference from the car engine and the road outside nearly rendered the conversation inaudible. The tape began with Leonard midprompt. "And what were you, what was said to him while he was yelling?" the detective asked.

"He said 'bullshit,'" responded Pete.

Leonard: "And then what happened?"

Pete: "He started screaming."

This was a fragmented recitation of the vague facts of the murder, which the boy and the detectives appeared to have already agreed on.

Confronted and threatened to shut up about their minibike theft, Pius had promised he wouldn't tell. But Brensic hadn't believed him and attacked him anyway, causing the boy to scream, intensifying the scrum.

Palumbo, concerned about the engine drowning out the audio, pulled over, and the detectives focused the narrative.

"Start from the beginning," Leonard demanded.

"Yeah," echoed Palumbo. Peter's ensuing account was plodding, stammering, and at times incoherent. He expressed all the emotion of a kid mumbling through a supermarket shopping list. The detectives in the front seat, like film directors, reminded him of his lines when he strayed from or seemed to forget the story.

Peter vaguely described the boys' night up until they stole the minibike. He said they were loading it into the trunk of Rob's car when Pius pedaled by. When the boys saw Pius while loading the minibike into the trunk, Peter said, Mike inexplicably yelled out: "Pius, you dick!"

Afterward, Peter claimed, Rob was alarmed that Johnny had witnessed the theft. "So then he said, 'Pius saw us,'" Peter said.

"That's better," Palumbo told Peter at this point in his confession, as if in encouragement.

"Let's get him," Peter then claimed Rob said of Johnny.

After stashing the minibike at the Quartararos' house, in Peter's telling, the boys drove back to the school. They saw Johnny biking toward the back of the school, piled out of the car, and chased after him, with one of the kids shouting: "Pius, come here!"

That's when, Pete said, Mike knocked Johnny from his Huffy and the boys told him to stay quiet about the minibike.

"And what did he say?" Leonard asked of Johnny.

"He said—oh shit, what the hell did he say?" said Pete, apparently straining to remember.

"I thought you said he said, 'I didn't even see you guys,'" reminded Palumbo. Pete then agreed that Johnny had promised he posed no threat to them.

But Rob pushed Johnny anyway, Pete said, and when the boy fought back "we all got on him." They were soon on top of Pius on the ground.

Leonard prompted: "What were you doing, kicking and punching or just—"

"Yeah," responded Pete. "Just like, everyone was just punching."

"He was screaming, right?" said Palumbo.

"Yeah," said Pete. "Then we shoved rocks down his throat to shut him up."

"Whose idea was that?" asked Leonard, to which Pete replied: "Rob."

In this way, the confession seemed designed to implicate each of them roughly evenly: Mike started the physical altercation with Pius, Rob intensified it, and now each of the boys contributed to the remaining major elements of the murder.

"I threw one in and then my brother threw one in and I threw another one in," Peter said, referring to how the rocks got in Pius's mouth.

"Threw it in?" Palumbo posited.

"Oh just, you know, tossed it in," Peter said, claiming that Rob was holding Pius down while Peter held open the boy's jaw with one hand and tossed in rocks with the other.

"And then he shut up and we dragged him over the woods to the, ah, hill," Peter said. The labor of dragging Pius's body and his bike was also equally distributed among the four. Tom and Rob each grabbed a foot, and Peter took a shin. Mike pushed the bike. While dragging the body, Peter said he saw Johnny's wallet fall out in the middle of the field and kept moving.

Palumbo, still working on the lie that Rob and Tom had implicated Peter, asked: "Whose idea was it to bury him? They're saying it's your idea."

"It wasn't," Peter objected. "I think it was Tom."

Because they didn't want to waste time, Peter then explained, they didn't go home for a shovel or other tools to bury their victim. "So we just kicked leaves on him and threw logs on him," Peter said.

"Kicked leaves, and how many logs?" Palumbo asked.

"Two," Peter responded.

Palumbo: "Who put the logs on him?"

"I helped put one," Peter said, to which Palumbo murmured in assent.

"And Rob put the other one," Peter said.

As for his brother Mike, Peter said: "After he brought the bike over and threw it up against the tree, he just came over and started throwing leaves on him too."

Then Peter said they headed back to the Quartararo home. The four boys with no criminal record who had just bloodily murdered a peer were home by 9:00 p.m. "Oh, we just hung out there for a while," Peter said when asked how they filled the rest of the evening.

The detectives pushed for a little more, trying to draw out how the boys had sat down together and came up with the "make believe story" about the night that didn't involve killing Pius. But when Peter became confused, and started fumbling over the stories, Palumbo put a cork in it. The detective said: "Um, that's good enough."

As Palumbo turned the key in his car, he made a half-hearted reference to his previous ruse that they were out of gas. "Come on, you old beast," the detective remarked, his hand reaching under his seat to turn off the recorder. "Don't stall out on me now."

* * *

The tape left Spota, as it would anybody with a law degree, underwhelmed.

The most immediate hurdle was the fact that Peter Quartararo was in that car by himself with detectives in the first place. New York law required cops to immediately inform the guardians of any subject under the age of sixteen when they took them in for questioning. Peter was two days short of that birthday. And of course there were constitutional protections for suspects of all ages, requiring cops to inform them of their rights to remain silent and have a lawyer present. The Suffolk homicide squad was certainly aware of those requirements, as in the previous few years at least three convictions they had secured were reversed on appeal for not abiding by them. Spota could also probably hazard a guess as to whether the detectives had read these kids their rights.

Besides the question of whether the confession was obtained through illegal methods, there was the issue of whether it had any real evidentiary value. Spota barely had any time in on the case, but already he could see the glaring inconsistencies in the kid's account of the murder. Putting aside the difficulty of picturing four teenage boys beating and suffocating a child to death and then burying him in a matter of minutes in a busy corner of a residential neighborhood without anybody seeing, there were improbable physical logistics in the crime as Peter described it. Among them: from Rice Lane to the Quartararo house was almost a mile along slow-moving residential streets. Peter said they made that trip, stashed the minibike in the garage, and then returned. But by his telling, in that time Johnny only made it by bike to the front lawn of the school, a distance of about five hundred feet. And once they had parked in the lot and yelled at Johnny, causing him to try to bike away, how did the four kids, none of whom were track stars, catch up to him by foot?

A different prosecutor might despair. The murder was the biggest solo case of Spota's career, and it was already threatening to implode. Mike O'Neill's parents were already preparing litigation. Three other families were no doubt plotting another assault on the precinct at that very moment. Spota's only evidence thus far was a teenage confession any competent lawyer could likely get excluded from trial.

Spota, though, was a pragmatist. Rescuing this murder case from its current quagmire would just require the thirty-seven-year-old prosecutor to utilize a few specialized talents. Instead of being concerned, Spota was elated. In his mind, they had their killers.

What convinced him was a small detail in Peter's confession: the logs. "So we just kicked leaves on him and threw logs on him," Peter had said. One could picture Spota's blue eyes widening at that moment as he hunched over the recorder. Spota knew that Homicide was trying to keep the existence of the logs at the crime scene secret. "That had never been publicized before," Spota would later say. "We knew then we had the right people."

The problem with that, even excluding the possibility that Peter had been fed that detail by his interrogators, was that the logs were actually well publicized as an element of the crime scene within three days of the murder. The neighbor who had found the boy told journalists for both *Newsday* and the *New York Times* about the logs.

Spota immediately got to work fortifying the detectives' efforts to hang the case on the four boys. Spota had by then already been contacted by a lawyer for the Ryan kid, who had also called the precinct and ordered detectives to stop their interrogation and release the boy immediately. Spota nonetheless poked into the room where Ryan was being held. He asked in a concerned tone whether the boy was cooperating, and worked on him to take a polygraph.

A stretch of a legal cover story was in the works to explain the interrogation of the boys without their parents being informed. In this version of the day's events, the detectives still had Michael O'Neill as their chief suspect. They said they were doing surveillance of O'Neill, even though the location where they were parked offered a view of Ryan and Brensic's houses, not O'Neill's. When Tom Ryan and Peter Quartararo drove by, the detectives said they just decided to call an audible and bring the boys in to be questioned as witnesses about O'Neill. The four boys didn't themselves become suspects, the detectives maintained, until Peter, without prompting, began confessing.

Now Spota grabbed the phone to speak to Ryan's lawyer. Spota had told the lawyer he was going to call as soon as he got to the precinct to let him know whether Ryan was being held as a witness or a suspect. But Spota apparently had been slow to do so, and Robert Skigen, the lawyer who was a family friend of the Ryans, was irate.

"Look," Spota yelled back at Skigen before hanging up the receiver, "don't tell me how to do my job!"

CHAPTER 3

AMITYVILLE

For Tom Spota, it was not the most gratifying way to spend a Friday night: interviewing jail guards in an attempt to build an ultimately weak corruption case against an elected official in his own party. For most of 1975, he had been distracted, along with the rest of Long Island, by a far more primal crime.

So when the Amityville case came up in conversation with one of the jail guards, Spota saw an opportunity and scrambled for a phone.

A more senior prosecutor was about to sit down for dinner with his family when he picked up and listened to Spota's explanation. "Will you come out?" Spota asked when he was done, disguising his intent to commit some light professional extortion.

For this prosecutor, Gerald Sullivan, it was only a question of how quickly his orange Volkswagen could get him to the correctional facility in Riverhead. He was eager to trade in the home-cooked dinner for coffee and sandwiches with a jail guard in order to shore up the biggest homicide case on his docket, or for that matter, any prosecutor's docket in the history of Suffolk County. As for Spota, his motives were a bit more self-serving.

Spota, then in his early thirties, typically came across as too much of an overgrown schoolboy to be cunning. He wore perpetually loosened candy-striped ties and budget suits, and hair that looked like Mom had swabbed it down with her thumb. He was prone to fidgeting, including a habit of nibbling the ends of his eyeglasses. And then there was his manner of speaking, plumbed from the idiosyncratic depths of middle-class Nassau County. He was nasal and squeaky and had an accent reminiscent of Tweety Bird, pronouncing crime as "cwime" and over as "ovah." Nonetheless, Spota showed that night that he knew his way around the prosecutor's most essential tool: leverage.

Sullivan was at first largely unimpressed by Spota's find. The jail guard was named James DeVito. Sullivan pitied the guy. He was a short, portly man who spoke with a stutter. "He was almost too willing to please," Sullivan perceived. "I didn't think he was lying, but I got the impression that Jimmy DeVito felt he had to please almost everyone he talked to."

Still, as Sullivan interviewed the guard well into the next morning, he began to share Spota's appreciation for Jimmy. Here was a potential hole-plugger witness in a case that could not afford to have any holes. Sullivan's fear of failure in this trial was strong enough that he was easily willing to overlook both his concerns about the jailer as a witness, and the raw ambition in the eyes of the colleague eagerly awaiting his assessment.

Once he knew his mark was hooked, Spota made his demand. He wanted in on the Amityville slaying.

* * *

Thomas J. Spota III's childhood education, spent in New Hyde Park–area Catholic schools, was a boy's-only odyssey of flat tops, glee clubs, and picture day bowties. His high school, Chaminade, was a factory for future prominent Republicans, including Alfonse D'Amato and Bill O'Reilly. By 1966, when others in their midtwenties were protesting the actions of the federal government, Spota was intent on joining it. His newly attained law degree from St. John's University was supposed to be the final step toward his singular goal: becoming one of J. Edgar Hoover's G-men. But then he failed the FBI entrance exam.

Spota was crestfallen, but he found plenty of other clubs that would take him. His dad, Thomas Jr., was an insurance agent and son of Italian immigrants who found his America through frenetic civic engagement. Dad was on the committee that organized filet mignon dinners for World War II vets, reigned over the New Hyde Park library board before being ousted in an election, and petitioned the school district to pick up the tab to bus his kids to Catholic school. His son also became a tireless joiner, his focus being all sorts of boys' clubs: Phi Alpha Delta, the Young Republicans, the Elks, and perhaps most formatively, Long Island's peculiar nexus of volunteer fire departments.

There were, and still are, dozens of these outfits on the island. Starting in 1963, Spota volunteered for the Garden City Park Fire Department, in Nassau, and then that of Mount Sinai, in Suffolk. The firehouses were gleaming taxpayer-funded man caves, outfitted with pool tables and bars stocked with beer. The volunteers, nearly all white men, were the spiritual kin of cops, including the sharing of a persecution complex. The volunteers were constantly complaining about how ungrateful Long Island taxpayers perceived them: as beer-bellied amateurs who used local taxes as a slush fund for banquets, vacations, firehouse tiki bars, and tricked-out firetrucks.

The volunteer firefighters and highly paid county cops often worked in tandem, including responding to serious car accidents together. Some cops liked to lounge away their tours at the precinct firehouses, which were particularly popular with plainclothes investigators in between cases. Spota's early tenure as a firefighter was his first extended exposure to that rarefied, swaggering creature to whom he would latch on for most of his career: the Long Island police detective.

With his FBI dreams dashed, however, Spota's paying career was initially far removed from law enforcement. He joined a Hicksville law firm and hung a shingle in the arts of "general practice." The first of thousands of times Tom Spota appeared in *Newsday* was in 1969, with the headline, "Barbers Told: Not Too Much off the Top." It was a brief on his legal efforts to get permission for a barbershop to serve booze and outfit its female haircutters in transparent uniforms. It wasn't exactly *Loving v. Virginia*, and Spota's quest was squelched by a state official who didn't want barbershops offering a "peep show."

In search of quality health coverage for his family—Spota was newly married and would have three children—he found government work around the turn of the 1970s. At thirty, Spota was hardly on a path to becoming a legal titan. By day, he was a town attorney in North Hempstead earning $14,000 a year. At night he clerked at a liquor store and scrubbed toilets as a janitor at an asphalt plant.

His initial inquiry to the Suffolk DA's office in 1971 betrayed no particular passion for prosecution. "I am eager to make my home in the eastern portion of Suffolk County," Spota explained simply in a letter to then DA George Aspland. But he had made a useful connection to Aspland's brother Mike, a lawyer who handled some government work in Nassau County. Within a few months he was in the rookie prosecutor's outpost, district court, pulling in $236 a week.

Spota earned a solid, if not remarkable, reputation. Defense attorneys said he "tried his file." It was a mostly complimentary assessment that pegged him as a workaday prosecutor who didn't manufacture evidence. Beat reporters took little notice of young Spota, a backbencher who barely registered in a DA's office packed with macho attorneys. Moderate raises accompanied minor promotions. In 1975, Spota had been assigned to the anti-corruption bureau, which newly elected DA Henry O'Brien had formed upon taking office.

There is little to suggest that Spota would have been enthused by the assignment. Anti-corruption bureaus in Suffolk County law enforcement were, with some irony, often hives for using law enforcement powers against political rivals. And O'Brien was a Democrat, the first of that breed in the 128-year history of the Suffolk DA office. His election was largely seen as a fluke, owing to a confluence of circumstances including post-Watergate sentiment in favor of Democrats and a third-party conservative candidate who siphoned away Republican votes. When tasked with investigating the office of Suffolk's Republican sheriff, the card-carrying Young Republican Spota had to know such cases wouldn't do much for his long-term upward mobility.

There was only one case that mattered on Long Island anyway. Like almost everyone, Spota had been transfixed by the headlines: "Six in Amityville Family Found Murdered at Home," read *Newsday*'s front page on November 14, 1974. The photo accompanying those words was the first dose of the case's fantastic eeriness. It was a nighttime photo, shadowy and somber, of police and coroner officials carrying a full body bag down the front steps of a large Dutch Colonial house. The accompanying story introduced one of the most sensational crimes in American history: a married couple, their two daughters, and two of their three sons, children ranging in age from nine to eighteen, had been apparently executed by gunshot while wearing their pajamas.

The next day's front page showed the surviving son, twenty-three-year-old Ronnie "Butch" DeFeo Jr., bearded and appearing slightly manic in a jumpsuit and handcuffs. Cops claimed he had murdered his family for a $200,000 insurance payout. The day after that, *Newsday* cited police sources who detailed how DeFeo "calmly endured more than 24 hours of interrogation" before confessing and even acting out the crime for detectives.

The story became Long Island's version of *Helter Skelter*, with everything a limelight-seeking prosecutor could desire, including a mob angle. Butch's uncle Pete was a reputed Genovese crime family captain said to control New York City's banana trade. Butch had initially told police that mobsters were likely behind his family's massacre. After Butch's arrest, the DA arranged to have him arraigned in a prison chapel out of fear that a vengeful mob assassin might invade a Suffolk courtroom.

Spota wasn't the first Suffolk prosecutor to be jealous of the case. The DeFeo murders were originally assigned to one of the office's most senior prosecutors. Gerry Sullivan had been shut out. He had been a prosecutor a few years longer than Spota but was even younger than Spota and not much more qualified to manage such a high-profile case. Sullivan admitted in a later memoir that he had launched an obsessive campaign in reverse psychology to get the older prosecutor to think the case was a loser and trade it to him.

He wasn't lying in that the case was rigged with trip wires. There was little doubt that Butch was at least involved in the killing of his family with a .35 Marlin hunting rifle. But cops and prosecutors could not land on a satisfactory motive. The insurance story cited in that early news coverage was flimsy. With no real explanation for why Butch committed this horrific act, a jury might have been prone to finding DeFeo not guilty by reason of insanity. Which was where Spota's jailhouse find came in.

* * *

Sullivan was a stocky, self-serious young attorney who spoke in a clipped, quasi-European accent even though he was raised in Queens.

He looked down on the jail guard Jimmy DeVito, but that didn't mean he was above using him. DeVito detailed to Sullivan his conversations over the past several months with DeFeo following the accused killer's arrest the previous November.

"Mr. DeVito, you ought to know I did it," the jailer recalled DeFeo saying, before clarifying that he hadn't actually pulled the trigger. Instead, according to DeVito, DeFeo detailed a burglary gone wrong. DeFeo and a couple of accomplices had attempted to steal $75,000 his father had stashed in his house. When his parents caught him, his accomplices executed the entire family. DeFeo was a chatty sociopath, by his jailer's account, at one point also casually confessing to having drowned a man following an argument at a bar.

DeFeo's accomplices would "turn out to be bull," Sullivan wrote, but there was one part of DeVito's account that "could be blockbuster testimony." DeVito said DeFeo had quizzed him about the behavior of other inmates who had claimed insanity. The jailer told DeFeo about inmates who had set fires, appeared to forget the names of others in the prison, perched high up in their cells, and feigned suicide attempts—behaviors that DeFeo then shammed.

DeVito called it the prisoner's "crazy act," and it would be valuable in refuting an insanity defense. So when Spota demanded to be put on the case, Sullivan was in no position to turn him down. He arranged for Spota to be made second chair in the prosecution. "I couldn't blame him for staking his claim," Sullivan later wrote of Spota, describing "a striving that goes beyond ambition."

* * *

The DeFeo case delivered goosebumps to a tabloid-devouring public fascinated by the episode of pure evil in their backyard. This demographic was not overly concerned with the Amityville Slayer's constitutional rights. If anyone had been paying close attention, they could have spotted the classic recipe for a Suffolk County homicide prosecution.

It was a simple dish virtually always prepared the same way. You took a confession, extricated while the defendant was denied access to a lawyer, and garnished it with perfect witness testimony, typically plucked from a jailhouse snitch.

In the DeFeo trial, these witnesses were mostly Spota's contribution. Jimmy DeVito tucked in his gut for court. Sullivan kept the questions simple and focused on only one vital element of the jail guard's account, that of DeFeo looking for creative inspiration on how to play the part of a disturbed person.

"Right after I told him those things, he began doing them all and yelling at me to enter them in the log book," DeVito testified. "But I considered them silly, and refused to make any entries except for the incident when he tried to set fire to his cell." A second guard, who DeVito had introduced to the prosecutors, corroborated his account.

The third witness in this vein had markedly less credibility than even an eager-to-please jail guard. John Kramer was locked up next to DeFeo on robbery, rape, and other charges. His story was that DeFeo told him that he planned on beating the murder rap by pleading insanity, and then taking an insurance and estate windfall to Hawaii with his girlfriend. Kramer acknowledged that the DA's office had promised to help shave off years in his sentence in return for his testimony.

DeFeo's confession to the jail guard was the centerpiece of the prosecution's case. It came with the usual defense protestations, which were almost always ignored, that it was obtained illegally. A lawyer who was related to the DeFeos testified that on the day of the massacre, he went to a Suffolk precinct, and then police HQ, demanding to see Butch.

He said he had asked "to see my client and, if he was being questioned by police, to have them stop until I explained his rights." He was told Butch was not there. When he asked to record his request to see his client on a police blotter, the desk cops ignored him.

The homicide squad's version of the same events was that DeFeo was only in their protective custody that night, so they weren't denying his rights by keeping him from a lawyer. When DeFeo fell asleep on a cot in their offices, they maintained, he was a "sympathetic figure, a sole survivor of a mass murder, whose life might have been in danger from mob figures." It wasn't until 9:00 a.m. the next day, they claimed, that they made him a suspect after cops found rifle cases in his bedroom and spoke to friends who said he was a gun buff.

DeFeo's main interrogator, Homicide Detective Dennis Rafferty, was exalted by his colleagues for a nearly mystical skill for cracking murders. He was capable of getting information out of a dying man using hand squeezes to communicate from a hospital bed. But in his own court testimony, DeFeo said Rafferty was doing a lot more than hand squeezing for the roughly thirty hours that he was in custody immediately following the discovery of his family's corpses.

DeFeo testified that the detectives took him from a house they commandeered next door, to the First and then Fourth Precincts, and then to Homicide HQ, kicking and beating him in each place, denying him sleep or food, and demanding that he confess. The tactics he described would become well known, as they were the Suffolk homicide squad's favorite set of tricks. In DeFeo's case, he said it included detectives putting a phone book on his head and hitting it with blackjacks, presumably to avoid visible bruising. DeFeo also claimed they covered his head with a shopping bag and slammed it into a wall.

The testimony concerning a coerced confession was easy enough for the DA's office to bat away. It all sounded outlandish, and the county techniques of interrogation had not yet become notorious. The family attorney was derided as a lying, mob-connected lawyer. DeFeo did himself no favors with the rest of his testimony.

"When I have a gun in my hand, I'm God," DeFeo declared at one point. It was part of bizarre testimony in which he described a dreamlike state in which he, and perhaps his sister, Dawn, committed the murders before he also killed her. DeFeo vaguely defended the killings as self-defense but also claimed to have murdered a dozen other people, and said he had plans to kill every one of his relatives, including the Genovese banana captain. If it was insanity method acting or, as he later claimed, his lawyer coaching him to get a book deal, DeFeo was quite committed to the role. DeFeo at one point exploded when Sullivan asked him about confessing to the jail guard. "I did not say that, I have more sense than that," DeFeo shouted at Sullivan, his face an angry red slate. "If I had any sense I'd come down there right now and kill you."

And then there was the line of testimony that helped spawn a lucrative dynasty of horror schlock. "For months before the incident,"

DeFeo said, "I heard voices, and whenever I looked around, there was no one there, so it must have been God talking to me."

But the jury disregarded the voice of God and denied DeFeo his insanity verdict. Judge Thomas Stark condemned him to six consecutive sentences of twenty-five years to life. It would be another two months before supernatural forces officially became a part of the Amityville saga.

* * *

A *Newsday* headline in early 1976 started it all: "DeFeo Home Abandoned, Buyer Calls It Haunted." The article detailed the ordeal of a family, George and Kathleen Lutz and three children, who had purchased the DeFeo murder house, 112 Ocean Avenue, for $40,000 and then fled it within ten days because they said it was possessed. The story was accompanied by a photo of the house's front door, which appeared to have been partially ripped off its hinges.

The article had everything Hollywood could want. The family "reported seeing human shapes in the house, told of strange sounds and vibrations, and said that the power would fail for unexplained reasons." There was a priest who visited the house toting a large cross; the involvement of psychic researchers; and an Amityville police captain who visited the house and later told his colleagues of strange vibrations. The Lutzes had done their own amateur sleuthing, including seeking blueprints from the DA's office and other research about the property in which they learned that "a tragedy had happened to every family that had lived there."

The article wouldn't have caused a ripple if it was published in the *National Enquirer*. But this was a newspaper in regular Pulitzer contention, citing confidential sources in the Suffolk County district attorney's office, about a house possessed by demons.

In fact, DeFeo's former court-appointed attorney made a meal out of it. The Lutzes became William Weber's newest clients, and he announced that the Lutzes' experience in the house had prompted him to consider an appeal on behalf of DeFeo, a legal motion citing those strange vibrations.

The next year, author Jay Anson published *The Amityville Horror*, a book billed as a true story based on the Lutzes' horrifying experiences in the house. It sold millions of copies. The movie adaptation, starring James Brolin and Margot Kidder as the Lutzes, was one of the highest-grossing films in the 1970s. It spawned a seemingly endless, and bottomless, run of Amityville-themed movies still haunting America today.

Seemingly everybody who touched the case, except for Butch DeFeo himself, benefited richly from it. That included its young lead prosecutor. In 1976, the year after the verdict, Gerald Sullivan was promoted to chief of the Major Offense Bureau, which oversaw homicides.

Spota's role in the DeFeo trial was largely unknown. He wasn't named in a single news story chronicling the case. So he filled the void with his own lore. He later described being at the murder scene while it was still splattered with blood, though in reality he didn't join the case until nine months later. And in hushed tones, he described a harrowing encounter with DeFeo. Spota claimed that he and a psychiatrist interviewed DeFeo in a cramped room in order to gauge his insanity defense before trial. Spota said DeFeo recalled seeing the toes of one of his brothers twitch following the shooting, leading him to surmise he was still alive.

"And I said to him, when you saw that your brother was still alive, what did you do?" Spota recalled.

"And he says: 'I shot him in the head.'"

That story may have gone down easily over clinking glasses of scotch, but there was likely no more truth to it than the Lutzes being chased out of their house by ghosts. DeFeo was indeed quizzed by a shrink but, according to the book written by Sullivan, he and Spota were only given a transcript of the interview that concerned the murders. Though court testimony suggested DeFeo said he saw the legs of one of his brothers twitch following the shooting, the brothers were each only shot once, and not in the head.

Prosecutorial fish tales aside, Spota's career was also transformed following his behind-the-scenes role in the case. O'Brien made him Sullivan's top deputy in the Major Offense Bureau. Spota then secured the murder convictions of a seemingly endless conga line of depraved Long Islanders. He got life sentences for a chess genius who slayed his family; a Hamptons farmer who resolved to kill prostitutes to keep them off his beaches; and a deranged murderer who threw candy at the jury and reportedly clobbered Spota over the head with a book.

Spota's niche paired him professionally with the cockiest, and most powerful, figures in the police department: its homicide detectives. They were virtually beyond supervision, working out of the little Homicide HQ in Hauppauge, eighteen miles west of the Yaphank offices of their top bosses. A sign on the homicide office's wall read: "Thou Shall Not Kill." Their pay rivaled that of the police commissioner. Homicide detectives were held in such high esteem in the county that they could get a prosecutor promoted by complimenting them to the DA.

Prosecutors often intentionally keep their distance from the cops who work their cases. But Spota made a number of the homicide bulls his closest friends. He became something like an honorary member of the squad. The relationships were symbiotic. The detectives, with their magic knack for pulling a confession in virtually every murder they investigated, consistently gave Spota his strongest trial ammunition.

For his part, Spota had the power to authorize overtime that would pay the detectives major dividends until death. Most veteran homicide detectives were near retirement, and their pensions were based on their total compensation in their final year in the department. Racking up significant overtime on their last lap could make for very comfortable golden years.

Homicide detectives constantly hung around the Major Offense Bureau. Even when ostensibly on a case, that didn't preclude them from shooting the shit and flirting with secretaries. When a jury was deliberating in a murder trial, a process that could last for days, the detectives on the case joined prosecutors to wait it out at their favored Riverhead watering hole, Esposito's. The detectives' overtime meter was still running as they downed drinks. The secretaries at the DA's office knew to call Esposito's when a verdict was in.

The homicide detectives were, as one defense attorney who had represented police put it, "almost princes of the county, who go anywhere, do anything." By the mid-1970s, at least one of those princes had decided to aid the ongoing plot to replace Spota's boss.

* * *

When Pete Fiorillo got a call from a mob associate on behalf of the Suffolk police commissioner, he started to wonder what was going on out on Long Island.

Fiorillo was then an investigator for the Manhattan DA's office, and the mobbed-up caller was Jimmy Muce, a Colombo crime family soldier who Fiorillo knew from his Brooklyn childhood. Muce told Fiorillo he recently had steaks with a Suffolk County homicide detective, August Stahl, who had asked him for his help with a current assignment. The Suffolk police commissioner was looking for dirt on Henry O'Brien, and the persistent gossip was that the DA was a homosexual.

Muce knew Fiorillo had previously worked with O'Brien when he was aiding a special prosecutor in Manhattan. The mobster wanted to know if Fiorillo had any sexual dirt concerning O'Brien to share and assured him: "I wouldn't be talking to you if this wasn't legit."

Fiorillo knew a little bit about Augie Stahl, a Germanic homicide detective who loved to pound his suspects and whose every other breath was the n-word. He took a while to process it all before responding to Muce: "Legit? You're a fucking gangster!"

It was another day in Suffolk: the police commissioner assigning a homicide detective to dig into the DA's sexual proclivities, and the job getting outsourced to a mobster.

A tuned-in newspaper reader could have seen some of this coming, as the innuendo was in every profile of O'Brien since he announced his candidacy. The stories invariably mentioned that he was a "bachelor," and a "shy, private" one at that. They described his tweed suits and made vague reference to his "life-style," including his stubborn patronage of a "student bar" called Long Island Potato.

As DA, O'Brien was both elusive and aggressive. He hired Suffolk's first Black prosecutor in 1974 but also fought for the criminalization of consensual sodomy, which effectively outlawed gay male sex, arguing "there is a sanctity in the marital relationship." And he antagonized the GOP as if unaware Suffolk was one of the Republican Party's strongholds.

Spota most likely played a small role in advancing the feud between O'Brien and Suffolk Police Commissioner Eugene Kelley. The top cop was a hypermasculine sort who never missed an opportunity to publicly mount a police motorcycle in a handmade leather suit. Following the DeFeo case, Spota wrapped up the sheriff's office investigation he had been previously working on. It resulted in the indictment of Suffolk County Sheriff Philip Corso, a Republican, on felony charges that he had extorted jail vendors for $50 political fundraiser tickets. The case was derided as a product of partisan vendetta, one of many O'Brien had spearheaded. Corso pleaded only to misdemeanors but agreed to leave office.

The case no doubt contributed to Kelley's tribal ire against O'Brien. The commissioner yanked out of the DA's office roughly three dozen police detectives who had been assigned there. O'Brien announced he was investigating Kelley for "misconduct in office" and other crimes. But the commissioner beat him to the punch, thanks indeed to assistance from mobsters.

The police commissioner personally filed a criminal complaint charging the DA had committed misdemeanor sex crimes involving a twenty-one-year-old male burglar who had been O'Brien's client when he was a private defense attorney. The burglar, Roger Barry Petersen, claimed in an affidavit that O'Brien had forcefully performed oral sex on him while he was driving.

The underworld intrigue behind this allegation was later revealed. Before O'Brien was elected, a mob-connected professional informant and habitual criminal, William O'Gorman, had told his handler in the Suffolk DA's office about an ongoing blackmail scheme by Petersen to record then candidate O'Brien coming on to him in his car. Commissioner Kelley heard rumors of this intel and recruited O'Gorman to spearhead his offensive against O'Brien. Kelley dispatched two detectives to Texas, where Petersen was a fugitive. They flew the burglar back home, interrogating him along the way as to whether the DA was a homosexual. After they landed, Kelley threw together an 11:00 p.m. impromptu legal hearing in his office, with a judge present, in which Petersen made his allegations against O'Brien while not being advised of his right to counsel.

Petersen said of the deal behind his allegations against O'Brien: "I could either do five years in jail or go with them and do no time." Another young man who gave statements implicating the DA said he and Petersen both lied under police pressure.

The saga of the lawmen's feud, drawn out over a couple of years, became an open sore of embarrassment for the governance of Suffolk County. New York City had its own ongoing law enforcement melodrama, as former detective Frank Serpico had recently testified about systemic corruption in the NYPD. But there was something special about a jurisdiction in which the DA himself spoke in paranoid terms about a police "goon squad" and publicly admitted: "I am frightened for my life."

New York Governor Hugh Carey ultimately assigned a special grand jury to examine both the charges against O'Brien and the feud that precipitated them. His special prosecutor, Joseph Hoey, seemed reluctant to plunge too deep into the dark heart of Suffolk County. What he fished from the shallow end were troubling blips: Judges who disregarded constitutional procedure to advance partisan grudges. A detective who acted as a mole within the DA's office and filed false affidavits about what he saw there. A "tradition" by police brass of not reporting criminal conduct in the department to the DA's office. It all suggested a world of unseen chicanery, one the state's agents took care not to stir up too much.

For Sullivan and Spota, the feud was perhaps an even greater boon to their careers than convicting Butch DeFeo. The grand jury didn't bring charges against either Kelley or O'Brien, clearing the latter of the pending sex abuse charges. Despite the exoneration, O'Brien's tenure as DA was ruined by the phantom blowjob. In November 1977, voters ended the Democratic experiment in Suffolk County law enforcement by electing a figurehead of the old guard.

The new DA, Patrick Henry, was a jowly, hard-drinking forty-eight-year-old former Navy man. Before resigning earlier that year, Henry had been O'Brien's top deputy. His father was Lindsay Henry, whose own tenure as DA in the 1950s included overseeing the botched Lyde Kitchner murder case in Smithtown.

Henry fiercely embraced an ethos similar to that of Sullivan and Spota. He believed that innocent men didn't confess, jailhouse snitches were truthful, homicide detectives didn't violate defendants' rights, and prosecutors never knowingly introduced perjured testimony. His philosophy held it was better to take a weak case to trial and risk acquittal than not indict in the first place. He apparently had no fear of the other possibility, that an innocent person might be convicted.

Upon election he promoted Sullivan to chief trial assistant, making him the third most powerful attorney in the office. And Henry had a special affection for Spota. Henry slotted his protégé into Sullivan's old gig. Only six years removed from the toilets at the asphalt plant, Spota was made chief of the Major Offense Bureau, in charge of all murder prosecutions in the county.

That was Spota's role late on April 28, 1979, as he listened to the tape of Peter Quartararo's confession and had the same realization as his buddy Sullivan a few years earlier. He had some holes to plug.

* * *

In a Juvenile Aid Room in the Fourth Precinct, former elementary school teacher Carolyn Quartararo sounded out every word as if it were a foreign object in her mouth: "Did you and Michael help kill the Pius boy?"

She was talking to her son Peter, whose head hung low. His tormentor, Anthony Palumbo, sat with them. Peter quietly told the story again while his mother listened in stunned silence. He said he hooked his fingers inside Johnny's lips to keep the boy's mouth open so he and others could throw rocks in. He told how they then laid two logs on top of Johnny's body.

When he was done, Palumbo called for Peter's kid brother Michael, who had been brought by their mother to the precinct. The detective told Michael that Peter had just confessed to the murder, and now it was time for him to do the same. Mike exploded, insisting that he didn't know what his brother was talking about, and that he never even saw Johnny Pius that night.

Peter asked to be left alone with his mom, and Palumbo agreed. As soon as Palumbo left, Peter told his mother: "I didn't do it."

* * *

While the saga of Peter's on-again, off-again confession unfolded and the boys' parents sought to rescue them from police custody, an oblivious Tom Ryan and Rob Brensic were stashed in a nearby file room. They watched a tiny black-and-white television set. *Supertrain* was on first. Then came a *Saturday Night Live* rerun, which told the boys it was almost midnight.

From the moment Spota had arrived at the precinct, he had taken full control of the investigation. That was unusual, as typically the DA's office didn't get involved in a police case until there was an arrest. But in the week since Johnny's murder, the upper ranks of both the police department and the DA's office had grown restless over the apparent stall in a high-profile case.

In the view of the lawmen, this wasn't the fault of the homicide detectives who had spent precious investigative time interrogating teenagers seemingly chosen at random. No, it was the fault of the Smithtown neighbors, who had given authorities "complaints, not cooperation," as a police inspector put it. Spota was determined, in consultation with Pat Henry, to arrest somebody, or somebodies, no matter how loudly their parents protested.

Michael and Peter's father, Philip Quartararo, arrived at the precinct from his home in Queens near 11:00 p.m. that night. When his ex-wife had called earlier to tell him Peter was missing, the cocksure IBM salesman had told her to calm down and said: "Have no fear." He'd handle it. He was a former auxiliary Suffolk cop, after all.

He asked the detectives and the boys' mom to leave the room, and he spoke alone with his sons. He hugged them and said it was better to tell the truth now. Both boys adamantly denied having anything to do with Johnny's killing. Philip asked Peter why he would say he did something like that if he hadn't.

"Dad, you don't know what it was like in there," Peter explained. "They were constantly yelling and calling me names, and they were calling Mom names, and they were calling you names. They kept on saying, 'You guys and your brother are going to go away for twenty-five years.'"

Philip would get a firsthand taste of the treatment his son was talking about. Palumbo asked for one last session alone with Peter while his dad waited outside. Philip later described the shouting he heard inside: "A lot of fucks, bastards, sons-of-a-bitches, 'Why are you letting those Irish bastards get away with this?'" When the other cops realized the dad was listening, they physically ushered Philip out of earshot under the auspices of getting him a cup of coffee.

Spota huddled with Pat Henry and another top prosecutor. There was no denying that the case was weak. The taped confession was enough to indict Peter, but it would undoubtedly be challenged in court. And it would be considered inadmissible hearsay against the other three boys. So Spota made the decision to release them all that night.

Rob Brensic went home first, thanks to the help of a lawyer uncle. Then a detective showed up in the file room for Tom Ryan, telling him that though he had been under arrest for the minibike theft, he should now consider himself unarrested. Tom walked out of the room in rubber galoshes, as the detectives had demanded the JCPenney sneakers off his feet. Later, they'd seize the sneakers from the gym lockers of Brensic and the Quartararos. None matched the imprint on Johnny's face.

Tom Ryan, free after twelve hours, hesitated on his way out. He told a detective he had a junior permit that didn't allow him to drive after 9:00 p.m. The detective told him he was okay to drive with it, just this one time. Though the detectives now believed Ryan's car was the getaway vehicle for an extremely bloody murder, they apparently never considered examining it for evidence.

Before the Quartararos were released, the detectives had one last requirement for them. The cops later said having the boys take a polygraph was their dad's idea. But Philip claimed Palumbo had insisted that the boys were going straight to "the shelter," meaning juvenile detention, unless they took a test.

The testing facility was out in Yaphank, requiring a sad midnight caravan along the Long Island Expressway for the boys, their parents, and the cops. Tested separately, the boys were warmed up with a series of routine personal questions. When asked about the best thing that ever happened to them, Mike answered: "born." Peter answered: "stereo." Asked for the worst thing, both answered: "This." They denied having anything to do with Pius's death. But when they were done, the polygraph administrator reported that they were both lying. Nonetheless, a failed polygraph—known even back then to be an unreliable barometer of the truth—wasn't enough to arrest them.

What pissed Philip off the most was the way in which he was told his sons were being released, after hours of manipulation, lies, and abuse. "Phil, take your boys home," Palumbo said casually. "We got nothing."

The father exploded, ranting at the detective about how he was a lying son of a bitch. By the time the Quartararos got outside and to their cars, the sun was out and it was about seven o'clock the morning.

Spota and his colleagues had debated putting a wire on Peter to catch him and his brother discussing the murder. Spota decided against that idea. But he had a very specific goal in sending the four boys out into the Smithtown wild. Spota "hoped against hope," as he later put it, that the boys would run into their own version of Jimmy DeVito.

CHAPTER 4

PIT PEOPLE

Call it a family tradition or something more like inertia, but the kid's future was already laid out for him. James Charles Burke was born on October 6, 1964, at Peninsula General Hospital in Queens. His grandfather, James Vincent, was a city cop weaned in Ozone Park. His father, George, was also NYPD and settled in the neighboring Howard Beach. Cops breed cops, so it was a safer bet than most of the ponies running at the nearby Aqueduct Racetrack: Jimmy Burke was gonna be NYPD, and he was gonna live out by the JFK airport.

But shortly after Jimmy's brother Michael was born in 1966, their parents split up. Their mother, Frances, didn't move them far. They joined her parents in an Archie Bunker–esque railroad house on 91st Street in Ozone Park. Franny's dad was a baker. Her brother, Michael Lo Cascio, returned home from combat in Vietnam in 1968. For a time all six family members lived in a narrow home crowded like they were on the inside of the A train.

Almost every weekday for about a decade, Jimmy Burke and his brother walked two blocks to a mustard-yellow church campus on Rockaway Boulevard. The neighborhood was a Frankie Valli ballad come to life, and The Nativity of the Blessed Virgin Mary was its spiritual heart. Generations of gangsters from Vito Genovese to John Gotti had christened their babies and mourned their dead there while detectives snapped photos from across the street. But for Jimmy and Michael, it was just school.

Their uniform was slacks, a white shirt, and a red tie monogrammed with the school's initials: NBVM. Wardrobe infractions could get your knuckles rapped by the ruler-happy nuns. More serious misconduct would land you in the principal's office of Sister Marguerite Torre, sibling to Major League ballplayer and future legendary Yankees manager Joe Torre.

Jimmy's longtime classmate Karyn Follar explained that part of the reason parents signed their roughly $500-per-annum tuition checks to NBVM was to avoid their children falling in with the "wiseguy wannabes over on 101st Avenue." That street, around the corner from the school, was home to the Bergin Hunt and Fish Club, the not-so-secret headquarters of the Gambino crime family.

The mob may have been what the neighborhood was known for, but more residents were members of a far more unbreakable cabal: the municipal pension fund. John Ragano, an Ozone Park lawyer and close friend of Jimmy's uncle, said that most kids there didn't aspire to higher education, but instead aimed for civil service jobs, such as working for the subway system or the police department.

Ozone Park was in the city, but it felt like a small town. It was home to packs of murderous criminals, but many residents didn't feel compelled to lock their front doors. Since young gangsters hung out in the parks, Ragano explained, other kids stuck to the baseball diamonds, or to the street game called stoopball. "Nobody had a lot of money," Ragano said, "but you also didn't go without."

Jimmy's classmates remembered him as the brightest among them. "I wish I had a brain like his," Follar said. She described him as "always uplifting and funny" with his classmates and "really, really smart with very little effort." Jimmy, she said, was a straight-A student, a literal altar boy on Sundays, and neither a nerd nor a bully. "He just kind of floated above it all," Follar said. Classmate Joseph Addabbo recalled Jimmy Burke similarly, as the kid who was always shooting his arm in the air for the nuns to call on him. Addabbo, a congressman's son who is now himself a state senator, said Jimmy was a spelling bee monster who after defeating his class would then easily whup the champions of the other classes.

By the late 1970s, the certainty that Jimmy would mimic his cop father and grandfather had faded, along with his relationship with his dad. George was a police officer in Brooklyn's 75th, a precinct so rank with drug money and corruption that it had converted many cops into criminals themselves. By then George had remarried and had another son with his new wife. The boy was named after him, and everybody called him Junie, for Junior. He took over the legacy that had previously seemed slated for Jimmy. Junie grew into a hulking 275-pound NYPD detective and amateur football player.

George Burke would still come to some of Jimmy and Michael's school events and chat it up with the other cop dads. But their mom's brother, Lo Cascio, had by then become more of a father figure to the two boys. Family friend Ragano described Jimmy and his dad as estranged.

In 1978, the local pack of professional hoods capitalized on the proximity of JFK airport. The Bergin Hunt and Fish Club crew pulled off one of the most lucrative heists in American history, stealing roughly $6 million in cash and jewelry from the Lufthansa cargo hold. The story of the crime was later adapted into the film *Goodfellas*, with Robert De Niro playing the character Jimmy "The Gent" Conway, who was based on the heist's real life mastermind: an orphan turned gangster coincidentally named Jimmy Burke.

As it happened, 1978 was our Jimmy Burke's last year in Ozone Park. His mother married again, to a suburban businessman named John Toal. He lived in Nassau County, but in starting a family with Franny and her two sons, he bought a home in a booming far-off suburb called Smithtown. The home was a sprawling white hi-ranch with a portico, a two-car garage, and a rolling green buzz cut of a lawn.

At thirteen years old, every element of Jimmy's life changed. He had until then known only the city. His new home was a highway exit fifty miles east, population one hundred thousand. His mom's new husband was a straitlaced former Navy man who owned a series of suburban refrigerator repair companies with dad-joke titles like Weather or Not; Day and Night; Mister Frost.

When his name was called on his first day as a high school freshman in Smithtown in the fall of 1978, Jimmy shot up out of his seat and announced his presence. The other kids tittered at Jimmy's crisp dress slacks and tie and militaristic manner. But within a semester, Jimmy had scrubbed away all residue of the Catholic school spelling bee champ from Queens.

* * *

For Spota and the homicide detectives, an inconvenient thing happened while they waited for their four suspects to blab about having committed the murder. Somebody else did instead.

It was April 29, the day after Peter had confessed on tape. Three teenagers were outside of a house near the Dogwood school. A hulking eighteen-year-old named Robert V. Burke, no relation to James, hopped out of the passenger side of a friend's car. He brought up Johnny's murder. "Did you hear what happened?" he asked. "I did it."

"I shoved my cock in his mouth and he choked on it," Robert explained, according to one of the boys. The other boys remembered the wording slightly differently, but the substance of it was the same. Robert said "no one would know" about the sexual assault because he then put pebbles down the boys' mouth.

The detectives heard about Robert's boast, and a couple of weeks later had the boys sign statements as to what he had said. Perhaps it was nothing more than the tasteless shock humor of a teenager. Two of the boys appeared to interpret it that way. One of them wrote that he wasn't "paying much attention" to Robert. The other said he "didn't want to listen to Burke, so I turned him off."

With almost any other boy in Smithtown, empty braggadocio would have been a solid assumption. But Robert Burke was different, and the detectives had known it from the very beginning of their investigation. On the Monday after Johnny's murder, Gill and Reck met with a confidential source in the parking lot of the Smith Haven Mall. The source was an employee of the Smithtown Central School District. He was never identified, even in court proceedings, a precaution typically not even afforded to witnesses testifying against murderous mob bosses. The reason the employee was adamant that he not be named was because he was afraid of Robert Burke.

The employee told the detectives that Robert was the only kid he knew in Smithtown who was "capable of committing the type of crime committed on the victim." Even then, only two days after the murder, the detectives had already heard lots about Robert, noting in a report that his "name has appeared several times in the course of this investigation."

Everybody who had crossed paths with Robert Burke, including members of his own family, agreed that he was mentally disturbed and prone to extreme violence, sometimes of a sexual nature. The detectives heard anecdotes about Robert that brought to mind the manner in which Johnny Pius died. After Robert had knocked a kid unconscious behind Smithtown High School East, he kicked and stomped his victim's face. Robert's half-sister had accused him of molesting her, and afterward his parents found out that he "threatened to kill himself or someone else," the detectives learned.

Robert was the son of a city firefighter. According to his brother, Jose, Robert's budding propensity for violence was one of the reasons his family moved to Smithtown. They had previously lived in Jamaica, Queens, one of the roughest neighborhoods in the city. As a young teenager, Robert had become smitten by the idea of joining a gang after watching a kid wearing a "Savage Nomads" motorcycle vest saunter through a Burger King, belligerently eating fries from the tables of strangers. Robert started getting arrested frequently for fighting or stealing, including an instance in which he kicked through the window of a police car from the inside.

Robert Burke's family moved to Franklin Drive in 1975, directly across the street from the Pius house. Jose and Robert Burke befriended Tony Cannone, Johnny Pius's cousin, and often swam in the Piuses' pool. Robert's mom was Colombian, and he and his siblings were among the few non-white kids in Smithtown. Robert's nickname in Queens had been Bean, a term for the young kid hanging out with older boys. In Smithtown, his new neighbors quickly adapted his moniker into a casual slur.

Before his first day at Smithtown's Nesaquake Middle School, Robert shaved his scalp clean. He seemed eager for somebody to make a snide remark about it, and the captain of the football team obliged. Robert flattened him with a punch to the head. Jose believed this was his brother's way of introducing himself to Smithtown's version of gangs—the hulking white bullies who played varsity football and lacrosse.

Robert's behavior in the years preceding Johnny's murder went beyond fights at school. In 1976, he was evaluated by a Hofstra University psychologist, who found that Robert had "an anti-authority attitude and poor control over impulses." He seemed to be getting more violent, particularly after Jose left home to join the Air Force in 1977. "During this period, to be honest, Robert was a scary guy," said Jose. "If you were not on Robert's right side, you know, you'd get a good punch in the face."

Robert was increasingly prone to random violence, including running up on a woman on the street, removing her glasses, and punching her in the face. A probation officer once wrote that "when drinking heavily Robert Burke experiences anti-social behavior and seems to become extremely uninhibited sexually." Even one of his best friends, Cannone, later noted that Robert preyed on kids with smaller builds, like that of Johnny. "He loved to beat up smaller guys than him," Cannone said. "He had a thing about that."

Cannone considered himself an amateur detective in the murder of his little cousin Johnny Pius, including going around town with a hidden tape recorder trying to catch other teenagers confessing. He did not suspect Robert of the murder, but not because the violence was out of character. To the contrary, Cannone felt the crime scene showed too much "remorse."

In particular, he didn't think Robert would have placed Johnny's bike up against a tree. That was a telling detail, as it would later be undisputed in court testimony that Johnny's bike was found on the ground, and was only leaned against the tree following the discovery of the kid's body. "He doesn't have the smarts to do something and to clean it up," Cannone reasoned. "Like if he said he did that crime, he wouldn't put the bike back on the tree. He'd just get out of there."

The detectives had access to most of this information about Robert's proclivity for serious violence. But they were oddly apathetic about pursuing him. The detectives did show up at Robert's house a couple of times, but they didn't seem determined to track him down. They accepted his stepmother's word that he wasn't there even though they saw his parked car. She said he was at work at a factory, but she didn't know which one, and the detectives didn't ask her to find out.

The detectives didn't interview Robert until May 8, more than two weeks after Johnny's body was discovered. Unlike the other boys, the detectives allowed him to bring his father, the firefighter, to the interview. Robert said that on the night of Johnny's death, he was at a party at a girlfriend's house in St. James. He gave her name as Nancy, but he didn't know her last name. He said he was there from 8:00 p.m. and slept over until the following day, and that a friend of his, Chris Dixon, could corroborate that account. A few days after the interview, the detectives learned that Robert had previously told the three boys that he was the killer.

Even so, the detectives did not check out Robert's alibi until late June, after memories had surely faded. By then, the detectives were firmly latched on to the four other boys as suspects, even though Spota's plan to wait for neighborhood snitches to come to them was going slowly, and there hadn't been any indictments. When the detectives interviewed Robert's friend, Dixon, he corroborated that he and Robert had gone to a party thrown by a girl named Nancy. But the detectives didn't ascertain what time he got there, only that it was "early."

The detectives also spoke to the supposed girlfriend, Nancy Ness. According to the cops, she said that the party at her parents' house was the first time she met Robert, and that he stayed all night. But Nancy said she didn't know anybody else at her own party. The detectives didn't attempt to find any others who were there.

Gill later acknowledged that "the fact that she told us she was there," meaning that Nancy was at a party at her home as Robert Burke had said, "was the sum total" of their investigation of his alibi.

Even Robert's brother, Jose, noticed that the detectives appeared more concerned with clearing Robert than Robert himself did. "It was almost as if the police had to work hard to say, 'Hey, it wasn't you, knucklehead,'" Jose said.

The only professional sleuth seriously probing Robert's whereabouts that night was a private investigator by the name of Herman Race. Tom Ryan's family had hired Race, a former NYPD detective, shortly after the boys were interrogated. Race was familiar with the county players, as he had also been hired by the defense in Butch DeFeo's case.

In trying to backtrack the homicide detectives' investigation into Robert Burke's alibi, Race found a web of contradictions. Ness told him in an interview that Robert Burke had actually arrived at her house that night at 10:30 or 11:00 p.m., and not with Chris Dixon but with another male friend. Burke had then left at around 3:00 or 4:00 a.m. When Race interviewed the girl again a few days later, Ness said she now realized she had been mistaken, and that Robert had arrived at her party at 6:30 or 7:00 p.m. Ness was adamant, however, that the detectives' report that Robert had stayed at her house all night was "absolutely untrue."

Race prepared a report for the Ryan family in which he relayed his confusion about the police treatment of the Robert Burke matter. He pointed out that in a statement written by one of the boys to whom Burke had confessed, a sentence had been crossed out. The sentence referred to Robert Burke saying he had been joined in the murder by another friend with a criminal record, also a city firefighter's son.

Race didn't understand why the detectives had chosen their four suspects over Robert Burke. "Certainly, based upon these three sworn statements given by the youths, there would have been more than enough to present to a Grand Jury, it would seem," Race wrote. "Apparently at this point, [it's] only the fact that Nancy Ness puts him at her house early [that] absolves him. But if she is mistaken and it certainly seems that she is confused—now what?"

Spota had a simple answer. They already had their perps. "There were never any other suspects after Peter Quartararo confessed," he later said.

* * *

Anthropology teacher Suzanne Spina wasn't very interested in the good kids, probably because she used to be one herself. Smithtown High School East had more than its share of National Merit scholars and brainy overachievers. Journalist Soledad O'Brien and author Jodi Picoult were both early '80s graduates of the school. But Spina was drawn more to what she described as "kids who were on the edge, the Jimmy Burkes of the world."

She described him as a fascinating and charming kid, and one who was genuinely interested in an experimental curriculum she introduced in 1979. She asked her students to produce ethnographic studies of the customs of their own peers. Some of them wrote about teenage truancy, hanging out at the mall, and sexual activity. Jimmy decided to study what he called his own kind: the drug users. He had quickly become familiar with the slang Smithtown kids used to classify themselves. You were either a "jock," a "dexter"—equivalent to a nerd—or a "head," which meant you experimented with drugs. Classing himself as the latter, Jimmy undertook what he called a "three-year study of drug use." He claimed he interviewed more than two hundred fellow heads, drug dealers, and police officers.

Jimmy's findings were in some ways a clear-eyed critique of his new, sheltered environs. He said that Smithtown's wealth made drug use more prevalent, not less, as the students had the cash to buy the stuff. Kids smoked less pot in the winter, he observed, because most drug deals occurred outdoors, and the coddled suburban kids didn't like to freeze. Weather aside, drug use was much more common than their parents and teachers thought. "What I found out is that most adults have the misconception that only kids with problems use drugs," Jimmy said in summarizing his research. "More than 90 percent of kids that go to school here will try drugs in one form or another before they leave."

Spina's curriculum was bold enough to draw the attention of journalists. Her classes were featured in *Newsday*, *30 Minutes*—CBS's kid-focused version of *60 Minutes*—and even the *New York Times*. Jimmy commandeered the reporter for the *Times* when she visited the school. He gave her a tour of The Pit, the school's "outdoor cement lounge" where students smoked cigarettes. The Pit did not attract Smithtown East's scholastic overachievers. The kids who gathered in the dirty alcove (and tended to be heads, drinkers, and truants) were known as "The Pit People."

Spina called Jimmy "one of the most interesting kids" she taught in her career. And yet the highest grade he ever got in her class was a C. That was better than most of his other classes in his first couple years in Smithtown, where he was prone to Ds or Fs. He had done stints in summer school to make up ninth grade math and tenth grade English. Jimmy didn't like classroom rules, Spina observed, such as doing his assignments. And he may have gotten a bit too close to his anthropological subject matter.

According to Jimmy, he smoked his first joint at age fourteen, in the park across the street from his stepdad's house. He later blamed peer pressure: "I had moved from Queens to Long Island and was hanging out with older kids." When he got home, he said, Frances asked him why his eyes were red. Afraid to get caught, he swore off pot for about two years before resuming semi-regular smoking.

Later in his high school career, Jimmy said, he sampled harder stuff but just didn't have any luck. He snorted coke but didn't "get off," and determined it was a waste of money. Mescaline made him sick. A quaalude put him to sleep. He tried diet pills as a form of "ups," but they gave Jimmy stomach cramps. There is reason to suspect he understated his drug use, however. The source of these accounts was his later application to be a police officer.

But back in high school, he had self-identified, in the country's most prominent newspaper no less, as a "head." By then, according to the application, Jimmy's drug use would've totaled two marijuana joints, which if true meant he was The Pit's biggest poseur. His new friends in Smithtown included full-blown addicts with ready access to hard drugs. And Jimmy had such a well-known reputation for keeping up with those friends that even the yearbook committee took a snarky dig at it. In the student "prophesy" page one year, they called him the "next Jim Morrison." Jimmy Burke wasn't a musician. It was a reference to Morrison's overdose earlier that decade.

Spina wasn't the only teacher who was smitten with Jimmy. Social studies teacher Jack Breen recalled him as a "great kid in high school," and had no idea he was anywhere near trouble. It was evidence that even back then, Jimmy's defining trait was chameleon skin, an ability to shift between multiple worlds.

Christine De Vallee phrased Jimmy's salient skill more directly. She was Burke's high school classmate who then became a Suffolk County police officer, meaning that she got to know him over decades.

De Vallee said that though the teachers may have been fooled, most students knew that he was, like the rest of his crew of friends, a no-good kid deep into drugs, burglary, and violence.

But De Vallee allowed: "He's a great bullshit artist."

* * *

Shortly after moving to Smithtown, Jimmy had emerged as the leader of a group of neighborhood boys who didn't share his interest in snowing teachers or impressing a *New York Times* reporter.

There was George Heiselmann, from Dartmouth Avenue, a year younger than Jimmy. A school bus driver once caught Heiselmann choking on gasoline as he was siphoning it out of the bus's tank. After getting busted burglarizing a house on nearby Maple Avenue, he was by age thirteen a grizzled veteran of Family Court.

Danny Culotta of Fifty Acre Road was a squat kid with the rugged face of a boxer. In '79, his dad was sent to federal prison for smuggling weed. Danny inherited his extralegal expertise, which included a mental map of every nearby pawnbroker that would buy stolen gold. More impressively, he had an experienced criminal's knack for saving his own hide, including using a hidden body mic to catch those same pawnshops in the act of buying stolen merchandise.

Rounding out the crew: Donald "Chip" Brensic, Rob's wild younger brother. Chip was squirmy and fearless. He'd have one of his friends, usually Danny, go through the phone book calling houses. If nobody picked up, Chip would soon be wiggling through a basement window to grab indiscriminate handfuls of jewelry. Culotta would then use his well-trained eye to pick out the valuable stuff, and they'd throw away the rest.

Culotta estimated he and Chip pulled off about fifty to sixty burglaries in a matter of a couple of years. They obsessively tracked the price of gold which, in the late 1970s, happened to be skyrocketing. Culotta bragged that he made $1,600 from a single burglary in St. James. They operated with near-impunity because they knew, unlike Peter Quartararo, that until they turned sixteen, cops usually had to release them to their parents in less than an hour.

Naturally, the police in the Fourth Precinct knew this crew well. One patrolman estimated he had spoken with Culotta two dozen times. So the crew also became known to the detectives investigating Johnny's murder, who sought to sniff out every juvenile delinquent operating in close proximity to the Dogwood school.

True to their anti-documentation policy, the Suffolk detectives didn't produce reports naming any of Jimmy Burke's set as suspects or stating what, if any, alibis they had for that night. But Culotta later acknowledged that the detectives told him he was a suspect in Johnny's murder. And Jimmy described to Spina, his favorite teacher, a session with the detectives that sounded like an interrogation.

Jimmy told her that he had been questioned about the murder in police offices, and then the detective stepped away, leaving behind a folder he said the boy was not to touch. Naturally, Jimmy opened the folder. Inside were photos of Johnny Pius's bloodied body. "And he looked at those pictures and he was really shaken by what he saw," Spina said.

By the summer following the murder, nobody had been indicted for Johnny's murder. But every kid in Smithtown knew who the chief suspects were. There's no due process in a schoolyard, and Rob Brensic, Tom Ryan, and the Quartararo brothers were condemned as Johnny's murderers. The most extreme ire was directed at the Quartararos. The family was subject to prank calls and death threats, including one referring to them as "dirty, lousy wops." According to Mike Quartararo, Tony Cannone, Johnny's cousin, showed up at the Quartararos' home carrying a hammer and threatening to burn the house down. Later that same day, Mike Quartararo and Rob Brensic were riding their minibikes across Smithtown East grounds when Mike spotted Cannone and Robert Burke in a car. In an episode oddly similar to the police theory of Johnny's killing, Mike said Cannone got out of the car and chased him down. Cannone knocked Quartararo over and punched him upside the head, face, and stomach while yelling: "I'm going to kill you! Where's your brother? I'm going to kill him too!" As Quartararo managed to get up and run away, Cannone lit his minibike on fire.

Mike Quartararo said that being branded a murderer made him a pariah among the friends he used to hang out with. So he sought out the only crew that had no such qualms: Jimmy Burke and his burglar buddies. Jimmy became one of Quartararo's closest friends for a while. Quartararo said that Jimmy never referred to his cop dad in Queens, and he assumed the refrigeration repair guy was Jimmy's actual father. Jimmy, the plotter of the crew, did voice aspirations to join the police—but not because he wanted to serve and protect. "He said he wanted to be a cop so he could get away with breaking the law," Quartararo said.

Sometimes Rob Brensic, who was friends with Jimmy's kid brother Mike, would tag along with Jimmy's crew to smoke weed or drink beer. Rob remembered seeing the boys empty out pillowcases full of jewelry while discussing the current price of an ounce of gold. Unlike Mike Quartararo and his own brother Chip, Rob Brensic only vaguely knew Jimmy Burke, who he recalled as a "freakin' creepy dude as a kid."

There was an erratic and hostile quality to these relationships. Chip Brensic, George Heiselmann, and a third boy used their base-ment window trick to break into the Quartararos' house at one point. They smoked Mike's weed until Peter Quartararo came home and angrily chased them away. Another time a friend of the boys suddenly began calling Rob Brensic a "puss," and punching him in the face.

Their preferred hangouts were parks, fields, under bleachers, or by the train station, anywhere they could smoke weed and drink beer without their parents seeing. By the summer of 1979, several months after Johnny's murder, that investigation hung over these sessions, in-fusing them with posturing and paranoia. The kids were not unlike a crew of Ozone Park mobsters, attempting to carry on as normal while secretly wondering who would flip on the others first.

* * *

While some of their sons schemed against each other, Smithtown's parents were apoplectic over the stagnating investigation. Smithtown had been a place where nobody locked their doors, and now residents wanted klieg lights to be trained on every patch of woods in town. Parent-teacher association meetings devolved into shouting matches over the Pius case. Half the parents were outraged there had been no arrests, and the other half were equally upset about the Stasi tactics being used on their kids. At one meeting, a police supervisor in the Fourth Precinct shouted down the latter group: "If we have stepped over the line, it was not with intent to hurt, but to put an end to this mystery!"

But Suffolk's top law enforcement honchos also publicly blamed each other for the open case. The police deputy commissioner complained to a newspaper reporter that prosecutors were delaying indictments in order to pressure one of the suspects to turn state's witness. DA Henry called that a "cheap shot," and said his office would seek indictments only after the detectives provided "a sufficient amount of evidence."

The detectives were desperate to get that evidence the only way they knew how. They were trying to flip every kid in town, taking a special interest in Mike Quartararo's thirteen-year-old girlfriend. They showed up at her house and asked if she had questioned Mike as to whether he was involved in the murder. She said she had, but his sarcastic reply—"What do you think?"—wasn't the smoking gun the detectives were hoping for.

Spota offered the Quartararo brothers a deal that would have convicted them in juvenile court and left them without an adult criminal record. Spota then made similar overtures to Rob Brensic and Ryan. He demanded in each case that they admit to the murder and testify against the others, and the boys all refused.

At the same time, Spota was dealing with a small fire set by Manhattan interlopers. The *National Law Journal*, which billed itself as "The Weekly Newspaper for the Profession," was not read outside of the oak-lined studies of private clubs. But in June 1979, a couple of months after Peter Quartararo's confession, a writer for the journal took withering, well-researched aim at the methods of cops and prosecutors in Spota's purview.

In the article, titled, "When Suspects Are Abused: Allegations of Beatings, Forced Confessions in a N.Y. Suburb Are Widespread," writer Rafael Abramovitz detailed more than thirty recent cases in which suspects alleged they had been tortured or beaten into confessing. The piece contained allegations of downright creative brutality: detectives threatened to feed a suspect's penis into a shredder, or slowly ran over their legs with a police car, or put a gun to their head and threatened to pull the trigger, or pummeled them so badly that they vomited blood.

In some cases, the abuse had been virtually proven. After a murder suspect claimed detectives had beaten him over the head with a concrete block muffled by a phone book, doctors found gravel embedded in his scalp. That suspect's confession didn't match the specifics of the crime scene, and a judge dismissed the indictment. The suspect accepted $35,000 to settle a lawsuit against the county, which his lawyer said was rife with "third-degree police-state methods."

The article contended that Suffolk County prosecutors were well aware of the torture and abuse driving the confessions that they used to secure convictions. Abramovitz wrote: "Such methods are indisputably illegal. Why, then, have prosecutors permitted them to continue?" His answer was that Suffolk authorities appeared incapable of trying a homicide case without a confession. He found that twenty-seven of twenty-eight murder indictments in the previous year included a confession. It was a 97 percent rate, much higher than that of neighboring counties. The coerced confessions went hand in hand with the other Suffolk trick, which was to deny defendants access to their attorneys. Abramovitz found seven convictions, five of them in murder cases, that had been overturned on appeal due to Suffolk police ignoring that constitutional right.

Suffolk homicide detectives weren't too concerned about the *National Law Journal* story. The next time they had a picnic, the homicide squad, including those who worked on the Pius case, posed for a group photo in custom-made T-shirts reading "97%."

The *National Law Journal* story made brief reference to the stalled Pius case as another example of a homicide investigation reliant on a disputed confession taken out of the presence of a defense attorney. "There is a growing consensus among local defense attorneys and prosecutors," the story read, "that the rights of the youths may have been so seriously compromised that the chances of successful prosecution have been jeopardized."

Perhaps Tom Spota took that as a challenge. Two months later, a pair of detectives visited Jimmy Burke's house, and the kid took a stab at the first version of a story he would tell for the next eleven years.

CHAPTER 5

TRAPPERS

It looked like a casting call for Smithtown's juvenile delinquents and their borderline buddies. Tom Spota was seated at a large table splayed with documents, while a two-person crew kept a camera trained on him. "Keep it running," Spota instructed them. Sometimes a boom mic jutted into the shot.

The first kid to sit at the table that late morning—January 17, 1981—was John McCort, a lean, mostly monosyllabic sixteen-year-old boy with a mane of dark hair, accompanied by his mom. Michael Burke was next, Jimmy's fourteen-year-old kid brother who stared at Spota like a scared deer. Spota soothed him with some quasi baby talk. "These fellas over here are recording the whole thing on television," Spota said, and then indicated a stenographer, "and this young lady is taking it down on her machine."

Spota made for a chipper, gum-chewing presence that morning. He stammered and giggled, played with his pen, and flirted with the stenographer. Perhaps he felt he had reason to be giddy. With each Smithtown teenager who entered this mustard-walled room and told their version of the story, Spota was cementing a case many other prosecutors would've given up on.

Two months earlier, he had returned indictments against Peter Quartararo, Michael Quartararo, and Robert Brensic. That morning's roll call of Pit People wasn't just bolstering Spota's case. When it came to

Brensic and Michael Quartararo, they were his case. As for Tom Ryan, Spota had decided to momentarily cut bait, as he had zero evidence or witness statements against him. But he considered that a work in progress, with a different army of teenage snitches having been deployed.

The third boy to enter Spota's interview room had the most genial confidence of the bunch. A patchy unibrow crept down the bridge of his pudgy nose. He wore blue jeans and a light blue collared shirt with long sleeves tight around a trim build.

"Uh, my name is James Burke," the kid said when prompted, fiddling with his hands, which were folded on the table in front of him, and then added his address on Fifty Acre Road.

"Okay," Spota said. "Jimmy—"

The stenographer interjected, reminding Spota that they hadn't sworn the boy in. She asked the boy: "Could you raise your right hand, please?"

Jimmy hesitated. "Um, raise my right hand," he said with a sheepish grin, momentarily staring at his hands while trying to remember which was which.

* * *

"Come on, you old beast. Don't stall out on me now."

After Anthony Palumbo's muffled pleas to his car, silence filled the Riverhead courtroom. Judge Robert Warren Doyle asked: "That concludes the playing of the tape?"

There is nothing more sacred in a trial than the lunch break. So after they heard the recording of Peter calmly confessing to the murder of Johnny Pius, the courtroom occupants broke for the cafeteria. Rob Brensic and the Quartararo brothers remained seated at the defendant's table while the judge shuffled out to chambers and the lawyers collected their papers.

Suddenly a musclebound missile of a man came charging out of the audience, taking aim at the boys. "If they don't put you in prison, I'm going to kill you!" John Pius raged before he was grabbed by court officers.

His wife was screaming behind him while officers also restrained her. "They should cut off your hands, you murdering scum!" Barbara

Pius yelled at the boys who were being hustled out a side door. "They should crucify you!"

After lunch, with the bereaved parents back in the audience after a stern warning, the pretrial proceedings returned to the testimony of Detective Palumbo. Pending before Judge Doyle was the question of whether Peter's confession was admissible. After weeks of testimony, Doyle then split the baby. He barred the playing of the tape during the trial but ruled that Palumbo could testify about Peter's second confession that night—in which the boy told his mother, with Palumbo present, that he had committed the murder.

That decision was consequential on multiple fronts, including leading to Brensic being tried separately from the Quartararo brothers. And it also boosted Spota's chances of getting a conviction in a sly and significant way by saddling one of the accused, namely a Quartararo brother, with a hapless new defense attorney.

* * *

Judge Robert Doyle's chambers were a regal lair of cherry wood, dark carpeting, flags, and framed certificates. The judge himself didn't quite match the trappings. Bobby, as his drinking buddy and confidant Spota called him, was a well-fed fellow with a reddish-blond comb-over. He was a few years removed from representing auto insurance companies in private practice, scampering around a Brooklyn courthouse to finagle settlements. Though he now decided matters of life and death, his favorite subject of conversation remained the gas mileage on his Honda.

In January 1981, Spota and Nicholas J. Castellano, attorney for the Quartararo boys, entered those chambers for a meeting with Doyle. Since the judge had determined that testimony about Peter's confession was admissible, Castellano had decided it would be a conflict of interest to represent both brothers. But the Quartararo uncle paying Castellano's fees couldn't afford to hire another lawyer, so the second attorney would have to be appointed by Doyle. The meeting in chambers would decide that assignment.

Spota and Castellano were on the opposite spectrum of the legal establishment. Spota, who like Bobby Doyle was the son of an insurance man, had made his way to the third-highest rung of the

DA office hierarchy. His buddy Gerald Sullivan had left the office in 1980, partly to cash in on the Amityville frenzy with his book about the DeFeo case. Pat Henry had then given Spota the nod to fill Sullivan's old role as chief trial prosecutor.

Castellano, on the other hand, was an unwelcome entity in Suffolk County. Then in his midsixties, Castellano's everyday legal demeanor started at a low boil. He had a knack for enraging judges but winning over juries with his belligerent courtroom eruptions. When he wasn't being dragged out of a courtroom for yelling and shaking his fists at a judge, he was in traffic court successfully fighting his own ticket for driving his Cadillac one hundred miles per hour. In a horse-race-fixing trial in which he represented a harness racer, Castellano was charged with contempt for such antics as griping about the judge in Italian to the jurors. But he got the harness racer off.

The Quartararos thought—with some naivete—that a bomb-throwing outsider was just who they needed to win their boys' freedom.

Castellano brought to the meeting a short list of lawyers he felt were fit to represent Michael Quartararo. He suggested a young Italian-American attorney with whom he had previously worked, positing that he believed the guy "could do a hell of a good job."

Doyle's response, according to Castellano: "I don't appoint guineas."

Castellano pushed forward. "Maybe we can appoint Rivers from Mineola," he suggested, referring to a Nassau County attorney with whom he was familiar. Laughter filled the chambers, where a few other attorneys were also waiting to discuss their own matters with the judge. Castellano asked what was so funny.

"Rivers is a Black man," one of the attorneys who was waiting nearby explained, while the laughter continued. "An Irishman turned inside out!"

Doyle seemed to already know the outcome of this conference. "I guess I'm going to appoint O'Leary," he said to Spota. "How about that, Tom?"

Spota hid his joy well. William R. O'Leary was a reputed alcoholic who worked out of a tiny office above a jewelry store. He lived on court appointments and might as well have worked for the Suffolk

County District Attorney's Office given how adept he was at getting his clients convicted. He didn't have a car, so his clients had to drive him to a bus stop after meetings. Judges called it the "O'Leary easement," breaking fifteen minutes before 5:00 p.m. so he could catch the last bus. Even Spota later acknowledged: "He was not known to be the greatest lawyer in the world."

The judge didn't ask Castellano for his opinion. Unaware of O'Leary's reputation as a doormat for the DA, Castellano didn't know he had reason to activate his temper.

As for Spota, he responded, poker face intact: "That would be all right with me."

* * *

Two weeks before jury selection, the DA's office apparently still thought their case was a bit thin. Perhaps coincidentally, around that time, the break-in prodigy Danny Culotta told his buddy Mike Quartararo that he had gotten keys to a side door of Smithtown High School East. A couple of days later, on March 1, 1981, the boys went on a 3:00 a.m. tour of the darkened school, rifling through desks for anything worth pinching. In the principal's office, Mike found a set of four walkie-talkie radios.

Whether or not it was a trap, burglary wasn't the brightest move for a defendant out on bail on a murder charge. Later that day, Culotta, Mike Quartararo, and Jimmy Burke experimented with the stolen walkie-talkies. Danny stayed in his house, Mike went down one block, Jimmy went down another, and they barked ten-codes at each other.

A couple of days later, a detective came to pick up Culotta and bring him down to the Fourth. Culotta then debriefed cops there on various burglaries throughout Smithtown, a recital that was not unusual for him. According to Culotta, that's when the walkie-talkie heist came up.

Mike Quartararo got a call at home that day from Culotta. "Mike, bring over the radio," his friend said. "I want to look at it."

Quartararo began the quarter-mile stroll with the radios hidden under a suede, fur-collared jacket. The moment he saw detectives pop out of a car along the way, Mike knew Danny had set him up.

Quartararo was a month over sixteen, which meant he could be tried as an adult. He lied to the detective, saying he was only fifteen, but the ruse didn't hold up.

When Mike Quartararo was brought before a judge, assuming this was a scheme to interrogate him in the Pius case, he referred to *People v. Rogers*, a ruling finding it unlawful to interrogate a suspect without counsel when he had a lawyer in another case. Here was a budding hooligan accurately citing recent precedent in the courtroom. It was no wonder the Suffolk authorities hated Mike the most.

A lot of jurisdictions steered clear of using jailhouse snitches due to their inherent unreliability. Not Suffolk, where prosecutors seemed to find a cellmate with a story to tell every time they had a weak case, particularly in murders. It was another way of getting past constitutional hurdles, as you could snag an incriminating statement through a snitch even after a suspect had already been arraigned and gotten a lawyer. The cops legally couldn't speak to you without your lawyer present, but a fellow inmate faced no such restriction.

But before a jailhouse snitch can work, a suspect had to be in the jailhouse, and Mike Quartararo was out on $5,000 bail in the murder case. If the plan was to use Culotta to get Quartararo locked up in search of jailhouse incrimination, it almost worked. Quartararo was indicted on charges of burglary, grand larceny, and criminal possession of stolen property. Doyle, who arraigned Quartararo in both cases, set his new bail for the burglary at $25,000. But the plan didn't account for the incompetence of Suffolk jail guards. One of them misread Mike's paperwork and let him walk right out of district court and hitchhike home. Quartararo later paid his bail and avoided any extended stint in jail.

The strange burglary episode captured the amateur Machiavellianism of Suffolk law enforcement. It also showed how Jimmy Burke, along with Culotta, was on his way to becoming a Swiss Army knife snitch for the DA's office, handy in cases ranging from murder to grand theft walkie-talkie. Burke later testified against Mike Quartararo in the theft of the radios, even though the burglary was of little consequence by then.

A memo relayed from Bart Jones, a detective in the Fourth Squad, to Suffolk prosecutor Timothy Mazzei detailed the information Jimmy had to share about the walkie-talkie heist. The memo listed Burke's home phone number and concluded: "Det. Jones [said] he could be a good witness but he'd have to be cultivated."

* * *

In the trial of the Quartararos, which came before that of Rob Brensic, Mike's girlfriend was slated to be the star witness for the prosecution. The detectives had initially struck out in getting Gwen Fox to say that Mike had confessed the murder to her. But in the grand jury, and now at trial, Gwen testified that Mike had left little doubt when she asked him over the summer if he had committed the murder.

"I did," Gwen said Mike told her. "I killed Pius."

"I don't believe you," Gwen said she told Mike, to which he responded: "Believe what you want."

On a morning about a week after giving that testimony at trial, however, fifteen-year-old Gwen found Castellano in a hallway. "I want to come back to tell the truth," she told the lawyer for her boyfriend's brother.

She retook the stand and testified that Detectives Jensen, Gill, and Palumbo made her father leave the questioning room and then interrogated her for five hours. "They yelled at me and cursed at me," Gwen said. "They said if I didn't say it they could charge me with perjury and arrest me right here now."

In fact, Gwen now maintained, Mike never confessed to the murder. Following her recantation, the courtroom air exploded with arguments from every direction, including Castellano's declaration that the detectives should be investigated for suborning perjury.

O'Leary, the doormat who represented Mike but had been only halfway paying attention during this whole episode, sulked: "Not that anybody cares, but I have no questions of the witness."

* * *

Jimmy Burke's videotaped session with Spota was at least the third time he told his story about Mike Quartararo. Detectives had previously visited his house and taken written statements from him and his brother, and Jimmy had also testified before a grand jury. He seemed to be still workshopping the account.

He told Spota that Mike Quartararo had described being shown crime scene photos by the homicide detectives. "He said that he saw pictures of the body of John Pius," Jimmy said, "and that the body—he described the body to me, saying that it was blue and that its nose was smashed off, his nose was pushed to the other side of his face and it was covered with leaves."

If Jimmy mentioned this when he gave his statement to detectives, they didn't include it. And there's no indication that homicide detectives actually showed Michael Quartararo photos of Pius's body. Also, Johnny's nose was not "smashed off."

There was another piece of his recorded interview with Spota that wasn't in his written statement.

"Okay, now, did he say anything about—did he ever mention the word 'pigs'?" Spota prompted.

"Uh yeah, he did," Jimmy responded.

"What did he say?" Spota asked.

"He said, 'The pigs fucked it up,'" Jimmy answered.

"Okay, thanks an awful lot, Jimmy," Spota said.

"All right then," Jimmy said with a pleasant smile, and he strolled out of the room.

But in his testimony in the Quartararos' murder trial on April 21, 1981, Jimmy didn't mention either of those statements.

Perhaps Spota was just being economical with the testimony he drew from his witness. Or maybe he had decided his case against the other defendant was more in need of incrimination. Because the next time Jimmy testified about a buddy boasting to him about how the pigs fucked up the Pius case, he said those words had come out of Rob Brensic's mouth.

* * *

Jimmy's story wasn't the only one shifting. He was one of five kids who testified about statements they said Mike Quartararo made while they were hanging out behind a feed store near the railroad station in St. James in the summer of 1979.

Their testimony was meant to be corroborative, but the boys actually seemed to agree on very little. They differed on what types of beer were drunk and how many, whether pot was smoked and how much, and even who was present. Two of the boys said Danny Culotta's brother Chris was there, though the rest didn't mention him. And most importantly, they each testified to a different version of what was said, and some of their accounts were contradictory. The most significant point of confusion came over a question Danny Culotta had asked Mike Quartararo.

Jimmy Burke recalled that Danny had asked Mike, in an apparent bastardization of the police theory of the case: "How could someone kill a kid for just stealing a minibike?" Quartararo had allegedly responded: "If you were drunk and if you didn't want to get caught, you would do the same thing." Three of the other boys—Michael Burke, Culotta, and McCort—testified about a similar question and answer, though their wording differed in significant ways. Culotta himself would ultimately acknowledge that he didn't remember the exact wording of his question and said of Quartararo's response that he "didn't take it as a confession."

John McCort testified that Quartararo only said, "He put the bike up against the tree, but those guys beat him up." Jimmy Burke said Quartararo told them he had seen Pius the night of the murder but hadn't touched him, but "did say something about leaning a bike against a tree." Michael Burke said Quartararo told them "something like" that he had seen Pius that night, but he was "not really sure," and mentioned "something about leaning a bike up against a tree, or something." And Danny Culotta said that Quartararo told them "that John Pius had saw him putting the minibike into Tommy Ryan's car, and that he didn't do anything. That's all he did, was put a bicycle up against a tree. That was it."

The kid who delivered relevance to the knotted testimony was a nervous and mumbling out-of-towner. David O'Brien, who was seventeen, wore his dark hair parted in the middle over his birdlike face. O'Brien was a friend of McCort's from when they both lived in the town of Syosset, but he had since moved to Orange, Connecticut. O'Brien was in Smithtown visiting McCort on the night of the alleged conversation, and his version of the exchange was the only one, if true, in which Quartararo inarguably incriminated himself.

O'Brien said Quartararo told them Pius had seen them steal the minibike. "[Pius] said he was going to call the police," O'Brien continued. "They ran after him, up to the school, and they beat him up, and they kicked him. They stepped on his face, and then he [Quartararo] took the bike and he put it someplace."

In his summation, Spota stressed how trustworthy he found "the civilians," as he called the teenage boys. "Good friends of Michael and Peter Quartararo," Spota posited. "No motive in the world to lie. Spoken to by the police in front of their parents. Inconsistencies in their statements? Minor, yes. Natural? They're thirteen-, fourteen-, fifteen-year-old kids."

Spota gave special credence to the kid from Connecticut, who he said had no conceivable reason to lie: "David O'Brien doesn't know anybody in this thing, other than McCort."

Maybe so, but by then O'Brien was, by his own later account, already a practiced liar. Decades later, in a personal history, O'Brien recalled facing trouble in Connecticut a couple of years before the Pius murder when he and friends drunkenly broke some windows at an elementary school. "I got caught by the cops and lied to my mother and the police that I didn't do anything except be there and watch the other kids do it," O'Brien recounted in the document, which ultimately wound up in the hands of law enforcement investigators in an unrelated matter. O'Brien also wrote that in 1980, the year before the trial, he was driving drunk when he got into a car accident. He lied and told his parents that "something came out of the woods," and he had to swerve to avoid hitting it. He recalled with a certain satisfaction: "They believed me and I didn't get into any trouble at all."

* * *

The most consistent element of both Peter's confession and the teenagers' stories was seemingly a minor one.

Jimmy Burke had included it in the police statement he signed in 1979—"Later in the discussion, Mike said he put the bike up against the tree"—and then mentioned it during his on-camera interview with Spota and at the trial of the Quartararos. Michael Burke, McCort, and Culotta also referred to Mike Quartararo saying he put the bike up against a tree.

It was clear that the detectives saw big evidentiary value in the placement of Johnny's Huffy, which was leaned against a tree when police arrived behind Dogwood Elementary. Like the logs over Johnny's body, here was another detail of the crime scene that hadn't been publicized, that only the true criminal would have known.

Unfortunately, the police had failed to actually keep the bike's placement out of the news, just as had happened with the logs. In fact, *Newsday* had run a large photo of the bike against the tree the morning after the body was found.

Unchallenged court testimony further deflated the accounts of Mike and the bicycle. Sean Abinet, an eight-year-old boy who first found Johnny's bike, described it as being "on the side of the hill, laying sideways." Johnny's father also said that the bike was on the ground when he arrived at the school, and that his niece spotted its handlebar protruding from the leafy ground. "Don't move the bike," Pius had told her when she went to touch it. He testified that he "put it up against the tree or the stump, or whatever was there at the time." So it wasn't Mike who put the bike against the tree, but the victim's own father.

There was an obvious possible answer to how that false detail ended up in both Peter's confession and the testimony of the teenage witnesses. Gill and Reck, the detectives who were first on the scene and had interviewed the dad and Abinet, would have known who put the bike up against the tree. But it was Palumbo and his novice partner Gary Leonard who got Peter's confession. They were both assigned the case that day, a week after the murder. Leonard also took the statements from the teenage witnesses.

This gaffe was a potential gift for a defense attorney, but the Quartararo legal team missed it. O'Leary, who hadn't bothered to get the case file from his co-counsel before trial and later explained that his "game plan" at trial was to "lay back," wasn't the sort to seize on nuance. That put the onus on Castellano, who seemed distracted by a perpetual state of blind rage.

Castellano once house-sat for a legal client, a horse racing mogul, and set such a roaring blaze in his fireplace that the whole manse went up in flames. His legal strategy in the Pius case amounted to something similar. He antagonized Judge Doyle, telling him that he didn't have enough murder trial experience. He accused Spota of prosecutorial misconduct. He railed that the homicide detectives weren't "worth the powder to blow them to hell." And he was in a consistent fury over *Newsday* repeatedly referring to Peter's taped confession when it had been excluded from trial, calling the paper a "filthy rag" that employed "scurrilous sheep."

It was a strategy that had worked for Castellano before, making everybody in the courtroom hate him except for a swooning jury. But this Suffolk twelve didn't seem to be falling in love with him. And Castellano's biggest mistake—putting Peter Quartararo on the stand—would torpedo his client's chances. Peter's testimony opened the door for Spota to play the suppressed taped confession in front of the jury in order to impeach his testimony. Over the vociferous objections of Castellano that to play the tape was a "perversion of all justice," Doyle permitted it.

The rest was bleak formality. O'Leary filled his five-minute summation, for which he did not prepare and used no notes, with odd remarks he liked to say at the end of nearly every trial, such as: "I'm not a standup comedian." He also revealed in his closing remarks that he had barely followed the recantation of Gwen Fox, potentially one of trial's most pivotal moments. "She didn't come over that clear, but she said something, naturally, against my client," he mused of Gwen's testimony. "Because that's what they brought her down here for. And what happened? Lo and behold, she comes back the next day and completely contradicted what she said. Frankly, I didn't hear what she said the first day, to be honest with you. Be that as it may, you heard it."

Reasonable doubt was hard to find in Suffolk County when it came to accused killers. The county's jurors saw fit to acquit a total of about one murder defendant a year. With a legal defense that swung from volcanic anger to indifference, it was unlikely that the brothers would be the lucky defendants for 1981. The brothers were found guilty of second-degree murder.

The Quartararos maintained their innocence during their June 1981 sentencing, as they have ever since. Peter, eighteen, appeared slow to understand that life as he knew it was done. He discussed his Boy Scouts troop and complained that he lost a good bowling alley job when he was charged. Mike, sixteen, seemed to better fathom the gravity. "About the only thing holding me together is the fact that I know I'm innocent, and God knows I'm innocent," Mike said. "It is my belief that Mr. Spota and the police know it, too."

If Spota did know he had put away two innocent teenagers, it didn't put a damper on a nearly yearlong celebration. Upon hearing the verdict, Spota had popped champagne bottles with the Piuses in the DA's office.

Five months later, in October 1981, detectives dragged Tom Ryan out of the kitchen of Cousins II, the restaurant where he worked. Ryan was arraigned in his white work uniform and oil-stained boots. Spota had finally gotten the witness statement he needed to secure an indictment against the case's loose end.

For a moment, it seemed like Tom Spota was done with prosecutorial work. In March 1982, a flyer went around the office organizing what it called "A Farewell Salute for Thomas J. (Blue Eyes) Spota III." There was to be prime rib, cocktails, dancing, and five hours of unlimited liquor on a Friday night at the Harbor Hills Country Club in Belle Terre. Entrance was $25, payable to a homicide detective.

* * *

Spota had made $1,814 every two weeks as the third-in-command of the DA's office. It was a fine salary in 1982, if low for a seasoned lawyer. But his old prosecutor pal Gerry Sullivan had convinced him there was a fortune to be had if he followed his lead into private practice. They hung a shingle for Sullivan & Spota in an office complex in Commack.

Spota went from working alongside homicide bulls to defending them when they got jammed up. He was hired on retainer by the Suffolk County Detectives Association, the union for cops of that rank. The death of a folk singer on the Long Island Expressway also gave the new partners an early windfall. Lawyer Anthony Curto, who represented Harry Chapin's estate, contracted Sullivan & Spota to handle litigation against the trucking concern whose rig had plowed into the singer's Volkswagen Rabbit in 1981. Spota was once again Sullivan's second chair in the case, handling technical legal research while his partner took the lead in the courtroom. This time, the pay was better: Chapin's estate won $10 million, and Spota and Sullivan's cut was $800,000 each.

Business was so good that less than seven months after Spota left the DA's office, Sullivan & Spota was included in a *New York Times* profile of firms enjoying boom times despite a recession. The article allowed that Spota's connections had helped: "Mr. Spota said that people he knew from his old job in the Major Offense Bureau had brought in cases."

That was a coy way to put it. Even before Spota left the DA's office, he and Sullivan had brazenly mixed prosecution and private practice. When Spota oversaw the prosecution of Virginia Carole Maddox, who killed her husband in what she claimed was self-defense, Sullivan represented her sons in a civil effort to exclude her from her husband's estate. Sullivan's case was largely reliant on her being convicted of murder, and Maddox later accused Spota of vetoing a manslaughter deal one of his deputies had offered her. While Spota was trying the Quartararos for murder, Sullivan had represented the Pius parents in a civil negligence lawsuit against the Smithtown school district. Spota denied having any financial interests in the Maddox and Pius cases, and after he joined Sullivan's firm they dropped the Piuses as a client.

But even after Spota resigned to form that partnership, he kept one foot in the DA's office in a deal that made him an unholy hybrid of murder prosecutor and private attorney. By 1982, Spota had become the Boss Hogg of all things law-related in Suffolk County and felt he had a lot to gloat about. "If these are bad times," he told the *New York Times*, "I can't wait to see the good times."

* * *

The same month Spota resigned, a homicide detective drove out to the Riverhead jail for an encounter that lasted all of twenty seconds. The detective, Jack Miller, stared down the familiar inmate, all sunken cheeks and desperate eyes, who had beckoned him out there.

"What do you want, Brett?" sighed Miller.

"I still have valuable information on the Pius case," Brett Locke pleaded, "and if you get me out of jail right now, I'll tell you what I have."

"No way," Miller shot back, and walked out of the jail.

An informant had to torch Jack Miller pretty badly to make him break up with them. Miller was the homicide squad's designated snitch wrangler, and he was typically unconcerned about their long rap sheets and proclivity for dishonesty. But Locke—a habitual burglar, hopeless addict, and terminal flake—had finally proven far too unreliable, even for Suffolk homicide.

But Locke was desperate enough to dodge a potential decades-long prison bid that he decided to go above Miller's pay grade. Early in March 1982, when Spota still technically worked for the DA's office, Locke's attorney reached him by calling him not there, but at Gerald Sullivan's law office. Later that month, after Spota had resigned, he met with Locke and his lawyer not at the Commack office of Sullivan & Spota, but at the DA's office. If it was confusing, that's because it was a highly unusual arrangement. The next month, the DA's office made it official that Spota would continue to work on the Brensic and Ryan prosecutions for $300 a day.

Spota wasn't nearly as squeamish as his homicide detective about using a snitch who had already burned the authorities. In fact, during the meeting, he was the one doing the selling, puffing up Locke with quasi-legal boasts about how he could get his pending cases in front of a favorable judge.

The jailhouse snitch's involvement in the case had a familiar origin story. Back in February 1980, only two months after being indicted for murder, Robert Brensic said he made the foolish mistake of accepting some cash from a friend to sell a few rings at a St. James pawnbroker. Brensic claimed he never partook in the burglaries committed by his brother and friends, and until the Pius indictment he had no criminal record. But he still had a reckless habit of blindly helping them out, including giving them his driver's license for them to use at the pawnshops. In this case, Brensic said he wasn't certain the rings were hot but he had a pretty good idea. "I probably knew it was freakin' stolen," he later acknowledged. "I was stupid."

At around the same time, Tom Ryan found the door to his yellow Capri unlocked. That immediately aroused his suspicion, because he never left his pride and joy vulnerable with his Jethro Tull and Steely Dan collection inside. Stranger still, Tom said he saw a ring sitting on the driver's seat. Asking around about the ring, Tom learned that Brensic's neighbor had recently been burglarized. When he showed it to her, she exclaimed it was her engagement ring.

Soon afterward, cops arrested Rob Brensic on felony charges. The rings he had pawned for his friends were among items stolen from the same next-door neighbor. If the ring from the same theft was a ploy to frame Ryan, he had thwarted the plot by being honest about finding it. Brensic, on the other hand, was charged with criminal possession of stolen property, and spent the night in jail.

Snitching was so popular at the Suffolk County jail that in some high-profile cases authorities held pseudoauditions, trying out the various stories on offer before choosing an informant. The aspiring snitch's most useful tool were newspapers, delivered daily, reporting who had been arrested and often providing details of the alleged crime. The snitch then had information to work with.

Locke, alias John Preston, had this all down to a science. At the time that Brensic was locked up in the same jail as him, Locke was only twenty-one years old but had been doing burglaries since puberty. His current jail stint, for breaking into a liquor store, was nearing three years. He wasn't great at burglaries but he was very good at jail. He was an adept cellblock drug smuggler, and his role as a tier rep, in which he explained the rules to new guys, was a prime placement for a snitch.

Locke and a crony, Alton Thorpe, typed up a confession in the jail law library and tricked Brensic into signing it by telling him it was for permission to watch television late at night. Thorpe then brought the confession to Spota. The prosecutor was unimpressed and ended the meeting, but the chicanery didn't turn him off from using Thorpe's savvier buddy down the road.

Locke waited until the next year to bring his own Brensic story to the homicide detectives. He had gotten locked up again and was facing three burglary charges and a DWI that could put him away for more than twenty years. In August 1981, Jack Miller met with Locke in a holding cell. The prisoner said he had some vital information about Brensic but wouldn't tell the detective what it was until he was set free. So the detective got Locke released with the agreement that he would meet him at the homicide offices that afternoon. Instead, Brett Locke gleefully disappeared.

Seven months later, Miller had his exasperated twenty-second meeting with Locke at Riverhead. Locke had been rounded up and was once again on the hook for the devastating prison sentence. But in the subsequent meeting with Spota at the DA's office, Locke got himself a life-salvaging deal. Spota agreed that in return for Locke's testimony, the burglar only had to plead guilty to misdemeanors, ensuring that he wouldn't go to prison. Spota also threw in one more requirement: Locke would drop an existing Internal Affairs complaint against a cop who he claimed had beaten him up.

After two years of hype, Locke then finally told his Brensic story to the lawyers. In between that meeting and Brensic's eventual trial, Locke nearly died of an overdose, absconded from drug treatment twice, and announced he no longer wanted to cooperate. It didn't make matters easier that the trial was beset by years of delays, including a mistrial and the murder of the lead defense attorney. But Spota held on to Locke with white knuckles, seemingly determined to ride this snitch's story to a conviction at any cost.

* * *

Tom Ryan's undoing was an appropriately named Smithtown bar. Trappers was a sloppy dive frequented mostly by teenagers. The drinking age back then was eighteen, and Trappers wasn't strict on proof anyway. "You wouldn't take your girl there, let me put it that way," Ryan said when asked to describe the bar's level of classiness. Nonetheless, because the bar was a couple of doors down from his job at Cousins II, he went there every so often for after-work beers in the eighteen months following Pius's murder.

During this period, Ryan stubbornly attempted to carry on with his normal life. He was promoted from busboy to full-time counterman at the restaurant where he worked for six years. He was there in May 1981 when he learned via a phone call that the Quartararos had been convicted. His boss found him in a back room crying, and when he consoled him, Ryan insisted that they were all innocent, and he couldn't believe that a jury would convict the brothers. His boss fully believed him.

Everybody knew that the Suffolk authorities were on the prowl for Ryan to make an incriminating statement. "You need to leave here and stop living in Suffolk County," urged his friend Jodi Tramantano, whom he later married. But Ryan figured if he didn't say anything stupid, they'd have nothing on him.

But Trappers was the beer-soaked war room for Tony Cannone, Johnny Pius's vigilante cousin, who always seemed privy to the inner workings of the investigation. It was also Jimmy Burke's favorite bar. Kids gossiped there about their grand jury subpoenas, and what others had testified about. One girl said she had been threatened by Tony's sister for not testifying against Tom Ryan in the grand jury.

Suffolk authorities were sending to the grand jury anybody in Tom Ryan's orbit who claimed to have incriminating information. At least two kids said they answered grand jury subpoenas but were then turned away when they insisted to detectives at the courthouse that Ryan hadn't confessed to them. The detectives called them liars, and said they were saving them from perjuring themselves. Former suspect Michael O'Neill was also subpoenaed. He said during the grand jury proceedings that Spota tried in vain to get him to say Ryan had made an incriminating statement, repeatedly demanding: "What did Tommy say?"

After Tom Ryan was indicted, his family's private investigator, Herman Race, dove into the Trappers milieu as he tried to figure out what the Suffolk authorities had on the kid. A young woman named Anne Erickson emerged as a central figure. Race learned that she had testified in the grand jury as to incriminating statements she said Ryan had made. Erickson had dated Tony Cannone and was said to be on a first-name basis with the detective Gary Leonard. She and Ryan had a brief fling after meeting at the bar, but he said he dumped her.

From the patrons of Trappers, Race heard gossip that the detectives were threatening to expose personal facts about Erickson if she didn't cooperate. That she said she was afraid she'd go to jail for lying about Ryan in the grand jury. That she had previously told people she knew Ryan didn't commit the murder. Among those who Race spoke to was a seventeen-year-old kid named Dennis Sullivan. The stocky son of a New York City cop, he was a busboy at Cousins II. Sullivan told Race that in the summer of 1981 he had talked to Erickson about the case. Back then, Sullivan said, Erickson was defending the innocence of Ryan and the other three boys. Erickson "said she might know something that would prove that all of the boys were innocent of the Pius murder," Sullivan told the investigator, but she wouldn't say what that information was.

Race added in his report: "However, Dennis is frank to say that he doesn't like her and feels that she would have no qualms about lying if she were asked to do so."

CHAPTER 6

FIXED

In June 1981, a few weeks after the Quartararos were sent off to prison, a patrolman stopped a teenager who was jogging along 7th Avenue in St. James. It was five o'clock on a Sunday morning, and the cop was watching the street because a woman who lived there had reported a frightening phone call. She said a male voice that she couldn't identify told her he would be over in five minutes.

The cop asked the kid where he was going. Jimmy Burke, then sixteen, was nothing but polite. He explained to the cop that he ran this way, about two miles from his home, every morning before dawn as part of his training for a boxing tournament. The cop had no reason to detain him and let Jimmy run on, but later expressed his skepticism in a teletype parenthetical. "(Smelled like a brewery)," the patrolman noted.

In the couple of years between the Quartararo trial and those of Brensic and Ryan, Jimmy collected a lot of police teletype while staggering to the high school finish line. By his own conservative account, he finished off a six-pack after school most days and dabbled in any narcotic he could get his hands on. He was becoming a known entity to the Fourth Precinct cops. On another late night in the summer of 1981, a patrolman questioned Burke, Danny Culotta, and a third boy after spotting them drinking beer in front of a supermarket. "Known burglar in St. James area," the cop noted, though it wasn't clear if he was referring to Burke or Culotta.

Jimmy squeaked out just enough passing grades to offset all the Fs and earn his diploma. Things got suspenseful in his senior year, when he had to retake eleventh grade English while also finishing twelfth grade English, but he managed a triumphant D in both.

He still got his teachers to like him, among them Jack Breen, who taught social studies. Jimmy took his half-credit elective, a class called Criminal Justice Systems, that senior year. Breen described Jimmy as Brando-esque when playing a witness in their mock trials, "quick on his feet, street smart, and very clever." Breen's class was the first B Burke had gotten in two years. Breen himself was busy at night studying to become a lawyer, so he hadn't been following the goings-on of the Pius case. He was unaware that Jimmy's star turn as a mock-trial witness was informed by real life experience.

By default, Jimmy began preparing for a career repairing fridges and air conditioners alongside his stepdad. Most of his credits his senior year were gained through courses at a nearby technical center from which he was granted a certificate in "heating/ventilation/ air conditioning." In June 1982, he received his Smithtown East diploma. His final GPA was 1.52, putting him in the 12th percentile of his class.

Jimmy, seventeen, began toiling as his stepfather's helper. On the evening of Friday, August 6, once work was done, Jimmy jumped in his 1972 Buick Skylark and raced twenty miles to Long Island's South Shore. He and friends boarded a boat at Captree State Park, a marshy little area down Ocean Parkway east of Gilgo State Park.

They were going on a fishing trip, but as is expected of teenagers on a boat in the dead of night, they were primarily interested in catching a buzz. Jimmy later estimated that he drank more than half a dozen beers. By 4:00 a.m., he was, in his own words, "extremely tired and intoxicated." Even after Jimmy disembarked the boat, he chugged about four more brews in the parking lot before heading home in the cool, buggy summer dawn. He was well into Nassau County, and nearing New York City, when he realized he was driving the opposite direction of Smithtown. He pulled a quick U-turn and his rearview lit up with blue lights of a state trooper's squad car.

Jimmy later maintained that he "offered no resistance and was fully cooperative" with his arresting officer, who took him to the state police barracks, where he flunked a Breathalyzer. His mom came and got him later that morning. "I was young, foolish and immature," Jimmy later acknowledged, calling the arrest the "low point in my life." He made matters worse by blowing off his court date in November 1982, and a bench warrant was issued for his arrest.

It was an on-brand episode for new graduate Jimmy Burke. He was rudderless, flashing some ambition but ditching any effort before it got too real. He applied to be a New York City firefighter, but when they called him in to take the physical exam, he decided he didn't want the job. He lasted nine credits in a psychology course at the nearby Farmingdale State College in late 1982 but quit after a few months. In November of that year, Jimmy was licensed by the state of New York as a "home appliance repair employee," but even in that field his job prospects were grim. His stepfather laid him off due to a lack of work a couple of months later at the end of high season.

He did odd jobs around the house in return for spending money from his mom and stepdad. Much of it ended up in the register at Trappers. If Jimmy could avoid jail, his best-case scenario appeared to be seasonal work in the industrial arts, steering the company's Plymouth Volare to meet housewives who were panicking over the impending spoilage of their groceries.

But the Pius case showed Burke an alternative career track. Most of the other teenage witnesses in the case tried to spend as little time as possible in the company of law enforcement. But teenage Jimmy flanked Spota through the homicide offices like he was the prosecutor's work son. Some members of the homicide squad, including its commander, Richard Jensen, also took a shine to the kid. Others, such as Detective Bill Mahoney, who joined the squad in 1981, didn't understand why there was a child hanger-on in the homicide offices. "He was the only kid who walked around there," Mahoney said. "I just remember thinking, 'Who the hell does this kid think he is?'"

Jimmy was soon plotting on how to make his presence in cop environs more permanent. A friend, Anthony D'Orazio, said that around this time Burke confided in him that he didn't want any part of the air-conditioning business. He talked about his NYPD dad and grandfather, that old birthright he seemed to have left behind in Ozone Park.

Either he was oblivious to how poor of a police candidate he had become, or he knew that a white hat could fix anything.

* * *

Robert Brensic turned twenty-one during his murder trial. The delays in his case had been surreal and tragic. In the spring of 1982, the day before a pretrial hearing, his attorney Leon Stern was shot dead during a home invasion in Nassau County. Stern had been a veteran defender in high-profile homicide cases, his most famous being his representation of "Son of Sam" serial killer David Berkowitz. After Stern's shocking death, the Brensic defense became the responsibility of Stern's junior associate, Andrew Polin, who worked deep into nights trying to catch up. "I felt like the sun, the moon, and all the planets had fallen on me," Polin said, paraphrasing Harry Truman. Though Polin was a diligent attorney, his inexperience came across in overly zealous legal arguments. In one filing, Polin declared that the "teratogenic result of the prosecution's spasmodic sophistry has been to relegate due process and equal protection to the societal scrap heap, along with the hula-hoop and coon-skin cap."

Polin was fearful for Brensic. He had read the transcripts of the Quartararo trial and knew that a Suffolk jury could easily reach a guilty verdict even if the evidence was a thin patchwork of vague witness statements and detective supposition. So when he saw a chance to avoid trial, he couldn't ignore it.

Across the courtroom, the $300-a-day special prosecutor spearheading the case was perhaps missing the much higher rates of private practice. According to Polin, Spota offered Brensic an extraordinary plea deal, similar to what the Quartararos had turned down before their trial. Brensic would serve no prison time and emerge with a clean adult criminal record. The only catch was that he had to admit to the murder and implicate the others. Polin encouraged Brensic to take it. But on the Monday on which Brensic was set to sign the deal, he decided against it, saying he refused to admit something he didn't do.

Brensic's trial initially started the week of Thanksgiving 1982, but the proceedings only made it to the testimony of Tony Palumbo.

While sparring with Polin, the red-faced detective blurted out that Peter's confession was good enough to get the Quartararo brothers indicted "and convicted, I might add" the year earlier. It was an open secret throughout the Pius trials that the Suffolk County jurors knew all the prior twists and turns of the case, but Judge Doyle still had to at least pretend they weren't tainted. After Palumbo's outburst, Doyle had to declare a mistrial.

That was the end of Tom Spota as a trial prosecutor, though he stayed involved in the Brensic and Ryan prosecutions as an advisor. His former deputy Billy Keahon, who had become chief of the Major Offense Bureau when Spota left, now took over the Brensic case. Keahon was known for cooing to female jurors, pointing wrathfully at defendants, and crying during summations. It was also the end of Judge Doyle's reign over the Pius trials, though Rob Brensic and Tom Ryan would find little solace in the reputation of the man who took over the cases. Judge Stuart Namm's penchant for life sentences had earned him the nickname "Maximum Stu."

Due to all the delays, Brensic's full trial took place nearly two years after that of the Quartararos. This perhaps benefited the prosecution, as the details of testimony in the Quartararo trial may have faded from the collective memory. Otherwise the weirdness of Jimmy Burke's testimony might have been more obvious.

* * *

In the Quartararos' trial, Jimmy had been just one voice in a teenage snitch choir. But when Rob Brensic finally had his trial in February 1983, Jimmy began to distinguish himself. Jimmy was the only boy—now a young man—who testified about separate incriminating statements purportedly made to him by both Mike Quartararo and Rob Brensic. Perhaps he was the most trusted teenage confidant in his corner of Smithtown. Or there was another explanation.

When he took the witness stand against Brensic, Burke described a hangout with five or six others on a late afternoon in September or October of 1979. They were at a field on the grounds of the St. James Elementary School, fifty yards or so from the railroad station. He said somebody asked Brensic if he was in any more trouble with the Pius thing.

"He said that the pigs fucked it up and that they'd never get him," Burke testified. After that, Burke said, "we just continued on in the conversation we had. We thought nothing of it." Burke said he first told this story in Spota's office the morning before his grand jury testimony in November 1979, when asked if he "knew any more information."

Besides the statement not being fully incriminating, Jimmy's story was maddeningly blurry. When asked by Brensic's attorney who else was present for this conversation, Jimmy responded: "At this time I can't recall, sir." But he was oddly sharp on other details. He knew that they were on the southeast of the field for the conversation, and he even gave a brief weather report, recalling that it was a "hazy, overcast day, you know, semi-cloudy." It wasn't the passage of time that had sabotaged his memory about other elements of the conversation. Back when he testified in the grand jury, shortly after the alleged conversation took place, he also couldn't remember who else was present for the conversation or even what month it had occurred.

The oddest part about Jimmy's memory of Brensic's words was that it was a carbon copy of something Mike Quartararo was alleged to have said. In 1981, Danny Culotta and John McCort had testified to statements Mike Quartararo had made in a conversation, in August or September 1979 at the St. James Elementary School field, after somebody asked him if he was still in trouble with the police. McCort said that Quartararo had responded "that the police officers fucked everything up, and that, you know, he would get away with it." In Culotta's version, Quartararo said: "No, they fucked it up. They'll never catch us."

Culotta said that Jimmy was present for this conversation, but Jimmy didn't mention it in his testimony during the Quartararos' trial. In his taped interview with Spota, however, Burke had said that Quartararo told him the "pigs fucked it up" in regard to the Pius investigation. Now Jimmy was attributing almost the exact same words, uttered in the same location and in roughly the same time period by Quartararo, to Brensic.

* * *

After Jimmy, George Heiselmann the gas-siphoner took the stand. Heiselmann said that he, Jimmy's brother Michael, Danny Culotta, and Rob Brensic were under the bleachers of a ballfield at Smithtown High School East on an August evening four months after the murder. Heiselmann asked Brensic whether he was involved in Johnny's murder. Brensic replied: "If you were drunk, you would have done it." When asked why neither Michael Burke nor Culotta had mentioned this statement, Heiselmann said they didn't hear it because they "were walking away."

It was another murky repeat of statements attributed to Quartararo in the previous trial. Burke had testified that at the railroad station at around the same time in the summer, Mike Quartararo had remarked: "If you were drunk and if you didn't want to get caught, you would do the same thing." To believe these statements attributed to Brensic, you had to accept that he and Mike Quartararo busied themselves that summer and fall uttering nearly identical incriminating remarks.

The Brensic trial's denouement, of course, was the gift from Tom Spota before he returned to private practice. After an overdose, three attempts to abscond, and one case of cold feet, Brett Locke finally testified. Locke's jailhouse story concerning Brensic was rich in drama. He said inmates, including a character named Mad Dog, were hectoring a sobbing Brensic, calling him "Pebbles" in reference to Pius's manner of death, when Locke rescued him from rape or murder. Brensic then cried to Locke about Pius: "We didn't mean to kill him."

Locke said that Brensic unloaded on him an intensely detailed confession, complete with dialogue of each of the players, largely in line with the theory of the prosecution. "And he sticks pebbles and rocks in his throat," Locke said near the end of his testimony, summarizing what Brensic had told him. "And a little while later they realized he was dead. And Tommy Ryan said: 'Drag the body in the woods.'"

Brensic denied making any such confession to Locke. Polin's first question in his cross-examination of Locke was, "You wouldn't lie to us, Mr. Locke, would you?"

"Not about something like this," Locke assured him.

Brensic's jury took eighty-six minutes to convict him.

* * *

Two months later, it was finally Tom Ryan's turn. His trial was the only one in which Jimmy Burke was of no use, as the two boys had rarely if ever hung out. Instead, the chief witness was the ex-flame, Anne Erickson, who regaled the courtroom with dialogue ready for a Lifetime special. She recounted conversations that occurred in Central Park, in front of Ryan's house, and at Trappers. As was the trend in the Pius case, Erickson testified to remarks that were suggestive of guilt but could also be interpreted otherwise.

Erickson testified they had an argument in which she said she loved him, but he insisted she didn't. "Don't tell me how I feel," Erickson said she protested. "Don't try to shut me out."

He responded: "You can't love someone that took someone else's life."

In the trials of both Brensic and Ryan, Namm had excluded the taped backseat confession by Peter Quartararo, ruling that only Peter's statements with Palumbo and his mother present were admissible. Namm instructed the juries that they couldn't use that confession by Peter as evidence of the guilt of Brensic or Ryan, but instead only "to corroborate the testimony of other witnesses." In reality, that distinction was lost. Keahon repeatedly seized on the confession, including telling the jury: "Remember that Peter Quartararo showed his mother how he gripped his mouth to pull it open so they could get the rocks in."

As with the case against the Quartararos, there was no physical evidence tying the boys to the murder. Ryan's jury convicted him in five hours.

Judge Namm justified his "Maximum Stu" moniker. Brensic and Ryan were both sentenced to twenty-five years to life. Namm dismissed the notion that multiple juries had gotten it wrong. "Perhaps I'm too gullible and have too much faith in our system," he remarked as he condemned Ryan. "There have been wrongs perpetrated by juries before, but I sincerely doubt that there have ever been three trials, consecutive trials, in which three juries brought in the wrong verdict."

Both men, then in their early twenties, maintained their innocence. "You will find out the truth someday!" Ryan yelled as sheriff's deputies took him away in handcuffs. "It was all lies!"

Michael Quartararo, who became a devoted prison letter writer, penned a few missives to Namm, one of which read: "Sometimes, I get the feeling this is one giant conspiracy. There is no way to beat the system, even if you are in the right."

Namm said that all of these protestations fell on "deaf ears." "In 1983," Namm wrote in his later memoir, "my eyes had not been fully opened to the devious capabilities of those involved in Suffolk law enforcement."

* * *

Good things started to happen to Jimmy Burke after the trials were over. The first order of business was getting his drunk-driving case taken care of. The summer after his testimony, Jimmy handled the bench warrant with minimal punishment. He pleaded to a noncriminal violation and paid a $50 fine, along with losing his license for a couple months. He was said to have boasted that Spota "fixed" the Nassau County case for him, though the DA's office denied having anything to do with it.

Burke said he was a changed man in terms of drinking and driving. Now he only drove buzzed. He said in a later police application that he learned in court-mandated drunk-driving school that the body processes an ounce of alcohol an hour. "I have not driven drunk (while intoxicated) at all in the last twelve months," Burke wrote with evident pride in January 1985. "However, I have driven under the influence of alcohol approx. 2 to 5 times . . . When I must drive I 'nurse' my drink so that I can 'burn off' the alcohol and drive within safe limits."

Another fortuitous development helped Jimmy avoid the refrigeration repair business. His brother graduated from high school and joined his stepdad's operation. With a new helper secured, the stepdad officially gave Jimmy his blessing to instead pursue his dream of joining the police. The only obstacle still remaining was Jimmy's utter lack of qualification.

In high school, he had a school-wide reputation as a drug user, one that he had burnished himself in an interview with the *New York Times*. He was on the record as being close friends with the most notorious young criminals in Smithtown, ranging from known burglars to convicted murderers he helped send to prison.

Jimmy filed an application to join the NYPD, and the cops started probing his background in September 1984. His bench warrant for skipping court after the DUI might have raised eyebrows. But Billy Keahon, the Suffolk prosecutor who had Burke partly to thank for the conviction in the Brensic trial, returned the favor.

In November, Keahon wrote a letter to the NYPD on the stationary of the Suffolk DA's office. Keahon claimed in the letter that Jimmy was subject to a bench warrant because he had been due to testify as a witness in Suffolk County court on the same day he was supposed to appear in court in Nassau County for his drunk-driving case. Keahon said that his office told Burke to show up to Suffolk to testify and that they would inform the other court of the reason for his absence. "Unfortunately, before the District Court in Nassau was notified of Mr. Burke's court appearance in Suffolk County, a bench warrant had been issued for him due to circumstances beyond his control," Keahon wrote.

That explanation was apparently sufficient. The NYPD hired Burke in January 1985. There's no indication in available documents that the department ran a basic fact-check on Keahon's letter. If they had, Jimmy Burke might have never had a police career. A review of his trial testimony transcripts shows no appearances in any of the Pius-related proceedings in November 1982, when Burke skipped his court date and the bench warrant was issued. Jimmy himself contradicted Keahon's explanation when he testified in the Brensic case in 1983. Asked about the bench warrant, Jimmy said of his reasoning for not showing up in court: "I had a roofing job to do that day."

CHAPTER 7

K-A-K-A

B y the time he oversaw the Brensic and Ryan trials, Stuart Namm had been a judge for seven years. He acknowledged that the antics he observed of court officers like Billy Keahon "sometimes bordered on prosecutorial misconduct," but he did little to rein them in. He instinctively trusted prosecutors and cops. Detectives testifying in his court "still wore the white hats in my eyes," Namm wrote in his florid memoir, *A Whistleblower's Lament.*

Namm was a creative eccentric by the standards of Suffolk judges, a self-taught tap dancer who traveled the world with his wife. With big, dark eyebrows and a doughy face with folds like a rumpled pillowcase, he looked like an old man long before he was one.

But throughout the early 1980s, his bushy brows began to more frequently furrow on the bench. He grew concerned by the frequency with which defendants in his courtroom claimed to have had confessions beaten out of them. Among those was an accused spree killer who credibly claimed that detectives had battered him with a fifteen-inch dildo.

Namm had a creeping feeling that he, and his juries, were regularly being told lies. When Namm held a hearing to explore the systematic exclusion of young Black men from Suffolk jury pools, two prosecutors including Keahon claimed to have regularly seen citizens of that demographic among their trial's pools. Namm's own experience in Suffolk courtrooms led him to suspect the two prosecutors had just perjured themselves, though he couldn't prove it.

His skepticism came to a head with two trials in 1985, a couple of years after he had sentenced Ryan and Brensic to twenty-five years to life. The first of those trials, in May, concerned the murder of a cigar-chomping, well-connected, and heavily indebted defense attorney, Archimedes Cervera, who had been executed by way of five bullets to the head and chest. Homicide detectives had nabbed Peter Corso, a drug dealer client of Cervera's, for his murder.

But the case hinged on the word of a professional informant who himself was believed by his FBI handler to have been involved in upward of ten killings. The informant claimed Corso had confessed to him. In keeping with Suffolk practice, the fixation on confessions and informants completely eclipsed the gathering of physical evidence and other typical investigative practices. Namm learned during the trial that detectives had kept almost no notes or reports during their investigation.

More stunning to Namm was the matter of the answering machine in Cervera's office, potentially a crucial piece of evidence because it contained recordings of calls from the day the lawyer was murdered. The detectives never listened to its messages. Instead, they told Cervera's secretary to listen to them and let them know if she heard anything interesting. When Namm demanded that a prosecutor produce the tapes, he learned that the police department had sold the answering machine and its reels at auction.

The jurors acquitted Corso, and then belittled the police handling of the case. "I think they should take the Suffolk police and teach them how to conduct surveillance and do reports," said one panelist.

Namm compounded the humiliation: "There is an aura, which permeates the facts of this case, which makes it difficult, indeed impossible, to give credence to the testimony of the police officers involved," he said.

* * *

The Corso case reflected the arrogantly shoddy casework common to Suffolk cops and prosecutors. The trial that occupied Namm's courtroom a few months later was, in the judge's view, a showcase of the comfort those same people felt in committing perjury.

The defendant was James Diaz, a drifter accused of raping and stabbing to death a nurse in her Port Jefferson home. True to form, homicide detectives declared they had secured a confession from Diaz. On a page penned by a detective and not signed by the defendant, Diaz purportedly stated that following the murder he threw the knife into the woods.

But nine months later while Diaz awaited trial, the nurse's widower was playing Ping-Pong in the basement where her body was found when he discovered a knife, later shown to be stained with the victim's blood, under a stack of wood.

The knife was a double headache for homicide detectives. It showed how poorly they had searched an area just feet from where the body was found. And, like the bike up against the tree in the Pius case, it cast serious doubt on the veracity of Diaz's confession.

The detectives doubled down. On the witness stand, Detective Dennis Rafferty added that he had asked Diaz "if he wiped the blood off that knife before he threw it away. And he said no, he didn't." This detail wasn't in the written confession or any notes or reports previously prepared by Rafferty himself.

But to bolster the idea that Diaz had previously included the detail about the bloody knife in his confession to Rafferty, two prosecutors—again including Keahon—testified that the detective had mentioned it to them a year earlier. In Namm's estimation, the detective and the two prosecutors had clearly committed perjury. The knife claims weren't the only dubious statements made under oath during the Diaz trial.

There was a jailhouse informant who later testified that detectives, including snitch-converter Jack Miller, had coached him in lying on the stand by showing him Diaz's purported confession and telling him: "This is how it happened."

Detective James McCready testified about three railroad workers who he said told him they recognized Diaz from the newspaper and had seen him near the scene of the murder. That story was contradicted by the fact that Diaz's picture had not yet been published in the paper at the time of the alleged sighting. When McCready realized that mistake, he simply changed his testimony midproceedings and said that he had shown Diaz's mug shot to the workers.

The jury acquitted Diaz, and its members later told the press that they felt the homicide squad had lied to them. "If someone close to me was murdered I'd rather have a small-town police department investigate it than have the Suffolk homicide squad, with all its resources," one juror said.

Judge Namm was unequivocal. During court proceedings, he asserted that "a perjurer was brought before this court with an open eye by the prosecutor."

* * *

Such comments quickly lost Judge Namm his favored status among Suffolk County's prosecutors and detectives. They made their feelings clear through anonymously sourced smear articles in *Newsday*. "You lose, Stu!" Namm heard from a prosecutor's window one day as he left the courthouse, just before discovering that his Toyota Tercel had been keyed.

At the cop and lawyer bar Esposito's, the bathrooms bore graffiti about how Namm "sucks off little boys." And his unpopularity brought real threats to his livelihood, including an administrative judge making plans to remove him from cases. It was elementary-school bully stuff, except that the bullies had pistol licenses and indictment powers. In a nod to the slipperiness of his adversaries, Namm's paranoia led him to stop carrying a gun, leaving his .38-caliber pistol at home because he anticipated an incident where he might be intentionally provoked into using it.

On October 29, 1985, Judge Namm dropped a letter in the mail. It was addressed to New York Governor Mario Cuomo. Namm asked the governor to assign a special prosecutor to investigate misconduct in the Corso and Diaz cases.

"In two consecutive highly publicized murder trials I have witnessed, among other things, such apparent prosecutorial misconduct as perjury, subornation of perjury, intimidation of witnesses, spoliation of evidence, abuse of subpoena power and the aforesaid attempts to intimidate a sitting judge," Namm wrote to the governor.

Having knowingly kicked up a shitstorm with his letter, Namm and his wife used their airline points to go on a lengthy holiday to South America.

* * *

On a snow-heaped morning in January 1987, roughly 250 off-duty Suffolk police officers, or a tenth of the department, waved signs with slogans like "State Investigation Circus" or "Why Public Hearings? Trial by Media," while circling the parking lot of a government building in Hauppauge.

In an auditorium inside, six aged white men, lawyers from as far away as the alien region of Buffalo, were trying to figure out who was paying Tom Spota. An indignant Spota had interjected and deflected during the testimony of seemingly every witness the lawyers tried to question.

Spota's involvement made sense, at least during the testimony of the homicide detectives. After all, his law firm represented the Suffolk County Detectives Association. And this was a legal examination, spearheaded by the New York State Temporary Commission of Investigation, or SIC, the state body Cuomo had assigned to probe Namm's allegations of rampant police and prosecutorial misconduct in Suffolk County.

Spota, however, didn't hold any official position representing members of the Suffolk DA's office. But when the commissioners moved on to the questioning of a Suffolk prosecutor, Barry Feldman, Spota nonetheless remained on hand as if he were his lawyer as well. Earl Brydges, the commissioner from Buffalo, asked whether Spota was being paid to represent Feldman. Spota responded in stagey indignation. "It is because I am a friend," Spota declared, "and Mr. Feldman is a friend of mine. And I believe in what he is saying. That is why I am here today."

The audience, like in the parking lot, was full of cops in uniform, who burst into loud applause. "But I think it is unprofessional to ask that question!" Spota continued, and the hooting and hollering intensified.

"Stop, or all of you will be tossed out!" boomed SIC chairman David G. Trager. Trager's thick glasses jostled on his egg-shaped head.

As the dean of the Brooklyn Law School and former US attorney for the Eastern District of New York, he expected to be heeded.

"This isn't *The Price Is Right!*" Brydges scolded.

But the police in the audience were uncowed, cheering every interruption and utterance by Spota, and drowning out with boos the efforts of the commissioners to rein their hero in. Finally, Spota himself calmed the crowd. "There is no reason to clap," Spota intoned. "There is no reason to boo."

It should have been clear then to the six commissioners that, out here, Spota transcended—or trampled—the boundaries of the legal profession. To the crowd of angry cops in the parking lot and auditorium seats, he was the lone defender standing between them and outsiders intent on destroying the greatest law enforcement jurisdiction on Earth.

* * *

In the fifteen months between Namm's letter and the beginning of public hearings, the state-appointed anti-corruption commissioners and their investigators—former New York City homicide cops who thought their Suffolk counterparts were lazy brutes—had been conducting hundreds of private interviews. They had issued scores of subpoenas, waded through tens of thousands of pages of trial transcripts and Internal Affairs records, and filed more than a dozen lawsuits seeking compliance with their investigation.

It wasn't just the SIC personnel who were swarming. Federal agents from New York's Eastern District were also sniffing around, their efforts overlapping with those of the SIC so often that the two investigative bodies had to warn each other off their choicest targets. The Democrats of the Suffolk County Legislature even joined in with their own investigation, to the eye-rolling chagrin of the law enforcement good old boy network. "The assholes of the legislature are looking at this," was how one prosecutor summarized it.

Even the regional newspaper got in on the act—a real et tu, Brute moment for Long Island cops. *Newsday* had for years been largely friendly to the law enforcement establishment. Even as scandal brewed throughout the late 1970s, the newspaper had often served as a willing bullhorn for prosecutors and detectives looking to bolster or repair weak cases, including the Pius murder.

But in December 1986, two of the paper's top reporters, Thomas Maier and Rex Smith, published a five-part investigative series entitled "The Confession Takers," which took withering aim at Suffolk detectives and prosecutors' reliance on confessions above all else.

The reporters examined the cases against 361 Suffolk homicide defendants and determined that 94 percent of them relied on confessions. Many of those confessions were dubious and allegedly coerced through torture, brutality, or unlawful trickery. "At its worst, the Suffolk system has depended on confessions that violate the rights of suspects, substitute for extensive detective work, conflict with other evidence and strain the credibility of the county's cases in court," wrote Maier and Smith.

With confessions and dubious jailhouse snitches as the foundations of almost every case, it was no shock that Suffolk authorities had neglected their crime laboratory. The reports noted the forensics facility had mushrooms growing from cracks in the floor, and its scientists had botched a case by losing a murder victim's brain tissue.

And for all the tough-on-crime braggadocio—"We were the best," was how a homicide commander explained the unheard-of confession rate—the *Newsday* reporters found that Suffolk's methods actually ensured its accused murderers were more often unpunished. The weak cases resulted in more reduced charges, lenient plea bargains, and convictions reversed on appeal than in neighboring jurisdictions.

Perhaps no detail in the story said more than the chest-thumping quotes from homicide detectives, a tribe of white men who sneered at concepts like due process. "Ask any one of the parents or friends of anybody who's been murdered what their feelings are on it," retired detective Richard Zito told the reporters concerning the topic of constitutional protections of suspects. "They'll tell you to forget Miranda and every other goddamn ruling that's ever come down from the Supreme Court—and burn the bastard right there."

* * *

The *Newsday* series included, almost as an afterthought, the revelation that Suffolk's most prominent forensic scientist was a serial perjurer. Ira DuBey had put his stamp on numerous felony convictions, including those of the Pius case, through confident trial testimony that always seemed to precisely support the prosecutor's theory of a murder.

But Maier found that DuBey had repeatedly lied on the stand about his credentials. DuBey claimed to have a master's degree in forensic science that he had never actually completed, misstated where he had gotten his undergraduate degree, and listed specialized courses he had taken at several schools where administrators said they had no record of his attendance.

It emerged that at least two top prosecutors in the Suffolk DA's office, including Barry Feldman, had been warned that DuBey was fibbing about his credentials but had killed the allegations and allowed him to continue lying on the stand for years. The SIC commissioners had been questioning Feldman about DuBey's perjury when Spota put on his show for the cops in the audience.

When Spota wasn't lawyering on behalf of cops and prosecutors who had caught the attention of investigators, he was himself the subject of inquiry. Both state and county investigative hearings explored how Spota built his burgeoning private client base so quickly, and whether the answer involved a brazen arrangement involving C-note bribes.

Theodore Adamchak was a proud Suffolk police veteran. He was bothered by some of his less motivated colleagues, the ones who crowded the doorways of 7-Elevens shooting the breeze for hours over cups of free coffee, or who spent their shifts at local firehouses playing Ping-Pong and drinking beer.

But for the most part, Adamchak focused on his own busy job. Adamchak gave out a hundred summonses a month and made forty to fifty DWI arrests a year, big numbers that made him unpopular with jealous colleagues but filled his mantle with annual Excellent Police Duty Award baubles.

In the spring of 1982, Adamchak was in court to testify in the trial of a defendant he had arrested for drunk driving. According to Adamchak, near the end of his day of testimony, the prosecutor in the case took him aside. Adamchak said the prosecutor, David Woycik, gave him a business card. He told him that the next time he arrested somebody, to call him so he could refer the defendant to "the Spota law firm."

The prosecutor mentioned a $100 payoff for steering business to Spota. Adamchak played it cool, but his gears started turning. "I took that as bribery and I didn't want no part of that," Adamchak said. He was interested in stringing the scheming prosecutor along, building a case against him and maybe earning the transfer to the Rackets Bureau in the DA's office he coveted. He immediately reported Woycik's overture to supervisors.

The matter was assigned to James J. O'Rourke, bureau chief of the DA's Special Investigation Unit, and Alan Rosenthal, a detective sergeant who worked in the prosecutor's office. It turned out Woycik's alleged scheme wasn't much of a secret, as Rosenthal soon interviewed another cop who had been offered a similar deal.

On a night in early 1982, Woycik had accompanied Suffolk officer Bill Brown on his shift. During a drunk-driving arrest, Woycik made his pitch. Brown alleged the prosecutor told him that there were law firms that would kick back 30 percent of their fees for each referral. The prosecutor handed the cop a business card for Sullivan & Spota. Brown said he responded by laughing and continuing to process the drunk.

The alleged kickback scheme was, by Rosenthal's later acknowledgment, an unusual case because its broad strokes had been so easily corroborated. Adamchak provided the business card Woycik had given him and it bore a phone number leading to Spota's firm. The case had the makings of a serious corruption investigation, and O'Rourke and Rosenthal were seemingly the men for the job. The DA's chief law assistant referred to them as the "two best investigators in Suffolk." But their heart wasn't in this one. They failed to ask rudimentary follow-up questions of the two police officers. They never bothered to speak to Woycik, who later denied the allegations of a kickback scheme. And O'Rourke ruled out any wrongdoing by Spota and Sullivan after a single desultory phone interview.

"They denied categorically that they ever participated in such a situation or knew about it or authorized [Woycik] to do it," O'Rourke testified, though he didn't remember which of the partners he spoke to and hadn't made a report of the call. When asked why he simply took the partners' word, O'Rourke explained: "I just couldn't believe that those two individuals would be involved." But when asked about the investigation recently, O'Rourke reversed himself on that, saying, "I think it was true" that the firm paid cops for cases. "Apparently Gerry in all his wisdom told the assistant DA if you get me cases I will get you a referral fee," O'Rourke said, putting the onus of the scheme on Sullivan, who is now deceased. O'Rourke said he found the practice was "inappropriate if not worse," but that he was blocked from seriously pursuing it by his boss, DA Henry.

Rosenthal later acknowledged during testimony that the investigation warranted a C or an F grade. Woycik resigned, and nobody in the DA's office reported him to New York's Grievance Committee, which enforces attorney misconduct. A couple of years after overseeing the kickback investigation, O'Rourke left the DA's office. By the time his handling of the case was investigated in 1987, he was a partner in Spota, Sullivan & O'Rourke.

In September of that year, a sullen O'Rourke, who wore large, dark sunglasses, a part in his thinning brown hair, and a pursed smile of disdain, testified before the Suffolk County Legislature about the episode. O'Rourke, an amateur banjo player whose cocky manner earned him the nickname "Hollywood" from his peers, sneered when asked about Detective Rosenthal's relationship with Spota and Sullivan. "They were homosexual lovers," he responded. "I don't know if they kissed and made love. How do I know what they did?"

If that wasn't clear enough, O'Rourke left no uncertainty how he felt about the proceedings in another outburst. "I think this is a bunch of dog kaka, that's my state of mind if you wish to hear it," O'Rourke declared, before aiding the stenographer: "That's K-A-K-A."

PART II

RISE

SUFFOLK COUNTY POLICE DEPARTMENT
ROOKIE OFFICER JAMES BURKE, 1986

CHAPTER 8

FORTRESS MENTALITY

New York City police cadet Jimmy Burke spent the first half of 1985 hustling around corners in shooting galleries called Hogan's Alley and the "Fun House," blasting his Smith & Wesson .38 at cardboard bad guys.

He careened a NYPD squad car through a high-speed course. He completed a calisthenics program, including a one- to two-mile run every day. And the Smithtown kid with a minuscule GPA in high school became, in a police setting, a star student. He got 90 percent or higher in every academy quiz and earned second place in a speech competition.

This account of Jimmy's time in the NYPD academy comes from his Suffolk County police application. Judging from the veracity of other claims in the application, it is assuredly at least partly bullshit. Nonetheless, it seemed that Jimmy Burke made for a more than passable police cadet.

On July 2, 1985, his unlikely career as a cop officially began, when Mayor Ed Koch and assorted police brass presented him and a couple of thousand others with their badges and guns.

Burke, NYPD shield number 19999, had only one regret. "I missed being valedictorian by half of a percentage point," he later wrote. His first assignment was in the 109th Precinct in Flushing, Queens, where he graduated from a foot post to a sector car. But before he was even out of the academy, he was looking to parlay his "city time," as cops called a brief rookie tenure in the NYPD, into getting hired in his home county. Suffolk police jobs were much harder to get, partly because joining the Suffolk force was a bit like hitting the lottery. Adjusted for inflation, the average Suffolk cop earned more than $143,000 in salary and fringe benefits by the 1980s, a figure that would only rise over the next several decades. Due to exorbitant vacation and sick day allotments, they earned their salaries in far fewer workdays than cops in other departments.

In putting in for a Suffolk job, Jimmy faced the same hurdles that were present when he applied to the NYPD: the arrest record, the bad-news teenage friends, the drug use. Jimmy no doubt knew that in a police application, past drug use could be overlooked but getting caught lying was an immediate disqualification. So he copped to frequent marijuana use as a teenager—"approx. 75–100 times," he wrote—and a seemingly unlikely one-and-done history with harder stuff: the cocaine that didn't work, the mescaline that made him sick, the quaalude that turned him sleepy, the speed that gave him a tummy ache.

And once again, his status as a star witness in the Pius case proved pivotal to moving his career forward. Among his references was Richard Jensen, the homicide supervisor who in 1979 had interviewed fifteen-year-old Jimmy in his stepfather's living room. "He gave information that was instrumental in the arrest and conviction of the murderers of John Pius," Jensen wrote. "He was always candid, forthright, and cooperative, despite adverse peer pressure."

The Suffolk screening cop who conducted Jimmy's background check showed only a fleeting concern. It was related mostly to his spotty history behind the wheel, which included three accidents. Police Officer Francis Dwyer recommended "close supervision of his driving habits." Besides that, Dwyer acknowledged "some evidence of immaturity" in Burke's past but found that the candidate "appears to have improved in all areas." With that, Suffolk County PD unleashed Jimmy Burke on the area known as The Corner.

* * *

Suffolk DA Patrick Henry heaped into a seat in the offices of his nemesis, SIC Chairman David G. Trager. When the puffy-faced top prosecutor lifted his arms, a faded tattoo of chains, a souvenir from his long-ago days as a hard-drinking Navy man, peeked out of his cuffs. On this day in February 1987, he was in the enemy territory of a high-rise in lower Manhattan to give up the ship. "I probably can't run again," Henry said.

The two days of public hearings in Hauppauge the month previous had been bruising televised affairs during which Trager, in his scathing opening statement, had jabbed a meaty finger at Henry and Suffolk County Police Commissioner DeWitt Treder as the ultimate culprits for the law-enforcement morass his commission was about to make known. "Top management of these agencies must be held accountable for creating the atmosphere allowing misconduct, first, to occur and, second, to go unpunished," Trager had declared.

Henry knew that this was just the beginning. There would be more public hearings designed to shame and embarrass his office, gobbled up by television cameras and newspaper headline writers. And after Trager finally figured he had tortured his subjects enough, he'd publish a report damning enough to justify the plentiful time and expense spent on the investigation.

Henry reasoned with Trager about the policy changes he had already made and problem prosecutors he had moved around. In return, Trager charitably informed Henry that he didn't think that he was corrupt, just incompetent. The DA "wasn't watching the store," Trager lamented. And then Henry made an attempt to retain a sliver of power for his highest-level acolyte, suggesting to Trager that he should replace the SCPD's commissioner, who he described as weak and not up to the job, with a top deputy.

After the meeting ended, whatever spirit of conciliation had inspired it broke down. Henry insisted publicly that he would run for another term. And his office sued for a restraining order to stop the SIC from issuing their report. That only succeeded in delaying the opus, which was finally published in April 1989.

* * *

The 199-page report had a cast of Suffolk stock characters, including homicide detectives who couldn't decipher the most basic elements of a crime scene, prosecutors who fished for lies from repellant snitches, and narcotics cops who got high off seized evidence. It condemned Suffolk County's law enforcement chiefs back to the potato farmland days. The police department and the DA's office, the report declared, "have failed to meet the challenges put to them by a county as important as Suffolk has become."

The hearings had showcased lawmen who were belligerently incompetent at all-important jobs. A homicide detective didn't run a ballistics test on a .22-caliber bullet found in the pocket of a defendant because "every Black guy in Amityville has a .22." A homicide supervisor, when quizzed on what a lab could discern from crime scene blood, responded vacantly: "I guess they can tell you if it's blood." When prodded for more, the supervisor posited: "Maybe, if it's food."

In Narcotics, some of the busiest cops were regularly raiding the evidence room for a fix. When one of them unknowingly arrested the son of the police department's chief of detectives, top officials in the department and the DA's office falsely claimed that he was a criminal informant in order to get the chief's kid off on a misdemeanor. Cops repeatedly used an informant they knew was dishonest, including in a raid resulting in the arrest of twenty-three Black defendants. Prosecutors tried unsuccessfully to stash the informant out of state to keep him out of the reach of the SIC. He testified nonetheless, about how cops urged him to commit perjury to lock up innocent people.

Cops and prosecutors trampled on strict protocols regarding wiretapping, the most invasive tool in law enforcement. Back then pen registers, which only recorded numbers dialed and not conversations, didn't require a warrant. When it came to illegally jury-rigging pen registers with a speaker to record audio, Suffolk cops were nimble-fingered crooks. In one recording obtained by the SIC, the cops accidentally illegally wiretapped themselves, chatting for fourteen minutes before one of them remarked: "We didn't turn off the speaker."

It wasn't a few bad apples, but a jurisdiction in which misconduct was woven into the fabric of the agencies heading up county law enforcement. "This Report does not concern a narrow criminal investigation and does not point to a single 'smoking gun,'" wrote the SIC chief. Instead, they said, the smoking gun was the "day-in, day-out manner" in which the police and the DA's office "have conducted the business of law enforcement in Suffolk County so badly."

* * *

During its four-year odyssey in Suffolk County, the SIC had taken pains not to touch one of the most obvious cases of misconduct. Its investigators had early on collected records from the John Pius homicide cases, but they did nothing beyond what they called a "preliminary review." The SIC report explained that, since every Pius defendant had active appeals, they would await the results of those legal proceedings. By the time the report was published, those results had been delivered in the form of overturned convictions for all four defendants.

Rob Brensic and Tom Ryan were granted retrials after New York's highest court found Pete Quartararo's confession to be unreliable, in that it was one of several versions of the murder he recounted that day, "was obtained from a juvenile after lengthy custodial questioning and . . . was given under circumstances which suggest that it was induced by the hope of leniency." The New York State Court of Appeals also noted that each of the witnesses who testified about Brensic's incriminating statements—Jimmy Burke, George Heiselmann, and Brett Locke—"presented credibility problems."

A federal judge then ordered a new trial for Mike Quartararo. In a scathing 107-page opinion, US District Court Judge Edward Korman ruled that Quartararo's attorney, the reputed drunken doormat O'Leary, had been incompetent in several "unjustifiable" and "inexcusable" ways, from not bothering to get discovery material from his co-counsel in order to prepare for trial; to his "rambling, disjointed" summation that left unconfronted the many shortcomings of the case; to his failure to object to Spota's own "inflammatory" summation that went "beyond the bounds of proper argument."

Korman also wrote that there were "facts that cast doubt on the accuracy of statements allegedly" made by Quartararo and recounted in court by witnesses including Jimmy Burke. The judge found it "troubling" that those witnesses and Peter Quartararo himself had mentioned Mike Quartararo placing the bike against the tree when the "undisputed evidence" was that it was on the ground when the body was found.

"Similarly disturbing," Korman wrote, was the bizarre confluence of testimony regarding incriminating statements in both Mike Quartararo's trial and the trial of Rob Brensic. While Mike Quartararo was alleged to have said that "the police officers fucked everything up" and that "he would get away with it," Korman noted that "virtually identical words in the same conversation were placed in Robert Brensic's mouth" by Jimmy Burke's later testimony.

"John Pius died a horrible death," Korman concluded. "Justice requires that his death not go unpunished. Justice is not served, however, when the trial that resulted in the adjudication of guilt is so defective as to cast serious doubt on the fairness and reliability of that verdict."

Korman was even more strident the following year when he overturned the conviction of Peter Quartararo, the final defendant in the case. He found that Detective Palumbo had made a "patent and deliberate" failure to read Quartararo his Miranda rights, that Quartararo's confession was coerced, and that Judge Doyle had made several "clearly erroneous" decisions in allowing the taped confession to be referenced at all, much less to be played for the jury.

Korman referred to the SIC report that had only been made public a couple of months earlier, citing the Pius case as a clear example of the failings of Suffolk County law enforcement. "The Suffolk County Police here deliberately violated the Constitution of the United States and the laws of the State of New York to obtain a confession," Korman wrote, finding that the shoddy case was "characteristic of conduct long tolerated by responsible officials of the Suffolk County Police Department and the District Attorney's Office."

Following the overturned convictions, Suffolk officials nursed their wounds by coercing another confession, this time legally and in open court.

* * *

The boys convicted in the Pius case were now men in their midtwenties whose youth had come to an abrupt end in state facilities. None of them were under any illusion that the Suffolk DA's office was going to give up on reinstating their convictions. All of them had grown bitter, but perhaps none as much as Rob Brensic.

He had tried to make the most of his five years in max-security Sing Sing. About a year of it was spent teaching himself to play "Stairway to Heaven" on guitar. He learned plumbing, and how to solder pipes. In an effort to make himself feel better about the prison time, he said he focused on "all the stupid shit" he did when he was a kid that he had gotten away with. Maybe it balanced out going away for a murder he didn't commit. But the rationalization was flawed. The stupid shit was crimes like siphoning gas for his friend's car and trapping a teacher in his house by pushing his Volkswagen up against his door. "It doesn't really add up, because if you put all that stuff together I'd get two to three days in jail," Brensic said with exasperation.

So instead he stewed on why he was there, and who was to blame. He kept landing on the "Webelo," as he derided Peter Quartararo. It was a Boy Scout–themed insult even though Pete was far from that past while doing his own hard time at Attica. Rob was resentful that he and Tom Ryan had been able to withstand the same trickery and manipulation without confessing, including, according to Rob, when he was set upon by jailhouse snitches. But in Rob's mind, Peter's weakness had fucked them all.

He found himself somehow angrier at Peter than at Tom Spota, Anthony Palumbo, or Jimmy Burke. "They put me through so much shit for seventeen hours, and lied to my fucking parents," Brensic later seethed about the 1979 interrogation. "And then they finally get that stupid asshole to say some fucking shit. He signed that shit because they told him he'd go to fucking jail for twenty-five years if he did not sign that paper, and he signed it."

Perhaps this was just more rationalization, a way for Brensic to make himself feel better about his decision to return the favor.

Brensic's retrial was in 1988. His lawyer, Frank Bress, ran a legal services clinic at Pace University, and had recruited sixteen students to tackle Brensic's case. They prepared by poring through more than twelve thousand pages of previous trial testimony. Bress had reason to be optimistic. The retrial judge, Ronald Aiello, had ruled that Peter's confession was inadmissible in its totality. Even more significantly, they had finally gotten the Pius case out of Suffolk County. By conducting a survey showing that a majority of Suffolk County residents had already decided that the four defendants were guilty, Bress had successfully argued to move the trial to Brooklyn. "It was a whole different ball game when we got to Brooklyn," said Bress, salivating at the potential jurors: "Hasids, Rastafarians—it was finally a break from the Italian Catholic juror pool."

But Bress was far from cocky. He knew there was a chance that even a Brooklyn jury could reconvict Brensic. In that case his client could again face a sentence of twenty-five years to life. Bress had recently worked on a case in which the defendant, Patsy Kelly Jarrett, who was convicted of murder on scant evidence, had won a new trial. Prosecutors offered her a plea deal with no jail time, but she refused to admit she committed the murder. She was reconvicted and condemned to serve the remainder of her twenty-five-years-to-life sentence.

That experience haunted Bress, even as the proceedings in Brooklyn looked to be going Brensic's way. Without Peter's confession, Suffolk prosecutor Tim Mazzci was even more reliant on jailhouse snitchery. To complement Brett Locke, who was still valiantly hanging on, homicide detectives turned up another inmate. Rick Margolis also claimed Brensic had confessed to him when locked up for pawning the stolen rings. But in a pretrial hearing, Margolis did more damage than good for the prosecution, harpooning his fellow snitch by testifying that Locke had gotten his own confession out of Brensic through violence and threats.

Justice Aiello called the two lawyers into his chambers. "You're getting beat up," the judge warned Mazzei, according to Bress. "This case is not going well for you. You need to think about offering something."

* * *

Brensic began his denouement with the same question that Peter Quartararo had asked in the back of Palumbo's car nine years earlier. "Where do you want me to start from?" Brensic asked on May 18, 1988. "From the beginning?"

"Yes, please," responded Aiello.

But before Brensic could speak again, a female voice shouted out from the audience in downtown Brooklyn: "It's wrong!"

"Mr. Brensic?" Aiello prompted, ignoring the interruption.

"He's lying about something he didn't do!" came the voice again.

Brensic's parents, Frank and Audrey Brensic, were throwbacks. She was a matronly homemaker who wore dresses down to her ankles. He was a financier whose default mood was consternation. They raised their three sons and a daughter in an immaculate home on Marquette Drive. During the proceedings of the previous trial, they had daily shielded their faces—she with her purse and he with his cap—from news photographers.

But now Audrey Brensic wouldn't stop shouting, even as the judge threatened to remove her. "It's not right," she insisted. "It's not fair. You people have crucified us. It's ridiculous. Why do they make people lie? It's not right. I can't help it, it's not right. It's an awful injustice. We've had to live through this, this terrible thing they are putting on my son."

"What we've gone through for nine years," lamented Frank Brensic.

And then, when the outburst finally subsided, their son continued.

Rob told a halting, at times vague story that started with the theft of a minibike. As Rob was putting the minibike in the trunk of Tom Ryan's car, he said, Mike Quartararo saw John Pius bike past, headed toward the school.

"Michael and Peter jumped him," Brensic said. "Me and Tommy Ryan were involved a little bit but not much."

"What did you do, specifically?" Aiello asked.

"I might have punched him a few times," Brensic responded.

Aiello: "Where did you punch him?"

"Maybe in the arm or the back. And Peter was on his chest and he grabbed him with the rocks," Brensic said. "He's the only one who put the rocks in him, only Peter. He grabbed a handful. He didn't count them or anything."

When the judge asked if he did anything to prevent the murder, Brensic responded: "It happened so quick. He didn't mean to kill him, he just wanted to shut him up. And the next thing he was dead and that's it."

After answering a few more questions about dragging the body to the woods and leaving it there, Aiello asked prosecutor Mazzei: "Is the allocution acceptable to the People?"

Mazzei responded quickly: "If it's acceptable to the court, certainly, Judge, it's acceptable to the People."

After nine years of steadfastly maintaining their innocence as they attempted to claw out from under Peter's recanted teenage confession, the four were now back to where they started. Or worse.

Justice Aiello detailed the terms of Brensic's plea deal. The provisions were so favorable that Bress considered it malpractice to take the case to trial. Brensic pleaded to second-degree manslaughter, a conviction that mandated a four-to-eight-year prison sentence. Suffolk prosecutors had promised not to object to immediate parole. Brensic would not be required to testify against his codefendants. The Pius family agreed not to sue Brensic. And, for Brensic, the clincher was simple: he could be in his own bed that night. Brensic would be set free, and be allowed to leave the state, while his new sentence was pending. He said that after Bress told him that part, he didn't need any more convincing: "Fuck this, man, I'm going home."

At his sentencing, Brensic said: "I'm very sorry for what happened." Outside of court, he insisted upon his innocence, though such protestations now fell flat. His attorney, Bress, said Brensic wasn't his first or last innocent client to plead guilty to a crime in order to avoid draconian punishment. "One of the unconfessed secrets of criminal law is that defendants plead guilty all the time to things they didn't do in order to get the benefit of lighter sentences," Bress said. "Judges know it, DAs know it, defense attorneys know it. They'll usually never admit it because the practice involves swearing to something that those in the courtroom know didn't happen."

But Mazzei treated the plea as vindication. The prosecutor was a thin, fastidious fellow with a dark mustache, and a chummy member of the Tom Spota cabal. A few years earlier, he had been a partner in the law firm then called Sullivan, Spota, Molita & Mazzei.

"We never had the wrong guys," Mazzei crowed to the press following Brensic's plea. "This was one way to prove that we had the right people."

In its report published a year later, the SIC slammed the terms of Brensic's plea as "totally misguided and improper," declaring that "the District Attorney was seeking a public relations coup, rather than appropriate punishment or justice."

Brensic would learn that every deal has its fine print. He spent two years as a free man with his sister in Virginia, becoming experienced as a professional plumber. He then returned to New York for what he expected would be a couple of months in prison before getting paroled. But instead, the parole board, which wasn't beholden to any courtroom deal, refused to let him go. He ultimately was released in 1993, having served a total of eight years in prison.

Among the parole board's reasons for denying Brensic: his arrest for burglary the decade earlier, and his lack of remorse for killing Johnny Pius.

* * *

The New York State Temporary Commission of Investigation had, despite its name, been around since 1958. But keeping the commission alive required a high-wire act. Half of its critics, invariably including the targets of its investigations, complained that the body trampled on due process. The other half derided it as toothless.

The commission had a larger jurisdiction than any other law enforcement body in the state. It could issue subpoenas, hold quasi-legal hearings, give criminal immunity to witnesses, and publish reports. But since it couldn't issue arrest warrants or indictments, it was ultimately reliant on other agencies to take its recommendations. Even in the wake of the searing report, the teardown of the Suffolk County law enforcement system never materialized.

A few bad cops put in their retirement papers. Police Commissioner Treder resigned. John Gallagher, the Suffolk chief of detectives, became—at that time—the highest-ranking official of the department ever indicted for a crime. Ira DuBey, the forensic chief, pleaded to misdemeanor perjury.

And Patrick Henry, who the commissioners said "charitably can be described as having ignored the grave and demanding responsibilities of his Office, despite clear danger signals and warnings," didn't run for another term. But his career didn't exactly languish. He became a top judge in the state Supreme Court. And he left a legacy in having groomed the next generation of Suffolk County's legal leaders, with Spota chief among them.

The 1989 district attorney election to replace Henry was a clear referendum on the direction of Suffolk County law enforcement going forward. Democrats nominated a self-proclaimed activist, defense attorney Robert Gottlieb, who vowed top-to-bottom reform. Republicans put forth an ornery establishment figure whose central campaign promise was changing as little as possible.

Jim Catterson's only criticism of Henry, who had been his boss during a previous tenure as a Suffolk prosecutor, was that he wasn't in office long enough. Catterson, a wiry fellow with droopy facial features, derided the SIC as "slipshod in investigations and selective in their use of evidence," and said he would aim to "reshape the District Attorney's office without dismantling it." In most jurisdictions, that would seem an inadequate response to an official finding that the entire county law enforcement system was corrupt and incompetent. But those jurisdictions were not in the death grip of a police voting bloc.

The three unions representing cops in the Suffolk County Police Department—the Police Benevolent Association, the Suffolk County Detectives Association, and the Suffolk County Superior Officers Association—had members who voted, campaigned, and donated in lockstep with their endorsements. About a quarter of the NYPD lived on Long Island, and those cops voted the same. Throw in the Suffolk County Sheriff's Office and members of smaller departments throughout the county, and those cops' families and friends who voted in their interests, and the result was tens of thousands of cop votes controlling elections.

It was no mystery who they were backing. James McCready, the detective who the SIC had found "knowingly gave false testimony" in the Diaz case, publicly attacked Gottlieb, saying: "He doesn't have the experience to be the DA of this county." The cops loved even Catterson's worst traits. He liked to say that he suffered from Irish Alzheimer's, in that he forgot everyone but his enemies. That he had disowned his daughter because she married a Jew was included in a

fluff-piece newspaper profile as an example of his quirky stubborn-
ness. Catterson blurted out during a debate that he didn't plan on
prosecuting "every man who raises his hand to his wife and belts her
right across the face." But none of it mattered. Catterson won handily.
"The Cat," as he was dubbed, would enjoy a fearsome decade-plus
rule. But then he learned something: When you live by the cops, you
die by them too.

* * *

In March 1991, Los Angeles cops were caught on camera savagely
beating Rodney King. The tape became a media sensation—and
sparked a national conversation about policing the police. Predictably,
anger and paranoia among Suffolk cops reached a fever pitch. Two
weeks later, the SCPD offered its own bizarro version of the high-
profile police beating, in which a well-known homicide detective was
accused of drunkenly pummeling a fellow St. Patrick's Day bargoer.

Detective Jim McCready had been the picture of a swashbuckling
Suffolk homicide bull, operating on macho intuition, and earning
more than four times the national average salary. His hefty pay stubs
enabled him to retire and open a pub, called Digger O'Dell's, with the
half-sister of a kid he had put away on a dubious murder conviction.

McCready's version of the events of St. Patty's Day 1991 was pure
old-school Irish cop glory. He said he was enjoying a few beers at Harry's, a bar in Rocky Point, when a drunk grabbed a banner reading
"We Support the Troops" and ran off. McCready jumped in his Jeep
and found the thief at a gas station, where he ripped off the man's
clothes, leaving him in the nude. "You want your clothes, you'll get
your clothes back when you bring me the flag," McCready told the
drunk, according to a later deposition.

"Last time I saw him he was running down the road with two
garbage can covers on him, one in the front and one in the back,"
McCready remembered. "So I went back to Harry's and had a couple
more beers and I went home."

But that's not the way Jim Catterson, the newly elected DA, saw
it. The alleged beating victim, whose story was corroborated by witnesses and photographs of his injuries, said that McCready and three
others chased him down a darkened side street where they pummeled

him, leaving his face swollen and bruised. When uniformed cops drove up on two occasions, the banner thief said they ignored his pleas for help. Catterson charged six people in connection with the beating, including a felony assault charge for McCready.

This was the first of several instances of perceived betrayal of cops by the new top prosecutor. And in seemingly every one of those instances, Catterson was opposed by the one true friend of all Suffolk cops. McCready hired Spota, as well as his frequent sidekick Billy Keahon, to defend him.

Spota turned the case into a referendum on cops, claiming that Catterson had only charged McCready due to national unrest over the King beating. "Catterson surrendered to the pressure of *Newsday* and the media because of something that occurred three thousand miles away in Los Angeles," Spota declared.

On an early morning in the midst of the McCready trial, Keahon piloted his Mercedes-Benz the wrong way on Nesconset Highway, colliding head-on with the vehicle of a doctor who had just wrapped up an emergency room shift. The doctor was severely injured, and Keahon was charged with driving drunk, on a suspended license to boot. He later acknowledged that he had been struggling with alcoholism since at least 1981, the year before he took over as trial prosecutor in the Pius case. Spota handled the McCready case from there. When the verdict came back not guilty, the old homicide bull cried and hugged Spota while yet another audience full of cops cheered and hooted.

The message of the verdict, as if there had been any doubt, was that Suffolk County wasn't interested in police accountability.

CHAPTER 9

ENTER RATMAN

North Amityville was once a destination for middle-class Black settlers seeking refuge from the city, just like their white counterparts in Smithtown. But by the mid-1980s, the crack epidemic had transformed much of the hamlet into a sector as bombed-out and dreary as anything in the five boroughs. The focal point of the misery was The Corner, the intersection of Albany Avenue and Great Neck Road.

A brazen drug trade—complete with corner boys calling out "Jumbo dimes! Jumbo twenties!" while shaking orange-topped vials— corroded the surrounding neighborhood, devouring playgrounds and stores and homes in the once-bustling business center.

In their place: slumped fiends, drunks pissing on walls, and with increasing frequency, gunfire and other violence stemming from drug beefs or desperate addicts.

This sort of open-air drug market that appears entirely resistant to traditional law enforcement efforts to clean it up isn't a unique phenomenon. Criminal sociologists working on similar drug hot spots around the country have achieved success through counterintuitive—and time-consuming—measures, often involving clemency and counseling. But the Suffolk County Police Department wasn't sending sociologists to North Amityville.

The hamlet was part of the First Precinct, home to a large number of Suffolk County's Black and brown residents, with high poverty levels as well. The police department had a policy of assigning ineffective officers, or those being subtly punished, to the highest-crime sectors in places like North Amityville.

The First Precinct, and the neighboring Third Precinct, had for years accounted for roughly three-quarters of the brutality complaints in the department, which at the time had six precincts. And because only about 3 percent of misconduct complaints against Suffolk police were ever substantiated, sectors like North Amityville were a paradise for violent or otherwise problematic cops who could operate with little fear of consequences. As the Suffolk County Bar Association put it in a 1980 report: "Persons in those areas often see the worst, rather than the best, members of the Suffolk County Police Department."

North Amityville, or Sector 110 to a cop, was where twenty-two-year-old Jimmy Burke reported in 1986, commuting from his parents' house in Smithtown to his first assignment as a Suffolk County police officer, earning $666 every two weeks.

Burke quickly established himself as a thriving creature of the drug war. He learned that in a sector like 110, you can do the same thing every tour: pummel drug dealers, brandish your gun at crowds, kick down crack house doors. And the next time you punch in, the whole dismal tableau will be there unchanged, waiting for you to do it again.

* * *

Consider the case of Barry Veney, a supernaturally menacing crack dealer in North Amityville. Or at least that's how Veney was described in internal police paperwork detailing his June 7, 1988, arrest by Burke and his partner, Dennis Sullivan, the former Cousins II busboy who had been interviewed by a private investigator about the Pius case.

That account, signed by supervisors but clearly cribbed from the officers themselves, described the sudden appearance at the intersection of Albany and Great Neck of the young Suffolk cops, known on the street as Starsky and Hutch.

The monikers suggested a sarcastic assessment of how this cop pair went about their daily business. Though they wore police officer uniforms and drove a boxy blue-and-white Ford, they emulated the plainclothes television detectives screeching around in the red Torino. Everything was a car chase, a foot pursuit, a tackle of a dangerous perp.

Burke was Starsky, the streetwise one. He and Sullivan seemed forever intertwined. Sullivan grew up in Stony Brook and bussed tables alongside Tom Ryan. He and Burke had been NYPD partners in Queens before snagging Suffolk County jobs together and winding up in the same sector car again. They each mostly eschewed uniform caps and wore their black hair mussed in a lothario style.

A confidential informant had tipped them to the whereabouts of Veney, who was wanted on several warrants, according to the internal police account. Upon their arrival at The Corner, Veney scrambled and a chase began. As described by the cops, Veney managed to combine the characteristics of a ferocious predator and a ghost.

"Due to the duration of the chase and the surrounding terrain, the nominees were split up and were each subjected to attack with the perpetrator threatening to kill the nominees," reads the account, referring to Burke and Sullivan. Veney was apprehended but then broke free three times "by virtue of his violent determination to escape."

Cue the angry natives.

"During the melee the nominees were surrounded by a large and hostile crowd which greatly jeopardized the nominees' safety," read the police account. One of the cops—the police document doesn't specify whether it was Burke or Sullivan—engaged in "hand to hand combat" with Veney. The other drew his firearm on the crowd. Yet more "lengthy and exhaustive foot pursuit" and "extremely violent confrontations" later, Burke and Sullivan managed to subdue and arrest the accused crack dealer.

They were treated at a local hospital for "head, shoulder and back injuries and numerous cuts and bruises." The police records don't mention Veney's postarrest condition.

Burke and Sullivan's supervisors lapped up such stuff. For the Veney arrest, the pair won "Monthly Recognition of Efficient Police Service," an honor regularly collected by young Burke. Thanks to such commendations, breast bars—the cop version of a Boy Scout patch—weighed down the space above his left uniform pocket.

And newspaper reporters reprinted tales of his glory without asking too many questions. "Crowd Protests Drug Arrest," read the *Newsday* story about the Veney melee. The story regurgitated the police version of a "hostile crowd of about 15 people." But it notably did not include that one of the cops had pulled a gun on the bystanders.

This was just one hyperbolic episode among dozens for Burke, who could have had a second career as a writer of overwrought cop dramas. His internal accounts of pursuing two-bit street villains nicknamed G-Man, Worm, Murky, and Leech were full of floridly written heroics.

The menacing crowd was at that point a standby for Burke. Following another incident in which Burke struggled with an accused drug dealer who he said had produced a metal blade from her breast, the police account stated: "During the melee a large and hostile crowd formed, further jeopardizing the officers' safety."

Burke and Sullivan never missed an opportunity to infuse their daily adventures with some thrilling verbiage. When they ran after a guy on a bicycle, it was a "wild mid-day pursuit" during which they narrowly dodged cars and the perp, after being tackled, "struggled violently until subdued." A burglar Burke arrested in a home full of stolen shotguns, electronics, bolt cutters, and hypodermic needles was a "one-man crime wave." A recently released convict selling drugs out of a stolen car at Cee-Cee's Lounge, the official bar of The Corner, was "a heavy drug user with a costly habit."

The reports convey less a neighborhood patrolman in the American suburbs, and more an occupier attempting to bring law and order to a foreign populace whose very body fluids represented danger. In one report, Burke and Sullivan arrived at the scene of a stabbing and "were met with a large and hysterical crowd and observed a subject lying in the street with a gaping chest wound." Burke applied pressure with a field dressing, and his supervisor credited his "quick and intelligent actions, despite the fear of contagious disease," an apparent reference to the paranoia surrounding HIV/AIDS.

On good days, Jimmy described the crowds surrounding him not as hostile, but as adoring. "Neighbors were literally on their front lawn cheering as the owner was led away in hand-cuffs," read an internal report after Burke said he arrested the operator of a crack house. In another instance, after clearing a different crack house, Burke recalled that he "received a standing ovation by approximately 150–200 residents" after delivering a speech about his actions during a local town hall.

Not everybody in the police department bought Burke's act. Timothy Gozaloff was a plainclothes cop in the neighboring Third Precinct whose first memory of Burke was hearing about his renown for gaming the commendations racket.

Gozaloff, himself the son of a Suffolk County detective, said that Burke was only the boldest of several cops in the First known for publicly exaggerating their own heroics. He observed that they were particularly brazen about fabricating their role in noncriminal incidents of the sort that would not attract scrutiny from a defense attorney or judge. "You can make up all you want, embellish all you want, because that never goes to court," Gozaloff said, adding that there was a simple brilliance to Burke's self-promotion: "The bigger the lie, the more they believe."

For Gozaloff, Burke's most impressive coup in that regard came in 1991, after Burke and three other officers responded to an emergency call at a North Amityville home where the roof had caved in on a mom and her two daughters on a Sunday night. Their derring-do made the local television news, and *Newsday* gave the story prominent play near the front of the tabloid. "After the Roof Fell In, Cops Rose to Occasion," read the article crediting Burke and his colleagues for pulling the two little girls out from under the collapsed plasterboard ceiling.

A photo of Burke's smiling, mustachioed face prominently accompanied the article. "There's nothing that rivals that as far as getting an adrenaline rush or an emotional rise out of a police officer," Burke was quoted as saying. "It's like you become almost possessed—you'll do anything you have to to save a child."

Gozaloff said that he and others in the Third passed around the article with amusement at Burke's shamelessness. Gozaloff was particularly astounded by Burke's little boast in which he added, apparently in order to tell an even better story, that he had smelled gas in the air. Even the article stated that it was water damage that had caused the roof to cave in. So where did the whiff of gas come from?

"This guy's out of his mind," Gozaloff said he decided, and he and friends began to refer to Burke by their favorite part of the article. "That was a running joke for years: 'Whiff of Gas.'"

* * *

Wyandanch, an equally crack-plagued town in the First Precinct to the northeast of Burke's turf, had its own overzealous street cops.

On a late morning in December 1990, a pair of those cops rolled up on a guy who was walking along a main drag with something bulky wrapped in a pillowcase tucked under his arm.

Police Officer James Hickey, the cop behind the wheel, had in his notepad the description of a burglary suspect who eight days earlier was chased from a nearby house by its owner: "B/M 5'10" 160 lbs lt skin scar over right side lip scar left eyebrow 25-28, green nylon jacket."

This pedestrian with the stuffed pillowcase was an inch or two shorter than that. His scars didn't match those in the description. And the pedestrian's most prominent facial characteristics, a full mustache and goatee and a set of prominently distressed teeth, weren't in the homeowner's description.

Close enough. "What's in the pillowcase?" asked Hickey. The pedestrian responded that it was an amplifier that he was bringing over to his friend's house.

It didn't really matter what was in the pillowcase. Hickey already decided he liked this guy as the perpetrator of the attempted burglary in his notepad, and a couple of other burglaries as well. Now it was just a matter of how to prove it.

The lean Hickey was in his midtwenties with angular everything: protruding nose, arching eyebrows, high forehead, jutting ears. He had an unsettling habit of slowly slathering his lips with his tongue while his eyes blinked rapidly. The rodent likeness was so undeniable that Hickey fully accepted the resentful nickname given to him by the street denizens of Wyandanch, along with the one they gave his partner.

"I'm Ratman," he would say, before indicating the burly fellow riding shotgun. "This is Fatman."

Ratman and Fatman had methods for closing cases that were closer to frontier justice than police procedure. Hickey had only been on the job in Suffolk for four years, and he and his partner, Michael Crowley, were already notorious in Sector 102, their little slice of the First. They were the subjects of a combined eighteen complaints of abuse, which earned them a half-hearted talking-to about tactics from the precinct commander, but no real consequences. As was seemingly always the case with abuse complaints, every one of those eighteen was found to be unsubstantiated.

"Today's your lucky day," Hickey told the pedestrian carrying the pillowcase. "We're going to whip your ass."

* * *

In April 1992, as Judge Stuart Namm listened to Fatman and Ratman's testimony about that arrest, he wondered if all of his efforts had been for naught.

It wasn't the first time he had had that sinking feeling in the couple of years following the SIC investigation into Suffolk County's endemic brutality and perjury. From Namm's bench, it appeared that nothing had actually changed. In 1991, he presided over a murder case in which the defendant had confessed, and then two other men had implicated themselves in the killing. "I have seen a murder confession from somebody that didn't commit the murder," Namm said while dismissing the indictment.

Such decisions now received relatively brief news coverage, as the media seemed to sense that the tides had turned against Namm's movement. But the judge didn't let the apathy deter him from scrutinizing every case the same, even that of a thirty-six-year-old career criminal Namm was fairly certain was guilty of at least one of the charges.

Freeman was charged with multiple burglaries, and the police said that he had confessed in their custody. He had spent sixteen months in jail awaiting this day in court in order to fight for his freedom. A longtime drug addict, Freeman had been previously arrested more than a dozen times, and if he were convicted on these charges, he potentially faced a life sentence as a persistent felony offender.

Freeman told Namm in this pretrial hearing that after the cops encountered him, they handcuffed him and put him in their car without reading him his rights. Hickey and Crowley had switched seats, Freeman said, freeing up Hickey to menace him as they drove. The more Freeman insisted they had the wrong guy, the angrier and more threatening Ratman got.

They drove him to a truck yard, a storage lot for construction equipment behind an after-hours club called Bootleggers. There the cops asked some people warming themselves over a fire whether they knew the perp in their back seat. When the drifters said they didn't know—and thus couldn't implicate—Freeman, Hickey grew really upset, and they drove to a parking lot near the Wyandanch train station.

There, the cops told Freeman that he had one more chance to tell them the truth. But Freeman wouldn't confess, which he said prompted Hickey to start punching him in the face, stomach, and ribs. He said Hickey used a blackjack to batter Freeman's mouth, loosening his remaining teeth, and that the cop then took needle-nose pliers out of his glove compartment and threatened to pull out Freeman's incisors. Hickey yanked hard at Freeman's handcuffs, Freeman said, and punctured his knuckle with the pliers.

The cops then drove the bloodied, swollen Freeman to three different homes in Wyandanch and Deer Park that they accused him of burglarizing. At one of the houses, the residents berated and questioned Freeman, and demanded that the cops turn him over to them. On their way to the precinct, Freeman said the cops vowed to beat him more if he complained about what happened or asked for medical care. When Freeman told a detective at the First that he had been beaten, in Freeman's telling, it only prompted Hickey to enter the interview room and threaten to batter him further.

Freeman's court-appointed attorney presented photos taken shortly after his arrest. They showed an injury to his upper gum and lips around two of his teeth, both of which fell out a couple of days later. There was a puncture wound above his knuckle, and his hands were swollen. A doctor testified that within a couple of weeks of his arrest, Freeman had suffered a complete loss of feeling in his left hand, the likely result of lasting nerve damage from being tightly handcuffed for nearly an hour while the cops abused him.

The police would point out that Freeman's looming life sentence gave him every reason to lie. But it was the cops' own testimony, which Namm found "troublesome" and "incredible," that led him to decide the arrest was bogus.

Hickey and Crowley testified that Freeman was almost immediately cooperative. He volunteered that he had stolen the amplifier he was carrying. But he then suddenly ran from the cops, which forced them to tackle him, causing some of the injuries in question. Freeman next led the cops on a Suffolk Police–patented tour of confessions, pointing out all the homes he had robbed. Once at the precinct, he refused medical care for his open wounds and other injuries, and signed four confessions.

Namm allowed that there were inconsistencies in Freeman's versions of events, and that he suspected that the accused had probably actually committed at least one of the burglaries he was charged with. But he said that the credibility issues with Freeman's testimony "pale by comparison to the tale" told by Hickey, Crowley, and the rest of the prosecution, which did "not pass the test of logic and common sense."

He said the cops had no probable cause to detain Freeman except for that he was a slender young Black man of medium height. "God only knows how many Black males fit that description in Wyandanch on the morning of December 10, 1990," Namm said. He didn't believe that Freeman didn't ask for medical care, and he smelled conspiracy in the fact that recordings of radio transmissions from the cops had been destroyed.

The judge referred to the cops' history of similar allegations, involving beatings to the face and head and excessive use of handcuffs, and whose complainants were "virtually always Black persons who are allegedly referred to as 'niggers,' or 'Black son of a bitch.'" Namm said he was tempted to "jump to the conclusion that these two officers have a propensity to terrorize and assault Black suspects. The law prohibits me from reaching such a solution."

Expelling what he saw as brutal, lying cops and their shoddy cases from his courtroom was muscle memory to Namm at this point. "The bottom line is this court has no confidence in the case presented by the prosecution as measured by the testimony of the arresting officers, the investigating detective, and the physical and documentary evidence," Namm concluded, and dismissed the case against Freeman.

Namm issued a finding of "adverse credibility" against Hickey, meaning that his testimony was not believable. The DA's office was now required by law to inform defense attorneys about his history before he testified in any case involving their clients.

A brief newspaper story on Namm's ruling triggered another Internal Affairs Bureau investigation into the cops. The IAB lieutenant who led the investigation agreed with Namm that Hickey and Crowley's account was riddled with errors, falsehoods, and the same sort of conduct that had garnered them eighteen complaints. The lieutenant suspected Hickey of lying and playing dumb during his IAB interview, pretending to be oblivious of protocols even rookie cops knew.

While the lieutenant said that he couldn't prove Freeman's allegations of having been beaten, he believed the cops' odd behavior, such as not notifying headquarters that they had an arrest, was covering up for something. "It was certainly not for the contrived explanations they provided," the lieutenant wrote.

And yet, despite the seeming seriousness of the case against Hickey, credibly accused of beating a confession out of a Black suspect he had no reason to detain, fabricating reports, committing perjury in court, and then lying to Internal Affairs, it was nowhere near enough to incur significant discipline in Suffolk County.

With the help of his union attorney, Hickey, who was hit with seven substantiated allegations of violating police rules, pleaded to one: "Chapter 16, Section 10/VI.E (Time Checks), in that he failed to advise the Headquarters radio dispatcher, in a timely manner, that a prisoner was being transported and the requisite mileage."

If you didn't know a judge had called him a racist with no credibility and rejected his testimony, you'd think he had merely forgotten to relay his sector car's odometer. Hickey's punishment was the forfeiture of twenty vacation days, but he got fifteen of them back by avoiding further trouble over the next two months.

Consequences for cops, particularly in Suffolk County, are relative. Hickey wouldn't be charged with perjury. The DA's office quickly passed on that. His career would continue for decades and he would be cushily compensated: the six figures that even the lowliest veteran Suffolk cops made, as many as 200 days off a year, a plum pension, health care for life. He'd drive his take-home car with county gas to a comfortable home on a leafy cul-de-sac in Smithtown. But Namm's ruling did put a hitch in Hickey's trajectory. Future promotions and a small fortune in corresponding wages were no doubt lost because of the meddlesome judge who was more unwelcome in Suffolk County every day.

Hickey was transferred out of his assignment in the cowboy First Precinct. On the occasions that he still took the witness stand, the defense attorneys raked him on his credibility issues.

His career stagnated. And then came the rescue of his career due to the unlikely rise of a fellow product of the First Precinct a few sectors away: Jimmy Burke.

* * *

Newly elected DA James Catterson's response to the dismissal in the Freeman case suggested he wasn't any more concerned than his predecessor, Patrick Henry, about rooting out dishonest cops. He told the press he was "extremely disappointed in the cop-bashing Judge Namm."

The implied threat in such a statement from one of the top powers in Suffolk law enforcement was redundant by this point. The losers of the SIC probe turned out not to be the targets, but the whistleblowers. Guys like Ted Adamchak, the devoted cop who testified about the alleged kickback scheme involving Spota's firm, were a testament to the price of speaking the truth. His police union, which had accommodated its share of loathsome cops including those convicted of crimes, decided to make Adamchak the first one they ever expelled from membership. Partly out of fear for his safety, he left the department and fled to Florida.

Namm's own retribution came about six months after his ruling in the Freeman case. Like a doomed mob capo, he was done in by those closest to him. In Suffolk County, judges serve ten-year terms, and incumbents are typically reelected without issue.

But their candidacies were still subject to the whim of political party bosses and power brokers. Thanks to New York's system of fusion voting, in which multiple political parties can endorse the same candidate and virtually ensure their victory, the notion that average citizens elect judges is a polite lie. In reality, judgeships are a form of currency for political power—or punishment.

In late 1992, Namm learned that he would have no party's endorsement in the election for his seat that November. The two major parties had instead cross-endorsed the Babylon supervisor, Arthur Pitts, a Democrat, in a deal that then freed up that town position for a Republican. The arrangement had to be authorized by county Democratic leader Dominic Baranello, Namm's former law partner. When the judge confronted him, Namm said Baranello responded: "This is not your year, Stuart."

Namm was sent packing to a bitter premature retirement in North Carolina. The old judge later used his book to excoriate basically everybody in the county where he was no longer welcome: "The people of Suffolk County who only gave lip service to caring about the criminal justice system were effectively disenfranchised by arrogant political leaders and gutless attorneys who had chosen to bite the bullet. They were prepared to accept a few days of negative media attention and an unfavorable editorial or two in order to achieve a result which probably had its genesis on the first day that I began to publicly criticize the district attorney and members of the homicide squad in 1985."

* * *

Following Robert Brensic's guilty plea, justice, or its Suffolk County approximation, took an arbitrary course in the Pius matter.

The case against Peter Quartararo, whose confession was the sole reason any of the boys had gone to prison in the first place, was abandoned. After being freed on appeal in 1989, following eight years in prison, he refused to return to the trap that was Suffolk County. He made his new home in Buffalo, near the Attica prison. The only evidence that the DA's office had against him was the taped confession, which had been deemed inadmissible, and they ultimately dismissed the charges against him.

Timothy Mazzei, the Suffolk prosecutor who had helped engineer Brensic's plea, attempted to entice Thomas Ryan with similar deals. Ryan said that under one of the deals Mazzei offered, he could have been convicted as a youthful offender, meaning he'd have no criminal record and would not be required to recite the details of his crime in court. But he would still have to admit involvement in the murder, which he, and his wife, Jodi, agreed was a deal-breaker. "We were still stubborn and stupid," said Jodi, who had an infant son with Ryan while he was out on bail awaiting the retrial. "You think, 'Okay, this can't happen again.'"

Ryan's retrial hinged almost solely on the testimony of Anne Erickson, the ex-girlfriend from Trappers, who made for a less convincing witness than in the first trial. She struggled awkwardly and at length to remember the key points of her testimony, and only recalled the money line—"You can't love someone that took someone else's life"—after refreshing her recollection with a diary. Though Peter's confession was ruled out, homicide detectives Jensen and Reck found a sly way to reference it to the jury. They both mentioned that after speaking to Palumbo, who was interrogating Peter, they read the other boys their rights, clearly suggesting the boy had confessed and implicated them. Ryan was reconvicted, and again sentenced to twenty-five years to life.

The retrial of Michael Quartararo boiled down to the witness who seemed to make himself more useful with every trial: once a terse teenager with a vague and dubious story, Jimmy Burke was now a cop with photographic recall who commanded a cleared-out courtroom.

* * *

Mike Quartararo's second stab at justice in March 1990 was a study in what had changed in his life, his case, and in Suffolk County, and what hadn't. The insolent fourteen-year-old hard case with the hair hiding his face was gone. In his place was a twenty-five-year-old who realized early in his prison sentence that the toughest part would be getting out one day and having to prove himself worthy of society.

He had graduated high school and taken college courses in prison. In the two years he had been out on bail awaiting retrial, Quartararo worked two jobs—at a Manhattan printer's office and a deli—finished his college degree, and got married, becoming a stepfather to two girls.

The brother who had sat by his side at the defendant's table at the first trial was in strategic exile an eight-hour drive away. William O'Leary, the DA's doormat, was gone as Quartararo's lawyer, replaced by a Fordham University law professor. Ira DuBey, the perjurious forensic expert witness, was busy building a new career as a pharmaceutical exec. Also gone this time was Peter's confession. But unlike Rob Brensic, Mike Quartararo hadn't succeeded in getting the trial moved to a new venue, and the proceedings remained rich in Suffolk County spirit.

The case's new judge, Thomas Mallon, was flummoxed by the absence of the Pius case's famous key evidence. The prosecutor, Mazzei, acknowledged that he couldn't use the coerced confession, but he still wanted to allow the prosecution to elicit statements Mike Quartararo allegedly made at the precinct that night in relation to his brother's confession. Those statements included: "The only thing you got me for is stealing a minibike, not killing John Pius."

There was one problem with that: there could be no mention at trial of Peter's confession, or Peter at all, and Mike was talking to Peter at the time of the statements in question. Mazzei's solution was simple. He recast the scene. He decided he would have Detective Palumbo repeat Peter's statements. Even stranger was that the judge did nothing to stop it.

On three separate occasions in Mike Quartararo's second trial, Palumbo testified that he said something to Mike when in fact it was Peter who had spoken. It was a remarkable occurrence, even for Suffolk: a courtroom witness testifying falsely with the full knowledge of the prosecutor, defense attorney, and judge. Everybody, in fact, but the jury.

* * *

The retrial, coming about a decade after the original, felt like a class reunion where everybody had aged badly.

Former detective Tom Gill returned from his new post in Fort Lauderdale. The Pius case was his last big job in Suffolk, as he put in his papers a couple of months after the initial Quartararo convictions and began a second career in the Broward County Sheriff's Office in Florida, where he resumed his habit of making flimsy cases against teenage suspects via dubious confessions.

Danny Culotta took the stand, in a scratchy-looking sweater over a collared shirt for the occasion. He was only twenty-four, but heavy drug use had added another ten years to his doughy face. He estimated that by then he had been arrested fifteen times. He had also tried to make a new go of things in Broward County, but that had gone wrong in 1988 when a cop spotted him running out of a cruise agency and diving under a van while clutching a stolen VCR. He jumped bail and fled home to Long Island before being captured and extradited to Florida shortly before he was recalled to the proceedings in Suffolk County.

David O'Brien, the Connecticut kid fond of lying, had spent the two years following his testimony in the original trial "getting bad" into cocaine and alcohol abuse, according to the personal history he wrote, which ended up in a law enforcement file. So he moved to Florida in 1983 in order to "separate myself from all the drugs and drinking and the wild life that I was living." Naturally, he then joined and began rising through the ranks of the Flagler County Sheriff's Office. One of the reasons he liked being a cop involved his wife: "I would lie to her and tell her I was out working late," O'Brien wrote, when in fact he was out drinking.

The former teenage witnesses testified again about the conversation they claimed took place near the St. James railroad station, with Mike Quartararo making incriminating statements. As in the original trial, it was only O'Brien who said Mike explicitly confessed to Johnny's killing.

Television cameras captured the testimony of all but one witness, who the local cable news channel stated was not filmed due to a "special arrangement." The witness testified in front of a courtroom with no audience. Members of the media were allowed to stay in the courtroom only by agreeing not to show the witness's face or disclose his occupation.

It was a lot of pomp for an entry-level undercover narc. Jimmy Burke, twenty-five, had put in for the transfer to the Narcotics Section the year earlier, using his special blend of fudged facts and self-promotion to convince his bosses he was ready. He had processed his past disappointment at having missed police academy valedictorian by half a point by simply deciding that he hadn't fallen short after all. When applying for the transfer, he bragged of finishing first. And he said in his transfer application that his "vast working knowledge of the street," along with his "aggressive attitude towards police work" and "youthful appearance," made him a perfect drug cop.

He had certainly gotten more comfortable on the witness stand since his teenage years. The defense attorney repeatedly admonished Burke for volunteering information he hadn't been asked. And Burke pontificated for the first time as to why he hadn't gone to the police after hearing Mike Quartararo suggest he was involved in the Pius murder.

"To a certain extent I was afraid of what I had heard," Jimmy testified. "I couldn't believe my ears that this happened to one kid already. I didn't want to cross them. I didn't want to go to the police department. You know, it was kind of like a taboo thing. Plus my own safety was—I wasn't terribly frightened, but I was concerned to a certain degree about it, yes."

His court testimony, never carved in stone, continued to shift. The other witnesses blamed the passage of more than a decade for losing some of the finer details of conversations. But Jimmy's recall had only gotten sharper.

Back in 1981, during the taped interview with Spota, Jimmy had blanked on a little detail in the story he told regarding Quartararo's pseudo-confession. "When someone asked [Mike] who killed Johnny Pius, he said, 'Ask Brensic,'" Jimmy said then.

"Oh, that was not Danny Culotta who asked him that?" Spota had prodded back then.

"I'm not sure who asked him," Jimmy had said. "But someone did. Might've been Danny, I'm not sure."

But in March 1990, nearly eleven years after that alleged childhood conversation, Jimmy testified that he could "remember clearly" its details, including who posed the question to Brensic: "Danny Culotta asked him who killed Pius."

Jimmy's testimony differed in a host of small, convoluted ways: For the first time, he remembered Mike Quartararo referring to cops as "pigs"—specifically, that "the pigs had fucked [the case] up and too much time had passed." This sentiment had become an all-purpose incriminating statement that Jimmy customized depending on whoever the defendant was. During his recorded interview with Spota, he had attributed a similar statement to Quartararo. Two years later, he said it was Brensic who had uttered it. Now in 1990, it was Quartararo again.

Such discrepancies weren't presented to the jury. Their verdict was once again guilty. Four jurors interviewed afterward said that the most compelling evidence against Mike Quartararo was "his own words," meaning the statements attributed to him by Burke and his other former friends.

At his sentencing, Mike Quartararo spoke for twenty-four minutes, reading a meandering, at times bitter, statement about the case and his life. "It has been said that I failed to express remorse over the course of these eleven years," Quartararo said. "It would be difficult for me to apologize for something I have not done. But I will stand here and emphasize my deepest sorrow for John's family."

The lengthy statement outraged the prosecutor Mazzei, who in his sentencing remarks read Peter Quartararo's confession, which had been ruled involuntary and barred from use in court. When Michael's attorney objected, Judge Mallon overruled him, declaring: "The fact that it may have been involuntary does not make it untrue."

In his own remarks before levying a sentence, Mallon appeared to make clear that he believed Mike Quartararo was guilty before the onset of the trial. The judge said that the prosecutor didn't have "the strongest possible case," but the proof of guilt would have been overwhelming if Mazzei was able to use constitutionally barred evidence like the confession. He then read from a transcript of Brensic's Brooklyn courtroom guilty plea and declared that Mike Quartararo was "the prime mover in the death of John Pius." It was an odd juxtaposition, as Brensic had said Peter was the only one who had stuffed rocks down the boy's throat.

Mallon sentenced Mike Quartararo to the maximum he could, nine years to life, while asking parole to keep him locked up for at least fifteen years.

* * *

The month after Jimmy Burke joined the SCPD's Narcotics Section, the SIC published its report lambasting that unit for heavy drug use among its ranks, lax investigations, and its "gross failure to detect, investigate and punish police misconduct." All indications are that Smithtown High School East's "next Jim Morrison" fit right in.

In 1990, Burke spent a decent chunk of his service time drinking at a bar he and a couple of other cops were putatively targeting for drug sales. Details about the operation appeared in a lawsuit filed by a Medford man, Robert Michael Sexton, who claimed to have been wrongfully arrested, and who was represented by the newly formed law firm of attorney Ray Perini. Sexton's lawyer was presumably an authority on the tactics of the Narcotics Squad, as he had overseen the prosecution of all their cases through 1989, when he resigned after being excoriated by the SIC.

The lawsuit's allegations matched the commission's depiction of the squad, describing a scheme to boost overtime in which Burke and the others fabricated police reports, lied under oath, and put an innocent man in jail in order to pad a lieutenant's wallet on his way out the door.

The beneficiary of their alleged scheme was longtime narcotics lieutenant Michael Finsterer, who planned to join a wave of retiring cops in the wake of the SIC report. In order to fatten his pension upon retirement, the suit claimed, Finsterer wanted as much overtime as he could get—and didn't seem to care if any police work got done on the additional shifts. According to the suit, he enlisted his subordinates, including Burke, in racking up loads of overtime on the bar sting.

And when their work proved fruitless, Sexton's suit claimed, they justified the overtime by making arrests anyway. Sexton maintained he was innocent, framed by fabricated police reports, prosecutors who hid exculpatory evidence, and the perjurious court testimony of Burke and his partner.

After spending eight months in jail, Sexton was acquitted in April 1991. He filed suit three years later, and the county settled soon afterward, for an undisclosed amount.

The aftermath of the bar sting showed how little change had been delivered by the SIC spanking of two years earlier. The department's long-standing policy was to not open internal investigations of allegations in which there was a civil complaint, meaning that the gravest accusations went unexamined as a rule. There does not appear to have been an Internal Affairs investigation opened into Sexton's allegations. If there had been, its existence and findings would have been sealed from public view, like all IAB records at the time.

Seemingly every element of the criminal justice system in New York worked in the favor of cops seeking to avoid accountability for misconduct. When a defendant was acquitted or had their charges dismissed, all court records involving the case were sealed from public view. Ostensibly a measure to protect the reputations of the wrongfully accused, that law in many cases forever hid police testimony which, having been debunked as false, contributed to the case being scuttled. In Sexton's case, all that was left was a few dusty, vague court documents pertaining to a lawsuit quietly settled with taxpayer money.

What is clear from the record is that Finsterer became a big Jimmy Burke fan. In a 1991 evaluation, the lieutenant called Burke "a top performer who took great pride in his cases," and complimented his "comprehensive knowledge of laws, Department policies and procedures."

"His thirst for knowledge was insatiable," Finsterer wrote of Burke. "His assignments were completed in a timely manner and investigated to their fullest potential."

Burke kept moving up. In February 1991, at twenty-six years old, he was promoted to sergeant. He was transferred back to his North Amityville stomping ground in the First Precinct, this time with a group of young officers under him.

Burke's longtime supervisor in the First Precinct, Lieutenant John Lynagh, was effusive in his own praise of newly minted supervisor Burke. He evaluated the sergeant as a "'hands on' supervisor" of the sort who "comes along once in a lifetime."

Burke's ace card was his unparalleled knowledge of street activity. When a wanted burglar named Wayne started selling crack out of one of the flop motels in Lindenhurst, Burke knew about it. When a white female prostitute was robbing her johns, Burke got a tip-off on her identity. When a taxi service routinely ferried crack from Brooklyn to North Amityville, Burke learned of it from a confidential informant.

He knew when and where to wait to catch a courier making a drug delivery to The Corner via bicycle. And he frequently had the inside track on the identities, and operations, of Jamaican crack dealers in the area.

Burke boasted to his supervisors about the relationships that allowed him to know before anybody else what criminal activity was going down in North Amityville. "I have a vast knowledge of local street people and have developed a rapport with them," he wrote.

It would soon become clear just how close that rapport was.

CHAPTER 10

DEAR BOB

Lowrita Rickenbacker knew she looked good. It was an evening in May 1992, and she was outside a Quick Mart in North Amityville, wearing a suede skirt and high boots, and a matching blazer with sequins along the edges. The outfit showed off her sinewy build, and she had a new long weave flowing down to the middle of her back. The crack cocaine coursing pleasantly through her bloodstream helped her mood too.

The only problem she had that night was that her friend Marcy had just had her foot run over by a truck.

They were at the perpetually busy intersection of Sunrise Highway and Albany Avenue, which was flickering disco-style with the lights of emergency vehicles. Paramedics tended to Marcy, who was in agony. From a nearby huddle of cops who had responded to the scene, Lowrita could feel somebody staring at her. She knew who it was.

One of those cops had questioned her, asking her whether she was high. When she answered truthfully, something flickered in the eyes of the short and stocky sergeant with a dark mustache. Rickenbacker was relieved when the cop and his stare left the scene, getting back into his car to accompany the ambulance taking her friend to the hospital.

But when Marcy, now nursing a bum foot, next saw Rickenbacker, she had an update: *That cop wants to date you.*

"Man, you crazy?" Rickenbacker responded. "He's police."

But the cop wouldn't take a relayed rejection for an answer. Rickenbacker started hearing that he was kicking down doors of drug dens she was known to frequent. He didn't know her name, but he asked for her by an approximate address: the girl who lives in the front room on Waldo Street.

Finally he spotted her walking the streets a couple of times. He pulled over his cop car and frisked her. He filled her ear with chatter about how he didn't want her out on the street getting high.

The second time he stopped her, Rickenbacker said, the cop asked midfrisk: "Do you want to go on a date?"

Rickenbacker sold crack and heroin, among other criminal activities, partly to support her own habit. A cop booting down doors where she had been wasn't exactly good for business. So she agreed to go on a date with him, but only so he'd stop bugging her.

On the arranged-upon evening, he showed up in a blue Pontiac. The stiff-postured Napoleonic little cop had changed out of his uniform, and it seemed to Rickenbacker like he had swapped skins. He had dark, curly hair and was wearing Wrangler jeans that framed his ass, chunky Timberland boots, and, in the height of corner boy chic, a Triple F.A.T. Goose jacket.

So fucking cool, Rickenbacker thought, and thus began The Corner's version of Romeo and Juliet, complete with crack smoke and cunnilingus in a sector car.

* * *

When he wasn't stalking Lowrita, Jimmy Burke was plotting his ascent up the police ranks. His sergeant's stripes had only whetted his appetite, and his next promotion, to detective sergeant, was known to be imminent. But his sights were already set on the next big leap: little brass lieutenant bars pinned to his collar, and with it, a paramilitary reign as a platoon commander overseeing multiple squads.

Most promotions were at the pleasure of the commissioner. But in the department's window-dressing stab at meritocracy, three big ranks—sergeant, lieutenant, and captain—were determined solely by an officer's placement on civil service exams. So Burke headed to see a guru, former New York City police captain George Mullins, founder of a school that trained cops for civil service exams.

Mullins later recalled that within five minutes he was smitten with the ambitious young cop. Here was a bright, dedicated sergeant and an "outstanding person" of the type he sought to employ at Police Tutorial Service, Inc., or PTS. Jimmy had entered the meeting angling for some free advice and left with a lucrative side gig teaching for Mullins's outfit. Ultimately, he became Mullins's top instructor.

Jimmy had that effect on police silverbacks. He always seemed to have his supervisors snowed. They saw in him a "cop's cop." It was a term of the old school with an onion-layered meaning suggestive of tribal protectionism, adherence to unwritten rules, and a disregard for some of the written ones.

Once again, Burke was shape-shifting his personality to suit the audience. Kathleen Dominy, a masseuse-in-training, saw a different cop archetype in Burke. In 1993, she put up an index card in a police precinct lobby looking for practice bodies, and Burke was the first cop to respond. Dominy said he was not "anything but a gentleman." They became friends, she said, and Dominy recalled: "He reminds me of the police officer from the Dick and Jane books."

Burke's civil service exam classes also connected him to on-the-rise cops in various police departments. According to one of those new friends, this particular version of the Dick and Jane cop liked to manhandle dancers in the basement of a strip club.

Robert Grettler, a New York City police officer, led a stressful existence in the 1990s. A gleaming beefcake, Grettler was part of a crew of gym rat cops who injected each other's butt cheeks with steroids and palmed off eight-balls of coke at tanning salons. NYPD's Internal Affairs was also on his ass over a domestic violence allegation. But Big Rob had a time-tested method for blowing off steam. It involved stripping down to a thong to the sound of a heavy synth beat. Before he joined the force, he had been an exotic dancer.

He met Jimmy at a cop wedding in Bohemia. Burke was fascinated by the exhibitionist giant of a cop. "He clearly was enamored being that he was five-foot-fucking-two and I was six-foot-fucking-five," Grettler surmised, robbing Jimmy of about six inches, before adding: "He pursued me like a girl."

Want to hit the gym? Jimmy asked him in phone calls following the wedding. *Want to do lunch?* Grettler finally relented and they cemented their relationship over a boozy meal at Applebee's.

Grettler tolerated Burke's incessant overtures in the name of career advancement. Big Rob was hungry to get his stripes, and Burke offered to let him take his PTS classes for free. Thanks to Jimmy's teaching, Grettler fared well on the NYPD's sergeant's exam and was promoted. Burke then got him his own gig teaching other cops.

After their classes, Grettler learned what was in their relationship for Burke: he was to be his wingman and muscle at the titty bar. Their chosen haunt was Gossip, in Melville, which cops liked for the private cigar bar downstairs with privacy partitions, ostensibly for lap dances. They knew the manager, and the bouncer was angling to get a police job. That meant that many nights Burke's cherry brandy and the cigars he dipped in it were "on the arm," cop-speak for gratis.

And Burke's behavior? "Animal, animal, animal," Grettler recounted, defined by rough sexual encounters he claimed to observe between Jimmy and the dancers.

Their strip club outings made for an oddly lonely tableau. Sometimes Burke would bring along another cop or two from the tutoring outfit, but they usually had their fill of his antics after one night, leaving Grettler as his only consistent companion.

And then Grettler would observe Burke at PTS during the next "cram course," as the sessions were called, with his bump to dick sergeant coming any day now, back to being a cop's cop in front of a rented auditorium of a hundred or more. He was certified in New York State as a police instructor, and though he listed his specialty as criminal investigations and confidential informants, in reality Burke could teach everything, and well.

He had a savant's recall of New York's Criminal Procedure Law, as well as rules and procedures in the patrol guides for seemingly every major department in the state. Fatal car accidents, telephonic search warrants, deadly use of force: Burke was skilled at explaining the relevant laws and policies, and then issuing profane and entertaining instructions on how to navigate, and at times ignore, those instructions in the real world.

Rules were important for passing promotion exams, but Burke didn't care that much for them afterward. "You'd rather be tried by twelve than carried by six," Burke advised the supervisors of tomorrow, referring, respectively, to jurors and pallbearers.

* * *

In the early 1980s, around the time that Jimmy Burke was first testifying against his friends in the Pius case, Lowrita Rickenbacker had been a runaway in New York City with a developing taste for heavy narcotics.

During her adolescence in Massapequa, the more affluent hamlet west of Amityville, Lowrita was a puzzle to her friends and neighbors. She was the Black girl who sounded like a white girl, she said, raised in a nice house in a quiet neighborhood, who couldn't wait to leave it all.

Her drive to flee is not so much of a mystery now, after years of group therapy and court-mandated shrink sessions. Yes, she had a boat in her driveway. But from age ten, she said, she also had a circle of adult men, including her electrician father, and neighbors, who wouldn't keep their creeping hands off of her.

"It seemed like everybody in my whole life started touching me," Lowrita said. "I couldn't tell anybody because I let it go on so long. I felt like it was my fault."

So at age thirteen, Lowrita absconded to the city. She wound up in project housing in the Bronx. She said that over the next couple of years she shacked up with a procession of boyfriends, ranging from the middle-aged owner of several pharmacies to a pioneering rapper.

She snorted cocaine for the first time soon after running away, and by age sixteen, she was smoking crack. She found it allowed her to forget the sexual abuse. "It helps me and I wish it didn't," Lowrita said of getting high.

She ultimately moved back to the Amityville area, married a thick-necked corrections officer named Dwayne, and kicked drugs long enough to get an associate's degree in horticulture technology at Farmingdale State College.

Lowrita did not become a horticulturist, or stay clean. She said her sobriety, and her marriage, disintegrated after she learned her husband was cheating on her with his colleagues at Sing Sing. By the time the twenty-three-year-old Lowrita met Jimmy Burke, she had become a fixture on the streets of North Amityville.

Funding her habit required a ceaseless procession of slippery cons. Turn Lowrita's handbag upside down and you would get a cascade of other people's credit cards, driver's licenses, and personal checks. All came in handy during convoluted schemes. She might, for example, peddle a fraudulently mail-ordered leather coat to her church minister.

Sometimes Lowrita was the fiend in line for a fix. Other times, when she came into a significant amount of crack or marijuana, she was the pusher. By 1993, her rap sheet had a little bit of everything. Among the twenty-seven arrests were charges for robbery, larcenies—petty and grand—selling and possessing controlled substances, assault, stolen property, reckless endangerment, loitering, disorderly conduct, and prostitution.

Lowrita freely admits to a life of habitual crime, taking exception only to that last charge. According to Lowrita, she was wrongfully charged with prostitution when cops pulled up on her while she was in the car of a hooker servicing a john. Lowrita says she was only there to shake down the prostitute for some money she was owed.

The explanation doesn't fully comport with the rap sheet, which showed she was arrested for prostitution three times in 1990 alone. But Lowrita is insistent: "If I sold weed and sold crack, why would I prostitute myself for a few dollars? And I'm making big money, you know what I'm saying? It's all a lie, and I didn't appreciate it."

But when she had the crack use under control—usually after a lengthy stint in jail—Rita got her body back. She was an amateur bodybuilder who could bench press a buck-fifty and do one-handed pushups. And even at her scrawniest and most addicted, she never lost her swaggering, sweetwise confidence. Perhaps their similar personalities brought her and the cocky street cop Burke together.

More likely it was, as described by Lowrita, their shared enthusiasm for fornication and hard drugs.

* * *

On a couple of occasions, Burke bought her roses and took her to Chateau La Mer, a potted-palm-trees, prom-night type of place in Lindenhurst. More often, it was fast food burgers. Sometimes Lowrita cooked up the soul food Jimmy liked. But most frequently, according to Lowrita, they forgot about eating all together.

"We just fucked all the time," she said.

They'd go to motels where the clerk was a guy with cigarette-stained fingers behind bulletproof glass, their favorites being Sunrise or Hollywood, but never Rainbow. There were too many whores, pimps, and dealers at the Rainbow Motel in Copiague, all of whom would be well-acquainted with both Lowrita and Jimmy.

In a twist unforeseen to both participants, a detailed account of what Rita and Jimmy did in those motel rooms would later be shared with a roomful of the latter's blushing subordinates. Suffice it to say that their bond was resilient enough to withstand Jimmy's bottomless appetite for kink. "After a while, hours and hours of doing this shit, it was like, 'Okay, enough,'" Lowrita recounted.

According to Lowrita, it was the cocaine—both powdered and in crack rock form—that fueled Jimmy. She recalled that they smoked crack in his sector car, and had sex in it multiple times as well. Other times they'd have sex in his personal vehicle. Lowrita said that police once pulled her out of the vehicle thinking she was a hooker with a john. But after recognizing their colleague Burke, they peeled off.

It was an illicit relationship, but Jimmy wasn't bashful. According to Lowrita, one night he knocked on the door of Lowrita's estranged husband and father to her children, who then called to warn her that she must really be in trouble now, because a cop in uniform came around looking for her. On other occasions, Burke would use his sector car's loudspeaker to address Lowrita on the street, in full view of other drug dealers. "I love you," Jimmy would announce on The Corner. "I dream of you all day."

Jimmy lived with a girlfriend in a drab brown hi-ranch in Ronkonkoma, where he also rented out a room to a divorced lieutenant. Lowrita said one day she went to Jimmy's house and all of the girlfriend's stuff was packed up. He wanted Lowrita to move in. Lowrita, who considered Ronkonkoma to be another world, turned him down. "Too far," she said.

Jimmy could be strangely secretive. She said he told her he was from Brooklyn, and had been a housing cop, neither of which are true. She said it was only years later that she discovered Jimmy had gone to high school in Smithtown and was a witness in the Pius case.

Nonetheless, for two years, Lowrita said the only instances in which they took more than a couple of days off from each other was when she was locked up. After her jail stints, Jimmy would "really flip out," Lowrita said, and implore her to stay off the streets. He offered to go shake somebody down on The Corner for whatever drugs she needed, but according to Lowrita, she always refused and did her own shopping.

Lowrita is adamant that she never snitched for Jimmy, never talked drug dealer shop with him, and never pulled his card when she was arrested by his colleagues. "Any time I got into trouble, I ate it," she said.

Except for the time, she said, that she was sure she was going to be murdered after stealing two garbage bags full of weed from a Jamaican drug dealer who owed her money. The dealer had stashed the thirty-six pounds of marijuana at her cousin's house, Rickenbacker said, and the cousin had dimed her out when it went missing.

"Are you okay?" she recalled Jimmy asking, his standard check-in that didn't require her to divulge street matters.

"And this time," Lowrita recounted, "I said, 'No, I'm not.'"

Lowrita said she told Jimmy about her dilemma and even showed him her knapsack full of stolen weed. She expected Jimmy to kick the guy's door down with his .38 blazing. But he proved cleverer than that.

Instead, she said, Jimmy told immigration control where they could find some illegals: "He had immigration come in and take half the Jamaicans out of Amityville."

Between loudspeaker confessions of love and deporting Jamaicans by the score, Jimmy and Rita were doing a poor job of keeping their relationship under the radar. And unfortunately for them, most every regular on The Corner knew how to barter information in order to save their own ass.

* * *

In August 1993, Vincent Posillico, a sergeant in the Internal Affairs Bureau, headed to the Fourth Precinct on an assignment that felt like a waste of county gas. A drug addict under arrest told the cop booking her that she had witnessed a police officer smoking crack. But all the ID the addict had on the cop was the name of a fictional TV detective.

Posillico grabbed an office across from the female holding cells and took a statement from an eighteen-year-old addict named Desire, who told a story about the time she watched Lowrita Rickenbacker smoke crack with her boyfriend, a short cop with a thick mustache and tight jeans, known as Starsky.

Posillico pulled a little string on it. He learned of an IAB case the year earlier in which a North Amityville cop nicknamed Starsky was said to be stealing drugs from dealers. The allegations in that case were determined to be unfounded. Posillico got a photo of the cop in that case, and he added it to an array containing photos of other white police officers in uniform. He brought it to Desire, who picked out the same cop from the previous case, who she knew as Starsky: James Burke.

But Posillico also determined, with little investigative effort, that Desire's story was bullshit. It was co-opted gossip that she had learned from a friend while dancing at a nightclub called Starlight, which Desire deployed to get out from under her own case. She knew what Starsky looked like only from seeing him in his police car in North Amityville.

That was enough for Posillico to have closed the case if he wanted to. Burke had already been in the IAB system six times, with allegations including undue force, "lying/false statement," false arrest, and the drug theft case from the previous year. Every time, these cases were closed as "unsubstantiated," "unfounded," or "exonerated," which were the varying degrees of IAB acquittals, with punishment topping out at the recommendation that Burke seek counseling.

But Posillico could tell there was something to this one. He wasn't the sort to look for an excuse to ditch a case. The soft-spoken Posillico, whose dainty glasses and low crown of salt-and-pepper hair made him look more art critic than detective, had been in IAB since 1989. It required a special kind of masochism to spend several years in IAB.

The division's eighteen detectives and handful of supervisors were tasked with investigating any allegations against the more than 2,600 Suffolk officers. They worked out of the police headquarters in Yaphank. That meant that whenever they headed out for surveillance in "soft clothes"—police-speak for jeans and sneakers—with cameras and other equipment slung over shoulders, every cop who had something to hide would hear from a buddy at HQ that IAB was on the prowl. The watchdogs were blocked at every turn by the powerful unions of the cops they were investigating. They were pressured to close cases prematurely by supervisors who were eager to head off trouble.

Stay too long in IAB, as Posillico felt he already had, and you'd be a pariah in the department when you finally transferred out. He explained: "The longer you're there, the more cases you get where you're going to make enemies."

Investigating rising stars in the department, and those with powerful connections, was the real tripwire. Posillico gleaned quickly enough that he was up against that in the Burke case.

"How's that Burke thing doing?" Posillico said his boss asked. "Because you know, they want to make him a detective sergeant."

Posillico responded gingerly: "I wouldn't do that."

Desire might have made up her Starsky tale, but Posillico tracked down the women whose gossip had initially reached her. Their stories checked out better. Posillico took statements that started to fill out a portrait of Lowrita's boyfriend: "Super Cop," as Lowrita affectionately called him, comfortable enough with his felon girlfriend to smoke crack in his skivvies at her apartment with company over and his blue Grand Am parked outside.

Tracking down Lowrita herself made for a surprisingly lengthy quest, but in April 1994, Posillico learned that she had been locked up in Nassau County. She was doing time for a very Rita crime. It involved, in her version of things, an eye doctor friend of hers who had given her his credit card to buy some boots, but he just didn't want to fess up about their relationship to his wife in order to explain the charges. The prosecutors' version was larceny. Posillico and a partner showed up to the jail to interview her.

According to Posillico, Lowrita initially was reluctant to talk, but when the subject of Burke's alleged drug use came up, she adamantly denied it and agreed to cooperate. Lowrita had in the moment come up with a too-clever plan to play these cops, which mostly backfired.

She decided not to deny that she and Burke had a sexual relationship. She told them about meeting at the scene of the accident with her friend Marcy, and how Burke pursued her for the next several months. How Jimmy gave her roses, and money for food, which she then used to buy crack. How they gave each other oral sex, including in his cop car, though Lowrita insisted that they never had intercourse.

Her account was odd, full of half-truths and strange details that seemed conceived on the spot to replace what actually happened. She told the investigators about the time Jimmy was taking her to Roy Rogers and she had him stop on the expressway so she could collect pine cones for an arrangement she planned to make. He lost his gun that day, Lowrita said, and accused her of stealing it. The next day, he said he had found it at home, and apologized.

On another occasion she described, they went out to a diner in Babylon, and while they ate, he left his gun belt and uniform in his back seat. She told him she had to go home because she had left her door unlocked, and he gave her the keys to his car. Once home, she got high and stranded Jimmy at the diner. An irate Jimmy, given a ride by his partner, showed up at her house and demanded the gun.

Burke's carelessness with his service weapon was potentially actionable, and sex acts in the sector car also wasn't department protocol, but Lowrita was laser-focused on clearing one element of the allegations against her boyfriend.

"I know that Jimmy doesn't smoke crack," Lowrita said in an IAB statement. "Anyone who says they saw him smoke crack is lying."

Count Lowrita among the liars then, because two decades and change later while cooking pepper steak in her Wyandanch kitchen, she stated matter-of-factly to this author that Jimmy frequently smoked crack. She explained that the stories of Jimmy losing his gun made a lot more sense when you added in the part she omitted, that they were both high. Crack users, she said, don't go to diners and don't collect pine cones. In fact, she had left Burke not at a diner but at a motel, and her errand was to go get them more crack.

Still, during her interview with the IAB cops, she agreed to take a polygraph test. She said she used a simple gauge to determine her answers. "Anything that was illegal, I lied," Lowrita said, adding with a laugh: "I passed the polygraph, so it was the truth!"

When the investigators asked her to take a second polygraph, this one focused on her relationship with Jimmy, she refused. The reasoning she gave was rock-solid gangster moll logic.

"She stated her honest answers regarding Burke's non-use of drugs could only help him," read the IAB cops' later report concerning their interview of Rickenbacker. "She also stated she knew her honest answers to questions about their personal relationship could only hurt him. She stood by everything she said in the statement but would not take a polygraph exam that could be used against James Burke."

Posillico wasn't oblivious to Lowrita's overall strategy, as he later explained: "She told us things that were bad to be telling about a cop but steered us away from anything criminal as far as he was concerned."

Lowrita probably inadvertently screwed Burke. Even if she had alleged that Burke was a consummate crack smoker, it was her word, that of a felon, against his. And in such cases, IAB had a policy: the tie goes to the cop.

But her story of Burke losing his gun was partly corroborated by Burke's own hand. He had the year before reported the "loss/theft" of his Beretta .38 "at an unknown location," and then a week after that said he found the gun in his home. The fact that she appeared to have gotten that right made it more difficult for Burke to outright deny their relationship.

Still, Lowrita did her best to get Super Cop off. "A lot of people hate him because he's such a good cop," she wrote in her statement. And then the county prisoner asked, like a teenager in love, if she could see Jimmy's photo again.

* * *

For all her loyalty, Lowrita knew she wasn't the only apple of Burke's eye on The Corner. While her polygraph was being prepared, she mentioned to Posillico that there was another oft-arrested prostitute, Linda Kennedy, who she suspected had also been in a relationship with Burke. Posillico then found Kennedy at the Suffolk County jail in Riverhead.

Kennedy told him that she had met the cop she knew as Officer Starsky a few years earlier. Like Lowrita, she first encountered him outside of the Quick Mart, at the tail end of a long night spent turning tricks while strung out on crack.

Burke informed her she had warrants out for her arrest. He cuffed her and they drove to the rear of a Burger King on Sunrise Highway. According to Kennedy, Burke took the cuffs off and pleaded with her to straighten out for the sake of her three children. He told her to wait for him, and he returned thirty minutes later in civilian clothes, driving his own car. By now it was seven or eight o'clock in the morning.

They drove to a 7-Eleven, Kennedy said, where Burke bought Kennedy shampoo and cosmetics, and for himself, a six-pack of beer. He then went and got them a room at the Capri Motel in Bay Shore.

And there, Kennedy told the investigators, he drank a beer while she took a shower. "I went to sleep," Kennedy said. He came back to pick her up again a few hours later. As he drove her home, she said, he finished off the last of the six-pack.

Every so often after that, Kennedy would see Starsky in his police car. At times he'd have a six-pack with him, and she'd know he'd been drinking if his eyes were red. Sometimes he'd show her "jumbos," or vials of crack, that he had taken off a dealer. "I would beg him for the drugs but he told me he would never give them to me," Kennedy said. "I never had sex with him even though I offered it to him."

Rickenbacker and Kennedy were two members of what Posillico later called a "trail of prostitutes" he investigated for their encounters with Burke. They both seemed to be walking the same tightrope to avoid ratting on him in matters of sex and drugs. "They liked him," Posillico said. "They wouldn't say anything to hurt him."

* * *

In January 1995, Posillico was finally across the table from the subject he had been pursuing for almost two years. Burke, who was accompanied to the IAB offices by an attorney and a vice president both representing his union, the Superior Officers Association, sat down to be interviewed by three IAB officials, including Posillico and Lieutenant Patrick Cuff.

Patty Cuff was a pale man with large, benign facial features. He seemed born to be in the upper ranks of a police department, and it wasn't just the cartoon cop name. Cuff spoke fluent Spanish from his tenure as a US Customs agent at JFK airport and some years in a sector car in the heavily Hispanic Third Precinct. He was a creature of his sensible routines, which included daily 7:00 a.m. mass at St. John the Evangelist in Center Moriches, and peanut butter and jelly for lunch. He was squeaky clean, all the way down. In other words, the anti–Jimmy Burke.

During the interview Burke denied using, or ever witnessing Lowrita use, crack. He said he didn't drink beer in his car or keep crack he took from drug dealers, as Linda Kennedy had said. But he did admit what by then was common knowledge: that he had a "personal, sexual" relationship with Lowrita Rickenbacker.

He said the relationship lasted just six months, and that he would never initiate contact with her, but instead only respond to calls to his beeper. He said he'd meet her, always off-duty and in his personal vehicle, at various parking lots. They'd buy some beer and he'd take her to his home, or a motel, or another parking lot. He said he couldn't recall if he ever allowed her to sit in his sector car but insisted that they never had sex while he was on duty.

Burke claimed he had no knowledge that Lowrita was a criminal, or that she was addicted to crack. Burke said it was only when he began to hear rumors about Lowrita from "street people" that he terminated their relationship.

Posillico and Cuff were impressed by the sergeant's gall. Lowrita Rickenbacker's rap sheet was twenty-three pages long. Most of the crimes occurred in the First Precinct, where Burke and his bosses had boasted that he possessed an encyclopedic street knowledge. Posillico had even at one point taken a highlighter to sentences in Burke's commendations and requests for transfers that referred over and over to his "vast working knowledge of the street" and "familiarity with the criminal element" in his sector.

And yet Burke, until recently a narcotics cop, managed to keep a straight face while telling the IAB cops that not only was he unaware of Lowrita's record, but that he didn't know she was hopelessly addicted to crack. Even Lowrita hadn't lied on that one, telling the IAB cops that Burke used to poke fun at her about all of her arrests in his precinct.

In Cuff's opinion the farcical crescendo came when Burke, indignant at his line of questioning, declared: "Lieutenant, I have a sterling reputation in the police department."

Cuff usually played it straight. But he couldn't help but picture a scene Lowrita had described for him in graphic detail: the crack-addicted felon reclining across the front seat of Burke's cop car with the door open, while the sergeant in uniform knelt on the pavement outside and performed oral sex on her.

Cuff laughed right in Burke's face.

* * *

The IAB cops might have subjected Burke to a drug test, but they knew the union would have blocked it, and Burke could have flushed his system by then anyway. So for better or worse, Posillico considered Lowrita's polygraph-tested claims as his strongest evidence, both in implicating Burke on some counts and exonerating him on others. He pecked out his findings on an IAB typewriter and then, in the spring of 1995, his captain, Edward Vitale, reviewed and concurred with them.

Substantiated, IAB's term for proven: that Burke had failed to safeguard his service weapon, engaged in sexual acts in police vehicles while on duty and in uniform, and carried on a "personal, sexual relationship" with Rickenbacker, "a convicted felon known to be actively engaged in criminal conduct."

Unsubstantiated, meaning IAB didn't have enough information to declare it false or accurate: that Burke failed to invoice crack as evidence.

Unfounded, or proven to be false: that Burke smoked crack.

His acquittal on this last count was thanks to Lowrita's cool control during her polygraph and some possible reverse psychology. "Her professed admiration and support for Sergeant Burke" lent credence to Lowrita's story, Posillico wrote, in that even though she was fond of him, she had volunteered some damaging information about him.

Posillico called Burke a liar as politely as possible, noting that the sergeant's stated ignorance as to Rickenbacker's criminal activity and background "seems disingenuous." He was just as ginger in stating that Burke's open dalliance with a crack-addicted prostitute "has a tendency to destroy public respect" for, and confidence in, the Suffolk County Police Department.

Tom Spota then came to the rescue again, offering Burke the legal services of his law firm. Spota's then-partner, Thomas Spreer, handled some of the negotiation with the police. He formed a later bluntly-stated opinion on Burke's denials of some of the allegations against him, including having used drugs: "I think he was lying through his teeth."

* * *

Posillico was well-acquainted with Tom Spota, and liked him. Posillico considered the lawyer to be a genial, no-bullshit advocate for his cop clients when they were in hot water with IAB. He recalled a case in which a couple of cops had busted into somebody's home without a warrant and then lied about it. Posillico pulled radio transmissions that clearly showed they had fabricated their account, and he informed Spota, who was representing one of them, that his client would be administratively charged.

Posillico asked Spota if the cop might now consider coming clean. Spota huddled up with his client, returned to Posillico, and said with an exasperated sigh: "He's going to lie to you again."

"Spota was a political animal, a deal-maker," Posillico said, and it was an appropriate attitude for a secretive police disciplinary system in which both sides were typically seeking a quiet resolution.

Few cops ever took their IAB complaints all the way to a hearing, and when they did it was just another arcane, shrouded system where your lawyer's connections ruled above all. In most cases, the cop's attorney reached a deal with a department lawyer beforehand. The pair might then forget all about it afterward over steak and martinis.

At the time that Burke called him, Spota's private practice had its share of high-profile clients: the estate of the folk singer killed on the Long Island Expressway; the homicide detective who denuded the St. Patrick's drunk; a deranged firefighter who set a fatal fire; a *Seventeen* magazine–friendly case of adopted twin teenage girls who he helped connect to their biological mother.

But Spota's bread and butter, and the work that consolidated his own influence, was the cases that police secrecy laws ensured the public would never hear about, even as they contained revelations about the conduct of highly paid, and powerful, armed public servants.

Spota's relationship with his supposed adversary on the other side of police discipline was a great example of the chumminess of the system. SCPD Deputy Commissioner Robert V. Kearon, whose purview included IAB, was a genial career bureaucrat who carried himself like an accountant: six-foot-three in three-piece suits, with large spectacles and a dark, thin mustache.

Spota was his first boss in Suffolk County. Kearon started as a prosecutor in the Major Offense Bureau of the DA's office in 1978, and Spota evaluated him with his "highest recommendation." Kearon then bounced between the most powerful divisions of the DA's office, the police department, and the county attorney's office. He was consistently in the same foxholes as Spota. He railed against the SIC when he was a top lawyer for the police department and was a target of the commissioners who accused him of knowingly filing false affidavits to cover up police violence, a charge he denied. He had squared off against Judge Namm in the John Pius trials, arguing against turning over disciplinary files concerning the detectives involved in the murder investigation.

There's no indication from the correspondence between Spota and Kearon in Burke's case that they didn't consider themselves to be on the same side.

"Dear Bob," Spota wrote to Kearon on Valentine's Day 1995, "As you requested, enclosed is the original of the Stipulation Agreement executed by Sergeant Burke. Thank you for your courtesy and cooperation."

In the agreement, signed by Burke, he pleaded guilty to a single count of conduct unbecoming an officer. His punishment: fifteen forfeited vacation days.

* * *

After Lowrita got out of jail, she went back to her old ways, getting high and hanging around the Rainbow Motel. She didn't see Jimmy anymore and heard that he got transferred somewhere else.

One day shortly afterward, she said, a cop car pulled up on her and a lieutenant ordered her to get in. Lowrita said this cop drove them four miles to a secluded area behind a Wyandanch factory, where he forced her to give him oral sex.

As he zipped up, she said, the cop remarked: "I wanted to see what Jimmy was getting." Then he left Lowrita there to find her own way back.

She said she reported the assault to IAB, but after a couple of investigators took her story, one of them remarked to her on his way out: "Ms. Rickenbacker, not for nothing, we really came here to sweep this under the carpet."

Afterward, Lowrita said, cops continued to harass her. She realized that they thought she was the genesis of the IAB complaint against Burke. She was terrified, particularly because it wasn't just her out on The Corner alone.

There was a third party to her street love saga with the cop called Starsky. Her daughter had been born in November 1992, about nine months after she and Jimmy first hooked up. The IAB cops were aware of the baby, if not the identity of the supposed father. When Posillico marked up her rap sheet during the investigation, he noted, "5 months preg" in a margin alongside a 1992 charge for criminal possession of a controlled substance. She was a light-skinned baby, and as she grew older Lowrita wasn't wrong in claiming that she bore a resemblance to Jimmy. There were no DNA tests or legal claims, so paternity was not established, but in Lowrita's mind the kid was Jimmy's.

Lowrita raised her mostly on her own for a bit. Then her husband, Dwayne, begged her to come home, telling her how their other four kids were crying for her. Lowrita said Dwayne agreed to raise the daughter as his own, and they hid the truth from her as she grew up.

Lowrita said that every so often Jimmy would have a cop in the First stop her and ask how the baby was doing. Lowrita never lost her taste for crack. She kept committing crimes to support her habit, and her rap sheet kept growing. A couple of years after the IAB mess, she was being processed by an arresting officer in the Fourth Precinct when she saw him again.

Burke looked her up and down, and then, in front of the other cops, made a remark that she said left her embarrassed and heartbroken.

He sneered: "You're still doing this shit?"

CHAPTER 11

BROKEN WING THEORY

In the years following the Lowrita case, Burke made an effort to keep his head down, by his standards. At least he wasn't broadcasting his love for known prostitutes from the loudspeaker of his sector car. Maybe he would become that mild townie cop from those Dick and Jane books after all. He bought and moved into a house on Sammis Street, near the house at Fifty Acre Road where he spent his teenage years. His mother and stepfather still lived there, along with Jimmy's half-brother John, who was born when he was eighteen. The divorced lieutenant roommate moved with him, into his basement. Jimmy's stepdad died in 1998, and Jimmy, by all accounts a devoted adult son, would spend decades as his mom's part-time caretaker.

Professionally, Starsky got his wings clipped. He was transferred to the Fourth. It made for a nice commute, but it was a policeman's purgatory. It was home to sleepy burbs like Smithtown, where except for the odd thirteen-year-old found murdered behind the elementary school, nothing ever happened.

Burke was reduced to investigating versions of his teenaged hoodlum self. In one case, he and a partner spotted a Suffolk detective canvassing businesses on Smithtown's Main Street. Learning that the detective was investigating possibly related cases of attempted robbery and criminal mischief, Burke and his partner rounded up their teenage usual suspects. Within half an hour, they told the detective to meet them at the St. James railroad station.

It was the same location where teenage Jimmy Burke claimed to have heard Mike Quartararo's pseudo-confession in the Pius murder. Now a police sergeant, he was back at the railroad station waiting for the detective with a couple of boys he liked for the petty crimes. The cops then took one of the kids home, where he broke down and confessed in front of his mother.

It wasn't exactly the Lindbergh kidnapping, or even busting the likes of G-Man and Leech for slinging crack rock on The Corner, but Burke and his boss still did their best to make it sound like vital police work. "If not for the alert observations, dedication to duty, and perseverance of these officers, these crimes may have gone unsolved," read a commendation describing Burke and his partner's corralling of the accused Smithtown rapscallion.

Burke plied his unique charms in the Fourth. He latched on to a supervisor susceptible to Burke's platonic male courtship routine of booze, back slaps, and bawdy conduct. It seemed to work. His boss approved Burke's assignment to one of the Fourth's more desirable gigs, the Crime Section, a plainclothes unit.

But there was now an opposing force quietly in play. Gossip about hookers and drugs followed Burke to the Fourth. And Burke had inspired a fervent little faction of hate-watchers on the force, many of them connected to IAB, who felt he skated on the Lowrita case and flat out shouldn't be on the job. One IAB lieutenant kept a photo of Burke in his wallet as a wry reminder.

It wasn't just Burke's misconduct that made him a stand-out IAB target. After all, there were plenty of loathsome figures with badges in Suffolk PD, like a cop whose affinity for coerced blowjobs from prostitutes made him an official suspect in the murder of a couple of them. But the IAB guys considered Burke to be particularly dangerous because, thanks to his association with Tom Spota, he had political clout.

As his previous IAB investigator Vincent Posillico described, that clout surfaced in the form of bosses fixed on dragging his wounded career up the ranks against all reason.

Posillico felt like he couldn't get away from Jimmy Burke after wrapping up the Rickenbacker case. Even in an ensuing matter that at first had nothing to do with Burke, involving a couple of cops accused of beating a suspect, Burke turned out to be their sergeant, and had written a commendation in the case that Posillico judged to be carelessly fabricated. Posillico could have gone after Burke for it, but he let it slide because he needed a Jimmy respite: "I had Burke up to my eyeballs at this point."

Posillico then left IAB for a stint in Property Recovery, where his purview included checking pawnshops for stolen items. There he would of course cross paths with Burke again. A supervisor called Posillico and said Burke's task force was tracking some burglary suspects. After the suspects went into pawnshops, the supervisor wanted Posillico to shut down those businesses and go through their inventory and books to search for stolen items. Posillico objected that to close down a private business and seize its property without a warrant was unconstitutional.

The supervisor responded with a fed-up speech about how in his day they grabbed the store owner by the throat. Posillico read into it an eagerness to make Burke look good, and a frustration that he wasn't aiding them. Posillico later learned that following that phone call, the supervisor had branded him with a damaging label: "obstructionist."

This was Burke's new personal cold war: his infatuated bosses versus the saboteurs in IAB. By early 1999, the bosses were winning. Burke was promoted to detective sergeant, the rank he had been on the verge of achieving when the Lowrita dust-up began. It was a sign that the bosses had convinced top brass that Burke had served his time and was ready to again rocket up the ranks.

But then IAB struck back. Jimmy gave them an entrance, once again, with his eclectic love life. Jimmy's various dalliances then and later included a called-off wedding engagement with a school aide he met while clubbing at the Oak Beach Inn, a Suffolk prosecutor, a first grade teacher, and a wealthy socialite widow. In 1996, the object of Burke's desire was a Smithtown hairdresser known for her house calls.

She happened to have a very determined husband who did his best to foil Burke's efforts to keep a low profile. And it turns out that while New York's draconian police secrecy keeps members of the public, reporters, and even legislators from learning about a cop's disciplinary history, the Deli Man still knows all.

* * *

A toothy, excitable Smithtown fellow named Doug made a comfortable living peddling insurance to his neighbors. In his basement man cave, he built model aircraft carriers, complete with cotton balls for the missile plumes, and yelled at the television about the Dallas Cowboys. But Doug didn't stumble upon his life's true calling, as he saw it, until January 10, 1999, when he discovered a detective sergeant's badge in his wife's handbag.

His wife, Michelle, was in bed, and had asked him to grab her romance paperback out of the purse downstairs. Doug extricated the badge and read, with widening eyes, an inscription on an attached index card.

He tried to act as casual as possible when he handed his wife her book. "Who's James Burke?" he asked.

Michelle, just as casually: "Oh, I cut his hair."

But Doug and Michelle, who had a young daughter, were on the rocks already. So that badge ate at him.

The domestic situation worsened a couple of weeks later, when Doug was arrested by Fourth Precinct cops for allegedly stomping on Michelle's foot. Doug claimed he had stepped on her foot accidentally, and that it was her who had punched him. The charge against Doug was ultimately dismissed. But in the meantime, exiled from his house by a restraining order, he had nothing to do but stew over his wife, and that badge.

He ordered copies of his home phone records and discovered that somebody—presumably Michelle—was making brief calls several times a day to the same number. When he called it, the voice on the answering machine was that of Michelle's best friend, announcing a hair and nails service that Doug didn't believe existed.

Doug hired a private detective to dig up information on the phone number. The detective reported back that it was a pager belonging to a Jane Burke, on Sammis Street in Smithtown.

Jane Burke . . . James Burke. Doug felt red hot.

He swung his black Thunderbird—vanity plates: DOUG10—toward the Park Bake Shop in Kings Park. Doug knew the deli's proprietor, Bill, and that he was privy to the gossip of the Fourth Precinct cops who frequented the place for coffee and donuts.

Bill seemed to have been waiting for this line of questioning. In between ringing up Neapolitan cookies and chocolate cigars, he gave it to Doug straight.

The sector car guys all hated this detective sergeant named Burke, Bill said, and they talked about how he was in the Fourth because of some IAB trouble involving a prostitute. There is no question that Bill was well-sourced. Burke's IAB trouble concerning Lowrita was at the time still confidential and wouldn't be publicly revealed for more than a decade.

Bill broke it to Doug that the sector car cops gossiped about how Burke was banging a civilian's wife, named Michelle. "The cops here all know about your wife," Bill said. "They all talk about her, all the time, and Burke."

Thus began Doug's yearslong legal and procedural jihad against Jimmy Burke.

* * *

The insurance agent and his hired investigators tore through Smithtown interviewing storekeepers and horny male residents about what Doug termed his wife's mysteriously ample spending on a fur coat and other extravagances, and alleged dalliances with other men.

A theory formed, seemingly founded more on a hunch than hard evidence, and in March 1999, Doug brought it to Suffolk's Internal Affairs Bureau. In a complaint, Doug said that he believed Michelle was involved in a Smithtown prostitution ring with Burke, and that they facilitated their contacts using the pager.

A couple of investigators handled the probe, and overseeing them was a figure quickly becoming Burke's nemesis: Patty Cuff, the same man who had laughed in Burke's face during his Lowrita interview. Cuff had since been promoted to a captain in IAB. One of his lieutenants interviewed Doug eleven times. The IAB investigation into Doug's allegations brought into hazy view the beginning of a Smithtown plot combining hairdressing, prostitution, cops, and a sprinkling of cocaine. They learned of a client who said a hairdresser in Michelle's shop cut his hair naked and interviewed a retired Suffolk cop who acknowledged that he dated Michelle before Burke, after she cut his hair at his home. And they got an affidavit from somebody who said she had bought a small amount of coke from Michelle. IAB struggled to get further than innuendo and rumors, but it wasn't for a lack of trying.

A surveillance-state mentality descended on this small Smithtown love triangle. Cuff put a tail on Burke, and he started spotting them in his rearview. On one occasion he pulled up next to an IAB spy and asked, with a chipper smile, whether there was anything he could help him with. The IAB guy turned pale.

And Doug's investigators were doing the same to Michelle. One evening, an investigator outside of Michelle's house saw a person she assumed was Michelle get into her car wearing a long black wool coat, a black hat, and a black scarf over her face. The investigator tailed her to a house in Commack and then sat outside for more than an hour. When a dark-haired thirty-something-year-old man casually ambled out to the grill to cook up dinner, the investigator realized she had been duped. In a report to Doug, the investigator described the scheme, which allowed Michelle to lose the tail, as "an unknown individual that made a diligent attempt to impersonate the subject and manipulate field surveillance." Put more simply, it was likely Burke in light drag driving his girlfriend's car.

In June 2000, Doug managed to harpoon his white whale long enough to drag him into a Central Islip courthouse. Doug and Michelle were mid-divorce, and Doug's attorney subpoenaed James Burke to undergo a sworn deposition. Burke was flanked by Tom Spreer, Spota's law partner. Michelle and Doug were present for the deposition as well. Doug was so keyed up that Burke's lawyer had to ask him at one point to stop "leering" at Michelle.

Doug had hired a "really nasty son of a bitch lawyer," as Doug himself put it, and had given him a typed list of more than two hundred questions he wanted asked, along with a written instruction: "Please use all your expertise and ability and let's nail this crooked cop."

But Burke was no longer a cowed dick sergeant, working off an IAB rebuke. About six months earlier, he had tested into his long-awaited bump to lieutenant.

With the promotion, Burke was transferred to the Third Precinct to work nights, and he got cocky again. He spent many of his days moonlighting as a part-time cop in the little village of Nissequogue, pulling in $17 to $18 an hour. As for sleeping, according to a fellow cop at the precinct, he did that at the Third. He was a connoisseur of "cooping," the police practice of parking your car in a remote area to snooze your tour away. Burke was said to be unabashed about it, borrowing others' cars so that the GPS on his vehicle wouldn't give away his activity if IAB ever came sniffing around.

But during the deposition, Burke played the part of exceedingly reasonable and scrupulous cop. He described his relationship with Michelle as something far removed from Doug's allegations of a pimp with a badge. Burke said he had met Michelle around their shared neighborhood, and that she would visit his house on Sammis Street to cut his hair. Other times, he stopped by her and Doug's house, usually "to check on her welfare," Burke said.

They had become "the best of friends," Burke said, and he had learned that she was a "classic abused spouse." In order to keep in contact, Burke gave her his beeper number, and he had Michelle's friend record the greeting to hide their relationship from Doug.

The beeper was the "only way she had to get in touch with me—safely, anyway, at least in my estimation—and that's why she called me ten, fifteen, whatever, twenty times a day," Burke explained.

Burke said funds he gave Michelle, ranging from money for cold cuts for her daughter's lunches to $1,000 in cash, probably totaled "in the neighborhood of $10,000." The money was loaned, Burke said, but he kept no record of it and didn't appear eager to be paid back. He said he kept her in cash because Doug had abusive control over her finances. He had also over the past year taken her on jaunts to New York City, the Hudson Valley, North Carolina, and Key West.

Burke was disdainful of Doug. He wondered aloud if he "unlawfully obtained my subscriber information from the beeper company," and described as ludicrous the accusation that Michelle and Burke were involved together in a prostitution operation.

"Both of us are devastated about that terribly false, absolutely false allegation," Burke declared, though he wasn't entirely forthcoming in his own sworn testimony.

"I take it, sir, that you, then, have never involved yourself personally, other than on official police business, perhaps, with a prostitute?" Doug's attorney, Arnold Firestone, asked Burke at one point.

"That's correct," the lieutenant replied. Burke's attorney, Spreer, said of that response, which came five years after the Rickenbacker case that contradicted that claim: "I just rolled my eyes."

When Firestone moved on to the subject of a house Michelle had rented, Burke was apparently unaware that the line of questioning had tripped up Michelle when she was deposed several months earlier.

Doug's investigators had discovered that she put down a deposit for the house before the domestic violence arrest occurred. Firestone was focused on Burke's role in that move, which in his argument suggested the domestic violence allegation was a premeditated ruse.

During her deposition, Michelle initially maintained that she had used her own money to put down a deposit. But after Firestone confronted her with rental documents that contradicted that story, Michelle said she was mistaken.

"It came from my friend," Michelle said.

When asked to specify which friend had lent her the money, Michelle replied: "Jim Burke."

Now Firestone asked Burke whether he had helped her with the rental deposit, without tipping him off that Michelle had already come clean.

Burke was unequivocal. "No," Burke said, adding: "I believe she saved it up on her own."

* * *

Hell hath no fury like a passive-aggressive interagency law enforcement memo, and eight days after Burke's deposition, Pat Cuff's boss, IAB Commanding Officer Philip Robilotto, sent a classic example of the genre to the DA's office.

In the memo, Robilotto informed T. Michael Conlon, bureau chief of the DA's Public Integrity Bureau, of the allegation that Burke had been promoting prostitution. The IAB "has exhausted all available lines of inquiry," Robilotto wrote. "At this time we cannot substantiate administrative charges. For this reason, I am requesting that your office examine this case for possible criminal charges."

Robilotto added that there was already an agreement in place to loan an IAB lieutenant to Conlon as a liaison to "assist your office in the criminal investigation."

It was an odd memo, and to an attuned observer, an explosive one. Robilotto was acknowledging that they didn't have enough to charge Burke with even an administrative infraction, but he was attempting to get the DA's office to open a criminal investigation based on the same allegations. For the IAB to refer complaints to the DA's office was rare, and for them to do so when they couldn't substantiate an administrative charge of their own was unheard of.

The memo, on Suffolk PD stationary, was the clearest possible evidence of IAB going in for the kill on Jimmy. They were handing him off to a bigger bully capable of escalating the arms race. "We referred it because the DA's guys could get wiretaps," said Robilotto, acknowledging that Jimmy had defeated his own investigators. He had spotted their tail, and they were unable to even make a haircut appointment with Michelle to test the theory that it was a cover for prostitution.

The DA's office also had good reason to want to open a case on Jimmy Burke. For DA Jim Catterson, Tom Spota was getting on the radar as a potential problem. Spota had been floated as a possible challenger to Catterson in the 1997 DA election, but had ultimately not run. But Spota seemed to be a more realistic threat to run, and pose a serious challenge, in the next election in 2001. Catterson was notorious for using his law enforcement powers to intimidate and destroy political candidates. The value of having an open criminal investigation into Spota's longtime right-hand cop would not have escaped him.

The diaspora of current and former IAB cops who loathed Jimmy were gaining in influence. The clearest example of this came in 2000, when Robilotto was promoted to chief of department, the top uniformed position, while the criminal investigation into Burke that he had sparked was still ongoing. Jimmy likely didn't know at the time that he had been referred to the DA's office for possible criminal charges. But he was an experienced-enough investigator to predict the IAB's next moves against him, from subpoenaing his phone records to parsing his deposition transcript for perjury, and to know that they were never going to leave his rearview until they found the case to destroy him.

Jimmy would kvetch about all of the IAB guys, and how they would do anything to bring him down. But he retained a special reservoir of hatred for one in particular: Pat Cuff. He was an unusual choice for the role of archenemy. With his unblemished record, daily church attendance, and Spanish fluency, he was the Mr. Rogers of the Suffolk County Police Department. But Burke blamed Cuff for the IAB probe of Doug's allegations, which Burke read as a simple vendetta. He also saw Cuff as the main source of disparaging gossip about him and Lowrita Rickenbacker. And then, of course, above all else, Cuff had laughed in his face. It became Jimmy's favorite tune, particularly when he was drinking: "Fuck Pat Cuff."

Dennis Sullivan, Burke's former partner and one of his closest friends in the department, heard over and over again about Burke's hatred of Pat Cuff, the top slot on an enemies list that was getting ever longer and more obsessive. So did Jim Hickey, the former Wyandanch cop who became one of Jimmy's closest confidants and for more than a decade soaked in his rants that Pat Cuff was no good, a scumbag, an IAB rat fuck who deserved retaliation. It was a mantra: "We need to get Pat Cuff."

It was a bit pathetic: a scandal-plagued midnight lieutenant under criminal investigation plotting to bring down a widely respected captain closely allied with the new police chief. But Burke was nothing if not a long-term plotter. And the only way he could save his own ass, and also fulfill his passion project of destroying Pat Cuff, was to bet it all on the rise of the man who had gotten him this far.

* * *

Hickey could point at his own stalled career as illustrative of what happened when you didn't have a political rabbi like Tom Spota to save you from your mistakes.

Hickey and Burke were like two controls in a science experiment. They both did a year of city time before starting out as twenty-two-year-old runts in the First in 1986. They were lauded by their bosses as highly active officers, and were on similar upward tracks, when they each ran into IAB buzz saws in the early 1990s. For Burke, it was the Lowrita case. For Hickey, it was being branded a liar by Judge Stuart Namm.

And then their careers forked. By the end of 1999, Hickey was a sergeant, having that year finally received his first promotion after more than thirteen years on the job. Burke was two ranks above him as a lieutenant and had loftier heights in mind if he could shake IAB.

Hickey knew the difference was Spota, Burke's fiercest defender and protector. As a close pal to some of the most venerable brass in the department, and a lawyer for the detectives' union, there was perhaps nobody better to have in your corner than Blue Eyes.

Back when they were street cops in the First, Burke roaming North Amityville and Hickey in Wyandanch, they each had only a vague enmity for the other. Their similarities made them rivals. But as Burke began to amass influence in the police department while Hickey stalled out, they saw opportunity in each other.

For Burke's part, he saw in Hickey a chance to test out his favorite management philosophy. Ever since the cop training gig and the bars on his collars, Jimmy fancied himself a guru. He was the Dale Carnegie of cops with plump IAB files. Among his philosophies was not to seek out subordinates just because they were good at their jobs, or even because they showed a strong loyalty gene.

No, Burke would rather have a compromised guy any day. Give him the liars, the loose cannons, the drunks, the womanizers, the gamblers. It was the "broken wing theory." Grant a perennial loser a second chance, elevate them higher than reason would dictate, and they will be so grateful, and limited in other options, that they will never betray you. And if they do anyway, their past will give you easy ammunition to undermine and destroy them.

Hickey learned that Spota also had a similar philosophy, which may have partly explained why he kept elevating Jimmy Burke. When Hickey started spending more time with both Burke and Spota, he likely realized there was potential for him to exploit their backward style of evaluation.

Burke, somewhere between a cheerleader and a bully, invariably brought up Hickey's IAB past in front of Spota. But rather than judging Hickey negatively, Spota bonded with him over it. Spota, after all, had gone toe-to-toe against Judge Namm too. Namm had been Spota's own version of Pat Cuff, an existential threat. Spota said that Hickey's own war wounds from battling the judge were a "badge of honor."

And to Jimmy, it was Hickey's broken wing.

CHAPTER 12

DEAR BOB, PT. 2

On an evening in the mid-1990s, Robert Trotta, then a young, on-the-rise Suffolk County plainclothes cop, was standing in the middle of Sunrise Highway. The road was closed due to a crime scene. An unmarked car pulled up, and an eager sergeant hopped out. He was a barrel-chested man with a standard-issue cop mustache, and he held out his hand for shaking.

"I've heard of you, you're a heavy hitter!" James Burke told Trotta upon introduction.

"Total stroke job," was how Trotta later described the beginning of that first conversation with Jim Burke, who complimented him on his high arrest numbers.

Burke's arm wrapped around Trotta's shoulders. He asked chummily: "Hey, do you know where I can find a snuff film?"

"What's a snuff film?" Trotta replied.

Burke seemed to be expecting the question. He uncorked a graphic definition of a porno in which a man, while having sex with a woman from the back, produces a handgun and blasts the woman's head off, causing her body to clasp onto his penis, pleasurably for him, during her death throes.

Trotta responded: "No, Sarge, I can't help you there."

* * *

If Burke was testing out a potential confidant, he couldn't have picked a worse guy in the department for it. Rob Trotta was not famous for his discretion.

At the police academy a decade earlier, Trotta was the college kid cadet who volunteered to his instructors in front of the class that he was late because he had the runs.

His fellow cadet John Rodriguez was sure Trotta was going to rat everybody out for myriad academy shenanigans. "He is an elitist rich kid who came into the academy and was green as could be," Rodriguez said, though Trotta actually grew up firmly middle-class in Commack.

Once Trotta graduated the academy, he turned his love of gab into a crime-squelching technique. He'd pull up on some of the most drug-infested intersections in his precinct, leave his gun belt in the car, and shoot the shit with the young dealers over a cup of coffee. That his visits killed their business for a few hours was just a bonus.

Trotta was known for his extreme doggedness. Even when he was driving his kids to a pizza place, he'd usually take a circuitous route to lay eyes on the home of a target under surveillance. His obsessiveness snagged him promotions and accolades, and in 1993, Trotta was named the department's "Cop of the Year."

He ultimately earned a role on a federal task force, which Trotta found suited his investigative style well. For example, most county cops would never deign to dig through a perp's garbage, a favored fed tactic. Trotta, meanwhile, spent more than a few mornings in borrowed coveralls holding on to the back of a garbage truck.

His penchant for strategic chatting got him in trouble with a judge at least once. He had an allegedly murderous cigarette smuggler handcuffed in his back seat during midday traffic, and during a lengthy, chummy conversation, Trotta asked the perp whether he was sure he wanted to follow his lawyers' advice and go to trial.

"They want a new boat!" Trotta told the smuggler of his lawyers. Trotta's manner of confiding was akin to that of a guy a few beers deep at a bar attempting to be heard over a noisy jukebox. A judge later ruled Trotta's remarks to the smuggler were "egregious" in that Trotta and his partner, the Burke-loathing Detective Tim Gozaloff, "tried to use their time alone with defendant, i.e. absent his attorneys, to convince him that he had no chance of prevailing at trial."

Trotta was a gangly sort, with a head that seemed to widen with age, an illusion due to an ever-receding little crown of downy hair. As a foe, he could be easily underestimated. For years after his initial encounter with Burke, he gossiped with other cops about his request. He wondered aloud if Burke was joking or gauging his response. He ultimately decided the sergeant was seriously seeking out a snuff film. Either way, his prognosis was becoming a common one among cops who had run-ins with Burke: "This guy's out of his mind."

Trotta had a fickle attitude toward politicians, which included DAs. Back in the late 1980s, when the SIC had cleaned Patrick Henry's clock so badly that he decided not to run again, the young cop Trotta had campaigned for Jim Catterson, Henry's heir apparent in terms of the traditional Suffolk County law enforcement way of doing things.

But over Catterson's next three terms, Trotta had soured on the DA. Most cops in the county had, largely because Catterson had prosecuted some of them in brutality cases. Trotta had more of a niche beef. He felt Catterson was singularly motivated by asset forfeiture, the practice of seizing allegedly illegal proceeds from those he charged. As a result, Trotta felt Catterson was prone to giving sweetheart deals to sophisticated criminals with well-connected attorneys in return for them not contesting large forfeitures.

Trotta despised seeing his hard-fought cases pleaded away to nothing so that the DA could afford some new toys. "Legal organized crime!" he railed to anybody who would listen. He said that during a meeting with Catterson's prosecutors, he berated them while hurling mug shots and rap sheets of hardened criminals who had gotten off easy onto the conference table.

"He's fucking crazy as the day is long," said Trotta's former fellow cadet Rodriguez, who had begrudgingly begun to like the guy. "Once he starts gnawing at a bone he doesn't let it go."

In 2001, the Catterson bone took him to the steps of a courthouse, where a challenger to the incumbent was announcing his candidacy for DA. It was an underwhelming event. The lawyer in question looked like an aging used car salesman. The crowd consisted of a few family members and friends and a reporter or two.

But Trotta was ready to pitch in against Catterson no matter who this guy was. After the event, Trotta declared as he shook Tom Spota's hand: "I don't care if you're Al Sharpton!"

Trotta recruited his kids to help him paint DumpCatterson.com on salvaged wood. The web address led to a campaign website of his own early internet design. He hung the signs on highway overpasses.

And during check-ins at Spota's de facto campaign headquarters in his law office, Trotta got to know Spota's ragtag team. It was a collection of cops and wannabes of every stripe, ranging from pinkie ring–wearing old retired homicide bulls to steroidal gym rats, phone banking, licking envelopes, and handing out fliers. They were all led by a rock promoter who wore long hair and sported an earring.

Trotta was amused to see that the caporegime of this odd brigade was his acquaintance from Sunrise Highway, Jimmy Burke.

* * *

Tom Spota always maintained that he was just a prosecutor at heart, and not at all a political animal. But he spent nearly all of Catterson's three-term reign up to that point situating himself as the perfect challenger.

When "The Cat" swiped at his own homicide bull supporter James McCready for the bar beating, Spota had been there to defend him and get an emphatic acquittal. Catterson then took even more direct aim at the police establishment, charging a Suffolk sergeant with helping hundreds of others cheat their way on to the force by gaming civil service exams. Spota's law partner, a former police lieutenant, was also indicted for allegedly helping the sergeant cover it up, charges that were ultimately dismissed. The growing belief among cops was that Catterson was out of control, and Spota was in agreement. He said he regretted his initial support of Catterson. "I worked day and night to help him," Spota said. "I thought he'd be a great district attorney. And unfortunately, that didn't occur."

By 1997, Spota was being groomed as a challenger to Catterson. He was eager to run, but there was a snag: Spota, like Catterson, was a

Republican. Spota would have to switch parties, and Democrats were reluctant to nominate him.

But Catterson had a way of motivating his opponents. He charged five officials in the Democrat-controlled town of Babylon with white-collar offenses, in what seemed to many like a purely political prosecution. Then a squabble between GOP top dogs over the glory for rescuing a kidnapped girl may have led to a courtroom spectacle in which Catterson was again pitted against Spota. Catterson and Suffolk County Sheriff Patrick Mahoney were said to have beefed over who would get to hold a press conference with kidnapping victim Katie Beers. The feud grew from there, and Catterson ultimately indicted Mahoney and his undersheriff, Eddie Morris, on dozens of criminal counts including using the jail as an illegal campaign headquarters.

Spota was once again on the other side. He represented Morris, who happened to be one of his best friends. By the time the case was in pretrial proceedings in 2001, Spota had been announced as the Democratic challenger to the DA prosecuting his client. The case felt more like an electoral spectacle than a criminal trial, a testament to how politics seeped into every hinge of the Suffolk justice system.

Richard Schaffer, leader of the county Democratic Party, decided this time he wasn't going to pass on Spota. Schaffer had been active in politics since he was a bucktoothed North Babylon ten-year-old, and had first run for office at age seventeen. His public-facing persona was that of an extremely dull and pleasant bureaucrat, a doughy fellow in a chunky sweater, who only reluctantly wielded the little power he had. But those who crossed Schaffer swore he was actually a cold-blooded samurai in the art of crushing his enemies.

The five Babylon officials Catterson indicted all reported to town supervisor Schaffer, and the smart money would be on the DA trying to put him in cuffs as well. Unless, that is, Schaffer succeeded in engineering the replacement of Catterson. Schaffer calculated his best shot at unseating Catterson was to nominate the keeper of the cop vote who, as a bonus, could charm civilians with his high-drama resume as a prosecutor in the DeFeo and Pius cases.

Even so, Spota was an underdog. That a hardline, death penalty–supporting prosecutor was so willing to become a Democrat for political gain was sure to inspire skepticism in voters of every affiliation. In order to have a chance, Spota needed a perfect Hail Mary from Jimmy Burke.

* * *

"I'm pounding 'em!" Burke yelled in Spota's law office, by way of a status update. "I'm pounding these lazy fuckers!"

Frank MacKay was pleased to hear it.

MacKay was a dude in his thirties whose ponytail and earring gave away his real occupation, which involved scouting out the next passable punk band to come out of Lindenhurst. He was the owner of several hole-in-the-wall rock clubs such as Dr. Shay's, popular with mohawked adolescents for its no-ID policy on certain afternoons.

But MacKay had stumbled into politics and found he loved the ruthless chess strategy of it. From there he had knifed his way up the org chart of a political party that embodied New York's electoral nihilism.

It was called the Independence Party. The name was key to its sneaky success. The party was ideologically bereft. An untold number of its two hundred thousand members—a collective that would more than double in size over the next couple of decades—had registered accidentally. They meant to pick no party at all.

By 2000, MacKay's leadership of this army that believed in nothing had made him a pivotal power broker. Notably, New York City Mayor Rudy Giuliani had invited him to Gracie Mansion so that he could lobby for MacKay's endorsement in his abortive senatorial bid against Hillary Clinton.

MacKay was ruthless in exploiting a flawed electoral system. He and Schaffer knew that Spota's greatest asset was the cops. And Spota's best conduit to the cops was this rough-around-the-edges lieutenant with whom he developed an odd father-and-son relationship. Schaffer soon found himself chatting with Jimmy Burke more than Spota.

MacKay was loath to entrust the campaign's success to Jimmy, whom he saw as a drunk and a lout. MacKay said he detected that even Spota sometimes doubted his protégé.

But for better or worse, there was nobody more enthusiastic or well-placed than Burke. The Spota campaign was like Burke's very own episode of *This Is Your Life*, filled with characters dating back to his teenage years. The retired homicide bull Anthony Palumbo volunteered for the campaign, and Burke recruited his old partner Dennis Sullivan to join as well.

MacKay's most Machiavellian ideas were implemented over eggs or bunless burgers, and so it was at the Peter Pan Diner in Bay Shore that he explained to a retired big league pitcher named Richard Neil Thompson that he wanted him to run for DA on the Conservative Party ticket.

Thompson and his wife looked back at him with stunned expressions. The guy had a 5.05 ERA over three seasons with the Indians and Expos, and his district attorney bona fides were even worse. He had been a lawyer for about five years, during which time he had worked as a baseball agent with no big league clients. He had never practiced criminal law.

But MacKay promised there'd be a pot of gold for Thompson if his plan worked. If Thompson could beat Catterson in the Conservative Party primary, it would rob the incumbent of having his name on the ballot under that line and cost him a vital chunk of votes in the general election.

"I thought that we could barely win but that we would win," said MacKay, adding that the only reason he chose Thompson was because police were impressed by professional athletes: "We picked him out of a hat just because the cops liked him."

MacKay gave Jimmy a new title—"the whip"—and assigned him to getting his fellow cops to hand over signed absentee ballots for Thompson, the former baseball player few, if anybody, in the county thought was qualified to be DA.

Burke insisting on absentee ballots for the primary contest, rather than trusting the cops to vote on Election Day, was essential to MacKay's plan. Without forcing a collection of these ballots, the cops might not vote Thompson, or they might not vote at all. Burke relayed to MacKay that he was struggling to make headway with cops who were afraid to piss off Catterson. At the time, absentee ballots legally required an excuse, such as a conflicting work shift, for why the person couldn't vote on Election Day. The cops expressed fear that Catterson might prosecute them for voting absentee in the primary when it turned out they didn't have to. Burke exhorted, cajoled, and blustered his way over those fears.

"Frankie Boy, Frankie Boy, I'm getting them!" Burke boomed. "They're hating me, but I'm getting them!"

Spota was a first-time political candidate at age sixty, and Trotta recalled that he was nervous about running a third-party operative to siphon off votes. "Is this electioneering?" Spota asked Burke, who assured him everybody did this.

Flagging down old ladies outside of a Waldbaum's in Ronkonkoma, Spota flashed a younger man's vigor for the election trail. His bumper stickers read: "Let's Put the Cat Out." He even won the endorsement of the leftist Green Party.

Newsday abandoned its decade-plus endorsement for Catterson in favor of Spota, who the paper's editorial department lauded for his "reputation for meticulous preparation and skillful trial work. Spota has the professional skills for the job but without Catterson's vitriol." The *New York Times* also endorsed Spota, citing his "solid experience" and "fresh ideas."

On the night of September 30, 2001, MacKay said he received a phone call. "You motherfucking genius!" squealed the voice, helium-high with excitement, on the other end. "Holy shit, you did it!"

Only when MacKay asked who it was did Spota identify himself: "It's Tommy!"

Thompson won the Conservative Party primary by just over one hundred votes. The general election was far from over, but Spota, and those in his campaign, felt they now had it locked up. Spota was fixated on ascertaining Burke's role in the coup. "Did he lift a fucking finger," Spota asked MacKay, "or did he just sit and tell jokes and get drunk?"

MacKay assured Spota that Burke was integral to the whole effort. Not long afterward, Burke asked to meet MacKay near midnight at the twenty-four-hour Millennium Diner in Smithtown. Burke was late, and as MacKay waited for him in the parking lot, a green Grand Marquis swooped up so close that it almost hit him.

Burke's voice rang out: "Frankie Boy!"

He was drunk off his ass, MacKay recalled, and after hopping out of his police-issued Mercury he immediately whipped out his dick and started pissing in the parking lot.

The guy was overjoyed, not just about the primary victory, but also about how MacKay had vouched for him when grilled by Spota. He made it clear that he was banking on Spota giving him a big job in the DA's office.

"This is a big deal for me," Burke said gratefully, putting his penis away and holding out the same hand for MacKay to shake. "I'm going to end up getting Rackets."

* * *

One of Spota's first acts upon being elected district attorney was getting Commissioner John Gallagher on the horn. Spota and Gallagher went to the same Sunday services, and the men knew each other well.

Suffolk cops mostly hated Gallagher, because he had never been one of them. He was a career bureaucrat appointed to the top administrative position as commissioner by the county executive in 1997. The jowly white-haired outsider was a little too at home in the bucolic environs of Police HQ, a low-slung, slightly decaying municipal building in the Yaphank hinterland.

Spota asked his fellow parishioner to appoint James Burke to be the commanding officer for the district attorney's office. Gallagher said he would talk with his commission staff and get back to him.

The commission staff were the SCPD's department bosses in all their paramilitary glory: a trio of three-star chiefs, one for each division—patrol, detective, and operations—and a four-star chief of department, Phil Robilotto, the top uniformed cop who laymen knew as the police chief. Robilotto, the former IAB boss, would have rather put Burke in handcuffs than a command in the DA's office, but he knew they didn't have much choice in the matter.

The chiefs gave Gallagher a history lesson about the feud, decades prior, between the two top dogs of Suffolk County law enforcement, resulting in Commissioner Eugene Kelley arresting DA Henry O'Brien for a coerced same-sex blowjob that may not have occurred.

Part of the agencies' reconciliation after the open warfare of the 1970s was a pact that allowed the incoming DA to appoint whoever he'd like from the police department to run the detective squad in his office.

It was a long story, but the simple moral was that Commissioner Gallagher, even if he wanted to, had no standing to block Spota from naming Burke to that top spot in his office. Nevertheless, that day or the next, a representative of the Internal Affairs Bureau told Gallagher there were a few things in Burke's file that they felt he should know.

Gallagher then called up Spota and confirmed he'd be transferring Burke. He ventured a passing mention of Burke's nose for trouble, that he had a checkered past with Internal Affairs.

"Yes, I'm aware of that," Spota responded.

Gallagher signed the papers.

* * *

Starting on January 1, 2002, Burke worked out of Building 77, three stories of rain-stained molded concrete and copper-colored brick labeled in Helvetica, as vaguely as possible: "Suffolk County Office Building." Inside, maintenance had just finished a fresh etching on a large window in the lobby, right over the county seal: Thomas J. Spota, District Attorney.

Spota's swearing-in ceremony had highlighted the odd optics of a lifelong Republican who had just turned Democrat in order to oust a Republican. US Senator Charles Schumer and then New York Attorney General Eliot Spitzer, two of the highest-profile Democrats in the state, sung Spota's praises as a figure of high integrity. Spota vowed that his mandate was to "enforce the law with temperance and without malice, to seek truth and not victims, to serve the law and not fractional purposes, and to approach these tasks with humility and respect."

Then he was sworn in by his beloved mentor whose reputation was the opposite of all of that: Judge Patrick Henry, former figurehead of a law enforcement machine derided as corrupt, political, and inept. Spota got comfortable in a corner office suite on the first floor. He was now in control of what was effectively the largest, richest, and by far the most powerful law firm in the county, with nearly two hundred attorneys on staff, as well as more than one hundred law enforcement investigators and a couple hundred more in support staff. Jimmy Burke was his chief digger. He got a no-frills office on the second floor and a lofty new title: Commanding Officer, District Attorney Section.

Old schoolers called Jimmy's unit "Rackets." He oversaw a few dozen seasoned detectives handpicked from the police department for the DA's use. With the job came the sort of resources cops drool over: easy access to wiretaps, virtually limitless overtime, and—most vitally to Burke—insulation from his actual employer.

Burke was technically still employed by the police department, which was a pleasant arrangement in terms of pay. Jimmy earned $144,000 in 2002, a steadily ballooning figure that would reach $200,000 by 2010. But in practice his only boss was now Spota, the most important man in Suffolk law enforcement.

Almost immediately, Burke felt the benefits of his protected perch.

The criminal investigation into whether he was involved in pimping out women in Smithtown was still technically active, almost two years after Robilotto had referred the matter to Catterson's Public Integrity Unit. But in May 2002, five months after Burke joined the DA's office, the new head of the unit, Jeremy Scileppi, declared in a letter to the IAB that the case was without merit.

Scileppi said he found the nature of the complaint "somewhat suspect" because its genesis was a husband fighting for assets in a divorce. "While reviewing the contents of this file it became clear that there is no definitive link between the subject and the activities alleged to be occurring, and no clear evidence of criminal activities by the civilian let alone the sworn Suffolk County Police Officer," Scileppi concluded.

That same day, IAB also declared the matter dead. "There has not been one individual who could provide firsthand information to corroborate any of these allegations," Cuff wrote to his bosses, the top men in the department. Both allegations in the complaint, that Burke was involved in a prostitution ring and that he had supplied Michelle with drugs, were found to be "unsubstantiated."

Later that year, as if to spike the football, Spota added a feisty memo of his own to scold Burke's detractors. The letter was to Robert Kearon, who had negotiated Burke's Lowrita slap on the wrist in his time as a deputy commissioner. Spota had already poached Kearon to serve as a division chief in his new administration.

"Dear Bob," Spota began. "To put it mildly the entire file is based upon nothing other than innuendos and baseless accusations," he wrote, calling Robilotto's referral "a blatant attempt to use the District Attorney's office to investigate Detective Lieutenant Burke for potential criminal charges."

The letter continued: "I believe we should return this file with a letter indicating the investigation was conducted with the clear intent to attempt in any way possible to destroy the career of Detective Lieutenant Burke and merits no further action of any kind." Spota closed with an order to bury the matter: "Please keep this file of confidential nature and do not disclose its contents to anybody else in this office."

All the letters and memos on official stationery telegraphed the same simple conclusion: Jimmy Burke was no longer to be fucked with. Robilotto, Burke's IAB nemesis who had risen to chief of department, certainly got the message. Within a couple of years of Spota's election, he effectively admitted defeat, putting in his papers and taking off for a department in Florida.

"A DA is something to be reckoned with—there's no two ways about that," Robilotto later explained. "And when you got one quite obviously in your pocket like Burke did, you weren't going to get much done against him."

* * *

Shortly after Spota vanquished Catterson in the general election, a prosecutor named Christopher McPartland sent his résumé over to the county attorney's office. For McPartland, the prospect of defending the county against civil suits and handling other municipal legal work would be a duller gig than what he had currently, and would mean a pay cut. But McPartland was certain Tom Spota, his new boss, was going to fire him.

Years down the line, McPartland would be christened behind his back with sinister nicknames that conveyed a grudging admiration, among them The Lord of Darkness and Bald Demon. But for now, he was just a midlevel prosecutor with two young daughters and an aging father with a hole in his throat. So he couldn't afford unemployment.

McPartland was the product of what his older brother, Terence, called "survival values." It was a remnant from his father, Ronald, a tempestuous figure whose own parents had fled Northern Ireland to escape poverty and persecution for their Catholic faith. Ronald at first seemed like an American success story, moving his wife and kids from New York City to Detroit to work for the Ford Motor Company and then, when Chris was around ten, back east to Suffolk County after he took over a truck dealership.

A newspaper ad for the 1976 grand opening of Mid-Island Ford Truck Sales—"Truck owners invited, Refreshments, Door Prizes Include C.B. Radio"—bore a photo of smiling, mustachioed Ron McPartland. Balding and in a polyester suit, Chris's dad appeared to have staked out a prosperous corner of the suburban boom for himself and his family. The reality was far more chaotic.

As his father's finances dipped into the red, he drank heavily and was abusive to the boys and Chris's mother, Thecla, who became cowed and withdrawn.

Throughout his early life, Chris had to tend to family and financial crises while his peers seemed blissfully untroubled. As a high schooler, according to Chris, his parents sent him multiple times on a most undesirable solo mission: to extricate his older brother from a West Virginia ashram the family considered a cult.

Chris got into Georgetown University. During his junior year abroad in Dublin, his parents called to inform him Ron had lost the truck dealership. They'd spring for his return ticket from Ireland, but otherwise Chris was on his own financially. Amidst his trust-fund classmates, he scraped together tuition and expenses through loans and a workaholic commitment to a catering business. He similarly hustled his way through a Hofstra University law degree, graduating just as his father was diagnosed with throat cancer. Now his father barked at his family through an electrolarynx.

In Catterson, who hired him straight out of law school in 1991, Chris McPartland got more tough love. Catterson demanded total loyalty from his assistants but didn't return the favor. He referred to prosecutors who had been in his office too long as barnacles, and he was fond of a periodic hull-scraping. Catterson also wasn't big on autonomy, as evidenced by the shields he distributed to his bureau chiefs bearing the Army axiom he adopted as his personal slogan: "Follow Me."

McPartland took well to the domineering dynamic. He happily devoted himself to the cases that some derided as political vendettas. When Catterson launched a lengthy grand jury probe of a county deal with a private health care insurance company that employed a former political rival, McPartland eagerly accepted the reassignment to the Public Integrity Unit to work on it. In the politically fraught prosecution of Republican Sheriff Patrick Mahoney, young McPartland was the designated workhorse. In a later memo, his more senior colleagues in that prosecution complimented McPartland's "intimate familiarity and immediate recall" of thousands of pages of testimony and his ability to deal with "witnesses who were often recalcitrant and unfriendly." The praise helped get him dibs on the next vengeance prosecution, Catterson's takedown of the five Democrats in Babylon.

These political cases were for the most part legal shit sandwiches that few young prosecutors could spin into anything substantial. Mahoney wriggled away with a misdemeanor and kept his job. In the Babylon cases, McPartland and colleagues secured a total of one misdemeanor conviction, following the noisy felony indictments and front-page perp walks of five officials. But Catterson seemed unbothered by McPartland's poor win-loss record in such grudge prosecutions. Even an unsuccessful prosecution intimidated potential rivals, not to mention it was financially and morally bruising for the defendant. For The Cat, apparently a big part of the joy was in the torture.

"McP," as he was referred to in office shorthand, became a connoisseur of leverage. He looked a bit miserable at trial, as if angry that his failure to jam a deal down a defendant's throat had caused him to waste his time proving his case to the rabble. His real calling was in the unseen elements of the job, such as hours spent in a wiretap room with investigators puzzling out nicknames and coded chatter, or in an interrogation room attempting to trip up a subject. His specialty was the white-collar conspiracy, which often required him to piece together casual conversations and verbal agreements like a criminal jigsaw puzzle.

McPartland was known as a knockaround guy, always game for more than a few drinks at The Printer's Devil, Catterson's boozy restaurant in Port Jefferson. In a testosterone-soaked workplace, knockaround guys sometimes got knocked around. McPartland's boss in Rackets was Marty Thompson, a weightlifter known for his love of horseplay. McPartland briefly went on worker's comp in 1996 after being accosted by Thompson. "He was tackled by his boss and thrown into a wall," read a doctor's note documenting his back injury. Thompson's own note concerning the incident dripped with the impunity characteristic of the alphas of the office. "I ran into Mr. McPartland and accidentally injured his back," Thompson wrote. "I should be more careful of my surroundings."

Spota's victory would bring the office hijinks to an end. McPartland had reveled in the job security that came with being Catterson's legal hatchet man. But the same cases that had saved McPartland from being subject to his boss's periodic barnacle-scrapings would likely doom him with the next guy. McPartland had helped prosecute a basketball team's worth of subordinates to Richie Schaffer, who happened to be the new DA's most powerful ally. If that wasn't enough, McPartland had also helped prosecute the undersheriff Eddie Morris, Spota's client and close buddy, who ultimately pleaded guilty to a felony.

So when McPartland saw Spota's thinning cowlick heading his way one day early in the new DA's administration, he must have figured this was his moment for the old man to exact his revenge.

Spota asked him about the county attorney's job, having been alerted to McPartland's application by one of his many spies. *Do you want that job?* Spota asked him. Chris explained that it wasn't really the new job so much as the likely end of his current one that had motivated him. Spota told him to stop by his office later.

For all the very strong reasons he had to expect termination, McPartland hadn't considered maybe the strongest factor of all: he was pure donkey.

* * *

There were a few Tom Wolfe fanboys in the office, the most influential being homicide bureau chief John B. Collins. He often referred his underlings to his favorite chapter in Wolfe's 1987 epic *Bonfire of the Vanities*, a passage of which he also had snipped in his desk. The book was about prosecutors in the South Bronx, and Collins said he valued the chapter "with respect to the doggedness that was required of a homicide prosecutor."

The chapter included an ode to the Irish "donkey," as Wolfe described those cops and homicide prosecutors who when caught in jams that were not always noble—"no matter what kind of stupid fix you got yourself into"—were without fail determined to go down fighting.

"The other side of it was loyalty," Wolfe further explained. "When one of them got in a jam, the others never broke ranks. Well, that wasn't completely true, but the game had to be pretty far gone before the Irish started looking out for Number One."

Collins, who is now a justice of the Suffolk County Supreme Court, said recently that what he gleaned from the chapter was the "pursuit of the truth" required by a prosecutor, not the stuff about fighting yourself out of stupid fixes.

Nonetheless, it would be difficult to build a more authentic specimen of the donkey archetype as described by Wolfe than McPartland. He was an assistant in his midthirties who had toiled over dubious political revenge cases to please his boss for little reward except more work. Now that his work had led to the potential loss of his job, he was ready to fight to keep it.

McPartland was a crier. Yes, when things in his life went south, McPartland was known to let loose the waterworks. Office rumors flew after his meeting with Spota that McPartland had wept and begged. It would be a sight: a large bald Irish-American who knew his way around a shotgun, shuddering with emotion.

So maybe it was the donkey thing, or Spota's affinity for broken wings. Or maybe it was just that McPartland was good with wiretaps, a rare talent for a prosecutor. Either way, Spota's decision not to fire McPartland, or Marty Thompson, the roughhousing bureau chief who had overseen all of those Catterson partisan prosecutions, came to look like contrarian brilliance. Obstinately playing against type, seemingly to the detriment of his own position, had become Spota's hallmark, and the key to his success, even if it was a hazardous game.

Tom Spota wasn't Irish—his grandpa was a stonemason who arrived on a boat from Italy in 1897. But he was more than a little bit of a donkey himself.

A coworker who had watched Chris McPartland walk dejectedly to Spota's office for their first meeting saw him on his way there again a couple of days later. The event this time was an impromptu gathering among the connected members of the office. Chris headed in with a twelve-pack of Heineken.

* * *

On an evening shortly after Spota took office, Rob Trotta was in Building 77 picking up a subpoena when the new DA, and his pal Burke, spotted him and harangued him to join them for drinks.

"He was fucking bombed," Trotta said of Spota. When they were at the Smithtown bar, Trotta downed a beer and left, not comfortable with the company of the man he had just helped get elected.

Spota later offered him a job working under Burke, but Trotta liked his task force. Years later, he would come to recognize that turning down that gig saved his life as he knew it.

Frank MacKay's golden touch in the Spota election helped make him a political mainstay. His Independence Party continued to gain the accidental membership of people who didn't want to be in any party. It became a powerhouse of nearly half a million voters and over the years endorsed a dissociative range of politicians from Michael Bloomberg to Ralph Nader to John McCain.

MacKay gained notoriety as a gadfly, launching his own local radio show that he taped in the baggage claim area of a Long Island airport. One of his guests many years later was the man he had helped put to power: DA Tom Spota.

During that interview in 2014, they shot the shit a little bit about scary old Jim Catterson. The Cat was dead by then, but Spota still tut-tutted the former DA for driving around in a pinstriped BMW seized from a drug dealer.

MacKay asked Spota, who he depicted as a consummate prosecutor of corrupt public officials, if he saw a common trait in those who had gone rogue.

"The first thing they have on their mind—many, many, many of the people that we have interviewed and that we have prosecuted," Spota mused, "is the fact that they love the power that they do have and they want to continue to have that power."

He added: "And that's when they start to do foolish, foolish things."

CHAPTER 13

GLAZED DONUT

At the end of his overnight tour on a September 2005 morning, Jim Hickey, then a Third Precinct lieutenant, stopped outside his boss's office to check in. Pat Cuff, the precinct's commanding officer, started his own workday when Hickey ended his. Cuff was usually a chipper presence. But today Hickey found him hunched over in his office chair, facing the wall. In place of his uniform, Cuff wore a suit.

Hickey rapped on the door. "Are you okay, boss?" he asked.

Cuff turned around, looking weepy. Hickey asked his boss delicately if he should come back later.

"No," Cuff responded. "Come in and shut the door."

Cuff confided in Hickey that he had been on vacation in Maine when he got a call from the Seventh Precinct. A detective there informed him that his eighteen-year-old son had been arrested for possession of two of Cuff's handguns. Cuff had apparently neglected to spin the padlock on the safe where he kept his old Customs .38 and his Glock service weapon. Somebody had called the cops to report his son, and when the police pulled him over, he had admitted the guns were in the glove compartment. The son was charged with a misdemeanor and given a ticket to appear at his arraignment.

The elder Cuff had been at that arraignment in a Central Islip courtroom that same morning. When Cuff's son was up, the prosecutors who had handled every arraignment to that point stood down. Another lawyer stepped in just to handle the Cuff kid's case, introducing herself to the judge as a representative of the Special Investigations Bureau. As in, the bureau that usually only handled serious and high-profile crimes. A bureau with Christopher McPartland at its helm.

The new prosecutor said that she planned to present the case of Cuff's son to the grand jury, which sent alarm bells ringing for Cuff. The grand jury could easily indict his son for a felony. Cuff sensed that somehow Jimmy Burke was behind this. As he explained this story to Hickey, he asked: "How would you feel if suddenly your own DA's office moved to upgrade a charge to a felony against your son?"

Hickey feigned empathy. But as soon as he was out of his boss's sight, he called his buddy Jimmy Burke at Building 77 to relay Cuff's sob story.

"That's great!" Burke guffawed excitedly. "Hang on, let me get Spota and McPartland on the phone and you could tell them."

Hickey patiently sat on hold in his office. When all three men were on speaker phone, Burke had him repeat the news a second time. So Hickey recounted the story again, making sure to include that Cuff had been crying. The hooting and hollering on the other end sounded like football fans whose team had just scored a crucial touchdown.

"Fuck that guy!" Hickey heard Spota bark.

"He's a fucking scumbag," chimed in McPartland.

"He's a rat motherfucker!" Burke added.

Hickey joined in on the celebratory laughter. For years, he had been working his way into Jimmy Burke and Tom Spota's good graces. His reporting Cuff's anguish, as petty as it was, seemed to be the clincher.

Two months later, Jimmy gave Lieutenant Hickey a little pep talk. He needed to get off the night shift, "get in the game," and become a career guy, Jimmy told him. And as it happened, a position had just opened up.

* * *

Jimmy finally had the power he craved. He could fuck his enemies and elevate a roster of broken wing cops to support his plays. Among the promotions was John Rodriguez, Rob Trotta's former fellow cadet who had become a toxic street cop.

The lanky, gruff son of Queens Colombians, John Rodriguez got his first policing job in a Bronx precinct. He called the NYPD "the biggest gang in the world," recalling colleagues who went to whorehouses during their tours and shot and roasted pheasants in Pelham Bay Park. After he joined the Suffolk force, he was one of the few cops in the jurisdiction equipped to understand MS-13, a street gang with Salvadoran roots. The secret, Rodriguez explained, was to give up on reasoning with its trauma-scarred teenage gang members: "It's like bringing in a frickin' Chechnyan rebel to try to talk to them." As for how Rodriguez did get information out of his gang subjects, he denied using violence, but also refused to conduct interrogations if there was a camera in the room.

Rodriguez's gang expertise got him a position as an investigator in the DA's office under Catterson. But in 1999, a "total schmuck" of a prosecutor kept him waiting to testify for ten hours, and after a shouting match escalated, Rodriguez said he "knocked him out." He was then exiled to the Third Precinct, where Jimmy Burke was lieutenant at the time. The two men knew each other by reputation. Rodriguez had heard about the half-Black offspring that the swashbuckling Burke had running around North Amityville, and Jimmy knew Rodriguez was a talented gang cop with control issues.

Jimmy stopped Rodriguez in the hallway one day before Spota had even announced his campaign for DA. Jimmy was clearly already deep in plotting, though. "Hey, I want to know something," he asked Rodriguez. "Would you ever consider going back to the DA's office?"

The answer was a no-brainer. In Rodriguez's estimation, there were two good jobs in a police department: homicide bull and working for the DA's office. And he had outgrown Homicide and its thirty-five-hour shifts whenever a body dropped. "Why is my life going to be guided by some shithead who gets killed?" he later mused. In Rodriguez's mind, the DA's office, where you worked long overtime-compensated hours and could plan them around your kid's piano recital, was far preferable.

Rodriguez thought Burke was just bullshitting. But immediately after Spota's victory, he found himself transferred to the DA's office to work under Burke as a member of their transition team. Rodriguez was in a cop's cop paradise, with a boss whose style he deeply admired. On weekends, he might spot Burke in the empty Building 77 knocking out some paperwork in shorts, T-shirt, and flip-flops, cop radio blaring while he inhaled beef jerky strips two at a time in between cigar puffs. "He reminded me of a kid whose fantasy it was to be police commissioner," Rodriguez said.

Rodriguez's affinity grew when he watched Burke haggle with the chief mob prosecutor, Marty Thompson, over a search warrant Burke wanted so that he could raid the home of a local Lucchese crime family boss. Burke acknowledged that most likely the mobster's home was clean. But he was in the mood for a show of force. "Fuck this motherfucker," Rodriguez said Burke growled to the prosecutor. "This guy's a boss. I just want my guys to grab up the guy's wife's panties in front of him."

Among Rodriguez's early misadventures with Burke's team was a bukkake sting, which was unlikely to go down in the annals of great law enforcement in the first place. Burke's guys had caught wind of periodic gatherings at a motel in Farmingdale where groups of men masturbated onto a woman. It was murky as to what laws if any were being broken. Gross, perhaps. But it appeared to be a consensual gathering, with no clear evidence that money was changing hands, as would be required for prostitution-related charges. Nonetheless, Johnny Rod volunteered to go undercover.

When he emerged from the target room following the mission, according to multiple people familiar with the incident, Rodriguez had an odd look on his face. Seemingly forgetting the next steps of his police work, he got in his car and drove off. His supervisor immediately suspected what had happened, and when he watched videotape from the bukkake session, the hunch was allegedly confirmed: Rodriguez, who later acknowledged he was identified in the tape by his "unusual pair of shoes," had taken part. The supervisor informed Burke, who just laughed and took the evidentiary videotape with him.

The bukkake case fell apart. Rodriguez later allowed that he stood there nude while his counterparts "glaze[d] her like a donut," and also that he threw away his unusual shoes afterward because he knew they were recognizable on the video. But he claimed he never masturbated on the woman, and that he only took off his clothes so that he wouldn't blow his cover.

* * *

Tom Spota didn't learn about every last one of Burke's shenanigans. But he appeared to tolerate those he did know about. Maybe he saw them as a necessary component of the Jimmy Experience. Maybe Spota didn't mind Jimmy's scandals because the old man was so adept at making them go away.

In the fall of 2002, Spota announced one of his first major news-making cases, a prosecution that seemed to signal that his DA's office wasn't beholden to cops. He charged fourteen members of what he called a drug ring: a musclebound, hard-partying crew who were allegedly caught on wiretaps, in surveillance, and via undercover operations hooking each other up with cocaine and steroids. They included four cops, members of the NYPD, state police, and the Suffolk department.

The NYPD sergeant arrested in the case was Rob Grettler, Burke's alleged sidekick from the strip club basement at Gossip. As defense attorneys will attest, there's no bigger baby than the cop about to go to jail. "I'm no criminal," beefcake Grettler had insisted in an interrogation room in Building 77, a floor below his old buddy's new workplace, as he begged for a chance to roll over on his friends. "I just like to party, and I got in with the wrong crowd."

Spota had links to some of the defendants, and he appeared to acknowledge it. At least three of the defendants—a Suffolk police officer, a car salesman, and a local gym owner—had worked on Spota's campaign. "It's disheartening to me," Spota lamented when asked about his relationship with the defendants. "But nonetheless, I took an oath to enforce the law."

For all his practiced new-sheriff-in-town indifference to the connections of his defendants, Spota didn't mention an initial prime suspect in the investigation: James Burke.

* * *

A flashy figure connected a lot of the indicted names in the drug ring. Marlowe Robert Walker III, a fast-talking wannabe film mogul, was Hauppauge's low-rent version of Jay Gatsby. He had wowed friends, especially cops, with his swell digs and apparent connections to Hollywood types like actor Danny Aiello. Starry-eyed cops from multiple departments had poured the excess from their hefty salaries into Walker's plan to build a film empire in Staten Island. Walker was pals with many of those indicted in the drug ring, and the father of one of the arrested cops had been named to the film company's board of directors. A detective sergeant in Burke's command had also invested tens of thousands of dollars and sat on the board.

A month before Spota was elected district attorney, Walker pleaded guilty to federal stock fraud. The aspiring movie-mogul cops lost most of their money, and Walker's buddies ended up the subjects of Internal Affairs eavesdroppers in a wire room in Hauppauge.

Among those targets was Burke. Larry Doyle, the IAB supervisor who ran the investigation, recalled that a photo of Burke was tacked to the wall of the wire room, along with that of his detective sergeant. The situation, Doyle acknowledged, was less than ideal—and showed the extent of Burke's insulation under Spota's wing. Any county wiretap had to be approved and overseen by the DA's office. So when Doyle's wiretap monitors reported that Burke was nowhere to be heard on intercepted phone calls, it was either evidence that he was clean, or that he had been tipped off by his colleagues in the DA's office.

Being the target of an investigation is far from proof of criminal guilt. It's feasible that Burke was a subject based only on a poor lead, perhaps from an informant looking to lessen a prison sentence. But when the case led to Spota touting the indictments of a group of drug-using cops—none of whom worked in his DAs office—Doyle and others were left to wonder if they had gotten them all, or just the ones Spota wanted them to get.

"It's like going fishing," Doyle, an understated cop, said when asked if he was satisfied with the case. "You never know if you caught the big one or not."

* * *

Bruce Barket wasn't a big Tom Spota guy, although he didn't have reason to doubt the new Suffolk DA either. Barket, a Connecticut native, was a former Nassau County prosecutor turned defense attorney. He was a droll, buttoned-up character whose clients tended to be the opposite. Barket's customers included Amy Fisher, the high school student whose attempted murder of the wife of her adult lover had kept supermarket tabloid publishers supplied with material for years.

Barket supported Spota's campaign despite knowing little about him, with the same reasoning as many: "He has to be better than Catterson." In return for a significant donation, Barket joined Spota in a luxury box for an Islanders hockey game. After Spota took office, Barket got a meeting with him to discuss new findings concerning the case against his latest headline-making client.

Martin Tankleff had been convicted in 1990 of using a watermelon knife and a sledgehammer to slash and bludgeon his parents to death two years earlier, when he was in high school. Combining gory violence, a lack of rational motive, and an affluent suburban setting, the Tankleff killings had captivated Long Island in a similar fashion to the Amityville and Pius cases of previous decades. By the time of Spota's election, Marty Tankleff was more than eleven years into a fifty-year prison sentence.

The case against Tankleff required leaps of logic. Detectives had explained the absence of blood on Marty's clothes and body by suggesting that he had murdered his parents while nude and then showered. His motive, they said, was a life insurance payout that he wouldn't even get for eight years.

From prison, Tankleff wrote to Jay Salpeter, a private investigator who agreed to examine his case for $5,000. Salpeter was immediately stunned by the dearth of evidence against Tankleff, and the leads pointing to better suspects who had been largely ignored. Salpeter brought the case to Barket, who agreed to represent Tankleff pro bono.

Early on in the investigation, multiple witnesses independently pointed police to the same suspect, a violent drug-world enforcer. A plot of pure Long Island noir emerged, implicating a business associate of Marty's father, Seymour Tankleff, who owed the dead man hundreds of thousands of dollars.

The associate, Jerry Steuerman, called himself the "Bagel King of Long Island" and wore a gold pendant of his signature food product around his neck. He was the last known guest at the Tankleff house during a poker game with Seymour on the night of the murders. He had shortly afterward cleared out his bank accounts, including one shared with Seymour, and fled to California under an assumed name. But detectives never seriously considered him as a suspect. "That man couldn't hurt a fly," explained Detective James McCready, displaying the signature Suffolk lawman gift for telepathy.

Barket filled in Spota on potential new witnesses, which included a convicted burglar who said he had taken part in the killings.

Spota seemed amenable to investigating the new findings. He made sure Barket was aware that he had a connection to that case, in that he had previously represented McCready, but didn't consider that to be a conflict. He said his office would look into it, and Barket left the meeting hopeful that his client could avoid a drawn-out legal battle to get the new evidence heard.

* * *

At first, Tom Spota had little interest in investigating the bad acts of public officials. After all, that kind of stuff had been a major element of Catterson's downfall, and Spota's mandate was basically to be the opposite of Catterson. But when a low-hanging legislator, as one investigator called Fred Towle, plopped down for an interrogation and sang like a mob canary, Spota and Burke began to think about hunting some larger game.

It started with an anonymous letter. Towle, a Brookhaven legislator, had been a usual suspect for chicanery going back a decade, to his days as a well-connected microfilm boy in the county clerk's office. After $100,000 in quarters had gone missing from that office, Towle crashed his county car and, according to lore, splashed coins all around the accident site. Catterson claimed there wasn't enough evidence to prosecute his fellow Republican for the missing quarters.

The new stuff was bigger than an alleged coin heist. The public didn't learn of it until Towle made a light-on-specifics guilty plea in a Riverhead courthouse, with McPartland silently watching from the prosecutor's table. Towle admitted to accepting bribes, and also to using his official position to grease at least one real estate deal. A well-prepped *Newsday* photog shot Towle as the grifter politician waddled sadly out of the courtroom.

What remained secret was that Towle had been a walking tape recorder for several months. Suffolk County residents had long derided his town as "Crookhaven," and now they watched its corrupt string-pullers paraded into courthouses in front of waiting cameras. Towle spilled dirt on some grotesque deep-sea creatures of Long Island politics: the no-show town employee known as Tony Tickets because he sold access to Republican fundraisers; a parks commissioner charged with trading town sand to a little league for a campaign donation; a building inspector whose alleged schemes included using a town worker as a babysitter and rigging a raffle for a Derek Jeter–autographed baseball.

Seemingly every dirty politician the investigation hooked was ready to roll over on their entire Rolodex. The Brookhaven arrests topped a dozen and kept running. John Rodriguez, used to interrogating gang members jaded by long rap sheets, considered it almost a vacation to build cases against criminal amateurs who, for example, didn't realize when they were free to leave. "The white-collar politician people, they're soft people," Rodriguez mused. "They're going to give you information not knowing they're burying themselves."

Political perp walks proved remarkably good for business. Spota and Burke each had their favorite *Newsday* reporters, some of them going back to the earliest days of the Pius case. They now put their public relations skills to work, infusing their efforts in Brookhaven with the excitement of an organized crime takedown. Spota's office had "beefed up its public integrity unit with seasoned detectives, interviewed hundreds of witnesses, issued scores of subpoenas and convened two special grand juries," read a breathless *Newsday* story about the Brookhaven probe.

"We are investigating an insular organization," Burke was quoted in the article. "You do wiretaps and bugs and utilize cooperators. That's how you make mob cases."

In an actual mob case, your ultimate goal is to bring down the don. But Spota threw felony charges at low- or midlevel perps, and appeared mostly disinterested in whether those charges would stick. The accused sand thief, for example, was initially charged with a felony but pleaded it down to the equivalent of a parking ticket.

When Spota did get a boss in his crosshairs, he turned transactional. There was a swap-meet nature to his prosecutions of the big guys. For example, by the time the public learned of the arrest of Islip town supervisor Pete McGowan for stealing from his own campaign fund, a plea deal had already been hammered out. McGowan agreed to forfeit to Spota's office the $1 million-plus in his campaign chest and serve a few months in jail.

While a DA usually slams the perp he just condemned to jail, in this case Spota told the media that McGowan "has done so much good for the town of Islip and the county of Suffolk." He vowed to return the forfeited campaign funds to McGowan's donors but ended up retaining the majority of it. His office spent the cash on cameras, police dogs, and "crime-fighting," which in his office had a broad definition.

* * *

Johnny Rodriguez didn't make it to the finish line of the Brookhaven probe. After he warred with supervisors around 2005, Burke interceded with what he deemed a better assignment for Rodriguez anyway: a newly formed Terrorist Task Force.

Burke and Rodriguez laid out their anti-terror plan in a meeting, essentially describing a Muslim monitoring operation mirroring a similar effort in the NYPD. SCPD would use undercovers to infiltrate mosques and other places whether Muslims gathered. They would then keep tabs on their targets by arresting and prosecuting them for even the most minor crimes. "The idea was to go in there and lock these people up for any crime that was observed and start documenting these people," Rodriguez later explained.

Among those at the meeting was Jim Rooney, the commander of the SCPD's Criminal Intelligence Bureau. Rooney, who sported spectacles and a giant white Monopoly Man–style mustache crawling from cheek to cheek, was a former colonel in the US Marines with a couple of master's degrees. He didn't hide how unimpressed he was with Jimmy and Johnny Rod's plan, but not because of the glaring civil liberty issues. The commander lectured them on the sophisticated planning that the FBI undertakes in advance of an operation like this, including deploying highly trained agents whose fake identities and background stories are well rehearsed and backed up by expertly doctored documents.

"Who are we going to get to do it?" Rooney said mockingly, the jostling of his absurd mustache contributing to the ridicule. He turned to Rodriguez. "You? You're going to do it?"

Indignant, Rodriguez shot back: "Yeah, I'll give it a shot."

Rodriguez spent the next week trying to figure out how he, a lanky Hispanic dude with a megaphone of a New York accent, would go undercover in a mosque. His cover story, he decided, was that his Turkish father had recently passed away, and that he was trying to honor his memory by converting. Rodriguez shared with Burke his plan to go to Queens to buy Muslim garb and a Koran, and to start studying.

"John, you can do this," Burke encouraged him, adding of Rooney: "Don't think I didn't notice the way that motherfucker spoke to you."

* * *

In 2003, Burke, always an ace on police tests, finished first among eight candidates on the captain's civil service exam. The exams, for promotion to the ranks of sergeant, lieutenant, and captain, were a mostly futile effort to rein in nepotism in the department. A typical rising captain would have transferred into the first command that came open. Burke couldn't stay in the DA's office as a captain, because union rules barred captains from investigative command. But those rules didn't work for Jimmy Burke, who had no interest in abandoning the protective bubble of the DA's office.

On October 17, 2003, James Burke wore white gloves, an eight-point cap, and the rest of the full dress uniform to a conference room at police HQ. It was his promotion ceremony to captain. On paper, he was transferred to the commissioner's office. But he never actually moved a paperclip. His run in the commissioner's office lasted one pay period. On November 3, Commissioner Gallagher promoted him to deputy inspector. The promotion allowed Burke to return to his gig as commanding officer of the District Attorney Section.

Less than a year later, Burke's little empire expanded. He was promoted to commanding officer of the Organized Crime Bureau. The bureau oversaw not only the DA Section but also Criminal Intelligence. Typically, the commanding officer of the Organized Crime Bureau reported to the SCPD's chief of detectives. Instead, the org chart was rejiggered so Burke reported to the commissioner, meaning he was largely free of oversight.

The following year, in February 2005, Burke once again broke out the eight-point hat and gloves. Gallagher had promoted him to inspector. The department standard was that every promotion triggered a transfer, the idea being that a boss supervising their former peers leads to potential conflicts of interest. An inconvenient rule was ignored in Burke's case yet again.

Soon after, yet another unprecedented personnel move ballooned Burke's team of investigators. The DA's office had two detective units: the squad of police investigators that Burke had run since 2002, and a unit of detective-investigators, or DIs, who were employees of the DA's office. After the DI unit boss retired, Burke was supposed to lead a search for a new chief of that unit. Instead, Burke emulated Dick Cheney's search for a vice president candidate and landed on himself. Spota duly named him chief inspector, putting Burke in charge of both sides of the house. He oversaw about fifty sworn police detectives and an equal number of detective-investigators.

So when Burke motherfuckered Jim Rooney for not appreciating his and Rodriguez's Muslim plan, it wasn't just hot air. He had the influence to punish even a top cop like Rooney for getting on his bad side. Rooney "got rocketed," the cop term for an unwanted transfer, to the Arson Squad. Burke peacocked about it to Rodriguez: "He won't speak to my fucking guys like that." In reality, banishing Rooney to a far less politically powerful unit was also Burke's way of freeing up the top job in a boutique unit, to be filled by a handpicked lackey.

A couple of months had passed since Hickey called to crow about Pat Cuff, and Burke hadn't forgotten the chummy feelings. So he reached down and grabbed Hickey, a largely unknown midnight lieutenant with a perjury rap, and gave him one of the most desirable positions in the department: commanding officer of Criminal Intelligence.

When Cuff heard of the transfer, he knew immediately what had happened. Any conversation with Hickey, he realized, had Jimmy Burke listening in too.

Hickey started to see what Jimmy meant by "get in the game." Jimmy's career was laden with perks, some more conventional than others. One of Hickey's first details in Intel was overseeing security at a counterterrorism conference at the Hyatt Regency in Hauppauge. Burke and Spota both hosted sessions. At the bar after the event, Spota hugged Hickey and said: "You're in the inner circle now." The closed-to-media conference was put on by a pro-Israel national security lobbying concern chaired by a real estate mogul. Shortly afterward, the group arranged for Jimmy to travel to Israel as part of a "law enforcement exchange program." It's unknown if Jimmy had time to check out the Sea of Galilee while he was there, but he was wowed by one element of the trip: the real estate mogul's much younger wife. After the mogul died a few years later, Jimmy and his widow were an item, with Jimmy being wheeled around in her Bentley.

* * *

Johnny Rodriguez said he dutifully spent more than a year, in traditional Muslim clothing and a beard, stalking Masjid Darul Quran, a major mosque in Bay Shore. After about six months, he reported "making mosque friends," he said, with leads on some drugs and weapons crimes. His goal was to get one of his targets to agree to buy a rocket launcher. None of that panned out. In the end, Rodriguez said the most serious crime he had was that of a halal meat merchant who may have been making illegal loans.

A top prosecutor overseeing the terror sting questioned the worth in charging misdemeanors. Rodriguez fumed, but eventually he abandoned the undercover project. After all, he hated it, particularly kneeling on a prayer rug and having his face next to an "older foreign man with green fungal toenails," which he said on a rainy day was "like being with a bunch of wet dogs."

"Nobody's heart was really in it, and I'm the asshole with a dirty beard," complained Rodriguez, adding that the detail was messing with his social life: "I can't talk to a girl because I look like a fucking Muslim."

For perhaps obvious reasons, the DA's office never publicized the abortive mosque sting. There is little evidence of its existence apart from a few surveillance photos of Rodriguez undercover that he keeps in a portfolio. They include a shot of the cop, in kaftan and skullcap and holding a flagpole, having joined New York City's Muslim Day Parade, or as he put it, "these idiots in pajamas on Fifth Avenue." Much like the larger NYPD Muslim surveillance program that it emulated, the Suffolk mosque sting went nowhere. The NYPD version led to litigation and class action discrimination suits. But to Rodriguez, the operation just showed how clever Jimmy Burke was.

"That was a year and a half assignment that the police department didn't even know about," Rodriguez said, adding: "This was Burke at his best. Nobody had the balls to do this."

* * *

While Jimmy was building an empire, his high school pal Michael Quartararo had spent more than a decade figuring out how to show remorse for a crime he maintained he hadn't committed. Quartararo had been sent back to prison in 1990 following his retrial conviction, and he soon became a human pinball in the correctional bureaucracy.

In 1992, his good behavior earned him access to a program allowing him to spend workdays commuting from a Queens prison to a job, and weekends at home with his family. *Newsday* found out and published a story headlined "John Pius Killer on Work Release." Barbara Pius demanded that the "sicko" be returned to prison. The DA's office made vague assertions about a fellow inmate who claimed Quartararo had said Barbara ought to be dead like her son. Quartararo was stripped of work release and stuffed in an isolation cell.

He was first eligible for parole that year, a process that turned into a Kafkaesque puzzle. Quartararo had an ongoing appeal, and anything he said during the parole hearings could be used against him in his case. Parole officials repeatedly assured him that he was under no obligation to confess his guilt. But then they punished him for not doing so. "We don't want to force you to show remorse or say anything that is inconsistent with your appeal," a parole board member assured him, and then asked if Quartararo had anything to say about the murder.

"I guess what I'd like to say is that I'm extremely sorry that John Pius died," Quartararo responded.

"Listen, you can't have your cake and eat it too," the board member interjected. "I mean, you can't say, 'I don't want to discuss the crime,' and say, 'Oh, I'm really sorry he died.'"

He went before the board every two years, touting his exemplary prison record, his acceptance to law school, his wife who needed him on the outside. The ensuing rejections were condemnations of his lack of remorse. "You have yet to confront and fully address the causative factors underlying your conviction," the board lamented one go-round. "Your intellectualism of the crime has given us an impression of insensitivity on your part," they ruled another year. "I don't get that you have internalized guilt in this case," a board member told Quartararo in a third session.

One board member was removed from Quartararo's case for improperly considering, in her decision to deny him parole, Peter's confession and news stories about the case. A judge ordered Quartararo released, ruling that the board "misconstrued its role, power and duty." An appeals court then overturned that order, and Quartararo remained imprisoned.

In 1998, US District Court Judge Joanna Seybert ruled on Quartararo's latest appeal, finding that the evidence in his retrial was not only "overwhelmingly weak, but insufficient as a matter of law." Seybert found that without Peter's confession, the case was built almost entirely on the statements of Jimmy Burke and other former teenage friends. She seized on Jimmy's oddly recycled testimony in the Quartararo retrial and Rob Brensic's trial, in which he said that each defendant said "the pigs fucked it up" and that they'd never be caught. "The striking similarity tends to diminish the reliability of the statement reportedly made by [Quartararo] in the same month and year and in the exact same location where Brensic's statements were made," Seybert wrote.

Seybert also found that even if Jimmy and the rest were to be fully believed, none of their statements, which she called "plagued with ambiguity," fulfilled the legal definition of the murder charge on which Quartararo was convicted. "No rational juror could have found the elements of intentional murder beyond a reasonable doubt," Seybert ruled. She ordered Quartararo released and even dismissed the indictment against him.

Suddenly a free man, Quartararo quickly found work at a Manhattan law firm. But then a higher federal court overturned Seybert's decision, attesting to the "combined inculpatory effect" of the alleged statements recited by Jimmy Burke and the others. Quartararo was forced to report back to prison, his appeals exhausted. Yet another judge then ruled that Quartararo had been wrongfully denied work release. In 2000, he returned to his job at the law firm. After four years of commuting by subway from his double-occupancy Manhattan jail cell to the litigation firm where he was rising up the administrative ranks, Quartararo was paroled at age thirty-nine. He had served a total of twenty-one years in prison for a murder that occurred when he was fourteen.

Tom Ryan was always the loose end. By 2002, he was the last man in prison seven days a week for a killing in which the prosecution admitted he was the least culpable. That year, a three-judge federal appellate court, among them future US Supreme Court Justice Sonia Sotomayor, granted Ryan's appeal. The judges found that the detectives' testimony hinting at Peter's confession could have tilted the jury against Ryan in a retrial where the evidence was scant, consisting only of Anne Erickson's coaxed-along testimony.

Ryan was freed on bail, and in 2003, the Suffolk DA's office—now helmed by Spota—prepared to take him to trial for a fourth time. Ryan had been in a similar spot thirteen years earlier, and he had turned down freedom in the form of a plea deal that required him to admit guilt. Because of that decision, he had missed all but the infant years of his son's childhood.

If it was just up to him, Ryan might've taken it to trial again to see how the testimony of his ex-flame from Trappers held up thirty years later. But his wife, Jodi, who had encouraged him to keep fighting at the previous retrial, needed her husband free more than she needed him vindicated.

"It was no longer can we help you prove your innocence," Jodi explained. "The question was can you get out of jail or are you going to spend the rest of your life there.

"I did ask him to compromise his principles," Jodi added. And when Ryan resisted, that ask became a demand.

On June 20, 2003, Ryan told a courtroom that on that April night in 1979 he had driven his friends back to Dogwood Elementary to search for Pius. He let them out of the car, and by the time he caught up to them, Johnny was motionless.

He pleaded to manslaughter. It was the third conviction in the Pius case, each of them with a markedly different account of the murder. Including Peter's eight years before his conviction was overturned, the four boys spent a total of fifty-five years imprisoned.

Spota watched Ryan's guilty plea from the second row of the courtroom audience. "I came to watch something that I started a long time ago," he remarked to a newspaper reporter, before snarking with a glance towards Ryan: "He's put on some weight."

That October, Justice Michael Mullen, Patrick Henry's former number-two, sentenced Ryan to five to fifteen years in prison. The maximum punishment was less than what Ryan had already served. "You have no feelings at all today, just that this is finally behind you?" the judge asked.

"I have feelings," Ryan shot back, but he said nothing more. He was free.

Jodi borrowed her dad's conversion van, and she and Tom loaded it with roughly ten boxes full of documents concerning the case. They headed up to a friend's house in the Adirondacks. There they fed the records into a bonfire. They drank beers and margaritas while watching the case that had ruled their lives turn into black ash.

The transcripts of nine murder trials, combined with three decades worth of related paperwork, can keep you warm for quite a long time. "The fire raged on for a while," Tom said.

* * *

Jimmy Burke, boss of one hundred detectives, still wasn't satisfied. James Hickey learned that while he, Jimmy, and Tom Spota were eating steak at Peter Luger in Great Neck. Conversation turned, as it always did, to how they were going to take over the county. Blowing a bit of smoke up the old man's ass, Hickey told Spota that he'd make a great police commissioner. He then felt a shoe plow into his shin under the table.

Jimmy later pulled him aside, seething. "Don't ever say that," he told Hickey. "Because some day, I want to be police commissioner."

But Jimmy's grand vision was always subject to revision. He realized at some point that the Suffolk police commissioner, who was on a set pay scale, made much less money than the Suffolk police chief. The commissioner also faced a far more arduous vetting process than the chief. So he outlined a new plan one day while driving around in his car with Hickey and another acolyte, Bill Madigan.

Hickey and Madigan were, not quite comfortably, lumped together as Burke's rescue puppies. Since 2004, Madigan had been the detective lieutenant in charge of the DA's Rackets squad, reporting to Burke. The reed-thin Madigan posed for his department photo with a creased frown and with his hand cradling his chin as if he were the Suffolk Thinker. After all, he was an intellectual, finishing up a law degree at Touro College in Central Islip. But the brainiac act wasn't extremely convincing. Madigan was prone to shouting fits and seeming ethical lapses. Seasoned cops didn't think much of his investigation skills either. All of that was fine with Burke, who preferred to have the biggest brain in his crew.

Jimmy told his middle-aged disciples his new plan. He'd be chief of department one day. Madigan would be chief of detectives. And Hickey would be chief of patrol. Jimmy said he would expect only one thing in return for putting his broken wings in powerful jobs: "Loyalty above all."

CHAPTER 14

THE ADMINISTRATION

The genesis of Burke and Spota's greatest coup came in 2001, the year before they moved into the DA's office, in the auspicious form of a coke buy in an Applebee's bathroom. Suffolk drug cop Phil Alvarez made the two-ounce undercover buy in 2001. When the involved parties returned to the bar, the coke dealer introduced Alvarez to a buddy. He was a slightly pudgy fellow with a small halo of stringy dark hair. In wiseguy character, Alvarez introduced himself as Mike, a contractor.

When the cocaine dealer turned his back, the pal pushed a cocktail napkin toward Alvarez. It was scrawled with his name and number. "I can get you a county contract from Route 110 out to Montauk, call me sometime," the guy said. When Alvarez rejoined his colleagues on surveillance outside, they informed him that the cocktail napkin character was a former Democratic county legislator by the name of Wayne Prospect.

Alvarez wasn't big on political corruption, but he knew a criminal lead when he had one. He called up Prospect and they became buddies, their favorite destination being Melville's most popular strip club for sketchy networking: Gossip.

Prospect swore the dancers, particularly the Russians, were infatuated with him. Alvarez bided his time, every so often needling Prospect about county contracts while watching the poor schmuck get rolled by his imaginary girlfriends. His patience began to pay off when Prospect introduced him to another pal, Stephen Baranello. Alvarez was getting closer to the heart of the Democratic machine in Suffolk County. Baranello's father, Dominic, was the former long-time leader of the county's Democratic Party, the very man who had authorized Judge Namm's ouster in 1992. Prospect and the younger Baranello were advisors to Steve Levy, an assemblyman preparing a run for county executive, the top elected position in Suffolk. Baranello in particular was Levy's right-hand man.

Once Tom Spota learned that Stephen Baranello was a subject of the investigation, Alvarez found himself abruptly transferred to the DA Section working under Burke and McPartland. He was told to bring his undercover tapes with him.

Spota had a couple of possible reasons for his interest in the investigation. The first reason was to create the illusion of fairness: he could use the case to avoid accusations of selective enforcement like his predecessor. "Now he had a chance to go after the Democrats, which would make him look like a bipartisan DA," Alvarez said.

The second reason didn't become obvious until later. Levy was, on paper, Spota's understudy in Suffolk County Democratic politics. He had voiced his own ambitions while watching the confetti fall on Spota's victory party at the Smithtown Sheraton. Levy grabbed Democratic leader Richie Schaffer by the arm and declared that he wanted to talk about running for county executive in 2003. Republicans had held the top spot since the late 1980s, but Spota's election signaled that Democrats were finally relevant again in Suffolk County. After Levy officially announced his candidacy, he followed Spota's lead by promising to clean up Brookhaven.

Spota and Levy both had amorphous political convictions. Spota had just switched parties to get into the DA chair. Levy's only consistent principle was that of fiscal conservatism. That put him on a collision course with the budget-busting contract demands of cops. Those cops, not the Democratic Party, were Spota's real base. He had reason to see Levy as a potential threat.

Jimmy Burke's ambition provided an even simpler motive for seeking control over Levy: the county executive got to choose who ran the police department.

* * *

Alvarez and his colleagues documented thousands of hours of undercover and wiretap tape, and Prospect and Baranello proved to be naturals in their roles as dirty politicians, with bickering worthy of a Coen brothers script. They loathed each other and tried to cut each other out of the graft. "Nervous Nelly!" Baranello berated Prospect, perhaps the first time that insult had been uttered on a criminal wire. In another conversation, Baranello hyped the undercover cop Alvarez: "Hey, listen, we're both moving up to the major leagues together."

Still a drug cop at heart, Alvarez's investigative philosophy was that if you're not speaking Spanish, you haven't bought enough cocaine—meaning, keep going up the ladder until you get to the boss. While it didn't pan out, at the time he believed that the kingpin in this case could be Steve Levy. Baranello had an extended conversation with Levy every night before going to bed. With wiretap reels running, Burke, McPartland, and Spota had unfettered access to the pajama talk of the man who might win the top elected job in the county.

Alvarez never got close enough to Levy to attempt to solicit a bribe or make any other sort of case on him. Baranello was too protective of his boss for that to happen. But Spota's office white-hatted a public works official who Prospect and Baranello tried to involve in their schemes. The pols discussed the finer points of bribery at a Hauppauge greasy spoon with a listening device hidden in a napkin holder. An undercover detective posed as their busboy.

With the investigation into his aides still a secret, Levy won election as county executive in 2003. He replaced police commissioner Gallagher with Richard Dormer, an old-school former chief of the department who still had the boyhood brogue of his native Ireland.

In 2004, the DA's office finally moved on Alvarez's targets. Baranello flipped on Prospect. At trial, Baranello insisted Levy had no knowledge of the illegal acts his right-hand man was committing, saying: "He probably would have punched me in the face." Prospect and Baranello were both convicted of bribery.

Long Islanders had to wonder about the wiretap tapes. What else did their county executive say on them? Spota refused to release the audio. The public got just a transcript of a single conversation, buried in documents in the Prospect trial, in which Levy ranted about how he needed a "set of eyes" in the Board of Elections and Public Works, and referred to a rival as a "fucking prick." Levy, who argued against the release of the wiretaps to the media, insisted there was nothing more damning in them than profane politicking. "Salty language," he said.

* * *

In the late 1970s, an epiphany struck mechanical engineer Gerald Jacino when he spotted the detritus of his kids' push-up ice cream pops on his porch. The plastic disc that pushed the ice cream up might work with other materials. Jacino and his brother Tony, a car dealer, spent months in their basements toying with the disc until they had transformed it into the obscure patentable device of their dreams. Next came the write-up in *Popular Science*, signing with Walmart, the bigness in Japan following a contract there. But engineering one of the world's most popular do-it-yourself tools for repairing car windshields—basically that ice cream pop disc connected to an epoxy syringe—tore the brothers apart. Next came accusations of theft, litigation, and, in the early 2000s, professional divorce.

In the split, Gerald got the company headquarters, a low-slung beige brick building in industrial Hauppauge. He now only needed a third of the square footage, and he put the rest up for lease. The man who rented the extra space seemed more concerned with discretion than feng shui. Their initial agreement was for $4,807 in rent for 4,600 square feet.

Gerald's employees knew not to ask any questions about the business of the new corporate neighbors, gruff men with gun bulges at the lower edges of their polo shirts. A computer company later rented space in the same building. Every once in a while, a corporate neighbor on a smoke break might see a harried-looking subject hustled into the building by one of these men. The smokers learned to avert their eyes.

Gerald agreed never to use his keys to enter the mystery tenant's portion of the building, even at night, without scheduling it first. If he had entered unannounced and gone down to the basement, he might have witnessed—according to an affidavit of a man who claimed he was brought there—such sights as a detective slamming a perp's head against a wall while being watched over by a foreboding bald man in a suit.

The only insignia on the building's facade was one of Gerald's trademarks: Blue Star. There was no indication of who had moved in, other than the dibs that the new tenants had put on choice parking spots. Small placards marking the two spots near the door read:

RESERVED

DA

* * *

During a 2014 appearance on Frank MacKay's radio show, Spota tacitly acknowledged the cloak-and-dagger operation at the secret location his office had been using for eight years. The DA explained: "We do corruption cases out of a separate location that nobody knows about, and when I say nobody knows about—it's in an area that, or in a location, that is, um . . . " Perhaps catching himself in mid overshare, Spota abruptly pivoted: ". . . and for good reasons. If we are asking certain individuals to come in to talk to us, to further our investigation, nobody will ever know that they were at our office."

The Blue Star building, rented with asset forfeiture funds, housed the newly formed Government Corruption Bureau, helmed by Chris McPartland. No longer would Burke's guys have to hustle perps into rented hotel suites for interrogation. And instead of having to swap out rickety and recognizable county cars while on surveillance, they contracted with a nearby Enterprise to use their rental fleet. It might cost upward of a thousand dollars a car per month, but with sometimes hundreds of thousands of dollars in forfeiture funds coming in from a single prosecution, there was no need to fret over the margins.

The business of government corruption—or combating it, ostensibly—was booming for Spota, McPartland, and Burke. Or as they referred to themselves, "The Administration." Spota was reelected without opposition in 2005, largely on the basis of his perceived corruption crackdown. He was cross-endorsed by Republicans. *Newsday* chided this agreement for robbing voters of a choice, but only half-heartedly. "Spota has done a solid, nonpartisan job of prosecuting political corruption," wrote the paper's editorial board. "Even so, this crucial office deserves a real contest. We would almost certainly have endorsed him, because it would have been difficult for the GOP to find a better candidate. But they should have tried."

The *New York Times* editorial board had that year denigrated Nassau County DA Denis Dillon by comparing him to Spota: "One need only look at his counterpart in Suffolk County, Thomas Spota, to see what an aggressive, creative prosecutor can do to clean up a rotted political culture."

Success only enhanced the cozy air of Spota's network. In 2006, Spota hired Anthony Palumbo, the old homicide bull who had secured Peter Quartararo's confession. He had retired from the department in the midst of the SIC investigation in 1986, cashing in his twenty-three years. When he came back twenty years later, his new boss was the key teenage witness from his career's biggest case. Because Palumbo was already drawing a police pension, Spota had to apply for a special waiver to hire him as an assistant special investigator. The waiver application declared that Palumbo would be tasked with "intensifying investigations into criminal activity in the following area: medicaid fraud, school district financial fraud and income/sales tax evasion."

In reality, the nature of Palumbo's work over the next several years was janitorial: he served as the mop-up man for public officials who Spota wanted shielded from criminal trouble. When a drunken off-duty Nassau cop bar-hopping in Suffolk opened fire on an unarmed cabdriver, Palumbo was on the case. He used a later-debunked confession to assist a prosecutor in charging the cabbie with felony assault. That prosecution was ultimately dismissed and the police shooting was found to be unjustified by Nassau's Internal Affairs. When Suffolk sheriff's deputy Thomas Pendick was under investigation for sexual assault charges, Palumbo took over the investigation and helped steer it toward a "sweetheart deal," according to Susan Onorato, the prosecutor who worked the case with him. Pendick walked, and he even remained employed with the sheriff's department.

Years later, Palumbo tried to use the handling of that case as a template for how they should give a pass to Spota crony Ed Walsh, a political leader accused of bilking his jail job. Palumbo asked of an Internal Affairs investigator: "Why don't you take care of the Walsh thing in-house like you did that rapist Pendick and stip him out to retire when he gets his time in?"

* * *

The beauty of the Government Corruption Bureau was the broadness of its mandate, which was to "focus on the investigation and prosecution of crimes arising from corrupt practices within all municipalities in Suffolk County." The Administration used that vague mission, and the bureau's inherent secrecy, to gather and wield valuable political intel for reasons having little to do with law enforcement.

Sometimes the plan worked too well.

Defense attorney Bob Macedonio was a conduit to all things sleazy in Suffolk County. He was thickly built with slicked-back dark hair, and so devoted to Polo Ralph Lauren that he eventually got its horseman logo tattooed on his left breast. He liked to roll up to court in a Bentley, wearing a mink coat and a diamond tennis bracelet borrowed from a rapper client. Half the Suffolk bar had heard rumors about his proclivity for fifteen-martini nights, a ceramic rooster said to be full of cocaine, and his chumminess with, as one judge friend put it, "50 Cents and 25 Cents and whatever these guys are." It was a reference to his relationship with the rap star 50 Cent and his oft-arrested buddies in the hip-hop collective known as G-Unit.

In the craggier corners of Suffolk County, Macedonio was an unpopular name. Back in the 1980s, Bob's father, a police detective named Carmine, had refused to drop a sex abuse complaint against a well-connected investigator in Patrick Henry's office who was accused of sexually assaulting a teenage girl. After getting sex charges filed against the investigator in Vermont, Carmine had been chased out of the police department.

So when an informant jammed up on a drug deal started dishing actionable dirt not on fellow dealers, but on his own attorney—Bob Macedonio—it got Tom Spota's attention. Macedonio was at the time exploring a run for Brookhaven Republican leader, which would give him control of the county's most notorious patronage pit. Eavesdropping on his phone conversations, then, was a conduit to gossip on practically every influential Republican in Suffolk.

John Gang, one of the narcotics detectives who got the initial lead about Macedonio, recalled they were called to a hastily-arranged meeting of the heavyweights of the DA's office, including Spota himself. Afterward Gang and the other detectives were informed that they now worked at the Blue Star building, and were not even to tell their on-paper boss in Narcotics what they were doing.

Macedonio was so awash in suspicious activity that the Government Corruption Bureau had several avenues to choose from in getting a judge to authorize a wiretap on his cell phone in 2007. Spota signed the eavesdropping affidavits, Burke steered the investigation, and McPartland at times manned the wiretap himself.

The calls showed that Macedonio was a political bag man, constantly boasting about backroom deals involving public officials breaking the law. Macedonio had no political position, and he eventually dropped his bid to be Republican leader. But the Blue Star cops found that he still had influence, writing after eavesdropping on his calls that "it has become clear that Robert Macedonio acts as an official representative of the Brookhaven Republican Party." Macedonio's wiretapped conversations lifted up a rock on the slimy mechanisms ruling Suffolk County governance. The attorney boasted of using his unofficial influence to barter judgeships for patronage jobs and discussed brazen schemes to circumvent election law. Perhaps most of it was coked-up braggadocio, but investigators found some of the sleazier schemes Macedonio described were partly borne out by investigation.

Macedonio referred to an arrangement that would alarm almost any DA. A deputy bureau chief, one of Spota's top supervisors, John Scott Prudenti, was regularly chartering his smoke-belching boat to defense attorneys whose clients he was prosecuting. Booking a trip on Prudenti's forty-seven-foot *Christina Marie* was notorious among the defense bar. Though Prudenti charged for the charter trips, the boat often wouldn't even leave the harbor.

The cops heard Macedonio chattering about having allegedly influenced Prudenti to mislead a judge in order to get a violent felon out of prison early. They corroborated the broad strokes of the allegations, finding that Prudenti had falsely claimed the felon had volunteered his cooperation in another case. The felon had in turn been resentenced, but Prudenti hadn't documented those resentencings in his case file. Spota's top lieutenant, Emily Constant, later said that investigators were unable to find physical evidence to corroborate Macedonio's claims, including the items the prosecutor was said to have received in return for helping to secure the resentencing: two jet skis.

Prudenti was chummy with The Administration, and he had bulletproof family connections, including a cousin who was one of the top judges in the state. After the wiretap went up on Macedonio, Prudenti's call frequency with the defense attorney "plummeted," as Constant later put it, and she assumed somebody "tipped [him] off."

The wiretap operation, which lasted most of a year, was shaping up to generate explosive prosecutions and months of front-page headlines. The widespread investigation included scheming politicians, judges, prosecutors, defense attorneys, and more traditional street criminals. The cops followed Macedonio's connections to evidence they believed could be used to indict at least seventeen participants in the illicit drug trade, including dealers who had peddled to Long Island high school kids. Burke's guys at one point thwarted a drug-den robbery in progress based on wiretaps connected to the Macedonio probe.

But when it came time to bring charges, those investigators— pulled from elite SCPD drug or white-collar crime units—watched with disdain as The Administration stalled out the whole operation.

Spota wouldn't allow the investigators to even question Prudenti about the resentencings, or why he stopped speaking to Macedonio on the phone. And Spota had attended at least one party on Prudenti's boat that was paid for by defense firms, so it was perhaps unsurprising that he wasn't up for a legal exploration of the ethics of the *Christina Marie*. He promoted Prudenti, who had been previously convicted of impaired driving, to bureau chief of the Vehicular Crimes Bureau.

Constant, Spota's loyal number-two, later said that Spota gave a pass to another top public official who was implicated by the wiretap on Macedonio's phone. John Rouse, then the Brookhaven highway superintendent, talked frequently with Macedonio, though not always eagerly. "That is fine, but I do not want to have that conversation on this phone," Rouse responded during one call.

Rouse, a Democrat, wanted to be a Suffolk County judge. In one recorded call, Macedonio referred to Republican-controlled judgeships that were set to become available, asking Rouse if "we give you one of ours, is that something you'd be interested in?"

"Ah, you know, let me call you back on another phone," Rouse said, before doing so and telling Macedonio: "I'd be interested in it."

In a later call with a buddy, Macedonio discussed an alleged scheme in which Rouse—who was not on the call—would supposedly trade twelve highway positions to the Republicans in return for the party's cross-endorsement of his campaign for a judgeship.

A search warrant affidavit signed by Spota detailed these calls, but appeared careful to put the criminal blame on Macedonio, noting that the highway superintendent "has not solicited or even discussed a quid pro quo for a cross endorsement, judgeship or any other benefit in any of the conversations intercepted." Rouse's current lawyer, Megan Meier, recently described Macedonio's talk of trading taxpayer-funded jobs for a judgeship as the empty boasts of a "drug-addled wannabe Republican power broker."

By the account of Rouse's own attorneys, McPartland's central focus as far as he was concerned was a financial contribution made to his campaign by a local masonry company at Macedonio's behest. The Government Corruption Bureau apparently smelled a violation of campaign finance law, which dictated that candidates could not knowingly accept contributions made in another entity's name. McPartland beckoned Rouse and his defense lawyer to his office, where he played them what he believed were incriminating snippets of wiretap conversations.

Rouse's lawyer, Terry Karl, said that McPartland then asked Rouse to wear a wire, but he refused. Karl said the interrogation amounted to a "fishing expedition."

But others in the DA's office described it differently. Law enforcement officials who were there said Rouse cried during the meeting. (His attorney recently denied that.) And Constant years later told federal agents, as commemorated in a FBI memo, that Rouse, a former prosecutor who had once been a colleague of McPartland's in the DA's office, "acknowledged illegal conduct." That FBI memo documenting the interview with Constant states: "Nonetheless, Spota decided not to prosecute Rouse."

Meier, Rouse's current lawyer, said that Constant is "not a credible witness" because she wasn't present for the meeting. Rouse would indeed get his judgeship after being cross-endorsed by Republicans, but his election was five years after the intercepted calls with Macedonio. He remains a Suffolk County Supreme Court judge. Meier denied he broke the law, writing that Rouse "performed his duties with the highest integrity and does not deserve to be tarnished with the wrongdoing of others."

But it wasn't just a future judge to whom, according to his subordinates in the DA's office, Spota gave a pass. He wouldn't even go after the drug-world traffickers and robbers the wiretap turned up. Possibly, Spota couldn't take anybody to trial based on the intercepted chatter without risking their attorneys getting access to the wiretap tapes. The tapes implicated some of Spota's closest allies, and also, according to law enforcement officials with knowledge of the investigation, showed how the operation had flouted strict laws about not recording calls unrelated to targeted criminal activity.

So Spota apparently decided to let them all go, with the exception of some light plea deals, maxing out at nine months in jail, for a few of Macedonio's criminal associates. The investigators had expected to at least drop the hammer on Macedonio himself, a man who they had come to believe was more gangster than defense attorney. "It was like listening to *Better Call Saul*," one of the officials said of Macedonio's phone calls. They had flipped two of his closest alleged co-conspirators and wired them up to meet with him. Burke's investigators had raided his law office and seized his bank accounts and property.

Macedonio, who ranted on intercepted calls to criminal buddies about the identities of suspected rats and undercovers, took to meeting in Home Depot aisles. He communicated by jotting notes on pieces of paper that he then flushed down a public toilet. Prosecutors estimated in sealed filings that Macedonio's criminal proceeds topped $4 million. In a plea agreement, McPartland referred to Macedonio's alleged criminal conduct between 2003 and 2008, including selling cocaine, engaging in mortgage fraud, laundering money, and violating election law—charges Macedonio has said were not backed up by credible evidence.

Regardless, McPartland agreed to forgo all those charges if Mace-donio accepted a watered-down plea offer. Macedonio only had to plead to a single count of possession of less than $50 worth of co-caine and forfeit $50,000 to Spota's office. He wouldn't serve any jail time, though the felony conviction meant the automatic loss of his law license.

It appeared that Spota had bitten off more than he could chew with Macedonio. The cocaine-fueled attorney was on his phone at all hours, spewed damning information about seemingly everybody Spota knew. Now the DA wanted nothing more than for him to shut up, which gave Macedonio an odd form of leverage.

Three years after he accepted the plea, Macedonio filed a legal motion to overturn his plea. The specific filing was called an Arti-cle 440. Typically reserved for the wrongfully convicted, it was the same sort of motion that the legal team for Marty Tankleff had been fighting Spota over for years. But now Spota readily went along with Macedonio's version even though the statute didn't apply to the situa-tion. Macedonio had his felony conviction reduced to a misdemeanor. Detective Gang said of that development: "I wanted to puke."

Shortly afterward, now sober, Macedonio got his law license back and resumed his busy criminal defense practice. During the 440 hear-ing, Judge James Hudson congratulated Chris McPartland, who han-dled the proceedings on behalf of the DA's office, for recognizing a reformed defendant. The judge declared: "He shows that he's concerned not just with the letter of the law, but the spirit of justice as well."

* * *

"Fuck you!"

When McPartland's colleagues heard him yell that into his office phone, they knew immediately who was on the other end. Like teen-age best friends, he and Burke reserved that special greeting only for each other. If the "Fuck you!" was heard in the late morning, odds were Burke would soon arrive at Blue Star to pick up McPartland for lunch.

At first glance, McPartland seemed to have very little in com-mon with Burke. McPartland was a minivan-driving dad to three daughters, often seen in Northport toting around a giant diaper bag or braiding his girls' hair. He was fluent in French, cooked Caribbean cuisine, and liked reggae. He used to passably impersonate a bit from one of Eddie Murphy's albums in which the comedian's senile grandmother would ask in a high pitch: "Honey, what time is it?"

In his relationship with Burke, though, McPartland seemed to ditch his own persona in favor of his buddy's mob boss bravado. Chris grew pudgy, with a Shar-Pei–like wrinkle developing on the back of his head, and adopted a seemingly permanent scowl. The former renaissance man transformed into a goonish Burke henchman.

To John Rodriguez, McPartland's makeover felt like method acting. The detective recalled an instance in which he phoned his boss Burke from the street after having located a suspected perp. "Be right there!" Burke had barked. He drove up with McPartland riding shotgun, and both men were smoking cigars. McPartland swaggered up to the handcuffed man, threw him against a fence, and started jawing at him about how he was going to cooperate. Then McPartland tossed Rodriguez a gritty parting line, cigar still clenched in his teeth: "Listen, if this comes up, I was never here."

It bugged Rodriguez, perhaps with a pinch of jealousy mixed in, that this lawyer thought he was a tough guy. So he shot back: "You're here."

McPartland put his stogie-reeking face close to the cop's. "Rod, I don't think you understand. I was never here."

"You're here," Rodriguez said again. "You want to come play detective, you're here."

Rodriguez assumed that McPartland and Burke were both buzzed that day. If so, it was very likely after a session at Butterfields. From Blue Star, the trip was muscle memory: two quick turns, a left and a right, past the mowed grass, constant sprinklers, and low-slung facades of extremely dull industrial suburbia, to Jim Burke's favorite hangout.

* * *

The interior of Butterfields looked like a low-budget movie set of a high-end restaurant: linens, bulk-purchased modernist paintings and chandeliers, contrasted with exposed overhead rafters and piping. On their website, the owners spun the odd decor as a "Sophisticated Industrial Vibe." One of those owners, Michael Shalley, had been both a cop and a firefighter in the city, and he quickly struck up a bond with Burke. The bar owner was entertained by inner workings of "the cabal," as he termed the DA's crew that frequented his place.

Back in the day, Suffolk homicide bulls used to gather at Rao's in the city. Butterfields was the Government Corruption Bureau's version, where they always had their table waiting for them. They rarely ate when together, filling their bellies with vodka instead. If one of their inner circle got promoted, or an enemy got fucked, it was nearly unspoken that they were headed directly to Butterfields to celebrate—which meant that for about a decade-plus, they were there on an almost constant basis.

In 2009, Spota once again ran for DA without a challenger, the result of a "mega-cross-endorsement deal" between parties in which Republican officials were also endorsed by every major and minor political party. He would have been tough to beat out for a third four-year term, even without the deal shutting down potential challengers.

The coverage of Spota in the region-monopolizing newspaper was nearly an in-kind campaign contribution. "Thomas Spota has enjoyed such a sterling reputation as Suffolk County district attorney that it is not easy to find people willing to say anything remotely negative about him," read the first line of a news story—not opinion—in *Newsday* in 2008.

It wasn't just the local paper. The *New York Times* ran their own story that was nearly identical in tone. In it, even public officials from the opposing party lavished praise upon the Suffolk DA. "It's an accepted principle among Suffolk Republicans that Tom Spota is nonpartisan and evenhanded in his prosecutions," the *Times* quoted John V. N. Klein, a Republican former Suffolk County executive. Republican lobbyist Desmond Ryan gushed: "With the support of the electorate, Tom Spota could be district attorney forever. He commands that much respect."

Both publications allowed that if there had been a misstep in his tenure up to that point—or as *Newsday* put it, "the first chink in Spota's shining armor"—it was his handling of the Marty Tankleff case. Jimmy Burke's guys made sure to express their displeasure over the blemish.

* * *

The first envelope arrived at Jay Salpeter's office in 2004. It was post-marked from out of state, and Salpeter's address was spelled out using numbers and letters cut from a magazine, like a ransom letter in a movie. After Salpeter opened the envelope, he immediately sensed who was behind it: "Spota's little boy witness," as he called Burke.

The private investigator had made himself an enemy of The Administration by doing his job extremely well. His doggedness on be-half of Marty Tankleff had produced so much exculpatory evidence that Spota was finally forced to drop his objection to a 440 hearing to examine it all. Salpeter had even turned up a possible murder weapon. The burglar who had confessed to involvement gave him precise directions to a spot in the woods where one of his cronies had dropped a bloody pipe. At the indicated location, Salpeter found a thirty-six-inch steel cylinder.

Witness after witness, ranging from a son of one of the alleged hitmen to the cabinetmaker who worked on Jerry Steuerman's bagel shops, testified as to the Bagel King or his hired guns implicating themselves in the murders. Even the accused lead hitman himself, Joey "Guns" Creedon, gave testimony that was a boon to Tankleff's legal team. Creedon denied the murder but did allow that he was an enforcer for a bagel-shop-based drug operation run by Steuerman's son, Todd. Creedon recalled that Todd wanted to hire him on his dad's behalf to cut out Marty Tankleff's tongue. When Creedon declined the offer, he said, Todd shot him in the arm and then paid him $10,000 to shut up about the incident.

The testimony of these witnesses produced a daily drumbeat of embarrassing headlines for the DA's office. And Salpeter had made himself an easy mark for a determined nemesis. The hard-boiled former NYPD detective was an excellent investigator but a shit husband. Inside the magazine-text envelope was a letter pasted together in the same ransom collage method. The letter detailed the names and addresses of the various women with whom Salpeter had been having affairs. The information was so accurate that either he was being tailed throughout New York City and Long Island, or there had been a tracking device on his Mercedes-Benz. Salpeter knew the letter had to do with the Tankleff case, and the unstated message was clear: stop digging or this will get worse.

Instead, Salpeter started ditching work early enough to get home before his wife could get to the mailbox. He succeeded in intercepting a similar letter that was addressed to her. But then his parents were in a severe car accident in Florida, and while he was down there, his wife called. She had gotten one of the letters identifying Salpeter's mistresses, including women named April and June. "What are you, going through the fucking calendar?" his wife, a schoolteacher, screamed. She divorced him not long after.

Though he realized his wasn't the most sympathetic tale, Salpeter was still bitter. Suffolk cops had conspired to blow up his marriage because he was finding lawful evidence to exonerate his client. "Listen, I gave them the ammunition," Salpeter said. "And they shot the gun. And they didn't have to do that."

But it wasn't just the murder case anymore. Salpeter had also turned up witnesses who testified to unseemly connections between prosecutors and private attorneys. It was common knowledge that Spota had represented McCready, the Tankleff case's lead detective. Thanks to Salpeter it also emerged that Spota's legal partner, Gerry Sullivan, had previously represented both Steuerman and his son, the latter for dealing cocaine out of the bagel shops. Witnesses testified to seeing McCready and Steuerman conversing before the murders occurred, contradicting the detective's claims that he didn't know the Bagel King. Weirdest of all, following Marty Tankleff's conviction and imprisonment, McCready opened a bar with the husband of the convicted man's half-sister, whose inheritance from their parents increased due to Tankleff's conviction. It all perhaps shed some light on why Spota, who refused to recuse himself from appeal proceedings, was fighting so hard to keep Tankleff in prison.

Bruce Barket, Tankleff's attorney, soon experienced his own version of Salpeter's ransom note. In October 2005, the 440 hearing was still stretching on. After a court appearance in Riverhead, Barket was driving home on the Long Island Expressway in his new hunter-green Range Rover Sport. It was a Friday evening, and Barket's mind was pleasantly occupied. His wife was expected any day now to give birth to their first child, and the Yankees were in the playoffs.

Then the cop car behind him flicked on its lights. The officer told Barket he had a warrant out for his arrest for not paying a 1993 parking ticket. Handcuffed in the back of the patrol car, and fully aware that you can't be arrested in New York State for an unpaid parking ticket, Barket thought about previous traffic stops. The lawyer had a heavy foot and a curt manner, so it was strange that none of the cops who had stopped him before had turned up this twelve-year-old parking ticket warrant. In the precinct holding cells, the other inmates saw his suit and started asking him for legal advice. Barket, preoccupied with worry that his wife was going to go into labor while he was locked up, shot back: "Get yourself a lawyer that's not dumb enough to be in here with you."

A police supervisor recognized Barket. Befuddled by the arrest, the supervisor made sure to get him arraigned and out of custody ASAP. Barket was out that afternoon, but not before he experienced a little rough treatment. At first, he was determined to get to the bottom of the episode. He filed a notice of claim, a legal precursor to a lawsuit, over the false arrest. But his plate was full, so he decided to let the matter drop. "Be happy they pissed on your foot instead of breaking your knee," a buddy who had been in the DA's office told Barket. He tried to follow that advice.

As the Pius defendants knew well, Suffolk County clung to its most troubled prosecutions with a death grip. After Tankleff's 440 hearing ended in 2006, Judge Stephen Braslow derided Salpeter's "cavalcade of nefarious scoundrels paraded before this court" and denied his client's appeal. But the next year, a state appellate court rejected Braslow's decision and gave Tankleff a new trial. Spota then cut bait. Though he maintained that "the alternative murder plot theory was 'not supported by the credible evidence,'" Spota admitted that he didn't think Tankleff could be reconvicted.

Marty Tankleff ultimately reaped millions of dollars in damages for the seventeen years he wrongfully spent in prison, six of them on Spota's watch. A footnote to the civil matter showed how tenacious Suffolk County's legal establishment could be outside of court. Barket received through discovery every document the DA had on the murder. The records included an obsessive cache concerning Jay Salpeter: directions to his house from the DA's office, a diagram of his block, information on subpoenaing his phone and credit card bills, a detailed log of his NYPD career, and even information concerning his daughter, who was studying in Buffalo during Tankleff's hearing.

Salpeter and Barket took it as confirmation that the DA's office had been behind the letters. The black ops against both the investigator and the lawyer never had a chance to actually stop the hearing. "I think for Jay it was sport," Barket said. "For me, it was a lesson."

The lesson as he interpreted it was to stay on his side of the Suffolk-Nassau border going forward. Barket sold the Range Rover, as the incident with the old parking ticket had killed the new car thrill. Other lawyers heard rumors of his arrest and assumed it was a DUI. Barket turned the incident into a funny story for cocktail parties and golf courses. But he didn't actually think it was funny at all. Barket knew that compared to losing seventeen years of his life like Tankleff had, an afternoon in lockup was nothing. But the experience still bothered him.

If it hadn't been for that dumb arrest, this whole saga might have turned out very differently. Barket later said he wasn't looking for a way to get revenge, but when an opportunity presented itself six years later, he certainly wasn't about to turn it down.

The body of thirteen-year-old John Pius, as police encountered it on the early afternoon of April 21, 1979, behind Dogwood Elementary School in Smithtown, New York.

Suffolk County District Attorney's Office

ius's wallet, found near his body.

uffolk County District Attorney's Office

Pius's bicycle was leaning against a tree near his body when police arrived. That fact would become a vital tell in the statements and testimony of various witnesses, including Jimmy Burke.

Suffolk County District Attorney's Office

Pius's bloodstained clothes. He was wearing Puma sneakers, which had on their sole the same diamond-like pattern as an imprint on his face, suggesting Pius's killer wore the same sort of shoes.

Suffolk County District Attorney's Office

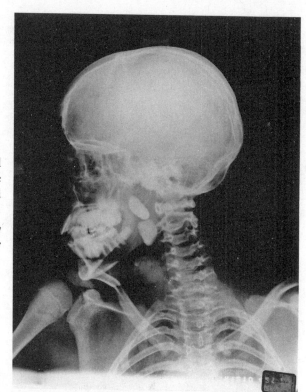

An x-ray of Pius's head and neck revealed the six stones jammed down his throat.

Suffolk County District Attorney's Office

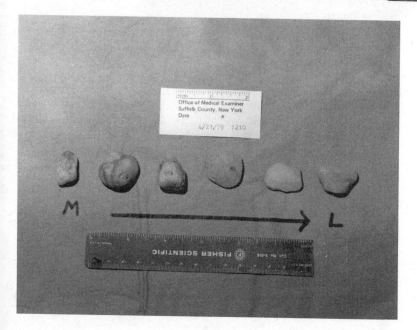

Police aerial photos showing (top to bottom) the area of Smithtown where the Pius family lived on Franklin Dr., the street leading off to the lower left of the photo; and the wooded area where John Pius's body was found. Cops and prosecutors said that on the night of April 20, 1979, Brensic, Ryan, and the Quartararos followed the trail from a beer depot to the Dogwood Elementary School.

Suffolk County District Attorney's Office

The junked minibike, with an estimated value of around $5, that teenagers Robert Brensic, Thomas Ryan, and Michael and Peter Quartararo stole on the evening of April 20, 1979. Detectives and prosecutors formed a theory that the boys killed Pius because he witnessed them with the stolen minibike.

Suffolk County
District Attorney's Office

The tape on which a detective captured the confession of fifteen-year-old Peter Quartararo, who had been in police custody for eight hours while cops lied to his parents about his whereabouts.

Suffolk County
District Attorney's Office

Tom Spota, a young prosecutor who had risen to a prominent position in the Suffolk County DA's office following his work on the famed Amityville slaying, led the Pius prosecution in which teenage Jimmy Burke became a key witness. The notoriety of the case later helped propel Spota to election as DA.

Suffolk County
District Attorney's Office

Thomas Spota

James Hickey's police career stalled when a judge accused him of perjury. But James Burke, who thanks to District Attorney Spota was on his way up the ranks despite his own checkered Internal Affairs history, saw potential in the compromised Hickey.

Eastern District of New York

Chris McPartland and Jimmy Burke; McPartland was Spota's top corruption prosecutor and Jimmy's best friend.

Eastern District of New York

The clandestine building in a Hauppauge industrial park where the DA's office ran their Government Corruption Bureau, led by McPartland.

Eastern District of New York

Butterfields, where the Government Corruption Bureau and its retinue plotted the takeover of Suffolk County, including how to replace its top elected official with a friendly.

Eastern District of New York

SCPD Organization Chart 2013–2015

Internal Affairs Bureau — Office of the Police Commissioner (Ed Webber) — Deputy Police Commissioner

James Burke
Chief of Department

GOVERNMENT EXHIBIT
801
17 CR 587 (JMA)

Dennis Sullivan
District Commander

William Madigan
Chief of Detectives

Mark White
Chief of Support Services

John Meehan
Chief of Patrol

Organized Crime Bureau

James Hickey
Criminal Intelligence Bureau

John Cahill
Deputy Inspector

Clifford Lent   Kenneth Bombace   Anthony Leto   Michael Malone

Burke's place atop one of the largest police departments in the country.

Eastern District of New York

GOVERNMENT EXHIBIT
301
17 CR 587 (JMA)

The highly paid detectives of the Lt. Hickey-led Criminal Intelligence Bureau, or as Burke called them, his "palace guards," counterclockwise: Kenneth Bombace (left, pictured with County Executive Steve Bellone, with whom he forged a close friendship), Michael Malone, and Anthony Leto.

Bombace/Bellone photo is courtesy of Bombace; Malone/Leto photos from Eastern District of New York

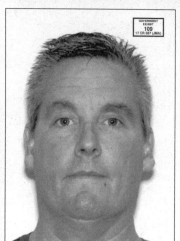

(Facing page) The participants in one incarnation of then-Suffolk County Comptroller Joe Sawicki's annual charter fishing trip, including Police Benevolent Association President Noel DiGerolamo (far left), Sawicki (second from left), Burke (third from left), Suffolk County Detectives Association President William Plant (fourth from left), County Executive Steve Bellone (third from right), and Bellone's then-aide Justin Meyers (far right). Burke never missed Sawicki's annual trip, and he was on the boat in June 2013 when he learned of the feds subpoenaing various cops about the Chris Loeb beating.

Eastern District of New York

Christopher Loeb, a longtime heroin addict and petty thief, unknowingly broke into Chief Burke's police truck early on the morning of December 14, 2012.

Eastern District of New York

A police photograph of Burke's stolen duffel bag in Loeb's room, carefully staged to avoid showing the porn, sex toys, and Viagra, among other embarrassing or illicit items in the bag.

Eastern District of New York

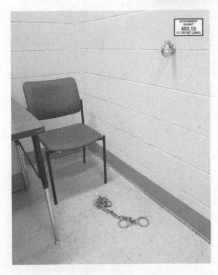

Loeb was beaten by Chief Burke, Bombace, Malone, and Leto while chained to the ground in an interrogation room in the Third Precinct.

Eastern District of New York

Members of Jimmy Burke's enemy list (from top to bottom): Patrick Cuff, whose offense was leading an Internal Affairs Bureau investigation of Burke early in his SCPD career; and Rob Trotta and John Oliva, who were removed from their gang task forces by a vindictive Chief Burke.

Eastern District of New York

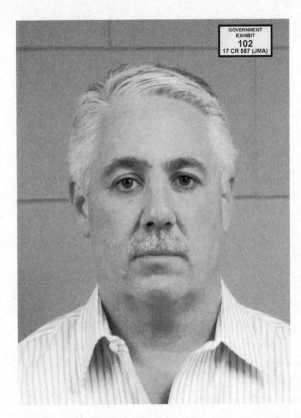

The federal mug shots of Jimmy Burke, following his indictment in December 2015, and McPartland (below left) and Spota (below right), who still led the DA's office when they were indicted in October 2017.

Eastern District of New York

CHAPTER 15

POWERPOINT JIMMY

All Kenny Bombace ever wanted to be was a soldier and a cop. Back in 1987, when he was a seventeen-year-old Commack North High fuck-up with poor grades and a brutalist mohawk, an Army recruiter showed up at his door at four o'clock in the morning. Kenny was expecting him, because he had enlisted at the recruitment center on Main Street Smithtown. His parents, on the other hand, were a bit surprised.

His dad, himself an Air Force veteran, at first refused to allow his son to enlist. But after Kenny pleaded, he relented, with a couple of requirements, including that his son join a branch of the Army that would teach him a profession. But Kenny didn't honor the deal, and just did basic training for the infantry. He only wanted to see combat.

Kenny was sent to West Germany. The Americans were warned that they were just a speed bump if the Communist troops decided to invade, as the East Germans and Soviets would outnumber them twelve-to-one. Kenny fantasized about what blend of bullets and grenades he'd use to mow down his allotment of a dozen commies. But then the Berlin Wall fell without warfare, and Kenny, slightly disappointed, returned to Long Island.

He had fallen in love with the lifestyle of the soldier: the uniforms, rules, ranks, patriotism, and the manly ballet of military tactics. Being promoted to specialist had imbued him with a new ambition, and he now considered himself a leader of men. But his career post-Army didn't quite match his self-regard.

He sold NordicTracks at the mall while taking every law enforcement exam he could get his hands on and studying for a bachelor's degree in political science. He eventually got a job as a sheriff's deputy making $24,000 a year. The Suffolk County Sheriff's Office was the brown-uniformed stepchild of local law enforcement. Deputies were paid much less than county cops and they were headquartered in the jail building. Bombace spent three years processing new arrests at district court before getting bumped up to driving prisoners around the state. He studied at night to get a master's degree in criminal justice and joined the National Guard, where he was promoted to second lieutenant with a specialty in military intelligence. Viewed by his colleagues as haughty beyond his station, Bombace eyed a switch to the more prestigious county department: "I wanted to be a cop, a real cop, so bad."

In 2003, he finally got his chance with the SCPD. But just as he was about to start onto the Suffolk force, he learned he was being deployed to Iraq. Bombace probably could have gotten out of it and had every reason to try. He had the new job, and he and his wife had two infant sons. But he couldn't turn down an opportunity to finally lead troops into battle.

After seven months training in Fort Drum, Bombace had become a captain by the time he arrived in Samarra, Iraq, in 2005. His mandate was to establish a seven-hundred-member civilian police department in a lawless city under daily mortar attacks. Bombace and military bosses tried to implement some of the niceties of an American police department, including holding an award ceremony for five Iraqi cops who distinguished themselves. Insurgents then killed all five. "Note to self," Bombace said. "No more award ceremonies."

He slept about an hour a night after days often filled with atrocities. A recruit staggered into the police academy with his arm blown off from a car bomb. After the five Iraqi cops were killed and Bombace observed their colleagues casually smoking cigarettes at the department, he berated them to get off their asses. "I'm tired of seeing dead Iraqi cops!" he yelled. "I want to see dead insurgents!" Soon afterward, the cops brought him a pickup truck with a bed stacked with the fly-covered corpses of men they had just killed. Bombace hoped to God they were all really insurgents.

The most affecting moment came after another car bombing, when Bombace was presented with a toddler in his pajamas. The boy looked unscathed, like he was asleep, but he was dead from a shrapnel wound concealed under his hair. "He was barefoot, and in the pajamas he reminded me of how my boy looks when he's running around my living room," Bombace said. The image never left him.

He returned home later that year with the Samarra police department fully operational, his quest for combat fulfilled, and a career as a real cop waiting for him. But rather than feeling accomplished, he was stricken with dread. Every time he opened a door, he was sure it was going to blow up in his hands. He couldn't sleep, and sometimes shook uncontrollably as he worked evenings in the Seventh Precinct. "I had no business being on patrol," he said.

In September 2005, Bombace and his wife were awoken by a noise like fireworks. They found their four-year-old son in his pajamas lying on the floor of Bombace's home office. Bombace saw his gun on the ground and with overwhelming relief registered that the boy was holding his ears and screaming. Bombace realized that after coming home from his tour, which had ended at eleven o'clock the previous night, he had forgotten to lock up the gun in his safe. Instead he'd left the weapon sitting on a closet shelf, where his son, who was infatuated with his dad being a cop, found it in the middle of the night. The bullet had ripped through two walls and the ceiling.

Bombace's wife later said that she went to call 911 when he took the phone from her hand. "I'm going to lose my job," he fretted. Instead of reporting it, he had the bullet holes spackled. His life continued to fray. He moved out of the family home, and in April 2006, his deteriorating relationship with his wife spurred her to report the September shooting incident to IAB.

When IAB investigators interviewed Bombace, they found him to be "contrite and most respectful" toward them. He came clean about the accidental discharge and blamed it on his own sloppy storage of the gun. The only difference between his story and that of his wife's was that they each claimed the other had stopped them from calling 911. The IAB cops clearly felt for Bombace, making sure to include in their report that Bombace was until recently in Iraq, "serving his country." He was penalized by the loss of four vacation days.

The incident pushed Bombace to confront his PTSD. He broke down crying in a shrink's office talking about Iraq. In 2006, Bombace started a nonprofit, the Suffolk County Police Veterans Association, a supportive fraternity for the hundreds of veterans working local cop jobs. Always a gabber, Bombace increasingly found himself chatting in the office of Commissioner Dormer, a grandfather-like figure who was also a former Army vet and military history buff.

Bombace had led an unusual career, full of frenetic stops and starts. It took a sympathetic observer like Dormer to appreciate Bombace's amalgam of experience. In 2009, Bombace received a call he was at first sure was a prank, in which a warm Irish brogue informed him that he was being transferred to his dream bureau: Criminal Intelligence. The rap on the bureau was that its members might as well hang up their handcuffs. Their job, on paper, was to collect criminal gossip, street names, gang affiliations, and any other intel from around the department, feed it into a central database, and analyze trends. When national politicians, candidates, or other dignitaries came to Suffolk County, the bureau also oversaw their security, sometimes in coordination with the Secret Service. A lot of cops wouldn't want to give up their street work for a desk chair or forfeit the regular endorphin hits of arrests, indictments, and court testimony. But for Bombace, a job in the Criminal Intel hive scratched his military itch.

His new boss, Jim Hickey, was a former captain of his New Hyde Park high school basketball team, and he ran Intel basically the same way. He was chummy and expansive with a handful of stars, inserting himself into their personal lives and inviting them over to his Smithtown backyard to gauge their ambitions and stressors.

But if you were riding the bench, Hickey didn't give a shit about you. The bureau's only Black member, Troy Gibson, described the series of insults that came with life on the wrong side of Hickey's system of Haves and Have Nots. Gibson said that the former street cop called

Ratman referred to him as "boy," denied him overtime, and gave his assigned vehicle away, among other insults.

Bombace was the right color at least, but otherwise he started at a disadvantage in Intel. Placed in his new position by an unpopular commissioner, Bombace already had a major strike against him: his brother-in-law was a fed.

His sister's husband, Ray Tierney, had previously been a Suffolk prosecutor, working on political corruption cases under Chris McPartland. Tierney had bitterly clashed with McPartland, Spota, and Burke over what he saw as their reckless disregard for ethics. At one point, the DA's office feuded with the feds over an informant. When McPartland directed his police investigators to escalate the interagency beef, Tierney warned those cops that they were risking criminal prosecution. McPartland reamed out Tierney for trying to steal his bureau out from under him, and punished him for insubordination. Tierney then left for a job as a prosecutor in the Eastern District.

Bombace's familial relationship with a Suffolk County turncoat made him a dubious figure in the eyes of Jimmy Burke and his mind-melded subordinate, Hickey. Bombace was initially barred from access to the bureau's most sensitive work, and instead Hickey made him answer office phones, or sent him out on drudgery assignments like writing down license plates at a mob funeral.

Hickey would say he ran a merit-based shop, but achieving merit rarely involved police work. Everybody knew Hickey was utterly beholden to Burke, the figure who had rescued his career. So the surest way to make it onto Intel's starting squad was to do something that made Burke smile upon you.

Among Hickey's Haves was Detective Anthony Leto. Before being recruited to Intel, he had spent most of his career in the hardscrabble Third Precinct, specifically gang-plagued Brentwood. Leto was the very picture of the sort of cop a perp would dread being left alone with in an interrogation room, with his icy eyes and a frame made sinewy through obsessive exercise. He was a devoted adherent to the tenets of martial arts, except for the one about only using it for self-defense.

But trapped in that hardened middle-aged detective's frame was a wounded kid from Rosedale, Queens. Back then, Tony was a quiet boy and poor student who used to spend class skillfully doodling superheroes and monsters. He was the son of a midlevel career criminal with mob bloodlines. Tony's dad, Joseph Leto, was brother to Frank "Chickie" Leto, a made man with the Colombo crime family, and he was cousins with Carmine Agnello, who was married to John Gotti's daughter Victoria. Joey Leto was co-operator of a Queens chop shop which those in the know might patronize for a Pontiac Bonneville nose of dubious provenance. Unfortunately for Joey—as well as his partner in the operation, 450-pound wiseguy cousin Mike Agnello—among those in the know were the NYPD's Organized Crime Control Bureau. Getting caught in multiple undercover stings, including an elaborate, yearlong operation in which detectives opened their own bogus auto rebuilding concern to trap him, meant he spent much of his son Tony's youth behind bars.

But for young Tony, the real trouble came when Dad was home. Leto learned not to let himself ever get into too good a mood, because even if he had the greatest day at school that night he could wake up to his parents beating on each other. The worst night came when he was six or seven years old, and he and his brother and sister ran downstairs to find their dad in the midst of choking their mom to death. The kids started pummeling their dad trying to get him off, Leto said, while they heard their mom gurgling underneath. Leto's sister was the oldest—around eleven—so she took the lead, stabbing their dad in the back over and over with a knife while his brother smashed a crystal candy bowl over his head. Finally, their dad let go.

That night was the beginning of the end of Tony Leto's childhood in Queens. His mom got an order of protection against his dad, and then a divorce, but those pieces of paper didn't stop Joey from trying to kick down the door every so often. The family ultimately moved with his mom's new husband to the Long Island village of Seaford. Leto kept with him a sliver of comfort from the violent nights in Queens: his memory of how the NYPD officers, radios crackling, brought peace to the traumatized family. Leto remembered that on the night his dad choked his mom, while he was on the front stoop of their house being comforted by his big brother, he could see inside a cop talking to his dad, who was lying on the floor of their kitchen with a towel soaking up blood.

Most kids might never want to get near a scene like that again. But Leto wanted to be that cop. As a teenager, that desire got even stronger when Edward Byrne, a young NYPD patrolman who lived one town over from Seaford, was executed by gangsters in Jamaica, Queens. "I wanted to do something noble," Leto said. Not to mention, he wanted to get the hell out of his mom's house but had done too poorly in high school to go to college.

Leto had no intention of joining the Suffolk force, with its notoriety for "squirrel cases," as he terms rural whodunits. No, Leto wanted the same uniform as the cops who used to make him feel safe: "I wanted to be a kickass NYPD cop."

Leto joined the city in 1991, and for four years patrolled East Flatbush and Crown Heights, then two of the toughest neighborhoods in Brooklyn. But he said he grew aggravated by the bureaucracy of the massive department—including being written up for what he believed were minor infractions—and he began to wonder why he was making the hour-long commute from his home on Long Island.

Leto's desire to be a noble cop took a few knocks in actual practice. It turns out that policing involves dealing with some pretty unpleasant people, and Leto wasn't one to let their insults roll off his back. "You deal with a lot of assholes on a daily basis, and they can be fucking really abrasive," Leto explained. "Yeah, I have smacked people before. Can I tell you what their names are? No."

However, Leto insisted he had standards. He said when he joined the SCPD in 1995, he met the "crusty fucking dudes" on the force who were the sort of detectives accused of beating confessions out of people, the department's longtime hallmark. But not Leto. "That to me was crossing the line," he remarked, before clarifying the reasons he had for exerting violence on a prisoner: "It was more or less to get respect or stop someone from acting like an asshole, that type of thing. I would never, ever beat a confession out of somebody."

Leto had Burke as his lieutenant when he was working overnight tours in the Third Precinct around 1998, and he also got to know Hickey, then the overnight sergeant for a different squad. There was no mystery as to why the two bosses took a shine to Leto, who was from the same unmanageable street cop mold as Burke and Hickey. Asked to describe his policing style, Leto mused: "I guess I had a reputation as being kind of a proactive cop, or . . . I don't want to use the word 'aggressive,' but I guess, I mean, I didn't take shit either, you know?"

Burke and Hickey didn't need a Rosetta Stone to decode those terms, as they too had been bruisers in uniform who liked to romp around a tough sector and knock heads. Burke referred to Leto as "Tony the Torture Expert," and enthused over the Brazilian jiujitsu devotee's knowledge of pressure points. In the hierarchy of parasites in the SCPD, Leto firmly latched on to Hickey, who himself was Burke's pet. Leto, by his own account, lacked for self-confidence, so he didn't take it for granted when he made detective in 2006, a promotion he knew was partly thanks to Burke's influence. And in 2007, Leto's buddy, Detective Mike Malone, recruited him to join him in the Criminal Intelligence Bureau under Hickey.

Leto was skeptical at first. One of the main jobs of an Intel cop was to show up at precincts when a perp was booked and grill them for information on their associates and knowledge of other crimes. Leto had seen Malone arrive for those debriefings with his "little fucking notebook," and heard the other detectives and supervisors criticize Malone for capitalizing on their hard work. But Leto's uncertainty about the bureau was overcome by Burke bragging up the bureau as a central hive where a detective could work on exciting cases with targets including the biggest bad guys in the county.

If Leto had thought about it hard, he probably could have seen the lie in that sales job. The first tell was the fact that they wanted Leto. A hard-charging street cop was an odd pick for a bureau in which detectives purportedly analyzed crime patterns, and even the "Intelligence" in the bureau's name was at odds with Leto's own self-analysis: "I guess I'm not the fucking smartest guy in the world, you know?" But what Leto lacked in actual qualifications for his new job, he made up for with those traits Burke and Hickey no doubt actually found attractive: he was loyal and unflappable.

Leto learned upon reporting to the new gig that detectives who labored over in-depth information gathering and analysis—the hallmark of the bureau—then saw their work ignored or even greeted with hostility. One of Leto's new colleagues, Detective Cliff Lent, for years spent every free minute at work catfishing gangsters on social media in order to build a database of cops from multiple departments—including the SCPD—who were consorting with members of the Latin Kings and other crime factions. In other departments, it could've been the beginning of multiple bombshell investigations, but Lent couldn't get his bosses to even take a look.

For new recruit Leto, it only took a few months for the real purpose of the bureau to dawn on him: it was a glorified goon squad, serving Hickey and Burke's political interests. "The focus really wasn't on getting bad guys," Leto said. "It was more about keeping control."

Leto, who had no interest in department politics, considered bailing on the new assignment and requesting a transfer back to the Third. But a buddy advised him that such a move would be career suicide. And Leto, who was married with three sons and a stepson, very quickly grew accustomed to the perks of the prestigious new job: a take-home car, lots of overtime, the flexibility to schedule his work around his boys' athletic schedules. So he went against his gut, and stayed.

"That's my biggest regret," Leto later said. "Because that's when I feel like I sold my soul."

* * *

Around 2011, after a couple of years of handling Intel's unwanted grunt work, Kenny Bombace got a break: Hickey told him that Jimmy had a job for him. Bombace's fed brother-in-law had warned him to be wary about Burke. But the detective figured there was nothing nefarious about a PowerPoint.

Jimmy had previously watched Bombace give a presentation to an FBI task force about his time in Iraq. In Jimmy's estimation, Bombace was an impressive public speaker, though of course not as good as him. But what really got his attention were those fancy projected slides Bombace used to move his story along, and now he wanted the cop to put together a slideshow for him.

Bombace had learned to hide his bemusement when White Shirts bloviated about "intelligence-led policing." It was a policing model that had originated in Europe, and had already been implemented in some way in virtually every major US police department. The concept, boiled down, involved using data and intel gathered from multiple precincts to inform the allocation of resources. Even archaic Suffolk County had borrowed from the model for years, including in the creation of the very bureau Bombace worked for. So any boss who seized on intelligence-led policing as cutting edge only revealed just how far they were from the vicinity of innovation.

Even those in the department who considered Burke to be an exceptional street cop knew he was also a Luddite who had nothing but scorn for policing methods rooted in academia. But Burke was an expert in delivering what his audience wanted. The demographic for his current quest required a new version of Jimmy Burke. So he asked Bombace to make him a PowerPoint about intelligence-led policing.

Bombace and his partner, Cliff Lent, threw something together quickly. Jimmy leaned back in a seat in a conference room and took it in, with only gruff tweaks: *Change that line. Take that stat out.* "All right, Inspector," Bombace assented. He made the changes and Jimmy enthused that the presentation was ready for his roadshow. And that's how Kenny Bombace became a Have.

* * *

For five years, over steak in Great Neck and vodka in Hauppauge, The Administration obsessed over how to get rid of Steve Levy, the county executive. The fixation began around 2006. It wasn't Levy showing himself to be anti-cop that drove their plotting. Everybody already knew that. It was Levy's incredible popularity with Suffolk County voters that made him a true threat.

The math had held for decades, with DA Henry O'Brien, Judge Namm, and DA Jim Catterson as proof: Suffolk County politicians who challenged the cops did not survive. But Levy was a pyrotechnician with accepted norms, and he had thus far torched this one as well. His most egregious affront, in the eyes of Suffolk County cops, was taking them off the Long Island highways in 2009. He sought to replace them with the bottom of the sworn officer caste system: sheriff's deputies. It was a direct shot at one of the Police Benevolent Association's (PBA) biggest cash cows, as highway patrolmen were experts at making their drunk-driving arrests right before their tours ended in order to rack up copious overtime. The union howled with indignation, fundraised for war, and attempted a hostile takeover of the Conservative Party in a scheme to oust the incumbent sheriff for the offense of agreeing to patrol the highways.

Going to the mattresses against the cop shops somehow only made Levy stronger. He had invented a new alchemy, in which he countered blowback from police by way of inflammatory race-baiting. Suffolk County, historically a KKK stronghold, had become a hive of violence against Hispanic migrants who had come there seeking work. In 2000, two Mexicans living in Farmingville, a town where white residents had previously railed against the influx of migrants, were brutally beaten and stabbed by white supremacists. Three years later, a Mexican family's home in Farmingville was firebombed. Levy saw electoral opportunity in the grim trend.

He ranted about "anchor babies," tried to deputize cops to be immigration enforcers, and directed a crackdown on overcrowded migrant housing, leaving dozens of laborers homeless. In 2008, the rash of hate crimes reached a predictable crescendo when Marcelo Lucero, an Ecuadorian migrant in Patchogue, was stabbed to death by a gang of white high schoolers. Levy was annoyed at the press coverage, complaining that if the murder happened elsewhere, it'd be a "one-day story." He issued a rare apology for that remark, but he likely knew it wouldn't bother his ever-widening base. Levy's rhetoric was effective because it clearly reflected a prevalent attitude in Suffolk County—especially among cops. A Department of Justice investigation into the circumstances of Lucero's murder found that SCPD had ignored previous attacks on Latinos, often classifying them as "youth disturbances."

In 2007, near the crest of the anti-migrant frenzy he kicked up, Levy won the endorsement of every major party and was reelected with 96 percent of the vote. Even Hillary Clinton wanted a piece of the Steve Levy magic, plastering his image on US Senate reelection flyers distributed in the Long Island suburbs. The *New York Times* waxed that Levy "bestrides this narrow island like a Colossus, while his political opponents—what few remain—walk under him and peep about."

Levy's Teflon status in Suffolk convinced him he deserved a larger stage. First he had to ditch the Democrats, whose statewide and national policies were now anathema to his own. In 2010, Levy announced he was joining the Republicans and entering the primary race for New York governor. But because Levy hadn't switched parties in time, he was forced to enter the Republican primary as a Democrat. That predictably diminished his chances, and he failed to collect the percentage of the vote required by party rules to permit a non-Republican to snatch the nomination at the state convention.

In June 2010, Levy returned, only slightly humbled, to Suffolk County. He was still almost certain to win a third term as county executive in the election the next year. He was expected to run as a Republican against Steve Bellone, a little-known town supervisor of Babylon. But by switching parties, Levy had lost the insulation provided by Richard Schaffer, the easily underestimated Democratic leader. The boys at Butterfields saw opportunity in Levy's unforced error.

* * *

Killing Steve Levy—politically—became the ultimate black ops project for the Government Corruption Bureau. Usually the bureau's major investigations were overtime-laden affairs with prosecutors and cops hunched over wiretaps around the clock and preparing eavesdropping affidavits as thick as novels. But the Levy matter was decidedly lo-fi, relying on the quaint art of extortion. Only McPartland and Burke knew the full extent. As for Spota, Jimmy looped him in solely when he was useful.

Jim Hickey was apprised of the status of the operation through pregnant statements made by Burke and the others at Butterfields. A boozy Jimmy Burke usually couldn't help but gloat about every detail of his covert activities. With the Levy matter, he was suddenly as guarded as Deep Throat.

But sometimes a development was too significant to keep discreet. Like when The Administration came to believe that one of Steve Levy's closest longtime aides was secretly gay. They discussed that revelation like excited schoolboys. There was no actual law enforcement relevance in the news that one of Steve's soldiers was in the closet. But if the name Henry O'Brien rang a bell—and the four men at the reserved table in Butterfields were all buffs of Suffolk County history—it was clear how politically useful that information could be.

Hickey, like the rest of Suffolk County, learned of what happened next via the release of two vague prepared statements on a Thursday afternoon in March 2011. The first was from Levy himself. It was an odd and meandering statement in which a politician known for his tireless, combative obstinance suggested that this whole politics thing had left him downright pooped. He announced he wouldn't run for the third term he was favored to win, citing those reasons politicians conjure up when they're avoiding mentioning an elephantine scandal: "Long hours, tough decisions, grueling debates, family sacrifices."

It took three hundred words of throat-clearing to get to the nut of the matter, tacked on like an afterthought: "Questions have been raised concerning fundraising through my political campaign," Levy wrote. "Since this occurred under my watch I accept responsibility. In order to resolve these questions I will be turning over my campaign funds to the Suffolk County District Attorney."

Minutes later, Tom Spota released his own statement. His version was laden with gloating but just as thin on details. Spota said that Levy was deciding not to seek reelection in order "to resolve a sixteen-month investigation conducted by the Government Corruption Bureau which began in the summer of 2009." He said that $4 million in campaign coffers would be returned to donors or donated to charity, and described Levy as fully cooperative: "He met with prosecutors and investigators on multiple occasions to answer questions and provide information relevant to our inquiry."

But Spota was maddeningly coy on the substance of that inquiry. "There is no question that while the investigation revealed serious issues with regard to fundraising and the manner in which it was conducted, including the use of public resources, I am confident that Mr. Levy did not personally profit," Spota wrote. "The forfeiture of his 4 million dollar campaign fund demonstrates his acceptance of responsibility for these failings."

Spota's statement displayed supreme self-confidence in his right to enter into a quasi-legal agreement on behalf of 1.5 million residents who were kept in the dark. "The decision to allow Mr. Levy to complete his term was carefully considered and involved weighing his conduct, the need for stability in government in these difficult economic times while affording a smooth transition after the 2011 elections," Spota said. "You can be assured that if I believed that his actions compromised his ability to govern I would have sought his resignation."

Spota predicted that his own tenure "will be defined by my aggressive and impartial investigations and prosecutions of corrupt government officials," and added that though the Levy matter was over, the "investigation will continue with respect to the conduct of others."

A law enforcement boss using his investigative privileges to unilaterally end the career of an enormously popular rival politician, with no substantive public explanation, was a development seemingly more characteristic of the Eastern Bloc than the suburbs of America's biggest metropolis. *Newsday* was at a loss. "What exactly did Suffolk County Executive Steve Levy do?" wondered the newspaper, which also quoted passages of Levy's statement followed by the phrases, "What does that mean?" and simply, "What?"

The *Times* was just as befuddled but more declarative: "Something strange and sleazy is going on in Suffolk County."

* * *

It felt like more information about the episode was bound to emerge. But then none did. The public, and journalists, were forced to stare at tea leaves for clues about what had happened to their county executive.

It wasn't that Levy, despite being a proponent of campaign finance reform, didn't have some red flags. There was a missing campaign disclosure, hundreds of thousands of dollars in contributions from firms doing business with the county, and most intriguingly, the matter of an old law school buddy and a sex club in Manhattan. The friend, Ethan Ellner, was convicted of a multimillion-dollar fraud scheme involving The Dungeon, where his co-conspirator's wife was chief dominatrix. Ellner testified in court that he had gotten work in Suffolk County by donating to the campaign of a "high county official." A process of elimination identified that official as Levy. Ellner later said he was interrogated by McPartland, who was investigating Levy for allegedly "taking kickbacks from people who did business with Suffolk County." Levy has denied any quid pro quo.

As titillating and leather-scented as it all was, none of it amounted to an answer. Levy himself had no interest in providing one. When he later self-published a 236-page memoir, most of it a screed against the media, Levy managed to avoid addressing the only matter the average reader might care about, which is how his political career had abruptly ended. The secrecy by all parties didn't help dispel the general suspicion that an extortion scheme was at play. Anyone within earshot of the boasting at Butterfields would have had their suspicions confirmed.

Burke ceded to Hickey that McPartland deserved all the credit. He had perfectly played the hole card of the secretly gay aide. When McPartland threatened to publicly out the aide, Burke said, he "crumbled" and agreed to cooperate against his boss.

The timeline lined up with the aide being a key informant. The aide left Levy's operation for a plum Suffolk County gig in the summer of 2009, around the same time that Spota said he began the investigation into the county executive's finances.

But it's unclear how much of the story of blackmailing the aide was exaggerated, or outright bullshit, on the part of Burke, McPartland, or Hickey. The aide's attorney, Anthony LaPinta, a loyal defender of Spota, later denied that the aide's sexuality had anything to do with his cooperation. "He had come out with that prior, it wasn't anything that was a deep, dark secret," LaPinta said. He acknowledged the aide had fed the Government Corruption Bureau information about his boss, but said there was nothing coerced about it: "[He] never 'crumbled,'" LaPinta said. "It wasn't a crumbling situation." Either way, the lack of a clear answer on how or why the aide cooperated spoke to the vacuum of information surrounding Levy's ouster.

Rumors also spread in law enforcement and government that Levy had stepped down due to the wiretap tapes from the decade-old Prospect and Baranello investigation. Law enforcement insiders gossiped that the tapes recorded him using offensive racial language, which Levy later denied.

There is a counterintuitive art to wiretap extortion, a skill at which Spota, McPartland, and Burke were perhaps the best in the country. Rather than playing a handpicked piece of damning tape for their target, the Government Corruption Bureau knew it was more effective to let a worried imagination run wild. With the knowledge that Spota had dozens or even hundreds of hours of Levy's unguarded bedtime conversations with his closest advisor, it didn't matter what he had actually said. The real power of the tapes was in their unknown possibilities.

Combine all that with some financial improprieties, even if they were the sort that often went unprosecuted, and Levy's sudden capitulation became less of a mystery. Perhaps Levy could have fought a criminal case, but if Spota indicted him or one of his aides or froze his campaign funds, his campaign would have been shot anyway.

McPartland's successful plotting against Levy lifted Jimmy's regard for him to new heights. He now considered the prosecutor to be his soulmate in scheming. Jimmy proudly introduced McPartland to other cops as "the man who killed Steve Levy." Among the cops they brought into their fold was Noel DiGerolamo, a boss of the Police Benevolent Association. Winning over the unions was a key part of the rest of their plan, an effort helped along considerably by the fact that they had just ousted the unions' least favorite person.

Jimmy's partnership with McPartland was also beginning to make Tom Spota superfluous. For Jimmy's next trick, he cut out the old man altogether. He called Richie Schaffer, the county's Democratic Party leader, and asked for an introduction to Steve Bellone, suddenly the new favorite to become the next county executive. And he also asked for Schaffer's blessing in his plan to become the next chief of the police department.

In discussing their moves with Hickey, Jimmy and McPartland said they'd get Spota on board when it was time. "Spota only thinks it's a great idea," they explained, "if it's his idea."

* * *

In December 2011, Steve Bellone sat at a big kidney-shaped table in a publisher's conference room in *Newsday*'s Melville headquarters. He had been invited by the paper's editorial board to gloat over his electoral victory the month earlier and outline his plans as county executive. But Bellone found himself distracted by the overwhelming greatness of Jimmy Burke's PowerPoint.

Bellone, a US Army veteran and attorney, was a centrist down to his bones. Even his perpetual facial expression, an unnervingly toothy grin, seemed designed to please everyone, though the somber, silvery eyes punctured his cheery air. It is perhaps doubtful that Bellone would have charmed Suffolk County voters without a boost from the machinations of the Government Corruption Bureau. His background appeared purposefully dull. He was a Babylon-born protégé of Richie Schaffer, who seemed to have schooled him on the fine art of projecting tepid harmlessness. (A *Newsday* profile during the county executive race resorted to this as a fun fact about him: "Has driven cross-country twice.") But the GOP was kneecapped by Levy's sudden dropout, and by the time they scrambled to nominate an alternative—County Treasurer Angie Carpenter—the momentum belonged to Bellone, along with a surprise PBA endorsement and cop campaign donations.

Bellone had plenty of stump topics he could've recited during the meeting with *Newsday*, from the nine-figure hole in the county budget to a signature plan to revitalize Wyandanch. But it was his plans for the police department that got the attention of Bob Keeler, a longtime member of the editorial board. County executives had in the past always appointed a commissioner, the top official in the police department, who then chose their own chief of department. But Bellone announced he was naming the chief of department—James Burke—and would figure out the commissioner later.

This was a friendly room, full of the same opinion writers who had endorsed Bellone several months earlier. Nonetheless, Keeler bluntly pointed out to Bellone, and wrote into a resulting editorial in *Newsday*, that appointing the department's top figures backward seemed like poor management. Bellone responded by launching into breathless, you-gotta-see-it praise of Jimmy's PowerPoint on intelligence-led policing. "Burke had snowed him so thoroughly about data-driven policing that he was like totally under his thrall," Keeler later recalled.

Keeler continued to press Bellone on the flipped appointments, but the professional compromiser refused to budge. "Any person that I would select as commissioner would love Jim Burke," Bellone said finally. "And if they don't, then they wouldn't match up with the kind of commissioner that I want."

* * *

Tim Gozaloff hunt-and-pecked at his keyboard in his office at the police academy building in Brentwood. He had only one rule for his letter: no secondhand sources. Either he knew it directly himself or the information came from somebody who was there. When he was done, he pulled several copies of the document off his printer while wearing latex gloves.

He showed it only to his partner in the Career Criminal Investigation Bureau, Rob Trotta. Without touching the piece of paper, Trotta read the first paragraph, giggled, and said he was too nervous to read any more of it. Gozaloff then used a bottle of water and his gloved fingers to seal the letters in envelopes.

The two cops weren't exactly the bleeding heart liberals of the Suffolk County Police Department. Gozaloff's dad, Gerard, was a retired homicide bull, with war stories including having interrogated Butch DeFeo in the Amityville Slayer case. Gerard was friends with Spota, and for decades they had rubbed elbows at detective's picnics. His son was raised to be skeptical of the criticism of so-called police reformers, and sympathetic to men like Tommy Spota.

Rob Trotta wasn't the whistle-blowing type either. He had participated in some on-the-job shenanigans that neared or may have even crossed the line. Trotta was sued seven times in federal court, and in 2010 a treasurer for a Bronx mosque claimed that the cop had illegally seized $16,503 from his truck during a traffic stop in Mastic. Trotta denied it. After the mosque treasurer sued, the county settled for an undisclosed amount.

Neither man had a personal ax to grind against Jimmy Burke. Gozaloff had mostly observed Burke's career from afar, starting with bemusement at the street cop's self-aggrandizing commendations and fawning news articles. Trotta still considered himself to be on Burke's good side, even sending him a bases-covering email of congratulations when Burke was named chief of department.

But they both found the idea of his impending promotion to that position, which had been reported in *Newsday*, to be repugnant, something that could bring down the whole SCPD. "Everyone knew that he'd be a disaster," Trotta said. "You had a criminal running the police department." All they were trying to do, the cops later said, was save their workplace from what they saw as inevitable mortification if Bellone went ahead with the plan.

Gozaloff drove to a post office far from his house so the postmarks wouldn't give him away. He dropped the letters in the mailbox, half-expecting Burke's goons to soon show up at his office demanding to search his computer. But then they didn't, and he and Trotta didn't know if anybody even read their manifesto.

CHAPTER 16

SAMMY
TO THE RESCUE

Shortly after Bellone's victory, Billy Madigan, the scrawny bulldog who headed the DA's Rackets office, strode into the police brass sanctum in Yaphank. He had been promised a spot here years earlier in a pep talk in Jimmy Burke's car. The SCPD's four chiefs—of patrol, detectives, support services, and above them all, chief of department—had their offices here, as did their deputy chiefs. This was a White Shirt paradise, the dominion of middle-aged or elderly white men whose pull was conveyed via the number of gold stars on their collars.

Madigan tended to wear baggy suits that looked like he had raided his dad's closet to get dressed for a wedding. But he knew that soon he'd get some of those gold stars for his own. He yelled so all the silverbacks could hear: "Come January, there's going to be a lot of changes around here!" Then he strode out of the building.

Disgraceful, thought Pat Cuff, working out of Yaphank as a deputy chief, four ranks higher than Madigan.

As is the case in many workplaces, job security in the SCPD got scarcer the higher you climbed. The rank of captain was granted by civil service test-taking, but everyone above that—the inspector and chief positions—served at the pleasure of the commissioner. As a result, the chief chairs were referred to as ejector seats. Whenever a new county executive appointed a new commissioner, that usually meant new top cops. Nobody had ever taken as much glee in the turnover as incoming chief of department Jimmy Burke.

On December 15, 2011, all the Suffolk chiefs were in downtown Manhattan, doing cop boss things. They had met with NYPD brass about the Occupy Wall Street protests and then strolled out to Zuccotti Park to observe the "domestic disturbance," as they termed it. Then the Suffolk chiefs' BlackBerrys began buzzing with urgent emails from their offices.

Jimmy Burke, who was by then fishing pals with the top dogs of the Superior Officers Association, had let them in on it before he told anybody else: "The chiefs are all getting whacked."

Whacked with them: any odds that the Suffolk police would solve the biggest case in its history.

* * *

Two days earlier, Suffolk cops had pulled an intact skeleton out of a marsh in Oak Beach, a little gated community on the barrier island off the southern shore of Suffolk County, just over the border from Nassau. It took just a glance for the cops to know it was the skeleton of the woman they had been looking for, though often not very hard, for more than nineteen months.

The quick ID was courtesy of the metal plate in the skeleton's jaw. Cops knew Shannan Gilbert, the sex worker whose disappearance near this beach had led to the horrific discovery of a serial killer's dumping ground, had reconstructive surgery after being socked by her boyfriend.

The Long Island Serial Killer case, as it had come to be known, was like so many other cases out here: bizarre, interminable, and defined by flabbergasting police miscues. The saga began on May 1, 2010, when a panicked young woman came running out of a wood-shingled home into the buggy darkness of predawn Oak Beach. She had called 911 and was ranting, terrified, into her phone—"They're trying to kill me!"—as she ran down the street, banging on doors. One of the residents briefly let her in but then she fled again, and he and another neighbor called 911 as well.

Then the woman was gone. Shannan Gilbert was never seen by her loved ones again. Her boyfriend filed a missing persons report in

New Jersey. So too did her mother and sister. The family members included in their report that they had received a bizarre phone call two days after Gilbert's disappearance in which Dr. Peter Hackett, an Oak Beach resident, said he ran a home for "wayward girls" there and that he had tried to help Shannan.

It all seemed like a job, perhaps, for the Suffolk County police.

But the cops didn't connect the missing person reports with the 911 calls, a failure they later blamed on authorities in New Jersey, where the reports were filed. It took more than three months for the Suffolk County police to perform the most cursory investigation of Gilbert's case, including canvassing the street where she was last seen. It turned out she had been driven there by an associate to service a john. The cops' diligence was such that they didn't ask for the town's surveillance footage until eight months after Gilbert disappeared, long after it had been taped over.

The case—if you could call it that—of the missing woman appeared doomed to sink. But in December 2010, a cop who was training a German shepherd to find cadavers visited the brackish beach along Ocean Parkway, and sure enough the dog got a scent.

It was a skeleton wrapped in burlap, just a few miles west of where Gilbert was last seen. But it wasn't Shannan Gilbert. The real shock came when cops found three more disposed of in an identical manner, about one-tenth of a mile from each other, within the next few days.

In spring 2011, the cops found four more bodies, closer to Oak Beach. The western end of Ocean Parkway was in Nassau County, and now that police department picked up the search for bodies as well. In April 2011, the Nassau County cops found another set of human remains and a separate skull.

It totaled ten victims, in addition to Gilbert's unknown fate. Some of the remains were matched to partial bodies found more than a decade earlier in another apparent dumping ground forty miles away. Most of the victims were female sex workers, though some of the remains could not be identified, including those of an Asian male and a toddler.

After the bodies started being found, the cops turned back to Oak Beach and the missing persons case they had largely ignored.

Oak Beach was the crusted-over heart of Suffolk County on an ocean spit. It consisted of severe, weather-beaten homes owned by lifers—including county cops and those with connections to them—who prized above all the locked beach gate that kept away outsiders.

Detectives had obvious suspects. They ranged from the eccentric doctor who made the bizarre call to Gilbert's family—and then lied about it until he was confronted with phone records proving he placed the call—to the overgrown frat boy who had hired Gilbert that night, and claimed she ran from his house in an irrational paranoid fit. But this being Suffolk, the cops fell back on their long tradition of excluding suspects based on gut instincts and polygraphs. They appeared to be waiting for the right guy to corner in an interrogation room, their preferred method for solving a murder.

The circumstances of this crime—which cried out for a high-end forensic investigation—seemed tailored to overmatch Suffolk County's homicide skill set. And more than anything else, the Gilbert case appeared to be hindered by outright apathy.

The brass overseeing the investigation acted exhausted by the whole affair. By the time the bodies reached double digits, Levy had announced he was forfeiting office, which meant a new county executive, and most likely a new police commissioner. Dormer, a septuagenarian lame duck, appeared to wish away the major case thrust upon his jurisdiction during his last year in office. "I don't want anyone to think we have a Jack the Ripper running around Suffolk County with blood dripping from a knife," Dormer said at a press conference, despite all the indications that such a person was at large.

The investigation was under the purview of Dominick Varrone, chief of detectives. He was a steely gazed old cop whose droopy white mustache framed a perpetual frown. Even though he had one of the top jobs in the department, Varrone developed a grumpy air of underappreciation. It didn't help his mood when the county executive handed the department reins to a chief of department instead of a commissioner. And to James Burke, of all people. Varrone, like most in the top brass, was appalled that Bellone had chosen Burke, who was unqualified even if you disregarded his checkered IAB past. "Limited managerial experience, no degrees, he was sheltered at least the previous ten years in the district attorney's office," Varrone ticked off. "There's no way he had the expertise to run and control the department."

Varrone knew that in a less dysfunctional county and department, he would have been in the conversation for top chief or commissioner. Varrone had a master's in criminal justice leadership, a spotless police career dating back to the Nixon era, and had checked off the requisite inculcations at prestigious academies like Quantico and Boston's Senior Management Institute for Police.

Like Dormer, Varrone acted like he considered the bodies along Ocean Parkway to be a grievous annoyance at a time when his career was in deep limbo. He told the Public Safety Committee it was a "consolation" that the killer wasn't "selecting citizens at large—he's selecting from a pool." It's hard to imagine he would've taken much consolation if the pool of victims had been soccer moms rather than sex workers. And in an interview with journalist Robert Kolker, the author of *Lost Girls*, the 2013 bestseller on the unsolved killings, Varrone bluntly insulted the victims of his highest-profile case. He remarked that as sex workers "most of them are in the business that they're in because it's an easy way to make money, and because they're greedy."

In December 2011, a year and a half after Gilbert went missing, cops decided to scour the Oak Beach area where she had last been seen. On the second day of the renewed search, they found her belongings in the marsh across the street from Dr. Hackett's house. A quarter mile away, a week later, on December 13, 2011, they pulled her skeleton from the marsh. Two days later, Varrone was fifty miles away with the rest of the brass, studying a protest that had nothing to do with his jurisdiction.

* * *

When Varrone and the other chiefs and their deputies phoned into Yaphank, they were connected to a member of Bellone's transition team who bluntly delivered the news. They had to put in their retirement papers before the end of the year—two weeks away—or they would be booted down to captain, the biggest demotion Bellone and Burke could legally hit them with. Only one of the four chiefs was being kept on. Chief of Support Services Edward Webber, an accountant known for his pliancy, was being made interim commissioner, Burke's designated pushover.

That the chiefs and their deputies were given only until the year's end had Jimmy's spiteful thumbprints all over it. In the new year, they would've accrued more vacation and other benefits, contributing to the lump sum they received when cashing out upon retirement. To force out decorated cops, all of whom had three decades or more on the job, without that final bump was an unprecedented level of vindictiveness. For cops, sabotaging a peer's retirement package is an unthinkable sin.

If Varrone had been canned because Burke wanted a new boss overseeing investigations including that of the Oak Beach dumping ground, it would be hard to find fault with the decision. Few would argue that Varrone had overseen the investigation flawlessly. But Burke's handling of Varrone's exit made clear that the state of the serial killer case was the last thing on his mind.

There was as much indignity in the transition at headquarters as Burke could manage. Normally, top cops enjoy a "walkout" ceremony, where they leave the HQ for the last time accompanied by their families, while peers and subordinates cheer and salute. Not this time. "A small thing," Varrone said, "but I'm sure he took great pleasure in denying all of us that."

More to the point was the radio silence of Burke or any of his delegates on the Oak Beach case in the final two weeks of Varrone's career, as he scrambled through the holidays to wrap up loose ends and get his cases in order. Burke didn't bother to have Varrone, or his top detectives on the case—both of whom he also removed—debriefed. Burke would be starting from scratch on an investigation that was now nearing two years old.

Spota, per usual, seemed only too eager to give cover to Burke's kneejerk actions. The biggest question concerning the bodies around Oak Beach was whether they were all the work of the same killer. Particularly with the discovery of Gilbert's corpse, the dumping ground had become a confusing morass. The official police line, espoused by Varrone, was that Gilbert's death—despite leading the cops to the work of at least one serial killer—wasn't itself a homicide. Varrone believed that Gilbert was in a "drug-induced stupor" when she ran from the john's house and ultimately into the thick marsh where she drowned. Even if you accepted this explanation, which Gilbert's family and their lawyer certainly did not, it was unclear whether all of the other bodies were also connected.

Commissioner Dormer had made clear that he believed it was one killer. And the same day that the chiefs all learned they were being whacked, Spota held a press conference to lash out at Dormer for that theory. "I think that the facts that have been disclosed so far do not bear out the single-killer theory at all," Spota said with evident anger, and then addressed Dormer: "You're misleading, more importantly, the friends and relatives of the victims who are going to be hearing this."

Inoculated against irony, Spota blamed Dormer for public comments that he said were a gift for the eventual defense attorney if they were to make arrests in the case. "That's the worst thing in the world," Spota seethed. "Top people in law enforcement feuding publicly." Over the next few days, Spota further attacked both Dormer and Levy. "I don't think the commissioner stood up for the men and women as he should have," Spota declared. "I think he supported one person—Steve Levy."

To Varrone, Spota's strategy was obvious, and an escalation of something the DA had been dabbling in for years: a "concerted effort to find issues with how the police department was being run and how Police Commissioner Dormer was running it." It helped to justify Bellone's pick of a new department leader who was far removed from the establishment.

But infusing the feud with an extra boneheaded quality was the likelihood that neither Spota nor Dormer had any solid basis for their claims about the killer or killers. Geraldine Hart, at the time an FBI supervisor in the Long Island field office who later became SCPD commissioner, said that their theories concerning the number of killers were based on nothing but speculation. "Coming from a background where what is said is carefully vetted and also based on facts," Hart described the squabble as stunningly unproductive. Just two old men, neither of whom had done anything to advance the investigation, using a serial killer as fodder in a larger political squabble.

* * *

Burke had plenty of motivations for his cold-blooded chief massacre. The chiefs were a rival hive of influence. The longer they were allowed to linger in office, the more resourceful they could be in undermining the new boss. Doing them in spectacularly and hurting their retirement in the process was a show of Burke's power, which now extended from the DA's office into the county executive's office, and the entire police department. But as was always the case with Jimmy, there was a more primal reason too. Recall that old Butterfields chant: Fuck Pat Cuff.

Perhaps his hatred of the guy who laughed in his face during the Rickenbacker investigation two decades earlier wasn't the sole reason he machine-gunned the entire chiefs' suite. But Cuff was surely Burke's most savored casualty. Of the ousted top cops, Patty Cuff was the least prepared for the vicious swiftness of Burke's takeover. Unlike the others, Cuff didn't have the money saved to retire. He was the only one who accepted the four-rank demotion to captain.

Six weeks earlier, Cuff, the highest-ranking Spanish-speaking officer in the department, had been in Israel receiving counterterrorism training funded by the FBI and the Anti-Defamation League. Following his demotion—which Cuff estimated will cost him a total of around $670,000 in lost retirement benefits commensurate with his former high rank—he reported to a warehouse where he was now in charge of invoicing evidence as captain of the Property Section.

The Administration made a special trip to Butterfields to celebrate what they called Patty Cuff's "demotion party."

* * *

The Administration's grand plans hit a speed bump when top officials started receiving the anonymous letters. Kevin Law, the businessman head of the police commissioner search committee—something of a laughable gig considering the way Burke had turned the process on its head—got one. So too did Bellone, members of the Suffolk County legislature, and Democratic leader Schaffer.

The letter was a righteous, typo-laden diatribe. It began: "This is an anonymous letter regarding a member of the Suffolk County Police Department; Inspector James Burke. It is composed by several long time members of the Dept. for the purpose of advising the incoming County Executive and his Transition Team of the character and history of this person."

The letter appeared to offer Bellone, and even Spota, a gentle out for being suckered by a master con man. "Burke is probably the best public speaker, most prolific spinner of facts and the most powerful person in the SCPD," it read. "He is charming and is a master at winning people over and gaining their trust. He can and has had very high powered people do his bidding all the while believing that Burke's intentions are true. This is not usually [the] case."

The anonymous writer continued that Spota "is a fine and upstanding man and he is beyond reproach," but that Burke had taken advantage of their father-son relationship. Burke often cites "the D.A. says," or "the D.A. wants," the letter said, when in fact Spota had no knowledge of what Burke was talking about. The letter referenced the Pius murder, stating: "Spota believed that Burke stepped up and helped the case. No one can ever speak ill of Burke to Spota, it is [a] strong bond."

After a preamble averring that the incidents in the letter were "personally witnessed by the writers or by firsthand witnesses, these are not speculation, rumors or tall tales, they are facts," came ten bullet points detailing Burke's outstanding malfeasance.

As a sergeant in the First Precinct, Burke "was known to frequent prostitutes and on one of these occasions the prostitute stole his service firearm," the letter read in a reference to Lowrita Rickenbacker. "In an effort to retrieve the weapon, he committed at least one armed home invasion. He was subsequently transferred out of the 1st Precinct as a result of that case."

The letter highlighted transfers, demotions, and forced retirements of cops who crossed him. "He routinely threatens subordinates with forced transfers, and tells them he is untouchable and that they have no protection and that he will ruin their career forever," the letter read. "He has succeeded on numerous occasions." It also referred to Burke being caught in a prostitution sting in New York City, but being let go after the cops there verified his employment with the DA's office: "Burke threatened everyone who was there that he would ruin them if they ever mentioned the incident."

Perhaps the most compelling stuff involved Bellone's predecessor, and how it came to be that Burke "owned Levy," as the letter said he frequently bragged, throughout his tenure as county executive. The letter detailed Burke's role as the supervisor of the case against Levy's former aides Prospect and Baranello, stating that Levy was "on the wiretap almost daily and he had made disparaging remarks against minorities." With the release of those wiretaps as a constant threat, Burke "could now direct the Police Commissioner, through Levy, to get anything he wanted, including manpower, transfers and the quashing of [Internal Affairs] cases and he did so regularly since."

The letter noted that a month before Levy's agreement to not seek a new term, he promoted Madigan, Burke's loyal acolyte, two ranks to deputy inspector. "Is this why Levy was never arrested?" the letter-writer wondered.

"It is only because of the protection of Tom Spota that this man has not been arrested or fired," it read in closing. "If he gets into a position of power, (Commissioner, Chief Etc.) he will decimate the Department. We are advising you of this because we are all dedicated hard working members of the SCPD and we do not want . . . Steve Bellone to be embarrassed or caught up in a scandal over the dealings of this person."

The Administration decided they needed to draft a rebuttal. It was written on Suffolk DA's stationery, with Spota's signature, even though the rebuttal was at least partly a McPartland production. "The letter is entirely replete with false allegations," Spota's response read, characterizing the allegations as "baseless rumor" of the sort one could find by anti-Burke posters on internet blogs. "It deserves emphasis and re-emphasis that not one shred of evidence has ever been brought forth to support any of this trash," Spota wrote to Law. "I should add that the prime authors of most of these blog posts have family members or friends convicted of felonies and sent to state prison or have been rejected for employment."

Spota's response, particularly in regard to the allegations about Burke's dalliances with prostitutes in the First, was a masterwork in obfuscation. Spota didn't refer directly to those allegations, no doubt because it was on paper in an IAB filing cabinet that Burke's relationship with a known prostitute had been substantiated. Instead, Spota expertly muddied the water. "Inspector Burke's off-duty firearm was stolen, among other things during the commission of a burglary at his residence in Ronkonkoma in the early 1990s," Spota wrote. "The burglary was one amongst a series of burglaries involving forcible entry into residences."

The DA went on to write that Burke's gun, with the serial number obliterated, was recovered following a later bar fight. "There is no evidence of an armed home invasion being committed by Mr. Burke whatsoever," Spota wrote. "Any such allegation is entirely false."

The burglary Spota cited was a separate incident altogether, in which Burke and his divorced lieutenant roommate reported being robbed in 1994. According to a report concerning that theft, a thief splashed soda on their walls and made off with Burke's Colt Detective Special, his gold and black onyx "JB" ring, a couple of watches, and $300 in cash. But the anonymous letter was clearly referring to Burke misplacing his gun with Lowrita, which both her IAB interview and department records indicated occurred in late 1993. Spota no doubt knew that, having represented Burke in the Rickenbacker case in which the IAB substantiated that he failed to safeguard his service weapon. But the unrelated burglary was seemingly a handy way to confuse the matter.

Spota's response was a manifesto of its own kind, the DA pushing his then impeccable reputation to the center of the poker table on Burke's behalf, daring any of the recipients of the anonymous letter to call his bluff. "I have known Mr. Burke for many years and have entrusted him with overseeing law enforcement operations in my office for ten years," Spota wrote. "He is highly regarded in the law enforcement community by his subordinates and peers alike."

One might expect the anonymous letter to be of particular interest to Steve Bellone, especially in its allegations of Burke having "owned" the prior county executive. The county executive–elect, presumably not wanting to be owned himself, could have performed the slightest due diligence concerning the letter. The only reason Burke even had a chance at the chief of department gig was that IAB records were secret in New York State. But there were provisions for government officials to obtain those files, and Bellone might have at least tried to see them. McPartland even appeared to anticipate that, as he requested the IAB records from the police department that month in a possible attempt to make it harder for Bellone to get his hands on them.

Or perhaps Bellone could have simply googled James Burke. That would have brought up reams of online police gossip about one of the most notorious members of the Suffolk department. Perhaps, as the incoming top elected official of Suffolk County, Bellone could have vetted some of those claims. Though it was online gossip, much of it, like many of the allegations in the anonymous letter, turned out to be true.

But whether it was because he was still gobsmacked by the Power-Point, beholden to the Government Corruption Bureau for giving him his new job, or some other reason, Bellone gave the letter almost no thought. He continued full steam ahead with his plan.

The stuff in the letter, Bellone later said, "seemed crazy to me, honestly. It didn't seem believable."

* * *

Chris McPartland later said he and Jimmy weren't drunk on the night of Saturday, December 31, 2011. At their favorite bar, on New Year's Eve, about to take control of the county. Surely our heroes were sticking with water.

They had dodged the anonymous letter and run out the clock to clinch the most audacious plan of their lives. Jimmy, who bragged to his colleagues about hog-tying a female colleague and was known to unabashedly drop the n-word, was becoming chief of department of one of the largest police agencies in the country, where he would rule over 2,500 cops.

Jimmy planned to, or already had, boosted his buddies and hangers-on to the top ranks of the department. The loyal Madigan would become chief of detectives, overseeing the force's investigative arm. He'd give Dennis Sullivan, his old head-knocking partner from North Amityville, the job of district commander, to spend nights dropping in on precincts throughout the county like a general overseeing a massive fief. Under the guise of "intelligence-led policing," in which field information officers were ostensibly assigned to collect information for a central database, Jimmy would plant handpicked spies in every precinct. And Jimmy bragged that he was banging an administrative professional who worked in the commissioner's suite, so he had eyes there too.

The spying infrastructure would be useful because Burke and McPartland were already looking beyond Spota. Even the old man knew it. He was annoyed at Burke for going around him in calling Schaffer to get introduced to Bellone. And he didn't think Jimmy leaving the insulating bubble of the DA's office was a good idea. But his response to the anonymous letter showed that Spota just couldn't quit Jimmy.

After the new year had been properly rung in, the two men wandered out to their cars, McPartland with his wife and Jimmy with a girlfriend. And then Jimmy almost fucked it all up. Within minutes of driving out of the Butterfields parking lot, Jimmy smashed into the rear bumper of McPartland's county-issued car.

The men certainly weren't calling the cops. And McPartland definitely wasn't going to report the accident, and the heavy damage to his car, to the county. Instead, Jimmy had a guy.

His name was Sanjiv "Sammy" Panchal. He was a cherubic former NYPD officer with a talent for tech. Jimmy had kept him around the DA's office since 2010, the crafty IT guy becoming Burke's personal version of James Bond's gadget master, Q. Sammy was paid just under $100,000 a year out of forfeiture funds, via vague invoices for "consulting services." The sketchier the job, the more comfortable he seemed doing it.

From Sammy's home in Smithtown, it was a short drive to the accident scene at Route 34 and Old Willets Path to bail out Jimmy and Chris. He got the car to a discreet mechanic, where Jimmy dropped around $5,000 of his personal cash to get McPartland's county car looking as good as new.

The following Monday, Jimmy Burke was sworn in as Suffolk's chief of department.

PART III

THE DUFFEL BAG

SCPD CHIEF OF DEPARTMENT
JAMES BURKE, 2012

CHAPTER 17

A TERRIBLE
FOREBODING FEELING

In an auditorium in Hauppauge, Acting Commissioner Ed Webber, a thin figure in a creased, dark suit befitting a mortician, made the mistake of thinking this was just another sleepy public meeting. He didn't realize he was the emcee for Jimmy Burke's frenetic coming-out party.

Jimmy, his suit jacket and white shirt laden with sixteen gold stars and assorted other paramilitary flash, never missed an opportunity to assert his dominance. So when it was his turn to follow Webber's seated and brief remarks, Jimmy said he'd rather stand. And didn't need a microphone either. "I believe I'll be able to carry it," Jimmy announced cockily, his salt-and-pepper hair and mustache accentuating his tuna tartare skin tone.

Jimmy held court for about two hours on that night in February 2012. He promised accountability for "each and every member of this department from a police officer on the street up to and including Commissioner Webber and myself." He vowed to eradicate hate crimes by scaring teenagers straight. "Hey, you see what those police officers just told you?" Burke imagined a convict telling some high schoolers following a lecture on racist attacks. "That was me last Halloween and I just got out of prison."

Next came his practiced riff on intelligence-led policing, while Bombace's PowerPoint slides flashed behind him. "The central nervous system of the Suffolk Police Department is going to be our Criminal Intelligence Bureau," Jimmy said of what he called the "warehouse for crime tracking and analysis." Jimmy described his plans to put field intelligence officers in every precinct debriefing arrestees. "Do you know anyone in the St. James area that's perpetrating or is trying to sell GPS devices and the like?" he offered as an example. They would also track what "criminals are doing on Facebook," he said, and the department's top officials would be "relentless" in making sure that "we know that our commanders know the crime picture."

The intelligence-led policing schtick had quickly become one of Jimmy's standards. It was intended to enrapture the audience the same way it had Steve Bellone. And the legislators, primed to adore any delegate of the police voting bloc, obliged. "You're holding up well under this, I'm telling you," one legislator said to Jimmy with a hint of awe.

"I physically have a headache," complained another. "I'm on informational overload."

"Intelligence-led policing," mused a third legislator, a volunteer in Jimmy's law enforcement infomercial. "Seems like a no brainer."

Burke fed off their praise. "It's policing," Burke assured the legislators, "with a purpose."

* * *

At Jim Hickey's direction, Detective Kenneth Bombace headed upstairs at the SCPD HQ in Yaphank and found Jimmy's tech consultant, Sammy Panchal, outside the chief's office.

Sammy explained to Bombace the mission of the day. Panchal had a couple of weeks earlier placed a GPS on the deputy commissioner's car. Now it was time to remove it, and he needed Bombace—the decorated combat veteran—to act as lookout.

Bombace had previously heard Burke gripe about Deputy Commissioner Risco Mention-Lewis. She was handpicked by Steve Bellone for the second-highest role in the department with the hope that she would help transform Wyandanch. For Bellone to appoint both

Mention-Lewis and Burke to top spots was a mad scientist move, albeit without the brilliance.

Mention-Lewis was Burke's policing antithesis. In her previous posting in Nassau County, she was a prosecutor who didn't prosecute, instead creating a program in which she intertwined herself in the lives of ex-cons, believing that all crime was the result of unaddressed trauma. Her favorite credo: "Hurt people hurt people."

Jimmy had gone to one of her meetings. As required, he shared the challenges and high points of his week with recently released felons who couldn't believe they were shooting the shit with the chief. But behind her back, Jimmy was aiming for sabotage from the beginning. It wasn't just their differences in policing philosophy that Jimmy loathed. She was a woman, the first to ever make it to Suffolk's top police ranks. Even worse, she was Black, and there was reason to believe that it bothered Burke. Bombace said he heard Jimmy unabashedly drop the n-word in front of him and others, including a civilian employee of the commissioner's office.

But like a good soldier, Bombace took his post on the north side of the Police HQ building. He watched the entrance for anybody leaving. Panchal scrambled over to Mention-Lewis's county vehicle, lay underneath it, and pulled off the GPS he had placed there.

The apparent idea behind the GPS was to catch Mention-Lewis doing outside work on county time, or otherwise engaging in some misdeed that Burke could use to oust or extort her. Even when he reached the peak of county law enforcement, Burke could never quit the machinations that got him there. Instead he plotted even more, now that he had an elite battalion beholden to his every whim.

Jimmy put the highly paid detectives of Criminal Intelligence to work as his black ops butlers. The chosen detectives were told to give Steve Bellone "dignitary protection," but that was a thin cover. Following the new county executive around like his security, the detectives "were really spying on him," Tony Leto later said, observing "who he would meet and things like that." The detectives then relayed the intel to Jim Hickey in order for him to brief Burke. Burke had Panchal install pole cameras outside of Bellone's house. It was ostensibly for security, but it also allowed the Intel guys to see who he had over. A passive-aggressive cold war broke out, the sad result being a county executive who took all his meetings at a Panera Bread in order to escape the surveillance state.

But even trapped in a chain bakery, Bellone was still proving himself useful. In 1993, Suffolk voters had passed a referendum limiting district attorneys and other elected positions to three terms. In 2012, Spota, who faced being term-limited out of office the next year, joined the sheriff and the county clerk in suing the county to overturn the limits. After a Suffolk judge ruled in their favor, Bellone sealed Spota's win with a letter to the county's lawyer on the case, instructing him not to appeal. "I am writing to inform you that I do not wish to pursue any further litigation in Spota v. The County of Suffolk," Bellone wrote. "I do not believe it warrants any additional expenditure of taxpayer dollars." The county had spent less than $4,000 on legal fees, the lawyer said.

Keeping control over Bellone was Jimmy's top priority. But he had plenty of other gigs for Hickey's men. Jimmy had them follow around the stepson of his girlfriend, in the hopes that the kid—who had become a pain in Burke's ass—would drive drunk or otherwise break a law that they could bust him for.

One might expect experienced detectives would find such work demeaning. But pay stubs like theirs had a way of making every assignment deeply gratifying. An Intel position meant virtually limitless overtime. That was the holy grail for a cop, in that it was not only paid out to them that year but potentially inflated their pension for life. In his first full year in Intel, Bombace's annual pay bumped up from roughly $132,000 to $186,000, mostly via overtime. It turns out those were rookie numbers. The year after that, in 2011, Bombace got his pay up to $216,000. Leto made $221,000 that year, and Malone $230,000.

But for Bombace, leading security details while in Intel gave him a glimpse of an even more rarefied class than overpaid cop. Close proximity to politicians began to give him flag-lapel-pin envy, and he wondered if perhaps it could be him speaking from a podium in front of an adoring crowd. He grew particularly close to Bellone, who, like him, was an Army veteran, and their families joined each other for barbecues. Bellone eventually started to openly flirt with the idea of giving Bombace a job in his administration, something like deputy county executive for public safety, and the detective salivated at the idea.

Bombace and his fellow Intel guys felt that all the good things that were happening to them were due to their close association to Jimmy Burke, the most powerful figure in Suffolk County. Burke even had the balls to shit-talk his lifelong mentor. Jimmy boasted that the DA's office was "stale," and bereft of any good cases since he left. He instructed his field intelligence officers to vacuum up all the actionable case information and not share it with the DA's squad.

Spota was furious, but poking the old man only served to grow Jimmy's legend among the Intel guys. They unironically referred to him as King Jimmy, and he had a name for them too: his "palace guards."

* * *

On a summer day in 2001, Tania Lopez got an assignment befitting a twenty-nine-year-old journalism intern. Her editor at a Queens bureau of *Newsday* wanted her to cover a pool opening. Lopez complained to one of her colleagues, who responded that her assignment was even worse: a machete murder in Brownsville. Lopez's eyes lit up, and she proposed a trade. The colleague agreed, but Lopez's next hurdle was how to get to a far-flung corner of Brooklyn quickly without a car. "Mine's in the shop," lied Lopez, who, having lived in New York City all her life, didn't even have a driver's license.

Their editor overheard and said Lopez could borrow her car. Not about to admit she couldn't drive, Lopez white-knuckled it over cross-borough freeways. Once there, Lopez took in the horrific scene of a woman who had been hacked to death by her boyfriend.

Brownsville was one of the most notorious neighborhoods in the city, which was likely why her colleague had punted on the assignment. But it didn't look all that different from the projects in Far Rockaway, Queens, where Lopez was raised. As a kid, her daily trip up to her apartment involved kicking away drug vials and averting her eyes from the crack fiend prostitutes in the elevator.

Near the scene in Brownsville, Lopez saw a girl tearfully hugging another woman. While the other journalists appeared to be keeping their distance, Lopez gingerly approached and introduced herself. In her boss's car with the air conditioning blasting, the machete victim's traumatized sixteen-year-old daughter recounted the murder. "Lord have mercy," the girl said her mom pleaded before her stepdad finished her with a coconut knife. Lopez phoned in her feed, and that quote became the story's lede.

When the boss's car died from the excessive air conditioning, Lopez had to beg another reporter for help with jumper cables. And her return trip to Queens was just as hazardous as the one out to Brooklyn. But with the knowledge that she had gotten the exclusive, Lopez felt invincible.

If there was a lesson to be gleaned from this early adventure in Tania Lopez's journalism career, it was this: she would rather risk arrest on the Jackie Robinson Parkway than cover a fucking pool opening.

Lopez had none of the indoctrinated self-seriousness common in her profession. At the age that some of her colleagues had edited their high school newspapers, this daughter of Guatemalan immigrants had loathed every minute behind the metal detectors at Far Rockaway High School. She spent her classes sketching out dresses, purses, and shoes in the style of *Mademoiselle*, *Vogue*, or *Harper's Bazaar*, magazines she toted around like holy books. Her main concern was survival, which at one point meant loading up her fingers with her brother's chunky rings and pummeling the face of a girl who was threatening her. But when it was time to think about a career after barely scraping her way through high school, fashion seemed the only natural direction.

An enrollment at Fashion Institute of Technology—complete with residence at the dorms in lower Manhattan—turned out to be a poor choice. Tania's "club girl" phase began, consisting of five or six nights-turned-mornings a week spent at strobing temples like Limelight or Palladium. Though Lopez stayed away from cocaine and other hard drugs because of her observations of the Far Rockaway crackheads, she missed classes, flunked out, and ended up back at her mom and dad's apartment. But Lopez had an infectious, authentic enthusiasm that seemed to endear her to employers. She went from selling high-end shoes to throwing cocktail parties for Macallan scotch, which had legendary journalist George Plimpton as its quasi spokesman.

Plimpton introduced Lopez to the brightest possibilities of a career in journalism.

After a doomed marriage left her as a twenty-three-year-old single mom, Lopez was determined to repair her academic and professional life. What followed was a yearslong blur of potty-training achievements combined with night classes and an entry-level copy-editing gig at the *Wall Street Journal*. Lopez parlayed her continuing education courses at New York University into full-time study in the school's prestigious undergrad journalism program, after which she ended up an intern pushing thirty at *Newsday*, desperate to work on stories with teeth.

She had learned by then that Plimpton, patrician pal to US presidents, was perhaps an unrealistic measuring stick for a life in journalism. She and her daughter followed reporting work wherever she could find it, which meant almost a decade of exile in the Midwest. She worked for the *Belleville News-Democrat* in harrowingly bucolic Illinois: "I'd never left Queens and here I am in this crazy-ass town full of, like, fields and stuff," she recalled. "Like, 'What did I get myself into?'"

She was then poached by the *Indianapolis Star*, where she realized her background put the risks of her job into perspective. When a purported gangster sent her an email threatening her life after she wrote an article about MS-13, her editors were alarmed but she was amused: "What kind of a thug sends an email?" she posited. Lopez's financial life was a perpetual struggle. Determined to keep her daughter in one of the best school districts in the Indianapolis area, her car was repossessed four times, and she was sued by credit card companies and collection agencies. She survived furloughs and pay cuts. When her teenage daughter, the love of Lopez's life, decided she wanted to move to New York to live with her father, Lopez did not let her do it alone. She got a job back at *Newsday* in 2011, and moved to Brooklyn, making the daily hour-long reverse commute to the paper's staid headquarters in Melville. A colleague's departure soon after she returned to *Newsday* made her the paper's lead Suffolk County reporter.

Lopez was thirty-eight when she rejoined *Newsday*, but she looked younger, and her unguarded personality could make her come off as naive. She didn't have fancy J-school credentials or big national awards, and a quick court database search of the sort readily available to cops, prosecutors, and journalists would bring up all those liens and lawsuits, suggesting somebody whose life was a mess. But Lopez was the sort who would show up at a crime scene and the cops, smirking, would let her see the body because they were sure she couldn't handle the gore. Being underestimated was her superpower.

At *Newsday*, Lopez saw that the paper was dutifully covering crime—which often meant regurgitating law enforcement press conferences and new releases—but not the police department itself. Lopez was far from a cop hater, but she was instinctively interested in scrutinizing their management. When she was a teenager, wearing her brother's baggy clothes and with a knife cutting a hole in her pocket to protect herself from rapists, she had always wished there were more cops around her housing project. But they only seemed to show up after somebody already got killed. In Suffolk County, where cops had long been criticized for ignoring their Hispanic constituents, Lopez perceived a potential rich vein for coverage and sought to make the management of SCPD her beat.

Which is why she took a special interest when one of her colleagues published the cop story equivalent of a pool opening: a downy-soft profile of the new chief of department.

* * *

The headline of the story, published February 2012, read: "James Burke: From Beat Cop to Suffolk's Top Cop." For a chief whose appointment had elicited a highly detailed anonymous letter from fellow cops recounting years of alleged misconduct, the profile conveyed zero trace of skepticism about his hiring. It was all fluff: the merits of intelligence-led policing; generic gushing quotes from supporters including Spota; and an unskeptical account of his role in the Pius case that didn't mention the part where federal judges had declared his testimony unreliable and inconsistent.

Another unmentioned elephant: that Suffolk County Executive Bellone had bucked tradition to name a chief of department first. And that his pick was the same figure in the DA's office who had supervised the murky investigation into Bellone's predecessor, paving the way for his election.

The story, which featured a photo of young Jimmy and Dennis Sullivan posing by the open doors of their First Precinct sector car, was a steroidal version of their old self-aggrandizing briefs from the North Amityville days. Burke wasn't just a top cop; he was an action hero:

A few weeks after becoming chief, Burke was leaving a meeting with Bellone in Hauppauge when he heard about a bank robbery in nearby Nesconset. He jumped in his car and joined a foot search for the suspect. "It was the first time in 10 years I had my gun drawn," Burke recalled.

It certainly wasn't jealousy that Lopez felt when she read her colleague's article. More like a flare-up of journalistic instinct. Firstly, the story should've been hers, as she covered the cops. The department instead granted the interview to a government reporter who had previously covered the Public Safety Committee meeting without skepticism. Secondly, the scrubbed quality to the piece suggested an over-sanitization, as if there was something to hide.

Lopez's curiosity was definitely piqued. She called up a department flack and wondered aloud: *Hey, when am I getting an interview with Chief Burke?*

Eventually, the department obliged. They invited her to come meet the chief in order to do a story on the SCPD's new way: intelligence-led policing. Lopez met Jimmy Burke in his wood-paneled chief's office in Yaphank. But she said that "the vibe I got from him was off." As she sat there jotting in her notebook, she was unnerved by his gaze. She had a feeling he was taking her in not as a reporter but as a woman he wanted to devour: "It was like, 'Are you looking at me, or are you *fucking* looking at me?'" Then there was the way that Burke and his deputies casually named confidential informants in front of Lopez, a cardinal sin in both law enforcement and journalism.

But most of all, it was the way Jimmy smelled. "He reeked of alcohol like he had a hangover," Lopez said. It reminded her of her dad, a former truck driver who after getting injured spent his days drowning himself in Bacardi. Lopez never wrote the article, partly because of Jimmy's weirdness and partly because she found there was no real story there. "All policing was intelligence-led," Lopez said. "You know, come on."

Shortly thereafter, Lopez's pursuit of another story involving the department brought her into a law enforcement official's office to see some records. Like most good investigative journalists, Lopez was more like a badly paid lawyer. The official appeared impressed with how diligent she was in proving everything in her story.

"What do you think of Jim Burke?" the official asked her abruptly.

"I don't," Lopez blurted, though she offered: "He seems to be somebody who has a nice following."

"You don't know the half of it," the official responded drolly, and they went back to the records at hand.

But afterward, Lopez started getting calls from cops and others gingerly offering her intel involving Jimmy Burke. Around Labor Day in 2012, at a Commack diner, she met with two Suffolk detectives— John Oliva and Willy Maldonado—who were accompanied by a couple of federal agents. Their story, that the new chief allowed the world's most dangerous street gang to fester in Suffolk County because of a petty squabble with the feds, sounded too crazy to be true. But they encouraged her to make some calls and vet it out.

Years later, Lopez asked that first official, whose identity she still shields, where that initial trust in her came from. The source shrugged: "Because you seemed like you knew what you were doing."

* * *

Detectives John Oliva and Willy Maldonado spent the Friday before Labor Day weekend in a Yaphank interrogation room across from a slight Salvadorian teenager nicknamed Unico. Without his frequently warm .25-caliber handgun, the kid was just a broken 120-pound boy still waiting on a pubescent growth spurt. The two cops studied the kid: it was always interesting to watch the eyes of a suspect to see the moment they realized they were going to grow old or maybe even die in prison.

Investigating MS-13 on Long Island was different than pursuing other organized crime factions. There was no head of the snake to cut off, or strategic lulls of peace between periods of violence. The don, as far as a low-level soldier like Unico was concerned, was often only another Brentwood teenager with a machete hidden from his mom under his mattress. A clique could be crippled by running out of ammo for their lone, shared 9-millimeter. The planning of a murder might consist of the seconds it took to register the wrong color or tattoo on a victim.

But that disorganization and senselessness just served to make the gang more deadly, and impossible to stamp out. Oliva and Maldonado, the top investigators of the gang in a suburban county that had become its American epicenter, could only hope to keep the body count under control by locking up killers as soon as they surfaced. It was like bailing out an overflowing bathtub with the spigot still going full blast. But the detectives were more successful locally than anybody before them. Oliva, in particular, was Suffolk County's reigning MS-13 pursuer, having been at it for more than a decade.

In 1999, the risk associated with gang policing was driven home when an MS-13 member Oliva was interrogating began calmly reciting details of the cop's life, including the speed bump near his home where he had to slow down to ten to fifteen miles per hour. That was a perfect place, the suspect explained, for an MS-13 member to consummate the "terminate on sight" order that the gang had out on Oliva and his previous partner. The gang called Oliva "The Cuban," and his determination to investigate them despite a shared Latin heritage contributed to their hatred.

Oliva's bosses offered to remove him from the assignment, but he refused. The department gave him a glowing-red panic button to keep at home, which only freaked out his wife and kids more. Oliva and his partner were written up in the *New York Times* for the contract on their heads, and the department brass expressed fierce pride. "I would like to think of them as two who exemplify the best of what we have," then-Commissioner Gallagher enthused to the *Times*.

Oliva felt he had found his career's calling in going after the Salvadoran gang on Long Island. His new partner, Maldonado, was a genial, seasoned investigator. Since 2010, they had been members of the Long Island Gang Task Force, in which local law enforcement agencies joined with the FBI to share intel and plan takedowns of gang members. They grew chummy with their federal colleagues. Maldonado, a comically massive man with a gentle nature, impersonated the stiffness of the FBI agents to their faces by walking around like a penguin. But past the jokes, the teamwork between the county and federal agencies was enormously effective, and an actual success story of intelligence-led policing, not just a PowerPoint. In less than two years, Oliva and Maldonado had helped lock up twenty-seven gang members linked to a dozen murders, including the one Unico was about to clear for them.

They had picked him up that morning on the basis of chatter from Oliva's street sources. Oliva was one of the rare officers in Suffolk County who spoke Spanish, and he had managed to cultivate an informant in every clique. The detectives suspected Unico for a murder in some woods off of Heyward Street in Brentwood. The victim was a *chavale*, or rival gang member, identified by tattoos showing he was a member of the 18th Street gang. Oliva had also learned that Unico was planning to murder a second 18th Street member whom he had been following. Within five minutes of them getting Unico in the interrogation room, the kid had confessed to the Heyward Street murder.

It was a quotidian murder, the kind Long Islanders appeared not to care much about. Gang-on-gang killings often didn't even make the paper. But the same killers who culled fellow gangsters also murdered civilians if not taken off the street. Among the gang-related murder cases Oliva and Maldonado had closed was the killing of a fifty-seven-year-old grocery store employee during an armed robbery. Each time the detectives locked up a kid like Unico, they theoretically saved multiple lives.

As they were going over Unico's confession again, Oliva's cell phone rang. It was the detective lieutenant who ran the Suffolk homicide squad. The commander abruptly informed Oliva that he and Maldonado had been transferred out of the task force and to separate precincts. "The powers that be wanted this done," he said.

He was calling from one floor above them in the Police HQ building, and Oliva demanded that they meet in person. They argued that this was more important than their own jobs. This was about fighting the worst kinds of crime.

Maldonado may have been a gentle giant, but he didn't suffer bullshit kindly. "Why are we being penalized and punished for solving over a dozen murders?" he demanded.

Oliva cut in, anger seeping into his sonorous voice: "Did anybody go to bat for us?"

Oliva said the boss didn't respond but the pained look on his face sent a message: *If I go to bat for you, I'm gonna be walking a foot post.*

Similar conversations were happening throughout the department between some of Suffolk's most skilled investigators and their bosses. Burke had also gotten Rob Trotta yanked out of the gang task force, where he had been working mostly drug cases. Other Suffolk cops were removed from task forces partnered with the DEA and the ATF.

Trotta returned from testifying in a money-laundering case in Costa Rica to learn that he had been transferred. In his new precinct, his first job was investigating the theft of copper pipes from abandoned homes. Trotta has an oblivious manner, but it's a false impression. In reality, he was well aware of the danger of his situation. He was seemingly inoculated against filtering his true feelings, and trapped in a department ruled by a vindictive boss who hated him. It seemed only a matter of time before those two factors detonated. So in order to save himself, Trotta began plotting his retirement, including ruminating on a nice sleepy second career for after he put in his papers. Such as politics.

As for Oliva, he left the assignment that he felt was his calling for the Fifth Precinct, where a gumball machine had gone missing from a truck. But unlike Trotta, Oliva considered himself nowhere near retirement, and he wouldn't let go of the gang work. He was still constantly on the phone with his former federal partners, sharing his intel on MS-13 targets, while the feds attempted to convince Burke to change his mind about the reassignments. Oliva felt sure that the reassignment was another example of the well-documented apathy toward Hispanic crime victims in Suffolk County. It was hard to imagine this going down the same way if the task force had been investigating murders of young white men in St. James, Smithtown, or Sayville. "It's almost like, 'They're whacking another gang member, or they're whacking an illegal guy,'" Oliva said. "And nobody really gave a fuck."

After getting pulled off gangs, Oliva wasn't terribly invested in his new post. "I didn't solve it, by the way," Oliva later admitted of his first case in the Fifth. "It's an unsolved bubble gum machine."

* * *

Jimmy Burke floated a few different justifications for the task force removals, one for every mood. A classic was that Jimmy, fiscal hawk, was cutting costs by keeping cops on needed departmental posts. Another was that Jimmy, a scrupulous manager, had learned that Oliva and Maldonado were responsible for an informant being killed, which the detectives denied.

But everybody around Jimmy knew his real reasons, myopic and petty though they were. The first was Jimmy's obsession with credit. He was of the belief that the only thing worse than a major crime going unsolved on his turf was for another agency to get the credit for solving it. That went double when it was the feds.

"We all hated the feds," Jim Hickey explained. When a Suffolk cop contributed to a federal prosecution, it was the feds who got the headlines and often a chunk of any assets seized. And the feds were the only major enemy that Jimmy hadn't either ousted or put firmly under his control. One of Jimmy's favorite tricks was planting spies in rival shops. He feared that by giving some of his top investigators to the feds, he was potentially turning them into spies against his own department. Jimmy's distrust of the federal government was apparent in the status of his top secret security clearance: unlike most chiefs of department, he didn't have any, even though some of his subordinates did. It would have been a hard sell for the feds to give him the clearance anyway considering his background, and the last thing Jimmy wanted was the feds undertaking the extensive investigation of his life that they required before granting access to closely held secrets.

So in regard to his cops being in task forces, it seemed unfathomable to Jimmy that in fact the feds were not actually interested in him—at the moment—but in busting MS-13 gang members. Jimmy railed against the Suffolk cops who, by simply doing their assigned jobs well, he perceived as dangerously consorting with the enemy.

"That they had become federalized," Jim Hickey later said in summarizing The Administration's view of Oliva, Trotta, and the rest. "That they have no loyalty to the police department. That they are just loyal to the feds, who we hate."

Said John Rodriguez of Burke: "He hated the fact that these guys would work for twenty years for some task force, grow their hair down to their ass, and not handle a frickin' real case. And he hated the fact that these guys were disloyal to the department that was giving them $200,000 a year. And a lot of these guys were running to the feds with their information, and he resented that."

Which brought up the central reason Burke had for stripping the task forces: one gangly cop with a mile-a-minute mouth. Rob Trotta scared The Administration like none other. Spota spoke often about Trotta's willingness to dig through his target's garbage, as if that were a sign of a truly dangerous nemesis. Removing the cops from the task forces was a way "to get rid of Trotta," Hickey said. "This was an opportunity and it would lessen Trotta's federal power base with his fed friends."

The move was incredibly cynical: removing half a dozen cops from life-and-death investigative postings where they were thriving, just to cover for detaching one of them from his federal handlers. Even more than that, it was brazen. Lots of county cop bosses hate the feds. Few of them try to do anything about it.

Shortly after Burke made his decision to gut the task forces, the feds demanded a meeting. There were a lot of dark suits streaming into Yaphank that day, as the feds brought in a delegation to plead with Burke to change his mind. Leading them were Nicole Boeckmann, the no-bullshit chief federal prosecutor for Long Island, and John Durham, her deputy who had directly overseen cases made by Oliva, Maldonado, and Trotta. On the other side of the table: Burke, Hickey, Madigan, and more top Suffolk cops.

The fed side made its case that they wanted to at least retain Oliva, as he was essential to active murder investigations. But Burke, as Hickey described it, was "unmovable, not open for compromise."

After the meeting, Hickey saw an unnerved Jimmy for the first time. "I have a terrible foreboding feeling that the feds are going to come after me," he confided. Hickey tried to assuage his boss that he hadn't done anything wrong.

But there was a funny thing about Jimmy. Even when he was rattled, he had only one strategy: escalate. He had tried to boot the feds from one of the two biggest criminal matters in the county, the pursuit of MS-13, and caught blowback. So of course, in December 2012, he cut out the feds from the other enormous case.

Nearly every high-profile unsolved serial killing in America gets scrutinized by the FBI's Behavioral Analysis Unit. In December 2012, an agent from the unit had agreed to visit Suffolk's homicide squad to prepare a confidential report profiling the killer or killers of the victims on Ocean Parkway. Instead, the detectives working the case were forced to make a sheepish phone call to the FBI profiler and tell him not to bother coming out to Long Island. On Burke and Spota's orders, he wasn't welcome.

* * *

Among the perks of life as chief was the take-home car, a gargantuan black GMC Yukon. Jimmy could've easily finagled a full-time cop chauffeur, but he liked driving. It was one of his favorite times to drink.

Being chief was a blur of schmooze-heavy events: get-togethers for the Irish cop frat called the Emerald Society, St. Patty's Day parades in the city, cigar parties, award ceremonies, speaking engagements, and multidepartment training sessions. Jimmy loved it all. About the only thing he used his work email for was RSVPs. When a police administrator asked him if he wanted to handle a couple of symposiums on street encounters, Jimmy responded: "Does Charlie Daniels play a mean fiddle?"

On the night of December 13, 2012—less than a year into being chief—Jimmy drove the Yukon home from a bar in Hauppauge where he had spent hours drinking. Jimmy had just gotten back from three weeks in Turks and Caicos the day before, and the night out had further fried Jimmy's already sun-addled brain. Later he'd have to ask his buddy Sammy Panchal, who tailed him to make sure he got home safe, what they did that night.

Jimmy and Sammy bonded over more than just spying on top governmental brass. They both had a Tony Soprano–esque affinity for cigars. Jimmy went nowhere without his portable humidor, and he relied on cigars as a barometer of a man's trustworthiness. If you claimed to like them and Jimmy spotted you smoking a stogie he deemed shitty, he'd shun you forever as a poseur.

But he respected Sammy as his equal in terms of cigar knowledge. The tech cop had given him a box of pricy cigars as a Christmas present that night. Undercrown, the cigars were called, by the Costa Rican cigar company Liga Privada, or Private Blend. Jimmy had stuffed the box into a Police Athletic League bag where he kept his own private arsenal of personal items.

Burke had, since his Lowrita Rickenbacker days, traveled with a party bag when he went to see girlfriends. And the next day he had a flight to West Palm Beach, where he planned to spend a long weekend with the wealthy widow of the real estate mogul he had met at the pro-Israel cop event.

After tucking Sammy's gift among the dildos, he tossed the bag into the roomy back seats of the Yukon.

Jimmy said his goodbyes to Sammy and stumbled into his house on Sammis Street in Smithtown. In his drunkenness he forgot to lock the Yukon, but not having to care about such details was another perk of being the boss. Who would steal from the police chief?

CHAPTER 18

PEE-PEE TOUCHER

In the first week of December 2012, Christopher Loeb squeezed next to his older brother Frank in the filthy double cab of Gabe Miguelez's red Dodge pickup. Chris was sleepily descending from a heroin high. When Chris awoke, they were in an area he didn't recognize. The three men hopped out and went right to their version of work: trying car door handles.

This episode of jigging whips was scattershot, even by their low standards. It was barely dark out, and the neighborhood was still awake. And Frank, a gray-haired wannabe wiseguy who had the New York Yankees logo sloppily inked on his right bicep, was hammered. Chris, whose nerves were still not used to petty criminality despite a decade of practice, was nervously pacing between cars when he saw it all go south quickly.

Frank was rifling through a parked car when a vehicle drove down the block. Gabe started hissing at Frank to get out, but Frank was too drunk to notice. The driver, probably just home from work, hopped out shouting that that was his car. A woman emerged from the house they were in front of, barking into her phone descriptions of the three thieves. Chris ditched his buddies and ran off into the nearby woods, finding a trail that led to Commack High School. From there, Chris flagged down a passing vehicle, whose driver warned Chris he was armed and would shoot him if he tried anything. This surly Samaritan gave Chris a ride to within a half-mile of his house in Smithtown.

When Chris finally made it home, he got in touch with Gabe, who gave him the score: Frank, busted with a stolen watch on his person, had been arrested. But because Gabe didn't have any contraband on him, the cops had let him go.

Down a member of their crew but undeterred, Gabe and Chris continued their never-ending quest for the next fix. That had been their lone mutual goal since they met about five months earlier. Back then, Gabe was a Roxicodone guy, though he had been hooked on one substance or another all of his adult life. The first time Gabe ever shot up heroin, it was Chris who found and flooded his vein in the latter's contraband-heaped Smithtown bedroom. Gabe was employed as a mason, and for a while he supported the drug habits of both himself and Chris. Gabe tried to get his buddy a job, but Chris slept through his first shift as a bricklayer. After Hurricane Sandy hit New York, Gabe's own work dried up, and so he and Chris turned to full-time larceny to pay Tommy, the friendly local heroin dealer.

With Frank locked up, Gabe moved into his former digs in Chris's mom's house. Gabe even took over Frank's prescriptions, impersonating the big brother in order to get a pharmacist to give them Suboxone—an opioid dependency treatment—which they promptly traded to Tommy for heroin.

Chris, though he didn't know it, was on borrowed time. A month earlier, his probation officer, Francine Ruggiero, had performed a random search of Chris's home. As it happened, that morning Chris had overdosed on heroin and Xanax in his mom's bathroom. While he was being loaded into an ambulance, Ruggiero found brass knuckles on his nightstand. She sent them off to the lab for a redundant, if legally necessary, scientific opinion on whether they were in fact brass knuckles, which would be a violation of Chris's probation. Ruggiero planned a raid on his home on December 12 in order to take him into custody. But Frank's arrest complicated her schedule because she was also his probation officer, so she moved the raid back two days.

If it hadn't been for Frank Loeb's drunken foray into Commack a week earlier, his brother would've been locked up while Burke was still on vacation in Turks and Caicos. And the DVD of a film called *I'm Here for the Gang Bang #2* would not have played a seismic role in transforming Suffolk County.

* * *

If only Shannan Gilbert's disappearance had gotten the same urgent treatment as the boss's truck getting robbed. Early on the morning of December 14, Kenny Bombace got a call from Jim Hickey. Hickey told him that the chief's vehicle had been broken into, and his things stolen. "You need to get all hands on deck," Hickey commanded.

Bombace roused the troops, calling up other members of the Criminal Intelligence Bureau. Hickey made more calls and, in the end, six of his detectives reported to Jimmy Burke's house in Smithtown. They combed the area for evidence and surveillance cameras and looked after Jimmy's elderly mom. When they heard about a probation search nearby that had turned up loads of stolen stuff, a couple of them went to check it out. After they then learned that a perp in the break-in was in custody, the rest headed to the precinct as a welcome committee.

The six detectives represented thousands of dollars per day of manpower, pulled off assigned duties that were ostensibly the most important investigative work in the county. The gangs and guns and all that other stuff could wait until after they closed the case of the jiggled door on Sammis Street. Hickey later explained why he put half a dozen elite detectives on the case: "Because it was Burke."

* * *

Brian Draiss was a highway exit cop. His purview for thirteen years had been the Fourth Precinct. Anything west of Exit 53 and east of Exit 61, or south of the Long Island Expressway, was irrelevant to Draiss, who had never been promoted. He made his $150,000 a year, stayed clear of pissing off his bosses, and planned to take retirement in a decade or so.

But now he was in Christopher Loeb's bedroom, staring at two dildos in a duffel bag alongside union cards reading "Chief of Department," and his mind was doing the Brian Draiss equivalent of racing.

The day had started innocuously enough. Draiss had been recruited by Fran Ruggiero to provide backup during the probation raid on Loeb's house. Like most every cop in the Fourth, Draiss had known Chris Loeb since the perp was a teenager, having responded to the woodsy brown house on Landing Avenue for one domestic disturbance or another. Officer Draiss didn't think very highly of Chris and his "self-chosen heroin addiction," at one point writing in a court document: "Again and again he has proven to have no redeeming value as a member of society."

That morning, Draiss, wearing a hoodie, jeans, and chunky sneakers, entered the Fourth Precinct offices holding a report from the crime lab that essentially said, Yep, those are brass knuckles. "I'm going to go arrest someone," Draiss announced. "Anyone want to go?"

Draiss and a partner were sitting in their Taurus about a quarter-mile away from the Loeb residence during the probation raid. When they heard "He's running out the back!" over the radio, they sped over to Teapot Lane just in time to see Loeb get peeled off the ground by a beefy, panting probation officer.

Once in the house, Draiss encountered Miguelez, who was claiming his name was Adrian despite the tattoo reading "Gabriel" in big letters down his arm. Loeb, in handcuffs, was initially planted on the couch next to the turtle tank. But he kept "peacocking," as Draiss described it, including yelling at his upset mom to shut up, so officers took him out to a cop car. Topping off the chaotic scene for Draiss was the archaeological layer of GPS devices and other stolen items in Loeb's bedroom. Draiss was in charge of invoicing each item, serial numbers and all, while hopefully avoiding impaling himself on a discarded syringe. It was a shitty morning. The contents of the PAL bag made it a shitty decade.

* * *

After word got out that the chief's stuff was there, the Suffolk police cavalry descended on the long driveway of the Loeb residence. Frank Catalina, the Fourth Precinct's squad commander that day, dispatched more men to the Loeb residence. Next, Intel guys started arriving at the scene.

As Officer Draiss loaded boxes of stolen items into a vehicle outside, there was Chief Burke himself. Draiss saw him peering through the windows of Gabe Miguelez's beat-up pickup truck. Burke then strode into the Loeb house, with Draiss joining his retinue. Burke took it upon himself to search for the gun belt, which was still missing, among the contraband in the house. He barked that the cuffs on it were special to him because they were from his police officer days. He then grabbed the handles of a duffel bag and lifted it off Loeb's bed as casually as if he were exiting a gym locker room. "Hey Chief," somebody interrupted. "We have to take a photo."

Kenneth Regensburg, a middle-aged detective from the Fourth with a digital camera, took a couple of snapshots of the duffel bag. The resulting photos appeared intentionally devoid of investigative value. Instead of removing the items from the bag as would be normal procedure, Regensburg just had it unzipped. All you could see inside was the box of cigars—Sammy Panchal's gift—Suffolk Detectives Association cards, and a packet of Shout-brand wipes.

And so, via mostly unspoken cop instinct, the cover-up began. Regensburg had already taken one glance at the Viagra prescription pill bottles with James Burke's name on them in the duffel, and immediately tossed them in the garbage. The dildos and some other items vaporized, either buried unphotographed in the bag or likewise tossed. Then there was the matter of the porn. Regensburg photographed on Loeb's nightstand one DVD with a cover featuring a woman giving a blowjob while three other erect penises surrounded her in apparent anticipation of their turn. The cops had actually found it in Burke's property, but they decided to gift it to Chris Loeb.

At least three law enforcement officers—Ruggiero, Draiss, and Regensburg—saw firsthand the contents of Burke's bag. Many others quickly heard the gossip. But they fudged their reports, sanitized their photos, and were prepared to lie under oath, all of it apparently to hide the fact that their chief kept dildos and porn at the ready.

Draiss later explained why he never even considered an honest inventory of what was in Burke's bag. "I could be transferred from one precinct to another. I could be counting cases or CCs"—cop-speak for case numbers—"down in central out in Yaphank in headquarters," Draiss said. "There's a whole host of things that could happen to you if you embarrass your boss's boss's boss."

Even a cadet on their first day in the academy knows a theft victim is not allowed to simply show up to an active crime scene and reclaim their property. Regensburg found it a little annoying that the chief was breaking protocol, but instead of confronting him, he said this: "You got some nice cigars there."

"Yeah, I know," Jimmy remarked as he left with his bag. "I don't want them to go stale."

* * *

Christopher Nealis was perturbed. The Fourth Squad detective wanted the first shot at Miguelez and Loeb. The arrestees were brought into the detective squad offices of the Fourth Precinct and shackled to the floor in separate interview rooms. But Nealis got only a few minutes with each of them, barely enough to read them their Miranda rights, when his boss, Catalina, told him it was now an Intel case. The purported rationale: Loeb and Miguelez were suspected of having broken into cars throughout the county.

Nealis, who thought of the Criminal Intelligence Bureau as "almost like a secret branch" of the SCPD, believed he could crack the case and they could not. It was a common prejudice against Intel: What did these desk jockeys know about interrogating a suspect?

The squad room was decorated in the style, common to police offices, of a demented man cave. Pieces of paper taped to the concrete walls heralded mottos such as "You Expect Too Much!!!!" and "This Is Your Butthole in Prison," with a large "O" next to it. For the three adrenaline-juiced Intel detectives—Bombace, Leto, and Malone—the guy they questioned first, Miguelez, was a pleasant enough warm-up. He was a hefty perp, stoic under pressure, who had plenty of experience in rooms like this. Miguelez calmly shoveled most of the culpability onto Loeb but nonetheless confessed to being the getaway driver while they were "lifting handles." Most important to the detectives, Miguelez admitted that they had broken into the chief's truck.

But then they entered Interview Room Number 3, and the vibe was all off. Loeb was purely belligerent. Cursing at them and demanding a lawyer was aggravating enough, but somehow it was the falling asleep that pissed the detectives off the most. Here they were in the biggest moment of their careers, and Loeb had the nerve to droop his head on his chest like he was at a Greyhound station. "He was just very nasty and he appeared to be, like, strung out," Leto later recalled with disgust.

Leto called what happened next "a bad combination of things," coupling Loeb's poor attitude with it being the holiday season. The detectives would rather be doing some gift-shopping before the Christmas rush than working on a case way below their pay grade. "I didn't want to fucking deal with this," Leto said. Contributing to their anxiety was a desire to get a confession. It didn't matter that the case wasn't much of a whodunit. It was the chief's truck, and they were going to close the case.

As a result, the detectives weren't a picture of patience that morning. Leto tried empty threats, including telling Loeb that his mother was going down for the stolen shit in their house, and that she would be raped in jail. And each of the cops tried violence, taking their turns hitting Loeb, who had no way to protect himself. With his wrists shackled inches from the ground, he couldn't even use his body to deflect the blows. When he tried to bury his head in his chest, Leto grabbed him by the neck so that he'd have to face their punches head-on.

Bombace later blamed a military-mind fugue state, where he was blinded to everything but his orders to get a confession out of this guy. As for Malone, battering Loeb represented an opportunity for a rebrand. Malone had a reputation for being chickenshit, and he embarrassingly didn't have an IAB conviction against him yet.

Tony Leto gets points for simple authenticity. His reason for kicking Loeb's ass that day: "He was being an asshole." When prisoners misbehaved, this is what Leto did.

But in Loeb, the three detectives faced a foe who had inadvertently prepared for this moment his whole life. Loeb had always been a magnet for other people's violence. If it wasn't his father, Loeb said, it was high school bullies. He blamed a beatdown over a girl, which left him with a fractured nose and sternum and a titanium plate in his jaw, for first leading to his addiction to prescription pain pills at age sixteen. Hard to believe back then, before the spiral of addiction, that he thought he was going to be in the US Navy.

Violence can produce diminishing returns, especially on someone who had experienced as much as Loeb. His response to the pain and fear inflicted on him by the detectives was to just put the shutters up. It badly skewed the expected power dynamic of the interrogation room. Here was a drug addict, facing serious charges, unable to even block his face from being punched, and yet the highly paid cops who were going home this weekend were the desperate ones. They soon were demoralized and needed a break. When they stepped out of the room to collect themselves, under the humiliating watch of the Fourth Squad guys who barely pretended to be busy with their own cases, the detectives were greeted by an odd sight: Jimmy Burke in a suit, waiting for an update.

They commandeered a break room where there was a television and a coffee machine. The detectives sheepishly broke it to Burke that Loeb was refusing to confess to burglarizing his car. This news seemed to stress the chief out, which wasn't particularly logical. After all, the cops had loads of physical evidence against Loeb. There was actually too much evidence, if you asked the hapless Fourth Precinct guys entering a seemingly endless amount of codes into their logs. But socking a confession out of a perp was never just about solving the case at hand. It was also about domination. King Jimmy wasn't going to leave this precinct with him and his palace guards beaten by a sticky-fingered serf.

The chief suggested he could go in there with them and talk to the guy. "I don't think that's a good idea," objected Tony Leto, but Jimmy was already on his way.

* * *

With the detectives hovering behind him, the chief used his left hand to grab Loeb by his cheeks. He brought down his right fist on the top of his head. He squeezed Loeb's face and asked: "Do you want to steal from me? You wanted to steal from me?"

Loeb, still chained to the ground, managed: "Get the fuck off me."

Jimmy angrily pushed himself off Loeb and started screaming about how he was going to hit him with every felony charge he could. Loeb, slightly tongue-in-cheek, asked the chief for an attorney. "You're not getting a fucking lawyer!" Jimmy boomed back, continuing on about how he was going to put Loeb, and his family, through hell.

Loeb looked up at the chief. "I know what I saw in your duffel bag," Loeb said. The insult he then spat at Burke has shifted in the telling. Sometimes it's "Pervert!" Other times, "Pedophile!" Or perhaps he slurred: "Pee-pee toucher!"

What hasn't changed is the way Jimmy responded. He used his left hand again to grab Loeb, this time with his palm covering his mouth. He told Loeb, his voice now low, that no one would ever fucking believe him, because he was a convicted felon and a dopehead. As Jimmy kept punching Loeb in the head and the body, and kneeing him for good measure, he told him he was going to give him a "hot shot," slang for a lethally laced heroin dose. Loeb screamed, groaned, and tried to cover up. Finally the three detectives interceded: "Boss, leave it alone, leave it alone." They had to physically pry him off the prisoner.

When they finally got him out of Interview Room Number 3, there was no longer an audience. The only cop left was squad commander Frank Catalina, who had cleared everybody else out. Jimmy was amped up, telling his detectives: "That was like the good old days!"

Burke and his Intel entourage streamed out of the precinct, later relaying a message: the Fourth Precinct guys could have their case back.

* * *

The cops who entered Interview Room Number 3 over the next several hours pretended like nothing out of the ordinary had just happened. Before the beating, a couple of the Fourth Squad guys had played the good cops. One of them had drawn out of Loeb the history with his abusive dad, his girlfriend's abortion, the origins of his heroin addiction. They were trying to build a rapport, and now another cop—Christopher Nealis—tried to pick up where they left off, as chummy as ever.

Loeb interrupted: "That was the chief?" Nealis, with practiced obliviousness, asked Loeb to describe who he was talking about. After Loeb was done, Nealis responded: "Yes, that was the chief." Loeb told the detective he had "nasty porn" in his bag, and Nealis quickly left the room. He returned about an hour later and, after asking a few questions about car break-ins, brought up the porn. "What are we going to do about this?" Nealis asked Loeb with a concerned voice.

"You're not going to do anything about this," Loeb sneered. When a second cop entered the room after a while, Loeb asked him for a lawyer. "I'll work on that," the cop assured him.

"That piece of shit put hands on me," Loeb remarked to a third cop, Detective Thomas Cottingham.

"What do you expect?" Cottingham mused. "You broke into his car." Later, Cottingham reentered the interrogation room holding Burke's gun belt with an air of triumph. They had found it hidden inside a dry vac in Loeb's basement. Cottingham said that because all the contraband was in his mom's house, they planned to charge her with grand larceny. "My mother has nothing to do with this," Loeb pleaded. "My mother has never committed a crime in her life." Cottingham had a few papers folded over with a statement written on it. Loeb agreed to sign the paper on the cop's promise that they wouldn't charge his mom.

At around 9:00 p.m., Police Officer Michael Kelly was told Loeb was ready to be "printed and photoed and lodged." Kelly had been there since that morning, when he saw Chief Burke enter the squad room. He had attempted to greet the chief, but Burke had walked right past his extended hand. Kelly then saw Burke and the detectives enter the interview room and close the door behind them. He heard yelling, and a "clap or a smack."

Kelly had since then been stuck handling the copious paperwork that went with the case. Now when he went to get Loeb from the interview room, he noticed the prisoner had red ears. He fingerprinted Loeb, had his mug shot taken, and brought him to his holding cell for the night. Loeb's neighbor was Gabe Miguelez.

"Some old guy in a suit smacked me," Chris announced to Gabe within earshot of Kelly. "It's the chief, and he said his best friend is the DA."

Gabe responded: "Oh, fuck me."

* * *

For the chief and his palace guards, the celebratory vibe to the rest of the day couldn't even be dampened by a gunman opening fire on elementary school kids across the Long Island Sound. Bombace saw the breaking news of the shooting in Sandy Hook, Connecticut, as he was leaving the precinct and called Burke to inform him. School shootings were, after all, Bombace's purview.

Bombace and Leto then headed to a bakery on main street Smithtown where they met with Cliff Lent, another Intel detective. They huddled over cappuccinos and whispered, not with any great concern, about the prisoner beating they had just administered along with the chief. When the three detectives then returned to the Fourth Precinct to help out with a few loose ends, the Intel Bureau's swagger was back.

Mike Malone in particular appeared to be having the greatest day of his life. Malone was a big, bounding golden retriever of a detective, with dull eyes, a salt-and-pepper buzz cut, and an all-consuming drive to impress peers and supervisors alike. As he sauntered through the Fourth, Malone bragged loudly of having pissed in Loeb's coffee cup, prompting Leto and Bombace to give each other a bewildered look. *What the fuck are you saying that for?* Leto said he thought: "It was stupid. It was really fucking stupid."

It's not clear whether Malone actually did piss in Loeb's coffee, though Leto recalled that the detective made a big show of bringing the cup to the precinct bathroom before giving it to the prisoner. Whether the boast was empty or not, it was the first of many times that Leto and Bombace felt uneasy about having Mike Malone as a criminal co-conspirator.

The Fourth Precinct guys turned over a GPS device believed to have been found in Burke's duffel bag, and the detectives took it back to the chief. They met Burke on the side of the Long Island Expressway, where the chief identified the GPS device as his and signed a statement about his items being stolen.

Jimmy wrote that after parking his truck at 10:00 p.m. the previous night, he had discovered at 6:00 a.m. that morning that "somebody entered it and stole my personal belongings." By his official account, this is what was stolen from his truck: a gun belt with two full Glock 9-millimeter magazines, pepper spray mace, a TomTom GPS device, a duffel bag, Ray-Ban sunglasses, a box of cigars, and lighters. The statement didn't mention the other contents of the bag, or that he had grabbed the stuff back from Loeb's house, or that he had ever gone to the Fourth Precinct. After signing the statement, Jimmy headed off to the airport to catch a plane to Florida.

Jim Hickey received excited missives about his detectives' big morning. Malone was gratified to have pleased the chief and jazzed to have peed in Loeb's coffee. Bombace reported like a proud soldier that they "took care of business for the chief." And Leto remained stoic, only saying that they "took care of Loeb."

None of them were as excited as Jimmy himself. Before he flew off on another vacation, the chief called James Hickey at his office in Yaphank to gush. The Intel detectives did themselves proud, he said. They beat the hell out of Christopher Loeb.

"Bombace was slamming his head off a table and Malone—Mikey Malone—peed in his coffee cup," Jimmy relayed. This impromptu performance review was as positive as one could get, Hickey later recalled: "Burke was very pleased."

* * *

Suffolk prosecutor Spiros Moustakas had heavy eyebrows, an acrid sense of humor, and an exacting legal mind. In his five years in the Government Corruption Bureau, that last trait could have caused a lot of sleepless nights. Moustakas had been the lead prosecutor on the Bob Macedonio case, in which Spota seemed to have avoided prosecution of dangerous drug dealers in order to give passes to his buddies. Investigators in the Government Corruption Bureau were still sore over that. Moustakas knew all the dark tactics of the cowboy bureau, from dubious wiretaps to "scooping" interview subjects off the street without anybody seeing, partly so they couldn't prepare by hiring a lawyer.

But Moustakas enjoyed the upward mobility that came with working in the DA's shadowy nerve center. And he slept fine because of his security blanket: ass-covering legal memos. Whenever he observed something dubious, Moustakas typed out a record memorializing it, and felt the absolution wash over him.

The Loeb case quickly had his memo-writing hand aching. His first encounter with the case came at eight o'clock on the morning of December 14. He got a call from Chris McPartland, his boss, informing him of the burglary and telling him to report to Building 77 rather than his customary Blue Star office. When Moustakas got there, McPartland was on his way out, heading to a Christmas party in the city with Bill Madigan. But he asked Moustakas to hang around to provide "legal process" to the break-in investigation.

Later that morning, Moustakas got a call from one of the detectives in the Fourth, who asked him to write a search warrant for Loeb's residence. The problem with that was that they had already searched the house. The detective name-dropped Jimmy Burke and talked about wanting to "dot the i's and cross the t's," but Moustakas found the request disturbing. He typed up a blandly worded memo. "The stolen property was already removed from 205 Landing Avenue and is at the 4th Precinct," Moustakas wrote. "Request denied."

Moustakas spoke to his boss by phone the following midnight. McPartland told him that he was to be at the Loeb arraignment the next morning. Moustakas oversaw long-term investigations, heavy on wiretaps, that typically involved corrupt public officials. But now McPartland was directing him to handle an arraignment on a Saturday for a car burglary. When Moustakas dutifully headed to the Central Islip courthouse the next morning, it became clear that Loeb had not been transported there for his arraignment.

Cops know that if you want to toy with a perp a bit, you can concoct an excuse to delay taking them to arraignment by a few hours. But missing the arraignment entirely is a serious matter. Moustakas called the Fourth and ended up on the phone with Catalina, the squad commander. Catalina explained that Loeb was "talking," and that his men were handling a fatal car accident anyway, so they wouldn't be able to produce him that day.

Moustakas scrambled to a corner of the courthouse where he knew there was a criminal procedure law book. He started reading to the detective sergeant about how a prisoner must be brought to court without "undue delay." Catalina was unmoved. Moustakas wrote a memo recounting the conversation. Then he parked it in the case file, to be seen by nobody in particular.

Loeb spent a full forty-eight hours in police precincts being grilled about various break-ins without ever seeing a lawyer. When he was finally arraigned that Sunday, he was kept in jail on $500,000 bail, an amount typically reserved for only the most serious of criminals. His codefendant Gabe Miguelez was ultimately released on $10,000 bail.

Afterward, Moustakas asked McPartland whether they should kick the Loeb and Miguelez cases to a different bureau. After all, the Government Corruption Bureau did not handle open-and-shut probation violations. But McPartland explained that there was ammunition involved and Moustakas was a "gun expert," having previously been involved in an investigation of weapon traffickers from the southern US.

"No," McPartland told his underling. "We are going to keep it here."

* * *

While Chris Loeb was sitting in the precinct waiting to be arraigned, Jimmy Burke was continuing his weeks-long vacation junket. The Wednesday after the beating, he returned from a six-day weekend in West Palm Beach with his wealthy widower girlfriend and drove directly from the airport to a party at a grand estate on Suffolk's north shore.

Gary Melius, the owner of Oheka Castle, was Jimmy Burke's type of guy: an eighth-grade dropout with a lengthy record, implicated in federal testimony as having stolen Cadillacs for a mob ring. He was an exemplar of the uneasy, but not uncommon, confluence between gangsters and cops. He had been the right-hand man to Richard Hartman, a gambling-addicted police union attorney whose brilliant and brazen contract negotiations were a significant factor in the ballooning salaries and unchecked power of modern law enforcement. In the 1980s, Melius scraped together $1.5 million to purchase a dilapidated 127-room estate built by a roaring twenties robber baron, and turned it into a lair for Long Island political power. A funhouse-mirror Joe Pesci with slicked-back white hair and faded tattoos, Melius made himself into a power broker partly through chummy relationships with both local cops and federal agents.

It wasn't a secret why cops liked Melius, besides the allure of a *Goodfellas* vibe. He threw them parties at his castle either on the arm, or at a steep discount. That included a two-hundred-guest shindig for Kenny Bombace's Suffolk County Police Veterans Association for which Melius never sent a bill. At the annual Criminal Intelligence

Bureau Christmas party at the castle that year, Bombace was the emcee. When Jimmy arrived, the chief immediately displayed that he was still riding high from the good times the week before in Interview Room Number 3.

A detective came and got Jim Hickey from another area of the party, telling him that his men and Burke were loudly discussing the beating. Hickey went to the bar of the Charlie Chaplin Room and saw Jimmy regaling Leto, Malone, and Bombace. As Malone chimed in with his own boasts, Leto fumed at the lack of discretion. He was especially wary of the civilian bartender standing there, underneath dozens of framed images of the silent film comedian, listening to these high-level cops laugh about having pissed in a prisoner's coffee.

But Leto was apparently the only one stressed about the whole thing. Hickey laughed along. Asked later to describe the tenor of the barroom conversation, he replied: "Celebratory."

Among his friends, Burke didn't bother hiding that he had roughed up Loeb. He told Sammy Panchal that the cigars he had given him were stolen, but that he "bopped" the thief on the head, making a hand motion like pounding pizza dough. Out at a bar with Dennis Sullivan, he said of Loeb that he "squeezed his cheeks."

The stress-free vibe continued until Hickey got a call that Rob Trotta was poking around the Fourth.

CHAPTER 19

ABSOLUTE PANIC

For Jimmy Burke, fucking Rob Trotta—stripping him of his little Costa Rican money-laundering adventures with the feds and yanking his buddies from their MS-13 task force while he was at it—felt great in the moment. But there were some unforeseen consequences.

He had put three of the most dogged investigators in the county in dead-end assignments. While they waited for fingerprints concerning the stolen bubble gum machine or a copper wiring caper, Trotta, Oliva, and Maldonado had little to occupy their attention except fucking the guy who had fucked them. And by virtue of their previous assignments, they happened to have iPhones full of contacts for equally pissed off federal agents.

Oliva heard about Burke being involved in beating a suspect at the Fourth within days of the incident. He immediately relayed the information to the FBI agents he knew. During the week of Christmas, Trotta called an old buddy of his who worked at the Fourth. But the friend, Chris Nealis, who nervously insisted that the allegations were "bullshit," was clearly scared to talk on the phone. Later, they met in a parking lot, where according to Trotta, Nealis was more forthcoming. (Nealis later denied giving Trotta any information, insisting he had none to give: "I never saw anything.") Trotta phoned one of the federal contacts to tell him: this thing really happened.

At the time, the feds seemed confident. "Don't worry," the agent told Trotta. "We got it."

Trotta, like any good mentally-checked-out employee, made a daily quest out of getting home as early as possible. So on a late morning in January 2013, when a colleague in the First mentioned he had to drop a small amount of cocaine at the department crime lab, Trotta volunteered to handle it for him. The lab was next to the Fourth Precinct, and Trotta lived nearby. He figured he'd do it near the end of his tour and get paid for the commute home.

He invoiced the coke and then wandered into the detective squad room to bullshit with the guys he knew there. One of the detectives made a circle in the air with his finger. It was his way of telling him that Burke had put a target on his back. Adequately provoked, Trotta asked loudly: "Did anyone see the chief"—he put his arms up to mime fisticuffs—"beat a prisoner?" One of the detectives, Tom Cottingham, took the bait, complaining to Trotta about having to enter the interview room and talk to the guy after Burke beat the shit out of him.

Immediately after Trotta left, Burke spies from the Fourth called Jim Hickey. They described the encounter down to the fisticuffs motion. Meetings were convened in Yaphank and over the phone. The Administration knew instinctively that if Trotta was aware of the beating, the feds were as well.

Spota and Burke's emotions swung on a pendulum. The DA again shared his almost animalistic fear of Trotta, and Jimmy—no doubt making a mental count of all the witnesses on that day—suddenly realized the stakes. But McPartland considered these moments his specialty. He used his legal expertise to try to calm the waters.

McPartland explained to his colleagues that a federal investigation of a police chief would require the involvement of the civil rights division in Washington, DC. Loeb's mug shot injuries weren't bad, so it was his word against that of the chief and the Intel detectives. McPartland didn't feel Trotta had the sort of horsepower needed to even get an investigation started, much less indict Jimmy.

Conspicuously absent from these discussions, and those to come, was the matter of whether Jimmy had actually beaten the guy. "We all knew that Burke did it," Hickey later said. "It was just a question of covering it up so that Burke doesn't go to jail."

That cover-up included planting a spy as an Internal Affairs Bureau supervisor. In January 2013, Frank Catalina, the squad commander who had cleared the room during Loeb's beating, interviewed for a promotion to detective lieutenant. Hickey was on the interview board, which was headed by Billy Madigan.

At the end of the interviews, the board ranked the candidates, and Catalina was topped by another lieutenant, John Rowan. Hickey called up Rowan and gave him the great news that he was being slotted in as a detective lieutenant in the IAB. But then Burke and Madigan told Hickey they'd decided to give the job to Catalina instead, because of Loeb. "Rowan can get it next time," Jimmy remarked.

* * *

In the months preceding the Loeb beating, Oliva had just about given up on *Newsday*. After he, Maldonado, and federal agents had met with Tania Lopez and given her information about their removal from the street gang task force, she still hadn't published a story. He figured that Spota or Bellone had succeeded in getting it squashed.

So Oliva and his comrades took the story to a competitor: the *Long Island Press*. The regional weekly paper assigned three journalists and scrambled a story into print in October 2012, two months before the Loeb beating. They described the detectives' removal as the result of a "turf war," teasing the scoop on the front page with an illustration of an FBI agent wearing a blue bandanna while an SCPD cop wore a red version.

The story included a response from James Burke, who blamed budgetary concerns. "Given these difficult fiscal times," he said, "we hope that we could work together in creative ways including having federal resources assigned to various Suffolk county police commands."

At the time, Oliva and Maldonado were still hoping the decision could be reversed so that they and others pulled from task forces could get those old jobs back. The pair arranged a meeting with Billy Plant, chief of the detective's union. Plant told them the department was within its rights to transfer them however it saw fit. He seemed unbothered by the loss of some of the best-paying and most coveted assignments available to a Suffolk detective. "Meanwhile, if this was with Steve Levy as the county executive, they would've blown a fucking gasket," Oliva later said.

Though Oliva and Maldonado's role as background sources had been kept confidential by the *Long Island Press*, they were named as subjects of the story. Given their anger at the transfers, it wasn't hard to figure out they were behind the article. Before the detectives left the meeting, Plant warned them: "Just make sure no more negative stories come out about Jimmy Burke."

Tania Lopez was pissed when she saw the local alt-weekly scooping a story she had months earlier. She felt she had enough to write the story nearly immediately, but her boss kept moving the goalposts. "I was challenged every step of the way," said Lopez, who ascribed her boss's overcautiousness to skepticism of a relatively new reporter's sources.

But by the turn of the new year, even Lopez's editor had to admit her story was bulletproof. Among those she had on the record criticizing the detectives' removal was Dominick Varrone. The recently deposed chief of detectives had been the one who initially agreed to loan the cops to the federal task forces. He now expressed skepticism that money was the reason for the transfers: "The returns for the manpower investment have been astounding."

Lopez also had quotes from family members of murder victims whose cases had been solved by the task force. "If they did their job so well," the niece of a victim said, "why would they pull them out?" Lopez's story finally went to print in late January. "The *Long Island Press* first reported the transfer in 2012," Lopez noted in the story, an intentional dig at her own editors for dragging their feet.

Out in Yaphank, Burke and his retinue had largely ignored the story in the *Long Island Press*, which had a relatively small readership. But getting trashed in *Newsday* was a new and deeply unwelcome sensation for Jim Burke. He considered himself a self-taught master of public relations, cajoling reporters and feeding them information intended to make them beholden to him. Among the most frequently dialed numbers in his Rolodex were one of the top investigative reporters at *Newsday* and the paper's best-read columnist, both decades-long fixtures at the paper. This was the first negative article the newspaper had ever run about Jimmy, and it had been written by a little-known reporter who had been there for just two years.

From that point forward, Lopez said, the SCPD's public information office largely stonewalled her. They only gave her records or information after the info was no longer useful, a significant detriment to a beat reporter on daily deadlines. But Jimmy saved his real ire for the man he figured was the source behind the article: John Oliva.

The detective only learned later that Jimmy and Billy Plant, the union official to whom Oliva had complained, were close buddies. "He gave me up completely," Oliva said of Plant. Up until that point, Oliva was mostly unknown to Jimmy, just a wannabe fed who was collateral damage in his move against Trotta. But now he had leapt to a spot near the top of Jimmy's enemy list.

* * *

About a week later, Emily Constant, Tom Spota's matronly chief assistant, sat at a table in her expansive office in Hauppauge and studied a crime scene photo. The photo depicted the DVD case of *I'm Here for the Gang Bang #2*, situated on Chris Loeb's nightstand. Tom Spota, standing in front of Constant and Spiros Moustakas while Chris McPartland perched on a couch nearby, wanted to know about fingerprints. Could they get them off the disc?

It was a workday in Suffolk County, population 1.5 million, and its top prosecutorial brain trust had scrambled this impromptu meeting in less than an hour after Moustakas told them about a meeting he just had in Riverhead. Moustakas was still the reluctant lead prosecutor of the Burke break-in case, and that morning he was scheduled to have a pretrial conference with Chris Loeb's defense attorney. Such meetings typically occurred in a judge's chambers while other lawyers waited their own turn. But as Moustakas was heading into the conference, Loeb's newly appointed attorney, Toni Marie Angeli, stopped him and asked him to step outside.

In a vacant jury room, Angeli calmly gave an ultimatum. The case had serious problems, she said, that neither the police department nor the DA's office would want exposed. Her client—who was still locked up on $500,000 bail and was at that moment in a nearby holding pen—had been abused and mistreated and would only accept a misdemeanor plea with a sentence of time served. With that, Angeli gave Moustakas a stack of papers.

At the following meeting in the judge's chambers, with Tania Lopez there taking notes, Angeli didn't disclose what she had told Moustakas. Instead she only asked the judge for a later court date so both sides could both look into the case further.

Angeli, the DA's office knew, was a bulldog. She had made national news in the mid-1990s as a thirty-one-year-old Harvard art student when a photo lab called the Cambridge police to report that she was developing nude shots of a young boy. When she arrived to pick up the photos, detectives were waiting for her. But the photos were of her son, for an art exhibit called "Innocence in Nudity." The cops claimed that in an ensuing scuffle, she threw a lamp at them.

Angeli was eventually convicted of disorderly conduct and malicious destruction of property and sentenced to probation and $229 restitution to the photo lab. But Angeli refused to pay a dime to the snitching photo lab and instead chose to serve a month in jail. When she got out, she decided a change of profession was in order. She was admitted to the New York bar at age thirty-eight. This background of righteous belligerence was one of the reasons the Loeb family liked her.

Now Spota, moving on from the question of fingerprints on porn, was read the documents Angeli gave McPartland. It was Angeli's discovery demand, typically a boilerplate legal record asking for all the general types of documents a defendant is entitled to. But, as Moustakas had already read, Angeli's demand was definitely not all boilerplate. She asked for "an inventory of the items found in the bag allegedly belonging to James Burke," as well as the identities "of any and all officers who were present at the 4th Precinct when complainant James Burke was allowed unfettered access to the defendant to interrogate and otherwise terrorize him."

Spota grew more agitated with every page. When he got to this demand—"The specific time at which James Burke arrived at the 4th Precinct on December 14, 2012"—Spota asked about surveillance cameras or a sign-in book at the Fourth. Moustakas didn't know, and McPartland intervened from the couch: "Doesn't matter if there's a sign-in book or not, everyone will remember James Burke. He's the chief of department."

The bosses told Moustakas to go and leave his file behind. As the prosecutor was leaving, Spota told Constant to call the Appeals Bureau, because "we need to get off of this." Assigning a special prosecutor outside of the Suffolk DA's office to handle this case was an obvious move, and had been for months, even if it weren't for the beating allegations. After all, one of the victims of this break-in crime, namely Jimmy Burke, had spent a decade as a supervisor in the DA's office. Giving up control of the case was still the last thing Spota or McPartland wanted to do, but there was an urgent rationale to cutting it loose now.

Spota couldn't, without arousing suspicion, simply cave to Angeli's demands for a misdemeanor and time served, given that they had already portrayed Loeb as a danger to society worthy of $500,000 bail. That same day, Tania Lopez had filed her first *Newsday* item on Burke being the victim of a crime. Though she played it straight, with no reference to misconduct by the chief—"Man Accused of Stealing Cop's Gun Belt Back in Court Next Month," the headline read—the online comments to the article made clear that the local rumor mill was well-apprised of the secret aspects of the case.

"Could it be that Burke is receiving preferential treatment," wondered a writer by the alias "fovbaker," noting the oddities of a top corruption prosecutor handling the case and the half-million-dollar bail. "Or perhaps Spota is secretly investigating the improper way in which Burke personally oversaw an investigation in which he was the complainant, was allowed to retrieve his property without first vouchering it into evidence like any other crime victim, and then had investigators assigned to him clear out the 4th Precinct so he could have a private 'conversation' with the defendant in an interview room. My bet is on the preferential treatment."

Burke's investigators printed out that comment, among others like it. Given that the gossip was already swirling—remarkably accurate gossip, time would show—there was no way to quietly shelve the case. With Angeli's allegations in the court record, Spota had little choice but to hand off the case to a special prosecutor. Typically, a DA's office would give the prosecution to the neighboring office to handle, which in Suffolk's case meant Nassau County, but Spota detested the then Nassau DA, Kathleen Rice. He considered her a blowhard who wasn't qualified to run a law enforcement shop. Worse yet, Rice had a reputation for being tough on police officers. The last thing Spota wanted to do was give her office control over a case that could destroy Jimmy Burke and, in the process, himself.

It was only the first week of February, but the giddiness of Christmas seemed a long time ago. The new mood, according to Jim Hickey: "Absolute panic."

* * *

Jimmy Burke—when he wasn't fretting about his fingerprints being on the X-rated disc—spent that month deciding on his story. "Should I say I wasn't there?" he wondered aloud one day to McPartland and Hickey.

"You can't say that," McPartland interjected. "Too many people saw you."

So Jimmy countered: What if he was only at the precinct to poke his head in? He had just wanted to see if he recognized the car burglar, and couldn't even recall if the interrogation room's door was open or closed. McPartland nodded, indicating that he was satisfied with the story.

They moved on to the next order of business: Hickey keeping his men—Bombace, Malone, and Leto—tight. No more boasts about pissing in coffee cups. "Deny, deny, deny," was the basic strategy. It wasn't just Jimmy and McPartland who told Hickey that it was imperative for him to keep his men quiet. Spota recited the same catechism whenever he ran into Hickey: How are they? Are they holding up? Are they toeing the line? Are they okay? Prior to the Loeb beating, neither Spota nor McPartland had cared at all how these cops were doing, so to Hickey their real concern was clear: "That they wouldn't tell the truth."

A plan took shape to keep the Loeb case under something approaching control. The plot relied on the borough thirty-plus miles to the west where so many of the figures in this saga had been born. The DA of Queens County, Richard Brown, was an octogenarian figurehead who couldn't lose a reelection if he tried, and he had ceded most if not all operations to his number-two, Jack Ryan. Spota called up Ryan, with whom he was chummy, and explained the situation. Ryan agreed that Queens would take the Loeb prosecution. They assigned it to Pete Crusco, a longtime prosecutor with an ingratiating manner and a rodentine mustache. Spota and McPartland were pleased. "Solid guy, good guy, Crusco," they reported back to Hickey. Crusco lived in Suffolk County and appeared happy to please his suburban counterparts.

For his part, Spota showed he wasn't quite a figurehead himself, providing some effective and obscure legal obfuscation to the maneuver. Giving a case to a special prosecutor required a DA's office to draft an affidavit that included the parameters of the investigation. That's because by New York legal precedent, a special prosecutor could not exceed "the limited scope of his authority," as specified in the original affidavit, or the resulting indictment would be dismissed. McPartland was certainly aware of this, having chatted with Crusco about this very topic while they prepared the paperwork. The Queens prosecutor even emailed McPartland the legal precedent for him to check out himself. Authoring that draft fell to Spota's chief of the Appeals Bureau: Michael J. Miller, a large, goateed man with a slight steampunk vibe siloed away in Riverhead.

So naturally, when Miller's bosses instructed him to write the affidavit, they didn't tell him about the misconduct allegations that had spurred them to finally seek a special prosecutor in the first place. Miller was by all accounts a thorough practitioner of his specialty. If he had known about the allegations of misconduct against Burke related to the Loeb case, he would have included them in the affidavit as part of the Queens DA's mandate.

The resulting affidavit only specified that the Queens DA was to be in charge of prosecuting Chris Loeb. Even if Crusco wasn't "solid"— which in Suffolk-ese meant not prone to disturbing a cover-up —his hands would have been largely tied if he did decide to investigate Jimmy Burke.

Spota and McPartland, presumably, were adding yet another layer of protection by appointing a Suffolk police "liaison" to the special prosecutor in Queens. This liaison was to monitor all police interactions with Crusco and report back to Spota and McPartland. There was never much doubt who would get the job. "Billy's the best guy for the job," Spota told McPartland and Hickey, referring to Burke stooge Madigan. "Billy's an attorney. He's trustworthy. He's one of us."

Planting a spy in part to make sure that Queens didn't veer off course proved unnecessary. In the end, Crusco seemed like he tried his best to demonstrate compliance.

* * *

On December 14, 2012, Fourth Precinct officer Mike Kelly saw Chief Burke, heard a slapping sound from the interview room, noticed Loeb's red ears afterward, and overheard Loeb telling Miguelez an old guy in a suit had beaten him. Those small observations could have helped bury Burke. But when Kelly testified in a state grand jury four days later, the prosecutor Moustakas didn't ask him about any of that, and the cop certainly wasn't going to volunteer it. A month later, he was promoted to sergeant.

Kelly was in supervisor's school in Brentwood in March 2013 when he got a call from Lou Tutone, a top official in the Suffolk County Police Benevolent Association. There had been a special prosecutor assigned in the Loeb case, Tutone told him, and the union was organizing a meeting to discuss it. The PBA didn't even represent Kelly anymore, as since his promotion he was now a member of the Superior Officers Association. But when Kelly, a thin cop with a black landing pad of hair, arrived at the PBA offices, the true purpose of the meeting became clear.

In the office with Kelly and the union officials were a smattering of other police officers who had been at Loeb's house or the precinct on December 14. A union attorney stood up and announced that since there were so many people present, the meeting would not be protected by attorney-client privilege. He then asked for each officer to tell their story of what had happened the previous December 14.

In the style of a class presentation, they each took their turns talking. Kelly told his story, leaving out the details that suggested a beating, and included that the interview room door was closed. "Yeah, I heard the same thing," Tutone mused. "But I heard that the door was open." Kelly suddenly felt anxious. He realized that Burke's story was probably that the door was open.

Later that month, Kelly went to a meeting with Crusco. The special prosecutor and his investigator, a detective, had commandeered an office in the New York State Police barracks near an airport in Farmingdale. Kelly was accompanied by a Superior Officers Association official and an attorney that the union had chosen to represent him. Kelly told his story again. He again left out the incriminating parts but this time said nothing about the door being closed, concerned that if he said the wrong thing again it would get back to the chief.

This was Mike Kelly's turn in the Great Story Straightening. Every cop even slightly involved in the Loeb incident had a similar experience. Before meeting with the special prosecutor, Fourth Precinct officer Brian Draiss went out to lunch with Tutone and a PBA attorney. At the barracks, the same union officials were present for his interview with Crusco. Draiss had never before had union representation at a meeting with a prosecutor about a case. At one point in the interview, Draiss listed for Crusco the items he found in Burke's bag that day. Shocker: he did not mention the two dildos. Draiss decided they were immaterial to the investigation. Also factoring into his omission were his aspirations to one day finally make detective, rather than exile to some far-flung desk assignment.

The Intel detectives got the deluxe version of the experience. Before their own trip to the trooper barracks, Hickey told them to go meet with Burke himself. They took seats around a table in Burke's office and the chief appeared to be in a screenwriter's mood, open to any ideas. *Did the chief come in the room? Was the door open? Was the chief even there? Was he even in the precinct?* These were some of the ideas that Tony Leto later recalled Jimmy "throwing out there." Spitballing aside, the story ultimately returned to the McPartland canon: The door was open, Jimmy poked his head in, asked how everything was going, and left.

When Leto showed up for his interview with Crusco, Suffolk County Detectives Association president Billy Plant pulled up in the barracks parking lot. He invited Leto into his car for a pep talk in which he assured the detective it was "all bullshit" and they had nothing to worry about. With Leto's union entourage present during the interview with the special prosecutor, Crusco apparently didn't even bother to ask about whether Burke had been in the interview room.

In Bombace's own interview, he was asked only "generalities" that would've conveyed a "vague understanding of what happened that day." Having gleaned that Crusco had been handpicked, Bombace feared anything he told him—even outside of the presence of the union officials—would immediately be relayed to Burke and McPartland. "It was almost unfathomable," Bombace said, "to think at that point to go into that room and tell the truth."

* * *

The *Mary Ann* was supposed to leave the Orient Point dock by seven o'clock. By the time everybody got their act together and out to the easternmost tip of the north fork of Long Island on the morning of June 25, 2013, they were fifteen minutes behind schedule.

Suffolk County Comptroller Joe Sawicki organized a charter fishing trip every year, drawing a cross-section of the white guys who ran the county. Over a couple of years, the trips included Suffolk County Detectives Association honchos Billy Plant and Russ McCormack, SCPD Chief of Patrol John Meehan, County Executive Bellone, and a couple of his top deputies: Kevin Law and Justin Meyers. Spota made it out a few times. Chief Burke was the only participant besides Sawicki who never missed a year. Jimmy, now also a member of the Smithtown Bay Yacht Club, loved few things more than boating and bullshitting with the boys.

The 2013 charter featured a cozy crew: Sawicki, Jimmy, Chief Deputy County Executive Dennis Cohen, a couple of financial consultants who worked with Sawicki, and the comptroller's orthopedist. The foot doctor and his fishing pals got quite a show that day. About twenty minutes into the charter trip, as they were about to drop their lines at Plum Gut—a nice spot for striped bass—the police chief received a call on his cell phone from Hickey. After he hung up, he rambled something about the FBI. "We have to turn around," Jimmy told Sawicki urgently. "You have to drop me back at the marina."

After the call with Hickey, Jimmy grabbed Sawicki's phone to reach McPartland. As far as he was concerned, his own cell phone was burned.

Shortly afterward, Tom Spota walked into Emily Constant's office in Building 77. Constant was Spota's administrative right hand, with a magnetic org chart on wheels in her office that showed every attorney they employed, with the big names up top.

"We are going to go to my house," Spota informed her.

"Okay," replied Constant, who had never been to her boss's home during a workday. "What for?"

Spota replied: "We'll talk about it when we get there."

* * *

Kenny Bombace initially tried to ignore the rapping on his door early that morning, thinking it was Jehovah's Witnesses, but it was persistent. He went downstairs and found a pair of FBI agents on his front steps. They told Bombace they'd like to ask him a few questions, but he said he couldn't do that. So instead, they handed him a piece of paper.

Once they left, Bombace launched a flurry of phone calls and texts. "Lieutenant," Bombace told Hickey, "I just received a subpoena from the FBI."

So had Tony Leto, roused from bed on his day off. The moment he saw the visitors in their suits, he knew who they were and why there were there. The week earlier, Tania Lopez had finally broken the story in *Newsday*, via an interview with Loeb's mother, that the prisoner was alleging Burke hit him. To Leto, FBI agents at his door seemed a natural, if disastrous, progression: "My heart sunk." The agents started asking about December 14, and whether he was with Burke that day. After he told them to call the union, they handed him a subpoena.

Leto remained stoic even as internally a heavy fatalism was taking hold. "Right there," he later mused, "my life took a shit."

* * *

When Hickey heard about the subpoenas, he tried Burke, but the chief wouldn't pick up. He finally spoke to McPartland, who was in full operational mode. The prosecutor told him that Jimmy was on a boat but aware of the subpoenas. He said that Hickey was to get his guys together, find out exactly what was said when the feds delivered the subpoenas, and what FBI office these agents were from. McPartland even added a somewhat patronizing explainer on 302s, the secretive memos FBI agents use to document interviews during an investigation.

Jim Hickey and his family lived in a three-bedroom on Tall Tree Lane in Smithtown. It was a little cramped, particularly when the fourth kid was home from college. But on a nice day they could all overflow into the spacious backyard where the Hickey family had a pool. On the morning of June 25, 2013, six of Hickey's detectives—the Haves—parked in the long driveway edged with obsessively cut grass. Hickey proceeded to pepper them with questions, alternating with checks on their emotional temperature.

Fourteen miles to the northeast, the executive suite pulled their own vehicles into the driveway of a home on Little Harbor Road in Mt. Sinai. Compared to Hickey's house, Spota's digs were courtlier, if still modest. Spota and his wife, Mary Ellen, were empty nesters, and Tom took a stubborn pride in maintaining the property, down to doing his own yard work and splitting firewood. Spota let his aide Constant in, and McPartland and Billy Madigan arrived shortly thereafter. It was a hot midsummer morning, and a bystander might conclude that the county's top law enforcement brain trust had decided it was simply too nice a day to spend in dingy offices in Hauppauge and Yaphank. But then came the weepy police chief.

First Burke told his audience about the subpoenas. According to Constant, Jimmy was adamant it was all over nothing, that he had never touched Loeb and that the investigation was only payback for stripping the federal task forces of manpower. He paced Spota's kitchen and deck. He kept repeating how he had done nothing wrong, and then he started crying.

If there was any good news, it was that Jimmy hadn't lost his biggest supporter outside of Tom Spota. *Newsday* had the story about the federal subpoenas by that evening. It included the following statement from County Executive Bellone: "James Burke is an outstanding law enforcement official and has helped lead our efforts to make Suffolk County a safer place to live."

* * *

Jimmy pulled himself together, converting his self-pity back into mob boss–style wrath. He called Hickey to tell him that his new full-time job was keeping his detectives quiet. He said the feds could be "up on their phones," meaning utilizing wiretaps. If they were studying call patterns, it wouldn't be unusual for Hickey to phone his detectives frequently. Jimmy told Hickey to relay to the guys that he had the two smartest lawyers he knew—Spota and McPartland—working on this, and that they were also going to hire attorneys for the detectives. "Real lawyers," Jimmy said. "Not shit union lawyers."

He then asked for the results of Hickey's temperature check on the detectives: "Who was the most nervous?" Hickey said it was Malone. Of the three detectives who had beaten Loeb, only Malone for some reason didn't get a subpoena, which had unnerved everybody because they couldn't figure out what it meant. Hickey said Malone had paced around, ranting about how he shouldn't even be involved in this.

Jimmy flew into a rage. He seethed to Hickey: "Tell Iron Balls Mike that if he wants to keep that million-dollar house and heat in his inground pool he'll keep his fucking mouth shut."

When Jimmy asked about the others, Hickey started: "They are all nervous—"

"There's two fucking questions," Jimmy interjected. "'Did you hit anybody? Did you see anybody hit anybody?' Answers: Two nos. Period. The end. Not that fucking difficult."

* * *

The detectives kept waiting for their union—highly paid officials whose stated purpose was to defend their interests—to care. "It seemed to us, at that point, this was a pretty big deal," Bombace said. But nobody reached out to him. Leto managed to speak with an in-house lawyer at the Suffolk County Detectives Association, but found the meeting uninspiring. The lawyer, a guy named Kranz, asked Leto for few details about the incident, patted him on the back, and said: "You'll be fine."

"Kranz was bullshit," Leto complained shortly afterward to union official Russ McCormack, Burke's boating buddy, who met him and the other two detectives at the Smithtown Starbucks. The detectives could have all the lawyers they wanted, McCormack assured them, and the union would pick up the bill.

But at a meeting with PBA president Noel DiGerolamo in that union's Bohemia office, the detectives learned of the strings attached in that offer. First off, if they admitted wrongdoing, the union would no longer pay for their attorneys. And secondly, the union wanted to handpick the legal counsel. Any lawyer the guys wanted to use had to be run by union brass first.

Kenny Bombace's brother-in-law, Ray Tierney, the former Suffolk prosecutor who had joined the feds, was at the time distracted by an ongoing trial he was handling. But he knew Burke well enough to glean exactly what had happened from the spare news stories concerning the Loeb incident. He felt certain that for wife's brother, this story ended in one of two ways: with Kenny cooperating or going to prison.

With the knowledge that the feds were investigating, Tierney had to keep his distance. So he called his friend Chris Clayton, also a former Suffolk prosecutor, and asked if he would talk to Bombace. "Get him unconflicted, non-PBA competent counsel," Tierney pleaded, "and tell him to tell the truth."

Clayton then called Bombace, and the detective brought Malone and Leto along with him for a meeting at the lawyer's house. They explained to him about the subpoenas, and Clayton advised them to cooperate with the federal government. The detectives thanked him for his time and left with no intention of following his advice. Their fear of retaliation made it unthinkable. "And not retaliation like you're going to get kicked out of your union, or even cops will think you're a rat," Bombace later explained. This wasn't a professional advancement thing anymore. The detectives felt they didn't have the imagination necessary to chart all the ways Burke could destroy their lives.

The detectives started catching glimpses of a separate plot to which they weren't privy. Kenny got suspicious when he started calling some of the most prominent defense attorneys on Long Island for possible representation. When he reached Joe Conway, a politically connected former federal prosecutor, the lawyer told him he couldn't represent him because he'd already been hired by Chief Burke. The detectives felt it was a sign that Burke was secretly moving to insulate himself. "I was fucking pissed," Leto said. After that, Leto, Bombace, and Malone emulated the drug dealers they all had experience pursuing, and purchased burner phones from convenience stores in order to communicate with each other. The goal was to protect their conversations not only from the feds, but also their bosses.

Bombace picked his own lawyer, Ed Jenks. But Leto was assigned a union lawyer, and he feared that anything he said to his guy would go directly to Joe Conway and Jimmy Burke. That suspicion was spot-on, as it turned out that Conway had provided PBA chief DiGerolamo with a list of federal defense attorneys to hire for the detectives and others in the Burke matter. Those lawyers and Conway then had a defense agreement to coordinate and share information. During his first meeting with his lawyer, Mineola-based Matin Emouna, Leto figured he might as well make that dynamic explicit. After telling Emouna he had no desire to cooperate with the feds, Leto asked him to drive them half a mile down Old Country Road to Conway's office. Leto waited outside while Emouna went into Conway's office and relayed Leto's message: that he wasn't a rat.

Leto took every opportunity to remind Hickey and Burke that he still had no plans to snitch. He said he did so because of his three teenage boys, one of whom had just started driving. He knew from the way Burke took pleasure in going after Pat Cuff's son that kids weren't off limits.

He pictured his boys being framed for drugs, or worse. Leto, the sinewy torture expert, was flat-out scared. "I feared for myself," he later said, "my job, my partners, my family."

CHAPTER 20

HICKEY'S BACKYARD THERAPY

On the same day that their colleagues, armed with subpoenas, sent more than a dozen cop households in Suffolk County into a predawn tizzy, FBI Special Agents Ryan Carey and Jeremy Bell showed up at the Riverhead jail carrying documents giving them custody of their chief witness. The two-hour return trip with Christopher Loeb to an interview room in Brooklyn felt like they had snatched a hostage from enemy territory.

The agents, who weren't much older than the twenty-six-year-old Loeb, started by taking down the story of his struggles with addiction. Loeb told them he first injected his girlfriend's heroin at age seventeen, kicking off a circuitous route to a meeting with Jimmy Burke's knuckles a decade later. He was blunt and seemingly honest about his relapses and his overdoses, and how before his most recent arrest he had been dealing thirty bundles of heroin a day to support his own habit.

Loeb's initial meeting with federal agents that day led to another debriefing a month later and a third within a few weeks of that. He chugged coffee and ate 1:00 a.m. muffins while sifting through photos to identify cops and straining to remember every detail of that day in the Fourth Precinct.

Back in the interrogation room in Hauppauge, he hadn't been able to keep his eyes open. Six months later, in a similar room forty-five miles west with the law now seemingly on his side, Loeb wouldn't shut up.

The agents' pens moved a little quicker when Loeb got to the burning question: What was in the chief's bag? Later, Carey and Bell compared notes and put it into bullets in a 302, complete with the FBI trademarks of a typewriter font and sporadic capitalization:

- Three pink anal beads in their original but previously opened packaging. The package felt greasy;

- A buttplug in its original packaging that had also been previously opened and felt greasy;

- One plastic baggie containing one tube and one bottle of sexual lubricants (not KY brand);

- Four or Five Pornographic DVDs. The DVDs were in DVD cases whose covers contained pornographic images. One cover depicted a photograph of a pre-adolescent boy who was smirking. His face was surrounded by penises. A second DVD cover depicted a blonde male teen having sex with an adult male. After seeing the two described DVDs and packaging, LOEB put the items back and did not look further into the side pocket.

That last bullet was certainly intriguing to the special agents, if also somewhat dubious. Traffickers in child porn did not typically adorn it with incriminating packaging. But even the minimal investigation the feds had conducted to that point indicated that the Loeb case had been handled against protocol in almost every way. And the more the feds learned, the more enticing the case became.

That said, targeting a chief of a major police department—particularly in a territory as famously insular and protective as Suffolk County—was a highly sensitive matter and bound to be challenging. Which is why it was perhaps odd that April Brooks, special agent in charge of the New York field office, gave the case to two greenhorns.

Bell, with a strapping build and a slightly stilted manner, was the lead case agent and an up-and-comer in the agency. But he was only six years removed from the academy at Quantico. The squat and bearded Carey, Bell's partner in the public corruption and civil rights squad, was a rookie. They were based in Manhattan, and Suffolk County was just an obscure territory a long ways down the expressway.

Their case up to that point had an unsurprising foundation: Trotta and Oliva. Federal agents had heard rumors of the Loeb beating almost as soon as it happened. But Carey and Bell's first official interviews with the two cops—deemed "cooperating witnesses"—occurred in May 2013. Trotta gave the feds the names of Fourth Precinct cops, Chris Nealis and Tom Cottingham, with whom he said he gossiped about the beating. The FBI also received an anonymous letter that month alleging Burke's beating of Loeb. By May 31, the feds were ready for the first step of any preliminary investigation: giving it a cool name. Thus, Shattered Shield was born.

The next month the special agents met with Loeb's attorney, Toni Marie Angeli, who relayed her client's allegations of finding prepubescent porn and being punched while shackled. Carey and Bell also received a cache of interview notes from the Queens DA's office, where the special prosecutor and his investigator had spoken to various cops and Loeb's codefendant, Gabe Miguelez, about the break-ins.

It was clear from the notes that Queens was staying clear of any questions of assault on the part of Burke. But the interviews with the special prosecutor still confirmed the odd handling of the case. Among the breaks in protocol were Burke taking back his stolen items rather than having them inventoried, and entering the interview room where Loeb was being kept. The special agents also learned from the notes that Miguelez claimed Burke had lubricant, sex toys, and a child pornography DVD in his bag.

There was a purposeful shock-and-awe quality to the agents both leafleting Suffolk with subpoenas and taking custody of Loeb on June 25. The decision of when to take a preliminary investigation "overt," as they did that day, was all rooted in some FBI handbook. They were trying to create a "prisoner's dilemma," in which witnesses rush to cooperate before their peers beat them to it.

But with the possible exception of McPartland, with his detailed questions about what office the subpoena-delivering agents came from, The Administration was too frazzled to realize that day what the feds' strategy also suggested: that they didn't have anything. As salacious as the allegations were, it was only the claims of two felons and hearsay from a couple of disgruntled detectives.

It wouldn't take much for the FBI to get something, though. The sheer number of potential cop witnesses at multiple scenes on the day of Loeb's arrest worked in their favor. The young special agents only needed one of those witnesses to tell the truth, and they'd be off and running.

The cops that their subpoena-serving colleagues encountered that day were for the most part as polite as could be. Frank Catalina, the Fourth Precinct squad commander, thanked the agents for acting like gentlemen and contacting him at home instead of work. But he apologetically told them that he had been advised by a representative not to talk about "the incident."

Mike Kelly invited the agents into his house, and started telling them exactly what happened. But then he figured he should call his union rep, Lou Tutone of the PBA.

While the agents were seated in his kitchen, Kelly told Tutone: "The FBI is at my house."

"No, they are not," Tutone responded in disbelief.

"Yeah, they are," Kelly insisted, and Tutone told him to politely inform the agents that he was no longer interested in speaking that day and would get back to them with an attorney.

Fran Ruggiero, Loeb's probation officer, didn't need any time or an attorney to get her own story straight. She too invited the agents into her home for a lengthy chat, and she even drew them a sketch of Loeb's residence. She then calmly proceeded to feed them a line of bullshit about what was in Burke's duffel bag: some comfy clothes, a toiletry bag, and a few other things, the most salacious being a few condoms.

When Carey and Bell got the reports from their colleagues about these interviews, it was a wet blanket tossed on the case. But they were still hopeful the subpoenas would scare an honest straggler or two into their offices. In other words, they had no idea what they were up against.

* * *

Jim Hickey knew his way around a big lie. It wasn't just that old brutality and perjury rap from his days in a sector car with Fatman, and untold other shenanigans they never got caught for. He also conducted his personal life as a series of conspiracies. He was a serial cheat, carrying on at least four yearslong extramarital affairs. Even though the street population of Wyandanch had decided via consensus that he looked like a rodent, Hickey was a popular suitor in Smithtown and Yaphank.

His mistresses included two civilian analysts who were his subordinates in the Criminal Intelligence Bureau, a woman who worked at a local beauty parlor, and an employee of St. Patrick's Roman Catholic Church. These weren't one-night flings. He texted one of the women up to a thousand times a month. Another woman he dated on the side for eight years. He lied to his wife about what he was doing when he was with his mistresses, and he lied to his mistress about his relationship with his wife. He cheated on a mistress with a mistress. Hickey's affairs endlessly tickled Jimmy Burke, who saw them as more fractures in a broken wing, ensuring Hickey would never betray him.

Being a successful philanderer requires meticulous multitasking, which Hickey believed was one of his greatest talents. And all he had to do was stay a step ahead of his wife, a nurse who he dismissed as unable to keep track of her cell phone. Hickey compartmentalized— and in his own clandestine way documented—his life with the help of a tear-away calendar on his desk. He neatly jotted down little scheduling notes regarding his daughter's kick line tournaments or his son's college orientation, and some less positive developments. "FBI subpoenas," he wrote in tiny handwriting on June 25, 2013. From that point forward, he jotted down a coded personal reminder of nearly every event in the cover-up.

Hickey's reason for such documentation, on a calendar on his desk that any passing cop could've scrutinized if they had bothered, was vintage Ratman. When—not if—the conspiracy fell apart,

Hickey wanted to be able to refer back to these dates in order to better cooperate.

In the summer of 2013, a long stretch of days on Hickey's calendar were marked with a "303." That was cop code for a vacation day. Jimmy Burke wasn't speaking figuratively when he told Hickey that the cover-up was now his full-time job. The day after the subpoenas, he ordered Hickey, who made about $174,000 that year, to no longer come into work. His Intel boss was more useful puttering around his backyard, on call at all hours of the day and night. Burke wanted Hickey on backyard duty any time Bombace, Leto, Malone, or any other cop feeling pressure from the feds needed bucking up. Hickey's only job was keeping Burke alive, keeping his guys calm, and keeping them from ratting.

"Hickey's Backyard Therapy," Jimmy termed it, though in reality the sessions were more for the chief's mental health than anybody else's. The detectives were expected to provide regular assurance that they were still loyal. Bombace, who earned $211,000 that year, discussed little with his boss, Hickey, besides updates on whether the detectives were remaining steadfast. After Leto's lawyer had him visit the Fourth Precinct to make a diagram of the interview room, the detective went directly to Hickey's backyard to assure him he hadn't gone rogue.

Besides the therapy sessions, Jimmy had all sorts of innovative ideas that summer, all of them increasing Hickey's stress. Another was reversing course on loaning detectives to the feds. Jimmy announced that he was assigning two detectives to an MS-13 task force. "Suffolk's Anti-gang Push," read the headline in *Newsday*. In the accompanying article, Burke made clear that the new move was not an admission that removing the detectives from task forces the previous summer had been a mistake. "Those decisions were made as a result of our intelligence-led policing model," he explained.

But Hickey knew the real reason that Jimmy made the move. The chief gave Hickey marching orders to relay to the reassigned detectives, Brian Keegan and Marcus Rivera, that their primary job was to spy on comings and goings at the federal courthouse in Central Islip. Jimmy used his power as chief to change the detectives' police supervisor from the homicide commander to Hickey. If the detectives saw any of the Intel guys in the federal courthouse, where they'd have little reason to be if not cooperating, they were to inform Hickey.

Jimmy had already been obsessive about the cover-up, but after the subpoenas he appeared to think of little else day or night. He released his stress by shoving it downward onto Hickey's psyche, forcing Hickey, in turn, to put that burden on his detectives. A couple of weeks after the subpoenas, Burke and Hickey pulled up alongside each other in their respective cars in the parking lot of Smithtown's Brady Park. They were driver's window to driver's window, in the vaguely belligerent manner of cops. A passing civilian might have thought about the hourly pay of these public servants and noticed the running of all that county air conditioning, and hoped that they were at least talking about police work.

Jimmy started by relaying Spota and McPartland's concern that Bombace was the most likely to rat, given that his brother-in-law was an Eastern District fed. "Keep us updated on any changes in appearances, or if any of the guys look like they are leaving the reservation," Jimmy said, and offered to pay for a private attorney for Hickey, which the Intel boss declined.

"I'm counting on you to keep me alive," Jimmy told Hickey. He then reminded his subordinate that he too had "skin in the game." If the feds were up on their phones, they knew that Hickey had been involved in the cover-up since day one.

He then drove off, leaving Hickey to digest his boss's remark. That was Jimmy's style, to cajole and threaten in nearly the same breath. Hickey's only way of regaining control was through his secret calendar notes. He memorialized the meeting in the park using his boss's initials: "JCB Brady."

After long days of talking detectives off ledges, calming his boss, and stewing in his backyard about a conspiracy he felt sure was doomed, Hickey would come in for dinner with his wife and kids. Earlier that year, about the time that Trotta entered the Fourth with his fisticuffs motion, Hickey began having a glass of wine with dinner, which he never previously did. Then he started treating himself to a couple of glasses, and the pours got more gargantuan.

By the time of the backyard therapy sessions, he was finishing off a whole bottle each dinner in two and a half glasses. After dinner, he'd switch to vodka: half a quart, or maybe the whole thing if it was a rough day. Sometimes he'd switch things up and sip orange juice and vodka with breakfast. Hickey knew he was playing with fire, as his father—a former US Marines drill instructor—had died from complications of alcoholism. But Hickey built up such a tolerance that he felt he was functioning fine, until a Friday morning in August when he suffered from severe stomach pain and was unable to keep anything down.

Hickey's wife drove him to the emergency room. "He is very tremulous, shaky with the wife at bedside," a doctor observed of Hickey, who continued vomiting while in the hospital and complained of anxiety and chills. The doctor diagnosed him with pancreatitis from excessive drinking. For five days he was locked in a hospital bed with gates up and alarms set if he tried to get up or fell out of bed. Hickey spent his daughter's thirteenth birthday in that bed suffering through alcohol withdrawal. After he detoxed, the doctors recommended an inpatient program. Hickey refused. Ditto for an outpatient program, or even Alcoholics Anonymous meetings. The last thing Hickey needed was a group meeting where you're supposed to bare your soul. He said he simply decided to never touch a drink again.

Hickey's coming-home present was a boss furious over his unexplained disappearance. Hickey explained to Jimmy about the pancreatitis and the detox. Jimmy seethed to Hickey that he thought the feds had grabbed him and Hickey had flipped, and that he was never to go incommunicado again.

Hickey's backyard therapy patients were a bit more sympathetic. Bombace and the other detectives didn't know about the emergency hospitalization, only that he swore off alcohol. The following Christmas, instead of giving him the usual bottle of liquor as a gift, Bombace headed to the mall and got him a tea set from Teavana. For the remainder of the conspiracy, Hickey was fueled by jade citrus mint.

* * *

Chris McPartland was once a drama kid—he had stunned in the Walt Whitman High School production of *Charley's Aunt*—and now he found an outlet as an acting coach in Jimmy Burke's office at Police HQ.

McPartland, Jimmy, and Hickey met there in September 2013 following more poor news on the Chris Loeb front. Loeb's attorney was claiming that his statements in the case were beaten out of him and that the search of his home was improper. The judge ordered a suppression hearing to determine whether the evidence was illegally obtained. In order to prepare for the worst-case scenario—Burke being forced to testify in the hearing—McPartland conducted a mock cross-examination of the chief.

But when Jimmy explained as if under oath that he only popped his head into Loeb's interview room, McPartland was unsatisfied. He proposed a fuller story, in which Jimmy was concerned about his sweet old mom, and drug use in the park across the street.

"Why did you stick your head in the room?" McPartland prompted.

Burke: "I wanted to see if I recognized the defendant from the neighborhood."

McPartland, drawing him out: "Why? Why was that necessary to recognize the defendant from the neighborhood?"

Burke: "Because my elderly mother lives nearby, and . . . there is the park across the street known for hanging out and using drugs."

They decided Jimmy nailed it.

But McPartland wondered: If they were successful in keeping the chief off the stand, who would testify instead? After all, if nobody testified, Loeb would win the suppression hearing and it would be obvious the department was hiding something.

Malone was too shaky, Jimmy pondered, so nerve-wracked about this whole thing that he had been visibly losing weight. And Bombace was too inexperienced at lying. So Leto would do the honors. Jimmy told Hickey that he was to give Leto the news. "He's not going to like it," Hickey said.

Jimmy became irate. "They want to make the most money, drive the nicest cars, have the nicest job," he snarled to Hickey about his detectives. "This is what they signed up for."

In the end, Jimmy's mock cross-examination proved unnecessary. Crusco, the ostensibly independent special prosecutor, happened to choose for testimony the very guy McPartland and Jimmy wanted: Leto. Informed of the decision, an upset Leto recruited Bombace and Malone for a visit to Hickey's for some urgent backyard therapy.

Leto made his case to his boss as adamantly as possible that he shouldn't be forced to testify. There were few shorter straws a cop could draw than being ordered to perjure himself in open court. The conspiracy was teetering on the precipice of collapse. If the truth came out, that Burke had beaten Loeb, which any number of witnesses might reveal, Leto's lies under oath would ensure his neck slid under the guillotine blade first.

Hickey was already thinking the same thing. When Jimmy and McPartland had been discussing which of his guys should perjure themselves so Burke didn't have to, Hickey felt he was witnessing the confirmation of a long-held suspicion: that Jimmy and McPartland's long game was to pin the beating on Hickey's detectives. Jimmy would skate, with the narrative being that Loeb had just thrown the chief in to make the story better. In that scenario, of course, it was Hickey who would take the ultimate fall for orchestrating the cover-up.

Hickey didn't say all that to Leto. Instead, he explained dispassionately that "they" did not want Chief Burke on the stand, and so it'd have to be Leto. As bosses are wont to do, Hickey simply passed down the bullshit like a baton. He told Leto: "This is what we signed up for."

Leto accepted it stoically. But ever since being handed the subpoena by the feds on his doorstep, he had a feeling in his gut that this was going to all unravel, and now the stakes were only becoming more catastrophic.

Leto prided himself on giving his boys a childhood free of trauma, unlike his own. But now all he could think about was the prospect of the feds busting down his door and dragging him out while his sons were home. That was the worst trauma he could imagine for them, perhaps worse—he began to consider—than coming home to their dad swinging from a rope. Or maybe he'd shoot himself with a service weapon, or crash his car in a way that would make it look like an accident. He realized that he should do it outside of Suffolk County, so that his colleagues weren't processing the scene.

He didn't tell his wife, with whom he had been an item since junior high, about the thoughts he was having. She had just graduated nursing school, and he didn't want to burden her with his problems. And he knew the dominos that could fall, including his guns being taken away, if the department learned he was suicidal. Instead, Leto confided in a female friend. That then became an affair. According to Leto, it was the first time he had ever cheated on his wife. Just another conspiracy to manage. "I was more or less in the state of mind like, 'Fuck it now, my life's fucked,'" Leto said.

Outside of his mistress, Leto kept all of this inner turmoil a secret. He started running ten miles a day, around St. James or in loops on the campus of Stony Brook University. Along the punishing routes, his mind raced too, with the unraveling of his marriage, the fear for his sons, that image of the feds at his door.

Like Burke, Leto had noticed the way a twitchy Mike Malone betrayed his guilt whenever he talked about the conspiracy. "You could see it physically, like he would fucking be like crawling out of his skin," said Leto. That wasn't Leto, who attempted to weather his own meltdown as unobtrusively as possible.

Before his testimony in the Loeb case, Leto was told to meet with Crusco for one more prep session. But instead of the neutral site of the trooper barracks, this meeting was to occur at Billy Madigan's office in Police HQ. And when Leto arrived, Chief Burke was exiting.

"Are you good?" the chief asked as Crusco waited for Leto to enter. The detective responded coolly: "Yes."

* * *

Over the course of 2013, Tania Lopez had become the clearinghouse for Jimmy Burke rumors. She got an email about how young Burke and Danny Culotta rigged the Pius murder case as teenagers. She door-knocked a retired cop in The Villages in Florida to ask about Jimmy being caught up in a Brooklyn prostitution sting. The cop's union in turn sent the publisher of *Newsday* a cease-and-desist letter. She interviewed a Smithtown insurance salesman named Doug about being cuckolded by Jimmy, but her editors spiked the story.

She spoke to Jimmy's old strip-club pal Rob Grettler, who had served his time in the drug-ring case and moved to Los Angeles to seek fortune as a screenwriter. Her bosses wouldn't spring for a plane ticket to meet him. She investigated whether Jimmy had been mentioned on a wiretap in that drug case, but as with seemingly everything involving the chief, the truth was like sand through her fingers.

Her reporting made Jimmy irate, though it appears he didn't want her or anybody else to know it. Instead he used the office of Steve Bellone as a bullhorn. In June 2013, Jimmy worked on multiple drafts of a letter to Lopez's editors. The missive castigated her for her use of anonymous sources in articles about the task force removals and the Loeb allegations. Jimmy wanted the letter just right, at one point making a correction in an email to Jon Schneider, Bellone's deputy executive: "Fourth paragraph should read: In these instances has *Newsday* done anything to verify the sources or is this an instance of a reckless disregard for the truth[?]" Once the fix was made, Schneider fired off the lengthy letter to *Newsday* as if he was the author.

By October of that year, chasing Burke rumors had led Lopez to the door of the Coram home of a recently retired sergeant named Vince Posillico. Unlike many of the others Lopez had spoken to, Posillico didn't have any great hatred of Burke. Sure, he thought the chief was a scandal waiting to happen, but Posillico had put in his papers a year ago so that wasn't really his business. And he figured Burke probably barely remembered him from his role in the Lowrita Rickenbacker investigation decades earlier. Unlike Pat Cuff, Posillico wasn't threatening enough to become a target for Burke. "I was just the flunkie little sergeant doing the case," Posillico said.

He agreed to speak to Lopez anonymously only because another retired detective had vouched for her. Before the interview, Posillico had dug out an IAB report, #93-152, which he had kept in his junk room for two decades, mixed in with a few banker's boxes of other records. He had often completed his reports at home because he found the office too distracting, but then never returned the records. They were confidential by law, so he technically should have gotten rid of them all when he left IAB, or at least when he retired in 2012. But retaining them didn't seem like any great scandal. The reports were kind of handy for looking up old cops during gossipy conversations.

During his interview with Lopez, which lasted about an hour, he used the report to refresh his memory. At one point, Lopez asked, referring to the report in his hand: "Can I have that?"

"Sure," Posillico said without thinking twice. He figured if she was doing a story on the case, she might as well have the source documents to make sure it was accurate. He expected one day down the line he'd read about the Rickenbacker matter in a column or a quarter page in *Newsday*.

That following Sunday, Posillico opened his apartment door to retrieve the paper. On the front page: Burke's photo. The words: "UNBECOMING: Inside 1995 Probe of Cop Who Later Became Suffolk's Police Chief." A graphic, made from an excerpt of the IAB report Posillico gave Lopez, was altered to look dramatically torn.

Other excerpts of the report were published in the layout of Lopez's three-page story, and *Newsday* made the confidential document, redacted in places, available online. Posillico realized the gravity of what he had done before he even shut his front door. He thought: *Oh man, they're going to go nuts.*

He spent that Sunday feeding all of his IAB files into a shredder in his home office. When the machine overheated, he'd wait impatiently for it to cool. As soon as he was done shredding, he hustled bags full of minced reports to the dumpster of his apartment complex. He was in a rush to get it all out of his possession before Burke's guys stormed through his door with a search warrant.

* * *

Lopez's article featured a mug shot of a strung-out Rickenbacker. Among the deeply embarrassing details Lopez quoted from the IAB report: "Rickenbacker told investigators Burke gave her small gifts such as roses, money for food—which she later admits she used to buy crack—and that the two engaged in oral sex in his patrol car."

The article appeared to put Burke's job in real jeopardy for the first time. Bellone didn't run to Jimmy's defense. For a week, he said nothing, suggesting that perhaps with the twin crises of the Loeb allegations and the Rickenbacker article, the county executive was finally fed up.

For Jimmy, who cared about little more than being feared and respected, the article was a debacle. The night before it was published after Lopez had called his lawyer Conway for comment, Burke had to undertake the embarrassing task of warning his top chiefs of what would be in the paper the next morning. Even Jimmy's ride-or-die sidekick, Johnny Rodriguez, couldn't contain his snickers when he read the article. "I was shocked," Rodriguez admitted, though he recovered admirably in order to spin the episode in Burke's favor. "You can never call him a racist, which his detractors must hate," Rodriguez posited recently. "But how can you? He was in love with this crack whore."

Though Spota also refused to publicly comment on the story, privately he was furious over the leak of the IAB report. "It's outrageous!" the DA declared. McPartland assigned Madigan the job of finding out who had given the report to Lopez. But before Madigan could even put his nose down to catch the scent, the gang had identified their suspect. And of course it was the wrong guy. For all their pride as investigators, The Administration never even suspected Posillico.

* * *

A week and change later, on the day that he had been ordered to perjure himself, Tony Leto dutifully headed to the Riverhead court facility. He reported first to a conference room within the part of the building occupied by the district attorney's office. He was there for yet one more prep with Crusco before the main event. In the conference room, Leto encountered a couple of the other Loeb-related witnesses, Brian Draiss and Mike Kelly of the Fourth Precinct. And on a table were a stack of FBI 302s related to the ongoing federal investigation of Jimmy Burke.

Crusco was given access to the confidential federal reports in order to hand them off to Loeb's attorney to satisfy legal discovery requirements. That much, arguably, was legitimate procedure. But Crusco leaving the reports in a conference room—whether intentionally or inadvertently—for witnesses to read was assuredly not protocol. Once Leto was alone in the room, he leafed through the 302s.

Among them: the report pertaining to the feds attempting to interrogate him on his doorstep, and a report documenting their interview with John Oliva. When his lawyer Emouna entered the room, Leto said he showed him the documents, and the attorney photographed them with his phone. The 302s quickly made the rounds from that point forward, with Jimmy later saying union boss McCormack had also seen them at the courthouse.

When it was Leto's turn to take the witness stand, it was immediately clear why Burke and McPartland wanted him there. With his muscular frame, tattoos, and knuckles the size of olives, Leto looked absurd in a boyish suit and tie. Here was a self-assured goon who clearly loathed having to speak complete sentences into a microphone. Counterintuitively, that made him a great witness. There was no overcompensatory dialogue, or nervous stammering, or trying to convince the judge he was telling the truth. Just a cop who thought this was all bullshit and desired lunch.

From the witness stand, Leto could see Billy Madigan and the union boss Russ McCormack watching him. They were sent there as eyes for Burke. Also in the audience was Tania Lopez from *Newsday*. But Leto appeared unfazed by the scrutiny as he testified that he had been assigned the case of the burglarized cars before he even knew Chief Burke was involved. The pattern of such crimes in the neighborhood fell within his purview as an Intel cop. He said that he, Bombace, and Malone debriefed Loeb in the interview room. Burke then arrived in the squad room, and he told Leto he wanted to see if he recognized Loeb from the area. He said he didn't recall if Burke said anything to Loeb. He didn't witness any assault. All that happened was Burke entered the interview room and looked at Loeb.

His whole testimony lasted just a few minutes. Toni Marie Angeli, Loeb's pugnacious original attorney, had exited the case the previous summer. She had cited a conflict on which she refused to elaborate. Loeb's new guy, Daniel Barker, didn't appear nearly as adversarial. He didn't challenge Leto on the basic premise of multiple Intel cops responding to the scene of a car break-in because of crime patterns. Instead he simply asked Leto about Loeb's allegations, including whether Leto had choked him and said he was going to rape his mother.

"Absolutely not," Leto growled dismissively. Barker had the notes from Crusco's interview with Leto at the barracks, and he pointed out that the detective never mentioned that the chief had entered the interview room.

"It didn't come up," explained Leto.

After Leto finished, Billy Madigan congratulated him for his good job on the stand.

* * *

In fact, all eight of the law enforcement officers who testified during the two-week suppression hearing did a good job, from the perspective of Jimmy Burke. Kelly kept his secrets about the smacking sounds, the red ears, and the complaint from Loeb that an old guy in a suit had slapped him. Probation officer Fran Ruggiero reiterated that her thorough search of the chief's bag had found nothing salacious. Draiss kept his omertà on the dildos. Not long afterward, Draiss, who in his fourteen-year career hadn't received a single promotion, was bumped up to detective. He interviewed for the promotion before a panel that included Jim Hickey and Billy Madigan.

Crusco was effective in making Loeb, who also testified in the hearing, look like an opportunistic dopehead with a rich imagination. Crusco wondered how it was that the bodybuilder Leto could choke and punch the shackled Loeb and not leave a bruise on the mug shot. He accused Loeb of fabricating his account in pursuit of a misdemeanor plea deal. When Spota recused himself, according to Crusco's theory, Loeb lost that gambit and was forced to instead peddle the story to the FBI.

"Mr. Loeb, it really didn't take too much to concoct this story, did it?" Crusco demanded mockingly. Though Judge Martin Efman ruled, over the objections of Crusco, that Loeb's attorney could subpoena Jimmy Burke to testify, Barker decided against it.

Following the hearing, Efman issued his ruling on whether Loeb's statements were admissible. He made clear that he believed the cops, particularly on the question of whether Burke had pornography in his bag. He said he found Draiss and Ruggiero's testimony on that point to be "credible and consistent." If the judge didn't believe that there was smut in Burke's bag—whether it be a single commercial DVD or Loeb's version, five discs including child porn—then he'd be hard-pressed to find any element of Loeb's story to be credible. Loeb finding the porn was what explained the chief's embarrassment and anger. Either way, Efman didn't even directly address whether or not Burke had beaten Loeb.

The judge did agree with Loeb's lawyer that the cops erred by not promptly producing him for arraignment, and by continually interrogating him without reminding him of his Miranda rights. Efman ruled that as a result Loeb's signed confessions were inadmissible at trial.

At first glance the ruling was a victory for Loeb. But it actually put him in an even worse spot. He was still a convicted felon caught on probation with a mountain of stolen items. Crusco could no longer use Loeb's confessions at the police precinct against him. However, during his testimony in the hearing, Loeb confessed on the stand to rifling through cars, including that of his most high-profile victim. "I went into Chief Burke's car," Loeb said under cross-examination. All that the hearing accomplished, then, was replacing a signed confession with transcribed admissions of guilt.

For Team Jimmy, the hearing really couldn't have gone much better. The lie had stuck, which at that point was all that mattered. And it had even gotten the county executive back on board. Bellone, who hadn't addressed the matter of Jimmy Burke since the publication of the Rickenbacker article a week earlier, issued a statement the evening after the last cop testified at the hearing.

"Based on the entirety of his accomplishments over 27 years in law enforcement, James Burke earned the position of chief of department and the results speak for themselves," Bellone said in the statement, which didn't directly address either of the crises swirling around the chief. He claimed crime was down because Burke "has helped implement reforms like intelligence-led policing, community-based policing and finding more efficient ways to put officers on the street."

Even better news came shortly afterward, when Chris Loeb finally cried uncle. He pleaded guilty to third-degree criminal possession of a weapon for stealing Burke's gun belt and high-capacity ammunition magazines. Loeb had realized that the case was unwinnable. Still, he loathed giving in, and at first he refused to allocute in court. But when the judge said he had to go to trial otherwise, Chris caved. "I'm sorry, I have to cop to it," he said, as if apologizing to himself. Chris tried to remind the judge that he was still upset about how he was treated, and that the police hadn't been held accountable for their actions. But the momentum was all on the cop side now.

Even though the judge had already agreed to sentence Loeb to three years in prison, police officers involved in his arrest wrote scathing missives to the probation department, seeking a recommendation of maximum prison time. Detective Sinclair wrote that Loeb's "continued refusal to accept responsibility for his actions was evident during this arrest and in all the proceedings that followed, as he lied repeatedly and attempted to place blame for his felonious activities onto the investigating officers and victims." Brian Draiss, the cop who went whistling by the dildos, wrote that Loeb was "unrepentant and selfish . . . and worst of all he blames his victims." The cops appeared to be referencing the pitiable Jimmy Burke, who on top of having his property stolen was then accused of brutality.

For Tom Spota, the relief accompanying Loeb's plea was so great that he sat down at his iPad and fired off a giddy email to the Queens pals he credited for keeping the case on course. "Peter was terrific, and, according to my prosecutors [who] were able to watch him in the courtroom, he's smooth as silk," Spota wrote to Queens' number-two prosecutor, Jack Ryan, in complimenting Peter Crusco. "Please understand that I had no idea the case would be as long and difficult as it was. Of course we had a weak judge to boot. Needless to say I'll be happy to reciprocate anytime."

Ryan returned Spota's thanks and quipped of Crusco: "I will forward to Pete after he completes his PTSD therapy in a year or two."

Spota had lots of reasons for his gracious mood. In November, he had been elected to his fourth term as DA after suing to overturn the term limits. He had coasted to an uncontested general election victory, again thanks to cross-endorsements.

More importantly, it was official: his lifelong protégé, the work son he couldn't quit, wasn't going to federal prison after all.

* * *

"I'm a good cop," Christopher Nealis had insisted to Special Agent Jeremy Bell in a phone call that summer. He'd tell the truth, but he needed to know about immunity from prosecution. Bell turned him down on that count. If he hadn't done anything illegal, Bell reasoned, he didn't need immunity.

When the good cop met with the special agents, he denied having told Trotta or anybody else that Burke had beaten Loeb. He did mention that his colleague Tom Cottingham told him that he saw porn in Burke's bag "with a bunch of dicks involved." He said he didn't know why Cottingham hadn't included that in his report. When the special agents interviewed Cottingham, he had referred to Loeb's claims about pornography as "full of shit."

Another Fourth Precinct cop, Kenneth Regensburg, testified in a federal grand jury that he had thoroughly searched Burke's bag and found nothing but cigars and the Shout disinfectant packet. But when the federal prosecutor referred to a 302 in which Regensburg was quoted as saying that there was lube and porno in the bag, Regensburg denied it. "It was not in a bag and I never told them that neither," Regensburg insisted. "So if they told you that I told them that the pornography was in the bag, they better have it recorded because I didn't tell them that."

This was how Shattered Shield had gone for the FBI special agents Carey and Bell. It felt like they had spent six months chasing their tail around the Fourth Precinct. They were contending with cops who felt, as Detective Keith Sinclair told them during his interview, that they were investigating Burke because they had an "ax to grind" due to the flap over the task forces. Lying to federal agents and in grand juries is a crime, but these cops seemed happy to do so if it was that or incur the chief's wrath.

The special agents just couldn't get past the hearsay stage. Sinclair confided in them, as if he were dropping revelatory gems, about Jimmy's relationship with Lowrita Rickenbacker. He told them how Jimmy's "rise from ashes to chief of department" could be at least partially attributed to Tom Spota. He said that Burke was a "good talker" who "could sell ice to an Eskimo."

This information was all either common knowledge or would be thanks to Tania Lopez later that year. The special agents waited in vain for one of the cops to break ranks during Loeb's suppression hearing. When that didn't happen, they conceded: they had nothing. On December 6, Carey drafted a "closing communication" stating that there was "insufficient evidence" to further pursue any of the criminal allegations in the investigation.

In the memo, Carey wrote that they had made some "concerning" discoveries. They included that the cops had searched Loeb's house without a warrant only after the discovery of Burke's stolen items there, and also that they had "staged" photographs of the evidence. Burke showing up at the house and the precinct also was of "considerable concern."

But all that stuff was below the purview of the FBI. The agents remained skeptical of the presence of child porn, and in fact they would never find credible evidence it existed. On the question of whether Loeb was abused, they said his mug shots "indicate no apparent signs of punching or choking on his head, face or neck," and none of the cops present "made statements directly or indirectly indicating Burke or others assaulted Loeb." With all leads exhausted, Carey concluded, "New York is closing this case."

There's typically nothing in it for the feds to inform a target when such a decision is made. And yet that's inexplicably what April Brooks, the boss three levels above Carey and Bell, who was in charge of the New York field office, did on December 18. Burke learned via a voicemail from Brooks that the investigation had been closed and he was cleared.

The Administration was elated. Jimmy told Hickey the feds had nothing, that they even sent Loeb's mug shot to Quantico and it didn't even show any injuries. "See what happens when you just hold tight?" Jimmy gloated. "The FBI is not gonna believe a junkie thief over the wildly popular police chief and decorated detectives."

Hickey won praise for keeping his guys in line. "They did great," Spota congratulated him. "Good job, lieutenant," said McPartland.

Chief Burke had dodged the biggest bullet of his life. The investigation had consumed him, and his closest confidants, with stress.

He had cried in front of his colleagues in Tom Spota's house. And here, granted by a benevolent lord named April Brooks, was an opportunity to start clean, stop fucking around, and finally focus on the actual duties of being chief.

But Jimmy only knew one speed. In January 2014, he called a meeting in which he was joined in the DA's office by Hickey, Spota, McPartland, and Madigan.

"It's time," Burke announced, "to fuck John Oliva."

CHAPTER 21

LEAKS

I n the wire room they custom-built to eavesdrop on John Oliva, six feet from Chris McPartland's office, Suffolk's three top prosecutors—Spota, Constant, and McPartland—huddled regularly so that the cops monitoring the wire could play them tape. Their main focus every day: the mean things Detective Oliva and his friends said about Jimmy Burke.

For McPartland, the wire's designated babysitter during those four months in 2014, the demands of that gig left no room for a vacation day or, depending on Oliva's mood, even a lunch break. The cops monitoring the wire around the clock pecked at computers taking down the details of his calls. Oliva "said he knows there was kiddie porn in Burke's bag but they just couldn't get it out," read one report. In another call, a Spanish-speaking FBI agent called Oliva with myriad unvetted Jimmy Burke dirt, including the tale of a confidential informant who was killed because he had information on the chief's neighbor. "I will have our buddy Tania Lopez give you a call," Oliva told the FBI agent.

The detective's own calls with Lopez, the monitors quickly gleaned, were the juiciest with gossip. The reporter updated Oliva on the progress she was making on notebooks full of Jimmy-related story leads. At times when Oliva and Lopez slipped into Spanish, the DA's office deployed multiple interpreters to translate it.

Lopez told Oliva about a woman who claimed Burke and McPartland had not pursued abuse allegations against her politically connected attorney husband. Gary Melius, the cop-friendly reputed former Cadillac thief, had survived a bullet to his head on Oheka Castle grounds earlier that year, and now Oliva gave Lopez information on how badly the department had botched the shooting investigation, which was still unsolved. "Burke's guys don't know what they are doing," Oliva said. He discussed the police department's obsessive hunt for whoever leaked Burke's IAB report, but promised to keep feeding Lopez intel regardless. Oliva was optimistic Burke would make some disastrous mistake. "He will fuck up," he told Lopez. "When Burke fucks up, a package will be on your desk."

Other times, the monitors picked up more casual conversations, like one about the Holy Trinity for certain reporters and cops: "Talk about working out. Talk about how much they drink. Talk about their children." Lopez knew that the Burke camp had initiated rumors that she and Oliva, who was married, were having an affair. Lopez certainly wasn't the first female journalist, particularly on a law enforcement beat, to have investigative subjects attempt to discredit her work by spreading such gossip without evidence. The wiretap logs of four months of frequent and unguarded conversations between detective and reporter made clear that that allegation was nothing but strategic misogyny.

McPartland would frequently call Burke with updates on what was being said about him on the Oliva wire. A couple of conversations got the DA's office particularly worked up. The first was when Lopez updated Oliva on her reporting concerning Burke's years-ago affair with the wife of the Smithtown insurance agent named Doug, who had obsessed over the cuckolding. Lopez said she got Burke's deposition in the divorce case. Lopez believed Burke had lied under oath by claiming to have never had any relationship with a prostitute, despite his former fling with Lowrita Rickenbacker. She was exploring a lead that Spota's office killed an investigation into the potential perjury. That call threw Spota and Emily Constant into a tizzy.

But the real wire room emergency came when Lopez told Oliva that she was heading upstate for a prison interview. She was finally meeting Lowrita.

* * *

The letter, dated June 10, 2014, that Lopez received from an inmate at the Albion Correctional Facility was neatly written on lined paper and exceedingly polite: "My name is Lowrita Rickenbacker and I am in receipt of your correspondence," it began. "I have taken the initiative to honor your request to speak with you for you [to] get my take on the story about James Burke in which I was featured."

The missive included confirmation, at least according to Rickenbacker, of a certain persistent rumor. "I conceived a child by Mr. Burke," Rickenbacker wrote, "and was prohibited to speak of but for the protection of this child it's important to use appropriate measures."

A second letter early the next month spelled out the measures Rickenbacker required to submit to the interview: a full copy of the IAB report received a week in advance, and for Lopez to gather Internal Affairs records concerning Rickenbacker's complaints of First Precinct cops harassing her following her relationship with Jimmy. "Ma'am in all due respect if these terms and condition[s] are not met this could mean the cancellation of such interview," Rickenbacker wrote.

Lopez decided, she said, those terms "were too stipulated for me." Instead, she'd just surprise Lowrita at the prison and see if she'd meet. She didn't make an appointment with the prison for an official media interview, partly because she feared Suffolk officials would hear about it and block Lopez from talking to Rickenbacker. But she did tell Oliva her plans over the phone.

Way back in his street cop days, his affair with Lowrita Rickenbacker had damaged his reputation, and his ego. Now his brain trust, jammed in the cramped wiretap room, feared the results of a jailhouse interview with Lowrita could prove even more destructive.

* * *

It was easy to forget, watching these top prosecutors obsess over Burke-related gossip, that the wiretap of Oliva was nominally about police officer safety. Extremely nominally.

After Burke announced that it was time to fuck John Oliva, The Administration had discussed the best way to go about doing that.

McPartland had volunteered that they should get up on Oliva's phone in order to, among other objectives, find out who he was talking to and add them to the enemies list. But they had to tread carefully. For the DA to wiretap a cop was a serious and potentially self-destructive step. In order to not incur the wrath of the unions, McPartland reasoned that only one "cover story" would do: that they were trying to save police lives endangered by media leaks.

After that meeting of The Administration, a bigger group was assembled to discuss leaks to *Newsday*. Nearly a dozen top prosecutors and police supervisors who worked in the DA's office gathered around a long table in an executive conference room in Building 77. First Spota asked whether he could subpoena Tania Lopez's phone records and tap her line. A couple of prosecutors in the Appeals Bureau said they had checked the case law and no, he couldn't lawfully do that to expose a journalist's sources. "Do you remember the Pentagon Papers?" asked Constant, reminding her boss of the forty-year-old landmark decision affirming the freedom of the press.

From there, the conversation segued to the finer points of a legal assault on John Oliva. A police audit of Oliva's work computer had confirmed that he had accessed documents that were later the basis of Lopez's stories, though the IAB report was not among them. The idea of a "scoop" was briefly discussed. That was the Government Corruption Bureau hallmark in which they surprised a target by pulling them off the street for an interrogation. After all, if Oliva's leaks were really endangering cops, alerting him to the investigation would surely put them to a stop. But the idea was quickly shot down, and the focus stayed on getting up on his phone.

Tapping somebody's phone, one of the most invasive tools available to law enforcement, requires thorough vetting. The authorities need to demonstrate that they can't gather required evidence against a target in any other way. Only a DA can sign a wiretap affidavit in order to get a judge's permission to go up on a target phone. Each affidavit gets you thirty days, and then it must be renewed with a document stating the reasons the eavesdropping must continue.

So McPartland would have to draft an affidavit explaining the wiretap on Oliva, and Spota would sign it for a judge's go-ahead.

One might expect that requirement might finally give Tom Spota pause. It wasn't just Jimmy Burke who had received a mulligan when the feds abandoned the Loeb investigation. Spota's blind defense of Jimmy, and his willingness to do his bidding at all costs, had nearly brought down the whole empire. When Jimmy decided to follow his barely getting away with the Loeb beating with yet another brazen double-down, Spota could have reasserted his status—on paper—as the most powerful man in Suffolk County law enforcement. At any point during the wiretap meetings, he might have posited that, you know, maybe it's actually time to do anything else besides fuck John Oliva.

Instead, Spota got busy figuring out how to really make those affidavits sing.

That same month—January 2014—Lopez published a brief article that was, by her recent standards, forgettable. It was about the police investigation of a string of armed robberies. But because Burke had barred Lopez from receiving typically routine information from the department, there were few easy stories for her anymore. She had to weave nearly every one of them, including this one, out of anonymous law enforcement sources. This story relied on such sources to reveal that the cops' suspect in the robberies was an employee of a body shop who they believed used its cars as getaway vehicles.

The Administration immediately suspected that Oliva was her source. They didn't have any real evidence that he leaked that specific story. And the information wasn't particularly sensitive anyway: a week earlier, the department had released a security camera photo of their suspect to media outlets. But none of that mattered. Lopez's story offered an opportunity.

The police department claimed that they had cops surrounding the body shop preparing to apprehend the possibly armed suspect when *Newsday* posted the story. Billy Madigan asked the paper to remove the story from its website, but Lopez's editors—predictably for any journalists—refused. The suspected armed robber and his girlfriend were then arrested without incident.

But a couple of days later, a stern group of well-fed white middle-aged men in off-the-rack suits gathered before news microphones in front of Police HQ. This could mean only one thing: a police union press conference. PBA President Noel DiGerolamo expressed his outrage over leaks that he said had endangered his officers, and he called for the DA's office to investigate "the dissemination of sensitive and confidential information about police officers and information concerning a then-current, ongoing criminal investigation."

Tom Spota was happy to oblige. He raved at his own presser, held in a claustrophobic corner of the police building, about the theoretical police casualties. "The results could've been very, very different, not only for the individuals, passerbys, who knows what would have happened," Spota said, before yelling at a reporter who tried to interject: "Let me finish!"

Spota explained that the article violated a pact he had with favored reporters. "You'll certainly get those scoops," he reasoned while waving his finger in a circular fashion to indicate the members of the media in attendance. "I have people—I'm looking around here— we have done it in the DA's office; we've done it on other occasions— rarely, thank God—we've asked you to cooperate with us, hold your story, he'll get the scoop because you've done a good job."

But instead of contritely pulling the story from their website as Madigan had requested, Spota lamented, "that particular media did something worse: they put it in a far more prominent position.

"There are four or five thousand cops living in Suffolk County," Spota said, "probably even more than that—those who live in the city—there are a lot of people that are really, really, really mad."

Spota's voice was high with anger as he stumbled over his words and pounded his balled fists on the podium. These sort of fits against the media had become Spota's default mode. Even when he clinched his fourth term the previous year, he testily refused to speak to *Newsday* at his victory celebration, angry at a vaguely critical article the paper had published. As he now railed against Tania Lopez, without deigning to name her, he was flanked by an arms-crossed cadre of top cops, among them Chief of Detectives Madigan, Police Commissioner Edward Webber, and Chief of Patrol John Meehan.

Spota reminded the reporters that he had been in Suffolk law enforcement since December 1971. "I've never seen anything like this, never," Spota insisted before scanning to see who was in the audience. "And thankfully to all of you, except one—whoever is here from that media—you've been cooperative with us and I think you can all understand the concerns of the police."

Spota held up the police document he said had been determined to be that on which Lopez had based her story. It was an Intel advisory, reading "County Wide Crime Pattern," that detailed fourteen armed robberies of gas stations and fast food joints. Spota used a finger to angrily flick the piece of paper. "Remember, that person, that reporter—it says 'for official use only, law enforcement sensitive,'" Spota said with indignation. "That reporter had to know whoever gave that to the reporter had committed a crime."

That March, a detective-investigator in the DA's office was beckoned to Blue Star, where he was told to put his name on a wiretap affidavit drafted by McPartland. The document spun a yarn in which the robbery suspect told the arresting cops that he "had seen [Lopez's] article and changed his pattern in response to it," thus putting police in danger. The DI didn't bother to fact-check that, saying later that he assumed surely McPartland had done his homework.

Even before Spota's press conference, Tania Lopez had used burners, those disposable phones favored by drug dealers because they are difficult to track. But Oliva didn't bother. After all, in January 2014, the phone he used for his conversations with Lopez was a holdover from his task force days. Surely a phone registered to the FBI was more secure than any burner.

And according to Oliva, he didn't worry about the investigation because it wasn't him who leaked the document about the armed robbery. There's no doubt Oliva was a key source for Lopez, as they both later readily acknowledged. But Oliva has insisted that the single document that officially kicked off the shitstorm wasn't from him.

His denial is credible on a couple of counts. The first was that Oliva primarily leaked Lopez documents pertinent to his singular obsession: MS-13. An advisory on pattern robberies had little relevance to the efforts to stop the street gang.

Secondly, even after the DA's office announced they were investigating the leak, Oliva never stopped talking on his phone. As a cop who had worked on long-term cases, he knew the stringent requirements for a wiretap. He later explained his thinking: "I'm not doing anything that fucked up for them to go up on my phone."

* * *

The prisoner that Bruce Barket met in a federal lockup in Queens in April 2014 didn't look at all like the scrawny, scabbed-over addict whose mug shot had made the nightly news. Christopher Loeb had weathered opioid withdrawal for what he promised himself was the last time, and his eyes and his skin were clear. After the federal investigation of Burke had dead-ended, Loeb had spent his ample free time inside bulking up, and calling lawyers about filing a lawsuit against the chief and the police department.

In that latter quest, Loeb had made a lot of unanswered calls. Suffolk lawyers were not enticed by the prospects of a long-shot civil action sure to piss off Jimmy Burke and the rest of the rulers of the jurisdiction where they made their living. By the time he called Barket, Loeb had already pleaded guilty to the case against him, the police witnesses had stood firm on their stories, and the federal investigation was declared over. It looked like a loser of a case.

But Barket was intrigued, partly because his colleagues considered Loeb so toxic. Toni Marie Angeli, the normally dogged attorney who midcase had declared a vague conflict and said she could no longer represent Loeb, was a former legal associate of Barket's. "The kid needed a lawyer," Barket said, "and nobody else would take the case, because everybody was afraid of [Burke]."

Barket had reason to feel a little cocky about taking on a client no one else wanted to touch. After all, in 2003, Marty Tankleff's criminal case had looked the same way. Barket agreed to represent Tankleff pro bono, won his release four years later, and then filed suit against the authorities for the wrongful conviction. Three months before his meeting with Loeb, the State of New York had agreed to pay Tankleff more than $3 million. Suffolk County was still on the hook in that civil suit, and Barket was aiming for at least three times that amount.

The lawyer was still buoyed by that win when he sat across from Loeb and asked him to tell him what happened the day of his encounter with Burke. Loeb did so in his frenetic manner. He struck Barket as having no guile about him. "I just believed him," Barket said simply. He next asked his partner to visit Loeb and give him her opinion, and she reported back that she absolutely believed Loeb's story as well.

Then there was the decade-old matter of the hunter-green Range Rover Sport. Barket hadn't forgotten about being handcuffed and booked for a parking ticket on what he was sure were Burke's orders, or the way the Suffolk cops had destroyed Jay Salpeter's marriage with anonymous letters. He agreed to represent Loeb on commission.

"I was perfectly happy to take that case," Barket said, "And to take another shot at these assholes."

* * *

McPartland ordered the wiretap monitors to pay special attention to all calls Oliva had with Lopez, Rob Trotta, Oliva's old partner William Maldonado, and their former supervisor Bob Doyle. That selection was yet another incongruity with the officer safety cover story.

Trotta had retired at the end of 2013, having been elected to the Suffolk County Legislature. He had made for an unconventional political candidate, given that by his own later account he had "zero" ambition to be a politician. His public platform was as a cost-cutter who wanted to go after county contract fraud, but in reality, he later explained, he knew Burke would destroy him if he stayed on the force, and he wanted a job that gave him a measure of power in the feud. "My ambition was to get rid of Burke, period," Trotta said, "and straighten the police department out." Doyle had also retired, so neither was in any position to obtain internal police documents. And Maldonado was never a suspected leaker.

Madigan had an idea to get the chatter going on Oliva's phone. He asked Hickey, who was in charge of publishing crime patterns within the department, to make them look enticingly negative—"put more red ink on it"—so that Oliva would leak the report to Lopez and they would all talk about it on the wire.

Though they weren't aware of the wiretap, Lopez and Oliva sensed a similar scheme was in the works. While a call monitor took notes, Lopez told Oliva about an alert she got concerning a top Nassau County official being indicted. Her editors tried to get her to call her sources about it but she held off. Lopez explained it turned out to be a hoax. "You have to be careful," Oliva warned her.

But Hickey didn't really need to bait Oliva with any red ink. Despite being yanked off the street gang task force, Oliva was still entrenched in the federal pursuit of MS-13. The wiretap monitors listened as his former federal handlers called him about subpoenaing him for testimony in his old cases, or to chat about confidential gang informants. Oliva believed that Burke, with Hickey's help, was covering up gang-related shootings, often by reclassifying them as reckless endangerment, in order to ensure that stats for gang crimes were down or flat following the dismantling of the task forces.

Seeking to prove that to Lopez, Oliva accessed the department computers and jotted down case numbers and other details about dozens of crimes, and he also printed out tour reports that included information on shootings. They were the sort of records that reporters could typically get from a police department via a simple request, but the SCPD had shut Lopez out. Oliva and Lopez's favorite meeting ground was Changing Times Pub, a hangout near Lopez's newsroom, where he gave her notes and records.

On a Friday night in April 2014, Lopez got a major scoop: Juan Garcia, a twenty-one-year-old MS-13 member, on the FBI's Ten Most Wanted Fugitives list for killing his girlfriend and her young son on Long Island, had surrendered in Nicaragua. He was on his way to Long Island on an FBI jet. Lopez, who was working with another reporter on the story, scrambled to confirm the information. An FBI contact confirmed the story was accurate but asked Lopez not to release it yet because it could be dangerous for the agents. Lopez relayed the concern to her editor. But after the Associated Press published a story on the arrest that night, she later explained in a phone call with Oliva, her editors pulled the trigger and published their story anyway.

She then heard from her FBI contact that the media leaks had angered Loretta Lynch, who at the time was the US Attorney for the Eastern District of New York. Lynch had sent out an email vowing to find out where the leaks were coming from, said Lopez's contact, who made clear he was also peeved: "I hope leaking the info was worth it."

Lopez in turn was angry at her editors, who she said could sabotage her sources. She told this story to Oliva and said her new policy was that she was "not going to tell the paper shit" until after it was clear to release.

In the wire room in Hauppauge, a kernel of an idea was forming as they listened to Lopez air these grievances. The DA's office knew they would face issues when it came time to indict John Oliva. If Spota took it to trial, they'd be forced to turn over the entire wiretap and all related affidavits. They had no clear evidence Oliva had leaked the pattern robbery info, and the eavesdropping on calls with retired cops and federal agents was legally dicey to say the least. Then there was the potential for embarrassment in turning over the rich vein of Burke gossip obtained by the wiretaps to a Suffolk defense attorney.

It would be much cleaner, The Administration decided, for the feds to indict John Oliva. Besides the logistics of having the federal authorities tidy up their mess, there was a poetry to it. Oliva was always talking about how the feds had a bigger hammer than the state. Perhaps they could see how he liked the bludgeoning end of it.

They began waiting for their opportunity, although no one told Billy Madigan. That spring, near the beginning of the wiretap, he rushed into Hickey's office full of giddy excitement. Chatter on Oliva's wiretap had confirmed he was leaking to the press, and Madigan considered it enough for a felony charge. Madigan explained that it was going to be great because Oliva didn't hit his twentieth anniversary until late June 2014. In other words, if they charged him now, he wouldn't get his pension. As the months passed with no arrest, Madigan, apparently oblivious to his bosses' plan to pawn off the Oliva case on the feds, started to get worried: Were they going to detonate this guy's life, or what?

On June 3, McPartland finally got what he was waiting for. Oliva was frustrated that without his input, MS-13 murder cases were stagnating even though he felt he knew who the killers were. In a call that afternoon, he told Lopez he'd hand over all of his case files. "I'll give you my cases," Oliva said. "I'm not working on them, so you could fucking work on them."

When Lopez asked if the feds were okay with that, Oliva responded that she should do what she had to do. They made plans to exchange the records the following week.

The next day, McPartland contacted Nicole Boeckmann, chief of the Long Island Criminal Division for the Eastern District of New

York. Boeckmann was already acquainted with the early chapters of the Oliva saga. She was among the feds who had pleaded with Burke, Hickey, Madigan, and others in the SCPD to leave him on the MS-13 task force. They had ignored her. Now McPartland—Burke's best friend—told Boeckmann that they had Oliva caught on a wiretap planning to give *Newsday* records pertaining to federal investigations.

McPartland's information prompted a hasty meeting between the two agencies. The Long Island division of the Eastern District is based in the Alfonse M. D'Amato United States Courthouse, an enormous white ocean liner of a building looming over the grubby suburbs of Central Islip. It so happened that Loretta Lynch was going to be out there anyway that Thursday. So Spota, Constant, and McPartland filed into a conference room to meet with a US Department of Justice murderer's row: Lynch, then Eastern District criminal chief James McGovern, Boeckmann, and FBI Special Agent in Charge Rich Frankel.

There's a queasiness in the gut with which criminals are often well acquainted. It occurs when a plan you've worked hard at is coming together seamlessly and the realization suddenly sets in, far too late, just how dumb that plan is. McPartland and his bosses sat down in a federal nerve center with Lynch, one of the most powerful law enforcement agents in the world and soon to be appointed US Attorney General, and her top deputies. For McPartland, it was less than six months since helping his buddy the police chief complete the cover-up of a federal crime under investigation by her office. Now McPartland was emissary to a proposal that the Eastern District adopt the paper-thin prosecution of the feds' favored cop, whose real crime was reacting angrily when he was removed from a life-and-death task force due to the same police chief's unconcealed hatred of Lynch's office.

The Suffolk prosecutors played the feds some tapes and made their pitch. They then shuffled out. One hopes, out of respect for his intelligence, that McPartland felt that queasiness as he walked out of that room.

Somebody didn't keep the meeting secret. Within days, the monitors in the wire room heard Rob Trotta tell Oliva: "Don't trust the phone."

* * *

Oliva got a little more guarded. But he only knew something was up, not that his phone was wiretapped. Somehow, he still didn't believe Burke and his gang were capable of that. And when Lopez called on the day he knew she had met with Lowrita Rickenbacker, he wasn't going to let it go to voicemail.

As Lopez hoped, Rickenbacker had agreed to the impromptu interview. Because she couldn't even bring a pen and notepad when she entered the visitation room, Lopez had to borrow a tiny pencil from a corrections officer and jot a few notes on a little scrap of paper.

It was a seven-hour sojourn from Albion in rural western New York back to her apartment in Brooklyn. When she got home, partly in an effort to keep the interview fresh in her mind to offset her chicken scratch notes, Lopez called Oliva to gossip with him about the interview.

Rickenbacker, who was sober and lively during the interview, recalled some uncorroborated details from her relationship with Burke. She told Lopez that she had seen Jimmy use crack and powdered cocaine. Lopez now had multiple sources telling her about the chief's past drug use, which she thought could be enough to put together a story. She didn't have the same hopes for the next bit, but she relayed it to Oliva nonetheless. Rickenbacker had described their sex life, in which Burke appeared to be a try-anything-once sort of guy. His ideas strayed from the goofy—turning her into a "fruit salad" by covering her with fruit and eating it off of her—to those that Rickenbacker found denigrating.

Jimmy always traveled with a party bag, Rickenbacker said, often stocked with implements with which they made creative use. Rickenbacker described to Lopez—in painstaking, highly scatological detail—Jimmy's adventures with a foreign object during one encounter, which Rickenbacker said led to her cleaning up a mess that would have otherwise threatened their motel room deposit.

Lopez in turn left out nothing when she related the story to Oliva, while the reporter and the detective were both "giggling like little schoolgirls," as Oliva put it.

It's safe to say their mirth was not shared by the police and prosecutors in the wire room in Building 77, where listening in on the lurid details of the top police boss's sex life was more than they had bargained for. In a handwritten call log, someone wrote as small as possible on the back of the page, along with some numerical information to locate the tape: "dildo call." They brought the wire down after that.

A few days later, on his way home from the gym, John Oliva saw his rearview mirror erupt into flashing police lights.

* * *

Before the wire came down, Lopez complained to Oliva of her suspicion that there was a spy in the newsroom. "It was awkward," she said as a wire monitor listened on. The reporter said that while she had been talking to her boss in the newsroom, another editor, Steve Wick, was "lurking behind." She had by then long believed she was being snooped on. The editor of the *Long Island Press*, with whom she was friendly, told her he had gotten a tip that *Newsday* had revoked her corporate American Express after she used it to pay rent. The disturbing part for Lopez was that the gossip was half-true: the paper had taken back the credit card after she swiped it to fill her car with gas, rather than go by policy and expense mileage. Then there was the fact that her cell phone had gone missing off her desk at work, and that she kept finding nails in her car tires. It was hard to know what was paranoia and what was real.

In the case of the lurking editor, a document stashed in the DA's file concerning the Oliva case suggests that Lopez's suspicions were indeed justified. The page, torn from a cop's notebook, contained a handwritten log of six phone calls between Wick and a person referred to only as "Tom," over roughly two hours on an unspecified date.

Wick, whose title in 2014 was enterprise and investigations editor, went way back with Spota. In the spring of 1979, when Wick was a twenty-seven-year-old reporter, he had covered the John Pius murder case. He had stayed close to Spota ever since. (He wasn't the only *Newsday* reporter for whom that was the case. Rick Brand, who was the first reporter at the Pius scene and ultimately became the paper's top political columnist, played tennis with Spota nearly every week. Brand said recently that partly due to that conflict, he didn't "cover" Spota, "because I didn't want to put my credibility at risk," though a search shows his byline on hundreds of articles naming his tennis pal.)

At 4:11 p.m., according to the notes, Tom missed a call from Wick. Tom called him back and they had three phone calls lasting twenty seconds or less. Wick then called Tom and they had a five-minute phone call. And finally at 5:49 p.m., Wick left a voicemail for Tom, according to the notes, "saying that Tania would be calling PIO"—meaning the police department's Public Information Office—"to confirm data."

When asked recently about those notes, Wick—who left *Newsday* in 2017 and is currently an executive editor of community newspapers on the eastern end of Long Island—said the information about the calls were "foreign" to him. But he didn't outright deny that he had provided information on Lopez's actions to Tom Spota.

Wick, who described Lopez's reporting as a "super-secret project" of which he had no involvement and would have little information to share, allowed nonetheless that the phone log must have referred to him responding to Spota seeking an update on her reporting. Wick said he used to call or visit with Spota two or three times a week. Though his desk was right next to that of Lopez's editor, Wick said he didn't purposefully eavesdrop. "Everybody knew at that point that Tom and I had been friends for a long time," Wick said, "so that may have drawn some suspicion."

As for Oliva and other targets of the investigation, they were spied on using more traditional methods. The DA's office employed Vigilant Solutions, a private service that uses vehicles equipped with license plate readers to fill a database with the various locations it has encountered a person's car over the years. Vigilant returned a record of sightings of Rob Trotta's Acura and Oliva's Nissan Pathfinder in places like the Smithtown mall parking lot, or outside Splish Splash Water Park.

And on certain days from March through July 2014, Suffolk cops hid outside of their colleague Oliva's home. It was a well-appointed colonial with a two-car garage, a flapping American flag, and a backyard pool with a diving board. They marked in their notebooks when the newspaper was still in the driveway, or when there was a bag of mulch outside, and when Oliva came out to check his mail. They followed him to Police HQ, and to his physical therapy sessions for an on-duty injury, and to the mechanic, and to Planet Fitness.

On a Monday morning in late July 2014, three investigators started surveillance on the detective's house at 6:00 a.m. At 9:25 that morning, they were on the move behind Oliva, who had a day off. Five minutes later, the marked police car accompanying the investigators put on its lights and Oliva's most frequent stalkers—DA investigators Tom Iacopelli and Paul Caroleo—walked up to chat with the detective.

Oliva was on the side of the road in a parcel of the sparse farmland that occupies some of the more remote swaths of Suffolk County. Across the street, a corporate steakhouse sat next to a poultry operation that stunk up the buggy summer morning air. The investigators asked if Oliva would accompany them to an interview at the Government Corruption Bureau. The detective, one of those people who become calmer in urgent situations, quietly refused, saying he should probably speak to his union. The investigators showed him a search warrant for his phone, and Oliva handed it over. They gave him a piece of paper and told him to call the phone number on it, that of McPartland.

Naturally, Tania Lopez promptly heard about the investigators stopping Oliva, and also that Maldonado had been stopped, the latter agreeing to an interview at the Government Corruption Bureau. She began reporting out a story. She called the Suffolk County Detectives Association's president, Billy Plant, whose job it was to protect the rights of Detectives Oliva and Maldonado, and he simply hung up after he heard her line of questioning.

Oliva began searching for a lawyer, and a knowledgeable friend pointed him to Stephen Scaring. The wiry, perpetually dapper defense attorney, a former Nassau County homicide prosecutor, had for decades been among the most respected lawyers on the island. He had worked as a special prosecutor in cases against Suffolk County cops in the wake of the SIC report in the mid-1980s. But unlike many top defense attorneys who gravitate toward the biggest cases, Scaring wasn't a bomb-thrower. He resembled a white-shoe litigation attorney and practiced like one too. He was a realist and a pragmatist who often steered his clients toward the least risky, though hardest to swallow, conclusion: a deal. Scaring and this DA's office—primarily, McPartland—were previously the mutual architects of the most intriguing plea deal in county memory, that of Steve Levy, Scaring's client who surrendered his career in politics under a cloak of secrecy.

After Oliva hired Scaring, the attorney called McPartland and learned about a case that could be termed Levy Lite. The DA's office was planning to charge Oliva with serious felonies—grand larceny and computer trespass—for leaking tour reports, intelligence reports, teletypes, and personal information about cops to Lopez. It was the first, and so far only, time that a Suffolk County cop was prosecuted for leaking to the press. But even beyond the hypocrisy inherent in the Oliva prosecution, the flaws in the case were glaring. The phone tap, outside of confirming Burke's fondness for dildos, had not been fruitful in a legal sense. Instead of boosting their case against Oliva, it was now just a liability, toxic proof of the frivolity of the investigation. They weren't eager to turn it over to Scaring, and if Oliva took a plea, they wouldn't have to.

As was the case in the Levy prosecution, both sides had an incentive to make the whole thing go away as swiftly and painlessly as possible. Scaring warned Oliva that if he took the case to trial, the legal labor of breaking down a nearly four-month wiretap would cost in the hundreds of thousands of dollars. And even then, Scaring explained, there was no guarantee that they would win. The fact was that by the letter of the law, Oliva had leaked records. He could bankrupt his family and still be convicted of felonies carrying jail time.

Outside of those legal fears were murkier considerations. First, Oliva faced the embarrassment of having his personal life turned inside out in a courtroom. There are indications in the DA's file that they were seeking evidence that he was having an affair, though nothing showed any proof. This was the default investigative mode of the DA's office: bruise your suspect with enough innuendo having nothing to do with the crime that they will do anything to extricate your tentacles from their life. Secondly, Oliva—just like Leto—was worried for his children. His son, who was looking to become a cop, was on the SCPD "list" for an open spot. And his daughter was hoping to start a career as a public school teacher. If he fought the case, Oliva believed, they would use every bit of subterranean influence at their disposal to blackball his kids and make their nascent careers as difficult as possible.

Oliva was under attack by every powerful force in the county where he lived and had built a distinguished two-decade policing career.

"Put yourself in my shoes," he later explained. "The union's involved. The district attorney's involved. At this time even the county executive is not siding with me; he's siding with the police department."

"I was done," Oliva decided. "They were going to do me any which way."

He had three proffer sessions at the DA's office. The purpose of the meetings, as described in a document prepared by McPartland, was to determine whether Oliva "will be permitted to cooperate." And McPartland made clear that for Oliva, permission to cooperate involved signing a confession. Most of all, McPartland wanted the detective to admit to leaking the report on the pattern robberies. Oliva didn't understand why McPartland was hung up on the document that, in the scheme of things, was probably more innocuous than those he readily admitted to having leaked. "If I had something to do with it, I'd tell you," Oliva said he objected. "I basically admitted that I gave Tania seventy cases. What does it matter if it's seventy-one?"

Only later did Oliva realize why McPartland was so focused on that single document: he and Spota had legally secured the wiretap by claiming that Oliva leaking the pattern robbery alert had put cops in danger. But they didn't have any direct evidence he had leaked the document. So if he didn't cop to it, the wiretap and any convictions based on it were arguably bogus.

At the third and final proffer session on a Thursday in early September, McPartland gave Oliva and Scaring an eleven-page draft document he wanted signed as part of a plea deal. Among the various leaks to which Oliva was expected to confess was the pattern robbery alert. "In January of 2014 the Police Department issued a 'SCPD Intelligence Countywide Crime Pattern' document that was for official use only and law enforcement sensitive," the draft confession read. "It listed details of each of the robberies. I obtained the intelligence report and called Tania Lopez and read the report to her. I gave her the dates, times, locations, vehicles used and information about the suspect. I did this because I was mad that I had been transferred."

Oliva was determined not to sign it. At 7:00 a.m. on Tuesday, September 9, 2014, Oliva and Scaring showed up at Building 77 for what was supposed to be his surrender. Oliva wondered if they would try to get him to sign the confession and when he refused, indict him and take him to trial. But it appeared Oliva had called McPartland's bluff. The detective was fingerprinted and had his mug shots taken, and he was brought to district court. There he pleaded guilty to official misconduct, a misdemeanor. Oliva had retired on a partial pension the week before, as part of his plea deal with the DA's office.

Police and their defenders love their "copaganda," and here was a detective for whom it wasn't even a stretch: Oliva had for decades risked his own life to save those of others. But instead of coming to his defense, the unions condemned him. The Suffolk County Police Benevolent Association said in a statement that Oliva's prosecution demonstrated that the department, "with its internal checks and balances, and working in conjunction with [the DA's office], is able to monitor and provide the proper oversight of its Police." Billy Plant, the Suffolk County Detectives Association boss, said: "I'm extremely troubled that a detective was involved in something like this." Tom Spota released a statement crowing that "members of the department should not be enticed by reporters who encourage them to commit crimes in furtherance of their own agendas."

Oliva, the MS-13 expert in a county overrun by MS-13, was home by noon, wondering how he was going to fill the rest of his day. He said it wasn't until that moment that the reality of the situation finally hit home. "I was in the twilight zone," said Oliva, who was forty-eight when he was forced to retire. "I thought it was just a really bad horrible dream, and I'd wake up and I'd go back to work."

Among the insults heaped onto Oliva was the department informing him that he was no longer permitted to keep a weapon. Federal prosecutor John Durham, who had worked closely with Oliva on the task force, wrote a letter to Commissioner Webber pleading that the retired detective "should be allowed to protect himself and his family."

"Detective Oliva now may be in greater danger because he may be perceived to be more vulnerable by gang members since he no longer works for the SCPD and does not have the protection or support of the department," Durham wrote after reminding Webber of the "terminate on sight" order the MS-13 had put out on Oliva. The SCPD relented and let Oliva keep his guns. Other insults remained, like Oliva's ejection from the PBA, and being denied a replica shield as a retirement memento.

For Chief Burke, the upside of ousting Oliva wasn't just the endorphin burst of fucking an enemy. There was a function to it as well. What they did to Oliva put the fear of God—or of Jimmy—into the rest of the department. For all the cops who had lied to save Jimmy's hide in the Loeb matter, this was confirmation they had made the right choice. Among those who got the message was Kenny Bombace, who read about the Oliva case in the paper and chatted with his fellow Intel detectives about it.

In their conversations, the arrested detective became a verb: to be "Oliva-ed." Bombace later explained: "It means if you were to cross the powers that be"—Burke, Spota, and McPartland—"you could be targeted like John Oliva was."

* * *

Six days later, Jim Hickey got a phone call from Brian Keegan, one of the detectives Jimmy had assigned to a federal task force so that he could spy on comings and goings at the federal courthouse in Central Islip. Keegan said he and Marcus Rivera, his partner, were in the middle of a proffer session at the courthouse when the feds suddenly asked them to leave.

If the feds ejecting Burke's guys was in response to the Oliva case, it wasn't particularly a surprise. The Eastern District's federal prosecutors had signaled their displeasure from the beginning with the investigation and prosecution of Oliva.

Back in January, when McPartland was still exploring the idea of wiretapping Oliva, he had learned that the detective was using an FBI phone. He emailed FBI supervisor Rich Frankel and requested specifically that Oliva "not be asked to surrender [the phone] during the pendency of our investigation." But the FBI retrieved its phone from Oliva the next day, with the explanation to the detective that they were routinely collecting their equipment. McPartland—his request resoundingly ignored—was forced to figure out Oliva's next phone, which was the one they ultimately tapped.

Then came the pathetic meeting with Loretta Lynch in early June. Suffolk prosecutors had gotten zero interest in pawning off their case against Oliva, and even worse, the meeting appeared to have kicked awake the Eastern District, particularly those in the Long Island division. The federal prosecutors there, who worked in the big cruise-ship courthouse named after Al D'Amato—the retired US senator long-rumored to have mob connections—were savvy to the ways of Suffolk County. Having been left out of the Loeb investigation, the division's chief, Nicole Boeckmann, became like a bloodhound for the Oliva matter. Before Oliva had even been pulled over in the traffic stop where he turned over his phone, she subpoenaed everything the DA's office had on the investigation, and hectored McPartland for months for various lingering documents. Perhaps McPartland was oblivious enough to believe that the feds were just belatedly taking an interest in the leaks he had tried to sell them on a couple of months earlier. But then came Keegan and Rivera's mid-September eviction from the proffer session in Central Islip.

Hickey called Jimmy as soon as he hung up with Keegan. Hickey didn't want to discuss the troubling development on the phone, so he asked to meet in person. Jimmy was at Building 77 and Hickey was at Police HQ, so they agreed to rendezvous at a middle ground: a carpool parking lot just north of the Long Island Expressway. Hickey told Jimmy about the detectives being booted from the courthouse, which to the Intel boss could mean only one thing: something was up.

"This is bad," Jimmy said. "We gotta call Chris."

Jimmy dialed McPartland and put his phone on speaker. As they apprised McPartland of the situation and he gave his thoughts, Jimmy was on hands and knees while wearing a suit, fumbling along the underside of his truck in the hunt for a federal tracking device.

You need to take the temperature of your guys, McPartland's voice blared at Hickey from Jimmy's phone. The chief was now searching his truck's console for a wiretap. *Find out what's going on*, McPartland continued. *Make sure that they're all quiet.*

Burke emerged from under his truck a frazzled mess and empty-handed. He told Hickey they needed to get both their trucks checked by Sammy Panchal for bugs and tracking devices.

Suddenly, they were back in the cover-up again. And McPartland had a new rat in mind. They had spent the year focused on fucking John Oliva, all the while ignoring Kenny Bombace.

CHAPTER 22

BAD PEOPLE

On the night of May 12, 2015, Jim Hickey got a call from Tom Spota. He was on his way from the airport and late for the big event, Spota explained. He wanted to know where to park, and he needed a suit jacket.

When the seventy-four-year-old DA drove up to the parking lot outside a Stony Brook University auditorium, he was dressed more appropriately for birding than the night's festivities. He wore khakis and brown loafers with gray socks, and a wide pink tie thrown over a blue button-down. Hickey was waiting there with a jacket, which he had asked his wife to ferry over to the campus from their bedroom closet. The detective directed an underling to park Spota's car while the two members of The Administration hustled inside.

Nearly the whole crew was there that night, with Tony Leto overseeing security. Jimmy wore his chief's silks: white shirt and black tie, dangling medals tacked all over him, and little golden wreaths adorning the bill of his police cap. Taking the lectern and speaking to an auditorium full of his subordinates, he looked the part of a four-star chief of department.

Seated on the dais behind Jimmy, to his right, were the cop brass. The three-star chiefs wore white gloves, which made them look not unlike Jimmy's butlers. Commissioner Edward Webber sat behind Jimmy, as did Risco Mention-Lewis, the Sammy Panchal–tracked deputy police commissioner. Behind Jimmy to his left were the county's political elite, including Spota, swimming in Hickey's too-big dark jacket and tapping his left loafer with nervous energy. Sandwiching Spota were a perpetually grinning Steve Bellone, county executive, and Tim Sini, Bellone's sad-eyed deputy for public safety.

Jimmy had hijacked the Suffolk PD's awards committee for the accolade he was about to give out, which wasn't a difficult feat considering his old sector car partner Dennis Sullivan was the committee's chairman. "Tonight we will present," Jimmy announced in a practiced public-speaking staccato while reading from a binder, "our first Thomas J. Spota Prosecutor of the Year Award."

Jimmy told the crowd of cops that Spota was a "true supporter and loyal friend to law enforcement." He recounted Spota's career from his tenure as a chief trial prosecutor "personally trying some of the county's most notorious and high-profile cases," to union counsel, "representing the interest of rank-and-file detectives."

"District Attorney Spota is serving an unprecedented fourth term and has meted out justice for the citizens of Suffolk County without fear or favor for the past fourteen years," Jimmy intoned. "This award is so named in his honor."

The chief then welcomed the award's recipient to the stage. While Jimmy intermittently petted his mustache and clapped, Chris McPartland shuffled up to a stripe of tape like a nervous kid in a school play. McPartland stared straight ahead, unsmiling, with his arms at his sides as if they were dead weight. He wore a boxy suit with fabric bunching up over his shoes.

Jimmy administered an ego bath similar to the one he gave Spota, recounting the various crime bosses McPartland had brought down, the many court-authorized wiretaps and grand jury investigations, his helming of the Government Corruption Bureau, and, of course, his partnership with the SCPD's intelligence-led policing model.

"We've all heard the term 'a cop's cop,'" Jimmy said as he reached the speech's crescendo. He had the bravado of a groom's best man who had completed six months of Toastmasters. "ADA McPartland is widely known as a 'cop's prosecutor' among the rank-and-file and bosses alike in the Suffolk County Police Department. It is his voice that you want to hear on the other end of the phone when there is a difficult issue that arises and an answer is needed quickly. It is his face that you want to see sitting across from you at a conference table when a complex, long-term investigation is being embarked upon. It is Chris McPartland that you want to see standing at the bar in a courtroom when our jobs as police officers are done and it is now time for justice to be served on behalf of the people of the state of New York."

Making McPartland the first—and as it turns out, last—winner of an award named after Spota was Jimmy's way of saying thank you to both men, respectively his mentor and his best friend. Besides, they all needed a self-congratulatory night off from their rapidly unraveling criminal conspiracy.

* * *

Kenny Bombace, whose disjointed career had been guided by compulsion—to be a soldier, to see combat, to join the police—had a new obsession: to quit.

His disgust with his current situation was cemented in late summer of 2014, soon after Steve Bellone invited him to join him on a South Shore boat trip with a legislator. Bombace considered Bellone his ticket to professional politics. As far as the Intel detective was concerned, their plan to launch that career with a job in the county executive's administration was still in play.

But an unexpected fourth boater joined them before they took off from the dock and changed the dynamic.

Tim Sini, then thirty-four, was a squat fire hydrant of a man with gapped teeth and an unreadable gaze. Bellone gave Sini's bona fides as a former federal prosecutor. He lived in Babylon, but he was an outsider in Suffolk law enforcement and politics. He immediately rubbed Bombace the wrong way, in the manner of a new acquaintance with whom your spouse appears slightly too enamored.

They boated over to Fire Island, where Bombace threw back a few beers and held court on how scholars consider postwar Germany the ideal democracy. When Sini insisted that America's system was better, Bombace fumed internally: *You motherfucker, I fought a war. What are you, questioning my patriotism?*

The next day at work, Hickey called Bombace into his office. The Intel boss told his detective that another cop had seen him with

Bellone and this former fed Sini on Fire Island, and he wanted to know why Bombace was meeting with them and what was said. Bombace was sure the line of questioning had come from Burke.

Bombace met Bellone in a parking lot later that day to tell him about Hickey's interrogation. Bombace saw terror creep into the county executive's face.

"All right, we cannot be seen together for a while," responded Bellone, who still spent most of his workdays in a Panera exile. "We need to lay low."

Bellone's open fear of Burke stunned Bombace. He wanted to tell Bellone: "These people work for you," but he didn't. Instead, he and the county executive kept their distance. Shortly afterward, Bombace learned that Bellone had made Sini his deputy for public safety, the same position he had once been promised. He realized that Bellone had invited him out on the boat to meet Sini in order to soften the blow of him choosing the other guy over him. And he knew then that his own political aspirations had been detonated due to his association with the Loeb conspiracy.

To that point, the hydraulic press of the federal investigation into the Loeb beating hadn't allowed room for any feelings except pure stress. But now, with the investigation looking dead, Bombace had time for another emotion: self-pity.

Bombace, as he was quick to remind people, had fought all the bad guys: Al Qaeda, MS-13, the Italian mob. "But because I slapped a violent felon, that's how I'll be known forever," he later bemoaned in what was a frequent refrain. "Look, people want to label me, no problem. Anyone who's done everything I've done and wants to come to me, I'm all ears. But everyone else, I don't remember you people complaining when I was almost blown up three times in Iraq."

The hurt feelings—and his opinion that he had been underappreciated, taken advantage of, and betrayed throughout his career—hardened in Bombace a sentiment that cops were petty, shallow, and disloyal. And now he no longer wanted to be one.

Bombace stirred this brew of resentment with his Intel partner Cliff Lent, who felt similarly. Lent was pissed that he couldn't get an audience for his elaborate social media analysis of cops associated with gangs, and was generally disappointed with his colleagues. "Ten percent of cops have their heart in the right place," Lent estimated. "Forty percent are pretty good. And the other fifty percent could care less about anything." This was Bombace and Lent's favored topic: kvetching about their dislike for other cops.

Bombace was nearing twenty years as a cop—usually the magic number for retiring with a pension. But seven of his years were as a sheriff's deputy, and he couldn't get a clear answer on whether he could combine his service time from both departments. He hectored the Suffolk County sheriff, Vincent DeMarco, for a meeting to enlist him for some help on that count. DeMarco dodged him, until suddenly he didn't, and invited him to meet him out at the new jail in Yaphank.

DeMarco was a diminutive, ballsy cop, who Bombace knew from their days as lowly deputies. DeMarco was immersed in his own highly political cold war with Spota. His feud centered on a deputy sheriff who also happened to be a top political figure—Suffolk County Conservative Party leader Edward Walsh—and was claiming on county time sheets that he was working at the jail when in fact, as DeMarco suspected, he was gambling, golfing, and politicking. Spota, who was Walsh's longtime buddy and the beneficiary of a perennial Conservative Party endorsement, refused to help DeMarco build a wage theft case against his deputy. As seemingly everybody in local law enforcement knew, DeMarco was using this rift to try to build a federal case against Walsh or even Spota, and to that end had been going into meetings with a tape recorder secretly running.

Bombace's antenna was thusly up when DeMarco sat across from him, armed only with a yellow writing pad, and began saying things that had nothing to do with combining service time. "Ken, I'm sure you are aware that I'm a witness for the federal government," Bombace remembered the sheriff saying, "and I need to be the best witness I can be." He then segued to Bombace refusing to cooperate in the Loeb investigation.

Bombace found it "comically obvious" that the sheriff was wearing a wire. "It was like he was reading it," Bombace later said. "Worst undercover operator I've ever seen." Bombace responded in line with his belief that the feds were listening, telling DeMarco stiffly that he didn't refuse to cooperate, but that there was never any follow-up on the subpoena he received.

The encounter illustrated the confused paranoia that had enveloped the governance of Suffolk County. DeMarco later acknowledged that he was dodging Bombace, even as Bellone called on the detective's behalf trying to set up the meeting, because the sheriff was aware of Bombace's involvement in the Loeb incident. "This whole thing stinks," DeMarco told Bellone in initially declining the meeting. But he had eventually decided to see what Bombace had to say. He later insisted that the feds didn't put him up to it, and that he wasn't in fact wearing a wire.

DeMarco's own suspicion was that The Administration had sent Bombace to the meeting in order to get information about the sheriff. Bellone at the time was floating the idea of an appointed rather than elected sheriff—a direct threat to DeMarco's tenure—and DeMarco's mind raced with the possibility that this was the first step to replacing him, perhaps with Bombace: "I didn't know what was going on, I didn't trust any of it."

He said he grilled Bombace because he didn't want to bring a dirty cop back to the sheriff's office, but he would've welcomed him if Bombace told him he was going to cooperate against The Administration. "I was just trying to get answers out of him, but he was being cagey," DeMarco said.

Bombace left the hopelessly guarded meeting frustrated that he was no closer to retiring with a fat pension. Like a good palace guard, he immediately called Hickey and informed him that he believed DeMarco had tried to set him up.

If nothing else, Bombace decided, he had to get out of Intel, which he now considered a toxic workplace. Shortly after the bad-vibes boat trip, Bombace went to Hickey and asked to transfer to an open position in a terrorism task force. He knew that, ultimately, Chief Burke himself would have to also agree to the transfer, so he wasn't overly optimistic.

But Hickey didn't even consider it. The Intel boss tried to frame it as Bombace being too valuable to lose: "I need to keep you right where you are at."

* * *

In the months following the removal of Burke's spy detectives from the federal task force, The Administration continued to wonder whether Bombace had flipped. Hickey, as the person tasked with keeping his detectives in line, served to absorb most of the group's anxiety.

In November 2014, Hickey went out to the Cherry Creek Golf Links for an "intelligence breakfast." Top law enforcement brass were discussing implementing some of Chief Burke's intelligence-led policing tactics in East End police departments. Tom Spota was there, and he cornered Hickey about the cop moles being thrown out of the task force. *Had he heard anything more about it? Are there any other developments? Are his guys holding tight? Does it look like any of them are cooperating or looking to cooperate?*

By the spring of 2015, The Administration had heard nothing more about investigations into Burke, and the dread had somewhat dissipated. "Things were good then," Hickey later said. That April, he and Spota arrived at the West Lake Inn in Patchogue for an event for the Emerald Society. Hickey held back and let Spota walk in first so the DA could soak up a big welcome.

As the party wore on, Hickey, Spota, Burke, and McPartland found themselves on the dance floor. They huddled closely in their own miserable version of a conga line. Spota wanted to know if Hickey had any updates on Keegan and Rivera being tossed from the federal task the prior September. He asked him how his guys were doing. *Are they holding tight, are they okay?*

"Everything's fine," assured Hickey. But it was clear from the dance-floor conversation that the Loeb conspiracy had created a permanent paranoia among its participants. Even when everything seemed fine, they would never feel safe. What wasn't yet clear was that the paranoia would prove self-fulfilling.

* * *

The resort was packed with beefy middle-aged white men in jeans and bowling shirts, ogling scrawny sales models who pandered to them through frozen smiles, all of it fumigated thoroughly with cigar smoke. And yet, Jimmy Burke couldn't enjoy himself.

He was on a road trip in early May 2015 to a cigar summit in central Pennsylvania with his fellow enthusiast Sammy Panchal. But he couldn't stop fuming about what his spies had told him was going on that morning back home: an initial conference in Chris Loeb's lawsuit against Burke, the county, and the department, recently filed by the firm of Loeb's lawyer, Bruce Barket.

Jimmy took out his cell phone and vented via text to a loyal group of eight acolytes, among them top Suffolk cops and union officials.

"The Loeb case was on in federal court today," Jimmy wrote. "There were proceedings in open court. That cunt Lopez was there. I'm sure I'm going to get crucified tomorrow."

"Bitch," seethed Chief of Patrol John Meehan, referring to Tania Lopez.

"She is a piece of shit," wrote another buddy. "You will get through it like before. It sucks that you have to go through it each time."

"Anything we can do?" wondered Billy Plant, the president of the Suffolk County Detectives Association.

The PBA president, Noel DiGerolamo, chimed in: "It will play out like every time prior. Truth is vast majority who read the paper don't give a shit or won't even read the article."

But the next morning, Jimmy was even more pissed off. He had read Lopez's story about the court hearing and, in his estimation, he had indeed gotten crucified. The worst part was that Brian Mitchell, an attorney representing the county, had acknowledged in court that the chief had shown "poor judgment" when he went to the precinct where Loeb was being held.

"Brian Mitchell is brilliant," Jimmy fired off to his text buddies. "He doesn't even speak to me before he goes into open court and unnecessarily and incorrectly opines on such a highly charged case. He may as well get a retainer from Loeb."

"Yeah!" joined in Chief of Detectives Billy Madigan. "Not a lot of thought went into that comment."

The ire of the text thread shifted firmly from Lopez to Mitchell. "Unreal," wrote DiGerolamo. "He probably prepared in the parking lot. Should have brought the check book with him."

"It was a dumb thing to say but otherwise the article was the same bullshit!" offered Meehan.

"A rehash of the same old rhetoric," concluded detective union boss Plant, agreeing that Mitchell's comments were "ill advised to say the least."

"Look at the bright side Jim," Plant told the chief, referring to *Newsday*'s coverage of the hearing: "no photos."

But Jimmy was beyond cheering up. CigarFest 2015 was totally ruined, and somehow, life got even worse from there.

* * *

On a Monday morning the following month, Kenny Bombace—who was absorbed with trying to figure out whether he could join his two police tenures in order to retire—got an urgent call from his attorney, Ed Jenks.

Bombace went to Jenks's law office in Mineola and absorbed a concise burst of life-changing information. Jenks said the previous Friday afternoon, he had been at the federal courthouse in Central Islip for an unveiling of a judge's portrait, a schmooze-heavy event over cubed cheese and Woodbridge. The lawyer was herded into a side room by a prosecutor for the Eastern District, James Miskiewicz, who told him matter-of-factly that the Loeb investigation was back on, and this time with more firepower than ever: Hundreds of subpoenas. People in handcuffs. The Queens DA's office as collateral damage.

It looked to be the entirely predictable result of the Suffolk wiretap and arrest of John Oliva, and in particular Spota and McPartland's ill-advised meeting with Loretta Lynch. Lynch had recently been appointed US Attorney General, making her the top federal law enforcement official in the nation. The meeting had failed to interest Lynch in indicting Oliva or any of his federal handlers, and instead put Suffolk's chieftains firmly back on the feds' radar.

The renewed Loeb investigation was no longer in the hands of greenhorn Brooklyn special agents for whom Suffolk County was an abstract concept. Instead, it had been taken over by prosecutors and investigators working out of the Long Island division of the Eastern District, based out of the Central Islip courthouse. The dozen or so federal mid- and late-career prosecutors assigned there were supposed to be out to pasture, working outside of major press scrutiny while enjoying pleasant commutes to suburban homes. In reality, those prosecutors felt an underdog pride at corralling a massive jurisdiction—with nearly 1,500 square miles of land mass and almost three million residents—that was hemorrhaging the sort of cases their big-city counterparts fought over.

Initially, this meant a flood of MS-13 murder cases, which had kept prosecutors particularly busy since the Suffolk PD had virtually abdicated its responsibilities on that front. But the Lynch meeting had driven home a reality that was becoming unavoidable: the Central Islip feds were working alongside a county law enforcement system that operated like an organized crime syndicate.

The lead investigator for the new incarnation of the Loeb investigation was Bill Hessle, a grizzled former postal inspector known for stony-faced interrogations in which he soaked up information and gave nothing back. And the top prosecutor overseeing the investigation was Nicole Boeckmann, who had been in the disastrous Lynch meeting and afterward personally hounded McPartland for materials in the Oliva case.

This news was enough to give any member of Burke's regime claustrophobia. The feeling was particularly acute for Bombace, whose brother-in-law, Ray Tierney, was one of Boeckmann's subordinates. In fact Tierney was one of the federal prosecutors stirring up the most shit for Spota and his allies. In January 2015, Tierney had indicted Walsh, the Conservative Party leader with the bogus time sheets, for theft of government funds and wire fraud. Tierney's chief witness, Sheriff Vincent DeMarco, had aided the case by secretly tapping a meeting with Spota in which he tried to get Spota to subpoena Walsh's golf records to show he was teeing off during work hours. The DA had dismissed DeMarco's concern and responded: "I'm not subpoenaing anything." Tierney and his colleagues considered Spota to be Walsh's unindicted co-conspirator. Bombace, who believed DeMarco had also worn a wire to meet him, felt like he was at the center of a Russian nesting doll of conspiracies.

Tierney never talked shop with Bombace, his wife's brother, and later insisted he had nothing to do with Bombace's lawyer being approached at the portrait unveiling. Whether or not Tierney had indirectly warned Bombace, the detective could see that the shit was headed in the direction of the fan.

During their meeting, Jenks told Bombace that the feds were going to issue a subpoena compelling him to testify in a grand jury about Loeb's beating and the later cover-up. Bombace would be given immunity for any crimes about which he testified truthfully, though he could be prosecuted for perjury if he lied. As a result of being immunized, he wouldn't be permitted to plead the fifth in order to avoid incriminating himself.

Bombace's first priority when emerging from Jenks's office was to tell Hickey about the meeting with his lawyer before the Intel boss learned of it from a different source. He showed up at Hickey's office at Police HQ and held out his phone. "Can we go talk outside?" Bombace asked Hickey. "I don't trust these things."

It was a chilly late spring day in barren Yaphank, and Bombace and his boss walked out to the patchy soccer fields behind the police building. Once Hickey heard what Bombace had to say, he was laser-focused. "You need to give me all the details," Hickey said. "They're going to want to know everything."

That night, Hickey drove to a parking lot outside of St. Patrick's Roman Catholic Church in Smithtown—where he prayed with his family on Sundays and also was schtupping an administrator—and waited for Burke. The boss also had some baggage near this location: directly across the street were the woods where Johnny Pius's body was discovered thirty-six years earlier.

When the nerve-wracked Burke entered the parking lot, they sat with their driver's windows to each other as Hickey repeated verbatim what Bombace had told him. Burke and Hickey knew that Vinny DeMarco, the Suffolk sheriff, was wired up and trying to bring them all down. They knew that Bombace's brother-in-law was the federal prosecutor working with DeMarco. And they knew that Bombace, a former sheriff's deputy, had met with DeMarco in his effort to join his two police tenures and retire. If Bombace retired, Burke and Hickey would lose control over him.

They were busy trying to talk through the muddy situation when Dennis Sullivan, Burke's old partner, entered the parking lot. Hickey and Jimmy drove to meet him. They all got out of their cars, and Hickey and Burke renewed their fast-paced conversation. Sullivan was lost, hearing names he didn't know and words—like "proffer"—he didn't understand. Hickey mused to himself that it was on-brand for Burke to involve his buddy Sullivan in the conspiracy by inviting him to this meeting for no clear reason. Jimmy had a habit of getting other people involved in his messes. "We need to talk to Tommy and Chris right away," Jimmy said as he ended the conversation.

Jimmy's girlfriend at the time, a mousy first-grade teacher, had three kids and had imagined a police chief would make for a stable partner. They had met at the wedding of the daughter of union boss Billy Plant. But since the beginning of the Loeb investigation—which Burke told her was "all BS"—Jimmy had become erratic, including using her phone for furtive conversations with his cop friends.

On the night he met Hickey in the church parking lot, Jimmy had been cooking dinner at her house when he got a phone call. When he returned from the meeting, he was in a frenzy, saying that the investigation was back on. He remained on edge all summer, pacing around while talking on her phone with Chris McPartland.

He kept saying the same thing: "If everyone would just be quiet, this would all go away."

* * *

The morning after the church parking lot meeting, Hickey was at Police HQ, just done with a briefing on a triple homicide in Wyandanch, when Jimmy Burke pulled him aside.

"Tommy needs to hear this from you," Jimmy said.

They took separate cars from Yaphank to Building 77. Spota's corner office, on the first floor of the building, was a comfortable if somewhat sterile sanctum a couple of decades behind in decor. It was all brown furniture—including Spota's large wooden desk and leather couches lining the walls—and bright white accessories like his landline phones and a standing whiteboard. Spota was unexpectedly an iPad enthusiast, and he kept the device propped up against thick legal books on his desk, in lieu of a computer.

When Hickey and Jimmy arrived at the office, Spota was behind the desk and McPartland was standing in front of one of the couches. "Tell me exactly what was said," Spota demanded.

Hickey started to relay again Bombace's conversation with his lawyer in which it was revealed that the investigation was back on, when Spota interrupted.

"Wait, wait, wait!" protested the old man, saying that it was "impossible" that the investigation was reopened because the feds had returned the Loeb file to the DA's office. Spota, in a moment of apparent disorientation, then directed Jimmy to call an attorney who hadn't worked in the DA's office in many years in order to verify that they had the case file back.

Hickey attempted to get back to Bombace's story, including the boast from the federal prosecutor about how this case was going to bring down the Queens DA's office.

"Wait, wait, wait!" Spota said again, overwhelmed with consternation. "Queens DA's office?"

Referring to the Loeb special prosecutor with whom they were chummy, Spota continued: "Why wouldn't we have heard that from Crusco—"

Jimmy had a possible explanation for why Queens might be in the crosshairs. "Maybe for Crusco leaving out the 302s for Russ to see," he offered, referring to the union boss Russ McCormack being allowed to see the confidential FBI documents.

McPartland, always the prudent manager of the conspiracy, interjected: "Don't say that out loud."

"Why?" Burke protested. "It's just us here."

"It doesn't matter," McPartland retorted.

Spota leaned into Hickey. "I don't even like talking in this room," the DA told the Intel boss in a low voice. "I don't trust this office. Usually when we talk we go downstairs to the basement, to the file room.

"Somebody's talking," Spota then told Hickey, "and you better find out fast, if it's not too late already."

"Tommy, call Joe Conway," McPartland chimed in, referring to Burke's lawyer. "Conway has all the lawyers corralled. Conway will know if anyone is talking."

And so Tommy called Burke's lawyer and left a voicemail. Spota then again addressed Hickey: "Who do you think has flipped?"

Hickey was aware that knowing who had flipped was his sole job. So he tried to deflect, and to explain how he could be so in the dark. "Maybe one of my guys got kidnapped," Hickey allowed—using a Suffolk term for when they scooped a subject off the street for an interrogation—"and I'm not aware of it."

"The feds don't do that," Spota shot back, leading to an impromptu rant. "The feds show up at your house at six o'clock in the morning. They go to your job. They try to embarrass you. They are bad people. They are bad people, the feds."

When Spota was done, his eyes, along with those of McPartland and Burke, came back to rest on Hickey. The Intel cop, feeling the pressure, began to analyze the suspects. He mentioned that Burke always said Detective Malone—"Iron Balls Mike"—was the shakiest. And McPartland, Hickey continued, considered Bombace the most likely to rat.

The men, watching Hickey regurgitate their own suspicions on who was the snitch, said nothing for a moment. Finally, Spota asked: "Who do you think it is?"

So Hickey gave Bombace a turn, recounting to the men how he wanted to retire and had met with that known rat, Sheriff DeMarco.

Spota had finally heard enough. "It's Bombace," he concluded, but then as if to comfort himself, Spota said of the Intel detectives: "Well, no matter what, these guys can't change their testimony now."

McPartland corrected him that actually only Leto had testified. "Regardless," Spota said, "changing their stories now would be the worst thing that they could do."

Hickey mentioned Bombace's high regard for himself, and his political aspirations. "Bombace sees himself as a United States congressman with flags flying behind him," Hickey said with an edge of mockery, "speaking to large crowds."

"He's dead in Suffolk County," interjected Spota. "He wants to work here? He'll never work here again, and I will see to it."

McPartland locked his eyes onto those of Hickey. "You need to give your guys a Lieutenant Hickey interrogation," he commanded. "One-on-one. Find out if anyone's talking, if anyone's cooperating. And if so, we will take immediate steps to discredit them."

There was a come-to-Jesus feeling to this meeting in Spota's office. The Loeb beating had loomed for years. And after all their obsessive scheming, the men were realizing they had still been too complacent, and now they were cornered.

"Tommy, can you believe this?" wailed Jimmy, suddenly appearing pathetic in his police chief regalia. "Can you believe that the feds are going to try to put me in jail for tapping some junkie thief on the top of his head?"

"I told you, you should have never left here," Spota scolded him softly. "None of this would have ever happened." As the meeting broke up, Spota reminded the crew: "Just be careful for bugs and wiretaps."

When Hickey started to leave, Jimmy got up and followed him, barking about the Intel detectives: "Remind those guys what happened to guys who go against The Administration."

"Just ask John Oliva," added McPartland.

Once he and Hickey were outside the office, Jimmy summoned up even more wrath, addressing the broken wing cop who had thus far failed him. "You tell those guys, I go, we all go," Jimmy fumed to Hickey. "Including you, the good lieutenant, Mr. Little League Baseball Coach, with your pretty little analyst."

Hickey got the message clear enough that Jimmy was threatening to expose his affairs, including one with an analyst in his office. But if The Administration had been attempting to light a fire under his ass with all the threats, the meeting had the opposite effect. Hickey felt the conspiracy was too far gone, and it wasn't even worth trying to figure out who was snitching.

As he left Building 77, Hickey realized—having just been threatened by the district attorney, the chief prosecutor for government corruption, and the chief of police—that his career was over.

CHAPTER 23

PLAYING CARDS
WITH MOBSTERS

Jim Hickey spent that paranoiac summer switching out cars from
the Intel unit, driving different routes in case the FBI was tailing
him, and waiting for the next hammer to fall.

But on a Monday morning in August, Hickey found himself with
a full day of non-conspiracy-related activities on his calendar.

There was a wake for the wife of Chuck Berger, an FBI supervisor
in Nassau County. And then his oldest daughter, Emily, was leaving
her kick line team due to a conflict with her coach, a personal crisis
for which Hickey—who despite his foibles prided himself as a top-
notch dad—planned to wait outside the school in order to offer moral
support.

Then Kenny Bombace called, and added a shot of all-purpose
panic to the schedule. Bombace's lawyer, Jenks, had once again urgently summoned the detective to his office, and Bombace was on
his way.

Hickey rang Burke, but the chief's secretary said he was in a meeting at the Sixth Precinct. So Hickey raced ten miles east and texted
Jimmy from the precinct parking lot: "R u still at sixth."

Jimmy emerged and Hickey told him that Bombace was once
again on his way to his lawyer's office. Jimmy's now-familiar response:
"We have to call Tommy and Chris."

When Hickey told Jimmy he was on his way to the wake of the wife of an FBI supervisor, the chief had a new idea. Richard Frankel, the former Suffolk prosecutor who became an FBI special agent and was at Spota and McPartland's ill-fated meeting with Loretta Lynch, would presumably be at the wake. Jimmy directed Hickey to find Frankel at the wake and ask him what was going on with the re-opened investigation.

Hickey sped west to Manhasset. He paid his respects. He saw Richie Frankel. But he didn't mention the investigation. He had decided that was not an appropriate thing to do at Chuck Berger's wife's wake.

Hickey got back in his car and drove the thirty-plus miles back to Smithtown. He had entered a multitasking frenzy, and so while his daughter broke it to her kick line coach that she was quitting, Hickey arranged to meet with Bombace on the school grounds to hear about his meeting with the lawyer.

They paced the Smithtown High School West grounds, the perfect-postured detective and his rat-like boss, and Hickey took in the information. It proved an even-worse sequel to the disastrous news from the last time Bombace had met with his attorney. The same federal prosecutor had once again pulled aside Jenks, but with a "harsher tone" this time. This time, the prosecutor had made clear it was more than a threat. Bombace was to expect a subpoena soon, there would be arrests, and it was his "last chance" to cooperate.

Jimmy was anxious to hear what Bombace was telling Hickey. He texted the Intel boss: "How is the kick line going?"

Hickey, aware that Jimmy was not actually invested in his daughter's kick line subplot, wrote back, referring to himself and Bombace: "We are still here."

"I want to root her on!" Jimmy texted. "She's such a good kid!"

Hickey told Jimmy via a lightly coded text to meet him at the "same place as sully," meaning at the parking lot of St. Pat's church, where they had met Dennis Sullivan last time.

Twenty minutes later, Jimmy texted Hickey: "3-6," police code for having arrived at a scene.

When Hickey arrived at the parking lot, he found Burke sitting shotgun in a parked car with McPartland at the wheel. Hickey got in the back seat and caught a big whiff of booze. Both men were drinking.

Hickey and McPartland happened to share a history in this church, as Hickey had coached basketball against McPartland's daughter at the court here. Now one girl dad greeted the other abruptly. "You lost control of Bombace," McPartland snarled at Hickey.

Hickey gave them Bombace's account of the meeting with his lawyer. "The feds are treating it like this big amorphous conspiracy," Jimmy complained.

McPartland had the unique perspective of a corruption prosecutor who made cases based on snippets of casual conversation between white-collar conspirators. He knew that such a case could look a lot like what he, Burke, and Hickey were doing while sitting in a church parking lot discussing who was ratting. "It sounds like they are building an obstruction case," he told those in the car. "And an obstruction statute is so vague and so poorly written that even our actions here would be considered obstruction."

"What do you think I should do?" Burke asked Hickey.

"You should quit," Hickey told him. "This is never going away."

"If I do that, I lose the power of the unions," Burke said. "I'm not Chief Burke, I'm just Mr. Burke."

Hickey got out of the car, and McPartland and Burke drove to a nearby restaurant named Golden Dynasty. They had their own schedule that evening, which included toasting Jimmy's mom's seventy-fourth birthday over Peking duck.

* * *

At a restaurant in Northport, Kenny Bombace watched the head of the detective's union get steadily drunker while urging him not to retire.

"You don't have to do this," Russ McCormack, whose thick frame, mustache, and thinning gray hair made him a Jimmy Burke doppelganger, told Bombace. The detective had gotten the news he had been waiting for, official permission to combine his service time in the police department and sheriff's office, allowing him to retire with a pension. And now he was explaining to his union rep, McCormack, that he no longer wanted to work under the cloud of the Loeb investigation.

McCormack made a show of pulling out his cell to make a call. When McCormack returned to their table, he suggested that the unnamed person on the other end of the call had just filled him in on huge news. "It's over," McCormack said of the investigation. "You don't have to worry about anything."

After dinner, Bombace went directly from the restaurant to Hickey's house. The detective and the Intel boss took a long stroll in the buggy August night, from Hickey's sleepy street toward a Dunkin' Donuts on a main drag about a mile away. Bombace told Hickey how he wanted to retire, and about McCormack's claim that the investigation was over.

Hickey stopped and looked at his detective. "Was he drinking?" he asked simply.

"Yes," said Bombace.

"Fuck that," replied Hickey. "Put your papers in."

It was a rare break in the campaign among department higher-ups to dissuade Bombace from retiring. Even Commissioner Ed Webber called Bombace to impress upon him how important he was to the department. It seemed odd for the commissioner to care about a midlevel detective taking his twenty years. Bombace saw it all as a desperate gambit to keep him under Burke's thumb with his grand jury testimony date looming.

Bombace had told virtually everybody with a badge—including union officials and the other detectives—about the pending subpoena, due to his fear of being perceived as a cooperator. The reaction was general alarm, and skepticism that the feds could make him testify. He assured them that—according to his lawyer—they could do just that. Nobody was dumb enough to tell him how he should testify, but Bombace knew the expectation was that he should keep up the lie.

The final boss in Bombace's full disclosure tour was Steve Bellone. The county executive had an election coming up, and Bombace wasn't sure how he'd react. "Who knew where he stood on this?" Bombace said later. "For political reasons did he want this to just go away and everyone to just shut up?"

But when Bombace told Bellone about the grand jury subpoena, the county executive surprised him with an apolitical answer: "The only way you can get in trouble is by lying."

Bombace didn't tell Bellone what he planned to say. He officially retired in September, the month before he was due to testify in the grand jury. He stopped answering text messages and phone calls from other cops, sure that they were trying to gauge his upcoming testimony. Those attempts became so incessant that Bombace grew afraid that cops were going to show up at his door and confront him or his family. So he dropped his kids off with his sister—and her husband Ray Tierney—and checked into a Nassau County hotel.

He went into the grand jury on a Tuesday morning in October. It had been Bombace's little secret that, despite all the other cops being outraged on his behalf that the feds were stripping him of his right to plead the fifth, he felt nothing but relief about it. As far as he was concerned, the cover-up was over. "I knew in my gut," he later said, "there was no way I was going to sit in a federal courtroom and lie."

Bombace didn't hide from everyone his intention to tell the truth. He wanted the other Intel detectives to know his plans so they wouldn't perjure themselves in the federal grand jury, if they hadn't already. "I was terrified that these guys already went in and got themselves in trouble lying for people who couldn't give a shit about us," Bombace explained.

So before he self-exiled to Nassau County, Bombace met Tony Leto in a field near Bombace's house in Mt. Sinai. "I'm going to testify, and I'm going to tell the whole truth," Bombace told his former colleague.

Leto looked him up and down and responded: "Are you wired?"

"No," said Bombace. "Are you?"

* * *

By the time of that conversation, in which he learned that Bombace was about to blow up the whole conspiracy, Leto's life had already completely unraveled. His wife had found out he was having an affair. At first, he tried lying to her but then decided: *You know what, fuck it, I'm going to tell her everything.* So, now he was getting divorced. But with the devastation of having wrecked his family came a small measure of sanity, a big lie he no longer had to keep.

But on the other big lie, nobody expected him to ever waver. Unlike Bombace, Leto didn't get any invite from McCormack to a nice restaurant in Northport. His version was a Chipotle meal that he wasn't even invited to. His buddy Malone, the detective who had bragged of whizzing in Loeb's coffee, informed him that he and the union boss were going to meet at the burrito franchise in Hauppauge. "I'm going to fucking go, too," Leto insisted. At Chipotle, McCormack regurgitated his talking points: that the investigation was all bullshit, that the feds were just trying to scare Burke, and that everything would be taken care of.

Leto had tagged along to be bullshitted. He felt increasingly like the redheaded stepchild of the conspiracy. His complicity was assumed; his perjury purchased with a burrito bowl.

After they learned that Bombace had gotten the grand jury subpoena, Leto and Malone then went to Hickey's house. The lieutenant delivered a little pep talk to assure them this was not a disaster. He told them he didn't believe Kenny would testify truthfully, mostly because the guy would never harpoon his own political ambitions. And even if everybody got arrested, Hickey told Leto and Malone cheerfully, they could all still retire with their pensions. The moral: they should all keep lying.

But then Leto had that chat with Bombace in the field in Mt. Sinai, and he realized he was being left on a sinking ship. Before, the image that had so scared Leto was that of feds storming his front door while his boys were home. Now he had a new fear: him and Burke, together at a defense table in a courtroom, codefendants, partners, plotting with their lawyers and scheming over discovery. The idea repulsed Leto. He decided: *I'm not on his team.*

Leto—who had half-tried to convince Burke not to go into the interrogation room with Loeb, who had fumed while Malone bragged about pissing in Loeb's coffee cup, and who pushed aside his dread to perjure himself on the chief's orders—realized that this time he had to finally act on his gut, and fast.

* * *

On October 21, 2015, Leto traveled to Brooklyn for a meeting with his lawyer, two federal prosecutors, and a special agent. Almost as soon as he sat down, Leto began to suffer cooperation agreement envy. He knew that Bombace got immunity in return for his grand jury testimony, and heard that the same was true for Malone. But the feds were blunt that immunity was just not on the table for Leto, and never would be. He had missed his chance back in the failed Shattered Shield phase of the federal investigation to beat the others to an immunity deal. The feds don't speak as obsessively about white hats and black hats as their Suffolk cop counterparts, but they employ the same general concept. They were stingier with the white ones, however, particularly for those who had blatantly perjured themselves and had a reputation for abusing prisoners.

The best they could offer: making Leto their "Queen for a Day," the appropriately demeaning term they used for the subjects of what are more formally known as proffer agreements. Under the terms of a proffer, Leto would provide to the feds all the actionable information he could and answer the feds' questions truthfully, under penalty of perjury. In return, the feds promised nothing, except that they couldn't use his statements as direct evidence against him. (Though, the feds made clear, they were free to go out and secure whatever new evidence they wanted against him with the information he gave them.) If prosecutors then deigned to find Leto worthy of a cooperation agreement, he'd have to plead guilty to a federal crime like witness tampering, with a maximum sentence of twenty years. And even at that point, all the government would promise, if they were satisfied with Leto's cooperation, was a vague carrot called a 5K1 letter. The document sent from a prosecutor to his eventual sentencing judge would detail his cooperation in order to potentially—but with no guarantees—lessen his punishment.

It was, in short, a shit deal. It would be attractive only to a perp who the feds already had dead to rights anyway, which is why Leto, on his lawyer's advice, signed it. He then unloaded on the table full of feds. "I told them everything, man," Leto said. "Every. Fucking. Thing."

That included even how many prisoners he had struck before Loeb. "I said around five times, give or take," Leto said later, remarking of the exact number: "I honestly don't remember."

* * *

Hickey's only job had been to keep his detectives in line, and by mid-October he knew that he had failed miserably. He wouldn't find out about Leto until a little later, but he and Burke learned that Bombace had gone through with his grand jury testimony almost as soon as he left the courthouse, thanks to lawyer Joe Conway's federal spies.

It was a blow to his ego. Hickey prided himself on his competence, such as his ability to balance his children's athletic schedules with the demands of multiple ongoing affairs. His failure to control the conspiracy left him in a state of paralysis. He knew the unraveling was too far gone to try to fix. Anything he did would just make the situation worse. But he also couldn't bring himself to toss his entire life in the shredder by going to the feds himself.

So, instead, he stopped going to work. He readied his retirement paperwork in order to get his pension, the only thing that was still guaranteed in his existence. He ceased sleeping. He spent most nights by his front window, chugging coffee while on the lookout for the feds or other intruders.

"Stressed to the max," he told his wife. He treated his insomnia like a new job, calling it "24/7 guard duty." Jimmy had told him to call him right away "if they came." Hickey, ground down by distrust and insomnia, started to imagine things, namely giant lizards. Hickey kept seeing them, crawling on cars or in one case driving a Cadillac, near his Smithtown house. He also watched from his window as men in trench coats got out of black SUVs to interview his neighbors on their front steps. A few days later, he saw SCPD cars blocking the entrance to his street, with cops all over the place. His wife, though, couldn't see any of that. When she walked in on Hickey talking to his son in their living room with a Mets playoff game on, she had to remind him that the kid was away at college. Hours later, Hickey couldn't remember who won the game. He got lost driving home. He started slurring his speech and losing his balance.

It came to a head on the early morning on October 22. Hickey called Jimmy and told him there were people outside his house. But when Jimmy raced over, he found only his right-hand lieutenant and his very concerned wife. "He's not right," she said, and told Jimmy she was taking him to the emergency room.

He arrived at Huntington Hospital at 1:27 a.m. He thought he saw at least one giant lizard along the way. "He has a stressful job," wrote one of the doctors doing intake. By 8:00 p.m. that night—with Hickey still not having slept—the staff found the lieutenant screaming about a girl in danger, having ripped out his IV and shucked his hospital gown while running toward an elevator. He was restrained by security guards and tied down on his bed while doctors administered antipsychotics. Early the next morning, Hickey still hadn't slept. He had spent part of the night seeing hallucinations of children eating ice cream he sold them in his hospital room. Hickey was transferred to the critical care unit and given a Precedex drip, essentially forcing him to sleep.

While he was asleep, his wife filled in his doctor. "Wife reports that the patient is SCPD detective and that his work has been very stressful as they reopened a case and coworkers have been issued subpoenas," read one of his medical notes. "She reports that he slept for less than ten hours last week due to increased hours at work, and fears of getting a subpoena himself." Hickey awoke asking for water, and with little memory of the previous thirty-six hours, but seemed to have largely recovered. A doctor diagnosed the lieutenant with "delirium due to sleep deprivation and stress," and he was discharged on October 26.

"I felt back to normal," reported Hickey, "Stressed, but back to normal."

But over the course of his hospitalization and the couple of days afterward, Hickey's little universe shifted on its axis. This was driven home by a phone call he got from Police HQ while making a follow-up visit with his doctor.

The man on the other line, Stuart Cameron, was a tall and craggy figure who spoke with a canned geniality. Stu, as Hickey knew him, was terminally competent. He was diligent, educated—with a master's degree and eleven weeks at Quantico—and was neither an ass-kisser nor a cowboy. In Jimmy Burke's SCPD, these traits rendered him a total loser, not even obtrusive enough to get on Jimmy's enemy list. When Hickey started his hospital stay, Cameron was chief of support services, the position for accountants who accidentally become top cops. But Cameron was that sort of stable, scandal-free company man who suddenly appears very attractive to organizations during crises.

Hickey took in what Stu had to say: Jimmy Burke was gone. Stu was now chief of department. And they wanted Hickey's guns.

* * *

The day before—Tuesday, October 27—Jimmy Burke had been beckoned into the office of Suffolk County Executive Steve Bellone. He could guess what this meeting was going to be about. Joe Conway's spies kept them apprised of federal grand jury testimony, so Burke knew it wasn't just Bombace who had caved in the grand jury. Leto—the steely gangster of a cop Burke always figured as the most steadfast of the detectives—had entered the grand jury on his volition and "collapsed," Conway had told Burke. On top of all of that, the last time he saw Hickey, his Intel chief, the guy was seeing giant lizards and about to be whisked to the emergency room. Burke could see as well as anybody else that his world was coming down around him.

But Burke was an optimist. As he headed into Bellone's office, he was armed with a document that in recent months had become an increasingly pathetic security blanket. It was Burke's "timeline," a piece of paper on which he had written his version of events, complete with talking points about how the feds were targeting him as retaliation for the removal of the detectives from the gang task force. His lawyer, Conway, had asked him to write the timeline after they learned of the reopening of the investigation. Long after it was of any use to Conway, Burke still leafleted his colleagues in Suffolk County government with copies of the document. So when Bellone started in on his explanation of all the reasons Burke had to go, the chief produced his timeline as if it contained the spell that would magically change Bellone's mind. It wasn't a completely unreasonable presumption. After all, Bellone had been one of Burke's easiest marks, a sucker for every exaggerated boast and untruthful denial he could squeeze onto a PowerPoint or official DA's letterhead. Was a warmed-over timeline full of misdirection all that different?

But what Burke didn't seem to comprehend was the thoroughness with which Bellone was a political creature. The truth about the Loeb beating, or Burke's overall suitability to be chief of department, never really mattered. The only relevant thing was that the tides were now unmistakably headed counter to Burke. At some point after hearing about the Leto grand jury, Bellone recognized that in order to survive he had to not only ride those waves but pretend he was the celestial body pulling them.

So in the face of Burke's protestations and his timeline, Bellone laughed. He told him that he knew he had beaten Loeb. And that he could no longer stay in office.

That said, Bellone explained that he was going to allow Burke to remain an employee of the SCPD for another two weeks while Stu Cameron handled his duties. The delay was to ensure that Burke could file his retirement papers, get his vacation paid out, and secure his pension. Bellone was by then aware that the chief of department had beaten a suspect and orchestrated an ongoing, top-level criminal cover-up, but there was no need to do anything hasty.

After the news broke that night, Conway issued a statement explaining that Burke was retiring for "personal and family reasons . . . unrelated to any speculation of a federal investigation." Commissioner Ed Webber, pliant to the end, released his own statement calling Jimmy Burke "one of the most outstanding supervisors, investigators, and trainers in the history of the Suffolk County Police Department."

Burke's policy with those on his enemy list was to not let bygones be bygones, even when they left the department. He found retirement parties of his rivals to be useful because their attendance exposed members of the enemy camp, and thus, gave him new names to add to the list. When his old nemesis Pat Cuff finally put in his papers in July 2015, even as Jimmy was in a panic over the reopened investigation, he found time to alert his text thread of cop buddies. "We need a friendly to go to Cuff's retirement party to take accurate attendance," Burke texted. "Tonite. Not sure where. Whoever goes has to be able to recognize faces. Enemies, bosses, actives and retired and politicians. Flier is hanging outside chief of patrol conference room." At his party that night at a country club in Manorville, Cuff looked across the deck and saw a lieutenant who was pals with Burke and knew exactly why he was there.

But as it turns out, the retirement party that Jimmy most thoroughly sabotaged was his own. Following his last day as a cop, Jimmy, his high school friend Tony D'Orazio, Dennis Sullivan, and Chris McPartland met at Golden Dynasty, the Smithtown restaurant. They tried to keep it cheerful, but inevitably the conversation turned toward the same thing it had for almost three years.

"It's a weak case," McPartland assured Burke of the arrest they all now assumed was inevitable. "No injuries, and Loeb has credibility issues. I'm not going to lie to you and say there's nothing to worry about, the feds have a lot of power."

Jimmy groused that he hadn't heard from Hickey in over a week, which was unusual, and that he was concerned he was cooperating. And he mentioned yet another little domino he learned had fallen in the ongoing federal grand jury: Brian Draiss, the cop from the Fourth Precinct who had been in charge of invoicing the items found in Loeb's bedroom, had testified that he recovered a dildo from the bag.

According to his figurehead commissioner, Jimmy Burke was just about the best cop in the history of Suffolk County. But the end of his career was marked by four sad men in a Chinese restaurant, fretting over a dildo.

* * *

Even in the days after Jimmy was gone, his tricks remained. Stu Cameron needed to speak to Hickey, he explained in that phone call while the lieutenant was at his doctor's office, because of what the new chief of department had heard while at a funeral for a city cop. A rumor "through the lines" of cops at the funeral had reached Cameron, something about Hickey being admitted to CPEP, a psychiatric emergency facility in Stony Brook. As a result, Cameron and Webber were considering taking Hickey's guns.

Hickey knew that only his wife and Jimmy Burke were aware that he had been hospitalized. Jimmy had spread the rumor to discredit Hickey in case he was cooperating with the feds. But Hickey quite liked his guns, particularly since he appeared increasingly to be a target of armed and desperate co-conspirators. "I'm going to go home, put a suit on, and I'll be in your office by two o'clock," Hickey insisted to the new chief of department.

Hickey summoned up that old Ratman charm. "I'm the same old Jimmy Hickey!" he told Cameron. The new chief of department apparently agreed. Hickey kept his guns, and in his frenetic style he then busied himself with the next thing on his to-do list: a family vacation.

His son's college basketball team was headed to Florida to face the University of Miami, and the exhibition coincided with his wife's fiftieth birthday. The Hickeys had decided to make a weeklong trip out of it, and the lieutenant wasn't going to let a nervous breakdown, or a looming federal investigation, halt the trip.

At 2:30 p.m. on Friday, October 30, the day before their scheduled departure, Hickey was at home packing for Florida. He heard a knock at the door and was greeted by two investigators with a federal grand jury subpoena.

Hickey didn't call or text a soul. With the subpoena notice in hand, he got in his car and drove directly to the Superior Officers Association in Brookhaven, about twenty miles away. The little pink building, with an ornate sign reading, "Suffolk County SOA," looked more like a small town's library than the power center for the top-ranking members of the massive county police department. When Hickey walked in, a secretary was heading out for the week, leaving only two union officials—including President Timmy Morris—in the building. Hickey showed them the subpoena, and they sent it off to the union's attorney.

And then Jimmy Burke walked in. Hickey's union president had dimed him out. Hickey heard Jimmy making small talk with the union officials about his resignation, and his plans to pursue consulting opportunities.

Hickey finished his meeting and then walked out to the parking lot with Burke. The chief no longer appeared optimistic about his consulting work. He looked scared and agitated. No uniform, no big black cop truck. Jimmy had arrived in a drab brown sedan Hickey hadn't seen before. In his hand: that damn timeline.

The sun had gone down, and Hickey realized he was alone in a dark parking lot with a dangerous man. "We need to talk," Jimmy said. "Jump in the car with me."

Hickey refused. "You follow me," the lieutenant said. "I'll pick a spot."

Brookhaven is in a rural part of Suffolk County, and as Hickey drove his mind raced about where there would be people. More to the point, where there would be witnesses if Jimmy tried to kill him. He finally settled on the only bustling establishment within miles: Ground Round Grill & Bar.

In the rear parking lot of the budget steakhouse, which was crowded with Friday afternoon diners, Hickey and Jimmy both got out of their cars. Jimmy told him about being humiliated in the county executive's office, and how Bellone had laughed in his face about the timeline. He told him that Leto had gone in on his own to the grand jury and collapsed. About how Conway was preparing bail packages for the likelihood that Jimmy was arrested. "I don't mind doing three years playing cards with mobsters," Jimmy postured to Hickey, "but I need you to be strong."

Hickey knew what that meant: standing tall, keeping the cover-up going, to protect Spota and McPartland from a federal conspiracy case. Jimmy added that they needed to stay in touch so that the feds monitoring their phones wouldn't notice any change.

Ratman assured him on all counts.

The Hickeys had a great time in Miami. Hickey was back to his competent self, cheering on his son and celebrating his wife's fiftieth while also firing off a few hundred text messages to three mistresses. And when he got back to New York, he had a purpose again. He drove to a high-rise near the Manhattan end of the Brooklyn Bridge.

In the parking lot, Hickey filled four pages with notes. In the elevator up, he read them over to make sure he hit the key points of the last few years, trying to make it all as clear as possible for his new lawyer, and the feds.

"It was over," Hickey later said. "The cover-up, the whole thing. I wanted to tell the whole truth and cooperate."

* * *

Just as Spota had predicted, the bad people came for Burke at six in the morning. And they tipped off *Newsday* beforehand, ensuring the paper had a photographer hiding outside Burke's driveway when the small gaggle of men in blue "FBI" jackets descended on Sammis

Street in Smithtown on Wednesday, December 9, 2015. Burke knew that trick well, as the arrest perp walk was an old Government Corruption Bureau standard.

When the feds got there, Jimmy was waiting for them in the driveway in mismatched blazer and slacks, no belt, and a dress shirt, his hair still wet and his face cleanly shaven around his cop moustache.

Across the street from the site of the predawn arrest was the park where Jimmy Burke, Catholic schoolboy fresh from Ozone Park, said he snuck his first joint about four decades earlier. Around a couple of corners was Dogwood Elementary, where Johnny Pius's body was found under sticks and leaves. And right next door: his old mom's house, where Suffolk detectives had come looking for answers, and Jimmy had made the first inroads toward joining their tribe.

Jimmy made for a jocular arrest subject. Even as the feds handcuffed him in his driveway, he was still smiling and cracking jokes, cop to cop. As he was being fingerprinted and having his mug shot taken, he was greeted by Geri Hart, the Long Island FBI supervisor. Burke remarked that he had been meaning to meet her, and referred to his federal indictment like it was just another PR headache: "The press is going to kill me on this."

* * *

"I need a shoulder to cry on," Chris McPartland told Tony D'Orazio, Jimmy Burke's high school pal, over the phone. That was odd, because Jimmy's two best friends weren't particularly close themselves. But D'Orazio, as requested, met McPartland at Golden Dynasty in February 2016.

It had been a long two months since Jimmy's arrest. At his arraignment, federal prosecutors detailed the "climate of fear" in the department under Burke and argued that he was too dangerous to release on bail: "His long association with some law enforcement officials ensures his ability to continue to intimidate witnesses while awaiting trial." In the proceedings, prosecutors said they had at least ten Suffolk officers cooperating against Burke, and all but revealed that Hickey was one of them, referring to a "commanding officer" who had been ordered "to find out if any of the eye-witnesses to the assault were cooperating with federal authorities, and to remind them of the potential for retribution should they cooperate." US Judge Leonard Wexler agreed with the prosecutors that "there is no way he can be supervised to the degree where he's not a danger to the community," ordering Jimmy held without bail in protective custody in Brooklyn.

And in January, McPartland, still DA Spota's division chief of investigations with an annual salary of roughly $175,000, was informed via a hand-delivered letter from the feds that he was the target of a grand jury investigation for obstruction in the Loeb investigation. The existence of the letter, and the investigation, was of course immediately leaked and then plastered on the front page of *Newsday*.

Inside the Chinese restaurant, McPartland told D'Orazio that the investigation had caused a financial burden he couldn't handle. From D'Orazio's perspective, what followed was an awkward, blubbery overshare from a tough guy top prosecutor he knew only superficially. Choking up while telling D'Orazio about how he had asked all his family members for help and had taken out a second mortgage and was also paying for his daughters' college tuition, then came McPartland's ask: a $25,000 loan.

D'Orazio, a burly, bearded man with a buzz cut, did well for himself in construction and property development, but he was not some titan of industry for whom that sort of loan would not be a big deal. He left the restaurant feeling surprised by McPartland's audacity, though it didn't take him long to figure out who would be better suited to deal with the plea for a loan. D'Orazio called John Toal, Jimmy's half-brother, and told him what McPartland had said, and they agreed to bring it up with Jimmy.

At the Metropolitan Detention Center in Brooklyn, Jimmy, in a short-sleeved jumpsuit, huddled around a table with D'Orazio and Jimmy's three brothers: Michael Burke, George "Junie" Burke, and John Toal. Mike was still in his stepfather's air-conditioning business, while Junie and John, half-brothers from Jimmy's parents' respective second marriages, were a detective and a sergeant, respectively, in the NYPD.

John, who had the same thin lips and drowsy eyes as Jimmy but a far more millennial haircut—shaved to the scalp on one side rising to a little tsunami wave of salt-and-pepper hair on the other—had leaped to action when his big brother, with whom he lived, was arrested. The biggest logistical issue was figuring out what to do with Jimmy's incoming buckets of cash. Modern policing is the rare career in which getting indicted and having to quit your job in shame brings with it a financial windfall. Burke had already received his first big check, $225,000 for unpaid vacation and sick leave, and had more payouts coming, including a fat annual pension for the rest of his life.

Jimmy told his brothers and Tony D'Orazio that day that he was going to take a plea deal. The feds were offering about four years, and if Burke didn't take it, he'd face as many as twenty-five. As they were nearing the end of the somber visit, D'Orazio mentioned McPartland's request for money for legal fees. According to John, Jimmy looked at him and remarked: "Oh, well, give him the money from the box."

The money from the box was an odd thing. Before Jimmy was arrested, he and John had opened a safety deposit box at a TD Bank in Smithtown in which they put about $40,000. John claimed it was cash found while cleaning out the house belonging to their mother, who was ailing from cancer. And the day before the jail meeting with Jimmy, John and D'Orazio had cosigned for another safety deposit box, this one without Jimmy's name on it, a few miles away in Centereach. John had then moved the $40,000 into that box.

Jimmy pleaded guilty the next day. And three days after that, John and D'Orazio went to the bank in Centereach and together counted out $25,000. D'Orazio then called McPartland and asked him to meet at Golden Dynasty. He waited in his car, and when he saw McPartland hustling into the restaurant, he honked his horn. McPartland joined him in the front passenger seat. Upon seeing the envelope filled with cash, he began to effusively thank D'Orazio.

"Chris, you know I'm not the only one you should be thankful to for this," D'Orazio said.

But before D'Orazio could mention Jimmy, McPartland—the professional expert on the finer points of white-collar conspiracy—stopped him by putting his palms out and saying: "Listen, all I know is I came to you for help."

Jimmy emailed D'Orazio from jail: "Did you give the cigar to the old man?" D'Orazio replied that he had.

Jimmy had gone full Ozone Park. If the envelope of cash in a parking lot wasn't clear enough, Jimmy was even more explicit upon pleading guilty. He asked Joe Conway to pass on a message to McPartland and Spota: Jimmy wasn't talking to anybody; he was a "stand-up guy."

* * *

That spring, Joe Sawicki, the Suffolk County comptroller, was playing some golf with Tom Spota when he remarked on their old pal Jimmy's predicament.

Three years earlier, it was on Sawicki's charter fishing trip that Burke realized the gravity of the situation, when Hickey called to inform him about the detectives getting subpoenas. Now Jimmy was awaiting sentencing, and Suffolk County itself was becoming Jimmy's least favorite descriptor: federalized.

Edward Webber had been replaced as commissioner by Bellone's thirty-something deputy and former federal prosecutor, Tim Sini. He and Stu Cameron had the task of rooting out from the top offices of their department actors in a criminal conspiracy that they had every reason to believe was still ongoing. They made each police official above the rank of captain file into their offices for one-on-one interviews. Cameron later stated drolly that "those interviews were very enlightening." Most of Burke's closest cronies were informed, subtly or not, that they were no longer welcome. Cameron assigned Hickey to the SCPD version of a rubber room. He ordered Madigan to stay home.

Jimmy's most vindictive decisions were lacquered over. Pat Cuff, who had retired with a captain's shield after Jimmy demoted him from assistant chief, was instead now given the higher rank's shield, a bauble that didn't replace the two-thirds of a million dollars his demotion cost him. John Oliva, who had been denied his retirement shield outright, was also given one by Sini and Cameron. And while they were trying to steam clean the stench of Jimmy Burke out of the curtains in Yaphank, over in Building 77 in Hauppauge the men who had for years propped up Burke—Tom Spota and Chris McPart-land—were still clinging to top positions in county law enforcement.

That was despite the somewhat cynical efforts of Steve Bellone, who was attempting an unlikely rebrand as a Long Island Eliot Ness. The county executive had held a press conference on the steps of the DA's office, calling it a "criminal enterprise" and demanding Spota's resignation. Spota responded with his own hastily arranged press conference in which he made thinly veiled references to purported skeletons in Bellone's closet. "I have never said it before, but I'll say it now," Spota railed. "The county executive has made and did make in the past, multiple personal pleas to me in the presence of other prosecutors, not to investigate or prosecute people that he was close to."

Spota appeared supremely confident that all he needed was his familiar arsenal of those kinds of threats and innuendo, even as his division chief wept for a loan in Golden Dynasty. Spota would surely bluster his way through this crisis just like all the others he had weathered over the previous four decades.

So when Sawicki mentioned that he felt bad Jimmy was going to have to do some real jail time, Spota responded like a man who didn't know he was next.

"Don't feel bad, Joe," he said before he took his next swing. "Jim did it to himself. He had no business going up to the precinct that day."

RATMAN'S REVENGE

On November 2, 2016, in the federal courthouse in Central Islip, Christopher Loeb addressed a fellow prisoner. "Today is the day I honestly believed would never arrive," he told James Burke, both men now felons and clad in inmate jumpsuits. "I thought you were untouchable. Now look at us both, we are both incarcerated. The difference, besides the fact that my sentence is about to end and yours is only the beginning, is that my actions reflected only me."

The strung-out junkie whose story nobody would believe, as Burke repeatedly described Loeb to his co-conspirators, was now muscular and clear-eyed. He had spent months crafting and rehearsing this statement while in prison. "Not only did you ruin your own career and reputation, but you ruined the careers and reputations of subordinates . . . whom helped you assault me and who you ordered to help cover up your criminal conduct," Loeb said. "Your rise to power makes many people doubt the legitimacy of the Suffolk County Police Department and the integrity of the political leaders who promoted you."

Burke had pleaded in court papers for the judge to sentence him to the eleven months that he had already served so that he could care for his sick mother. Now Loeb, clearly relishing a chance to publicly school this particular fallen top cop, noted that he had been unable to spend time with his grandmother before she died, and that he had missed funerals of those close to him. "You see, I already know what you are about to learn," Loeb lectured Burke. "When you commit a crime, your family suffers along with you."

Jimmy appeared beefy from jail food and largely unbothered by the proceedings, at times slightly smirking as Loeb unloaded. The courthouse audience was packed with cops. Many of them had sent the judge letters asking for leniency on Burke's behalf. In his own remarks before sentencing, Burke apologized to Loeb, his family— "particularly my mother"—the police department and people of Suffolk County, and his "subordinates that I engaged in these acts with," whom he explained he was only trying to look after: "This was, among other things, a misguided and wrongful attempt to protect them and myself."

Finding that Burke "corrupted a system not in one act, but for three years," US District Court Judge Leonard Wexler sentenced him to forty-six months in prison.

Two months later, Loeb's attorney, Bruce Barket, succeeded in having Loeb's guilty plea vacated, based as it was on a foundation of perjury. Loeb was released from prison.

Over the course of the next two years, while Burke did his time at a low-security federal prison in Allenwood, Pennsylvania, Suffolk County agreed to pay Loeb $1.5 million to settle his suit stemming from the violation of his civil rights. Burke, who the county refused to indemnify, was still on the hook. He had to separately settle his part of the suit for an undisclosed amount. "Confidential means confidential, but I can tell you this," Loeb's attorney, Bruce Barket, said. "He had money, and we had him by the short hairs. So we didn't let him go for a song."

* * *

For a man whose self-mythologizing was one of his favorite parts of the job, Thomas J. Spota's resignation letter from the DA's office where he was first hired forty-five years earlier, and had spent the last sixteen as top dog, was notably concise.

"To Whom it May Concern," Spota wrote, "Please be advised that at the close of business November 10, 2017 will be my last day of employment as Suffolk County District Attorney."

Spota and Chris McPartland had been indicted two weeks earlier on federal charges of witness tampering, obstruction of justice, and being accessories after the fact to the deprivation of Loeb's civil rights. Both men, booked while wearing suits and ties, looked pale and shell-shocked in mug shots taken in front of a white brick wall.

Spota, obstinate until the end, still stayed in office for weeks, citing his need to complete "normal administrative matters." McPartland also stayed on until the end of the year, before getting a job as an East Northport liquor store clerk, earning $16 an hour while awaiting trial.

Then began the tenure of the new DA, elected amid the chaos: Tim Sini, the former fed from Kenny Bombace's jealous boat trip.

* * *

Since the settlement, Chris Loeb didn't wash his clothes. Instead, he just bought new ones whenever the old garments were dirty. So in October 2018, he met me at a mall in Queens in order to do some replenishing.

Loeb arrived two hours late in a new Jeep Trackhawk with a customized sound system. He hadn't bathed in days, had open sores on his face and neck, and his clothes were caked in grime and blood. He had gauze wrapped around his left hand, which he explained was from jumping out of a third-floor window. He was eating from a bag of Gushers and reeked of cigarettes.

For Loeb, so cogent and sober at Burke's sentencing less than two years earlier, reaping his share of a seven-figure payout from the settlement was a potentially lethal disaster. His lawyer, Barket, knew that, and took steps to mete out the money as slowly as possible. So Loeb fired him. At Macy's, Loeb heaped clothes onto his bony shoulders—Polo socks, Hilfiger underwear, Armani cologne, Buffalo jeans—and when he ran out of space, he used my shoulders as well. While he shopped, he seethed about his lawyer withholding his cash, as if Barket was in the men's section with him. "Listen, I slept in my car numerous, numerous times because you weren't around to send over the fucking money transfer," Loeb said. "I'm a millionaire now. A million dollars in my bank account. I'm sleeping in my car?"

Loeb got impatient waiting for the line at the register, peeled off $500 from a wad of bills, and gave it to me to buy it all. Then he scrambled to the bathroom. He never went more than half an hour without an extended trip to the bathroom, and later he acknowledged he was both shooting heroin and snorting coke.

Loeb's central role in the ouster of Jimmy Burke and Tom Spota, along with the life-changing cash windfall and the ego-amplifying effects of heavy drug use, had imbued him with a new sense of purpose: to be an activist, or even a cultural icon. In his recounting, he no longer just happened to jiggle the wrong truck's door. Instead, he now said that he knew it was Chief Burke's Yukon all along, which is why he stole from it. Loeb said he was working on a book himself. It was hard to finish while constantly being in and out of jail, but he did have a tentative title: *It Started With an Ass-Whooping*. His immediate goal was to speak in front of the Suffolk County Legislature about dirty cops and compromised politicians. "Obviously, I got to work on my cursing," Loeb remarked, as if his use of profanity was the only thing that needed polishing.

Loeb said he couldn't get the events of December 14, 2012, out of his mind. "I'm always picking it apart and picking up new things," Loeb said after leaving Macy's with his shopping bags, peeling off bills for a beggar on the street. "It's like watching a movie over and over again."

The movie, he said, doesn't end at night. "I'm an insomniac," Loeb said. "If I have dreams, they're nightmares. I wake up screaming. In the dreams, everything is dark and I'm in my house in Smithtown." In his paranoia, Loeb had even turned against the feds, the law enforcement agents who saved him from Suffolk County justice. He described recently speeding up on a Chevy Tahoe on the highway that he was sure was driven by an agent monitoring him. He gave the guy—who could've just been a hapless commuter—the finger, and screamed: "Go to your office, and go cry to your boss and get yelled at!"

Leaving his $90,000 SUV at the mall, Loeb walked to a nearby studio apartment outfitted with surveillance camera monitors trained on the outside walls. "This is my safe haven right here, away from all the scavengers and bloodsuckers," Loeb said. "No one knows I live here."

For all his bluster, Loeb wasn't oblivious to his state. He knew that his relapse was a welcome, and depressingly unsurprising, development for his opponents. If an incarcerated Jimmy were to learn of Loeb overdosing by a needle filled with heroin purchased with the settlement cash, he'd no doubt consider the money well worth the result. "I can get clean," Loeb said while seated on his bed. "I know I can. I don't want to die before I finish telling the truth."

Five months later, Loeb was back in Suffolk police custody, dragged out of the Trackhawk after allegedly smashing into a cop car and then leading them on a 115 mph chase down the Long Island Expressway.

* * *

Spota and McPartland's trial was in many ways a trial of Jimmy. It gave the feds an opportunity to showcase witnesses and evidence they had shelved when he took his plea deal. The thirty witnesses included Jimmy's best friend, Tony D'Orazio; his sector car partner, Dennis Sullivan; his first-grade-teacher ex-girlfriend; his half-brother John Toal; and his cigar pal Sammy Panchal. But the figure who didn't testify—though he certainly could've delivered the case to the feds if he had—was Jimmy Burke himself. A stand-up guy to the end, he did his three or so years playing cards with mobsters, and didn't talk to anybody.

Which meant that for the feds, bringing home the prosecution hinged on the testimony of a single figure: Jim Hickey. There were other key witnesses. Kenny Bombace and Tony Leto confessed on the stand to their role in the Loeb beating, and they described the pressure they felt from above to cover it up. Former prosecutor Spiros Moustakas described the thoroughly unusual treatment of the Loeb criminal case, and the vendetta-by-wiretap that was the Oliva matter, designed to silence anybody who might challenge Jimmy. But in a case that featured no wiretap or undercover recordings, and in which the conspirators were far too sophisticated to put their schemes in writing, or to gossip to outsiders, the bulk of the evidence was alleged remarks by members of the tight inner circle. And Hickey was the only member of that crew who had fully flipped.

On paper, Hickey didn't look that much more promising: the feds' star witness, who the jury was expected to believe totally, was a declared perjurer who had been hospitalized with alcoholism and delusions, and who treated cheating on his wife like a second job. "James Hickey had a powerful motive to twist the facts," Spota's attorney, Alan Vinegrad, declared in his opening statement, "to shave the truth or even outright lie, take your pick, to help himself out of his own trouble, a witness with a long history of credibility problems going back years."

But Ratman had receipts. It wasn't just his little conspiracy-tracking notations on his office calendars. The feds showed evidence that calls, emails, digital calendars, and cell phone analysis mirrored Hickey's testimony about when and where various conversations had taken place, and details of their content. Others who seemingly had no reason to lie, like Sullivan or Burke's ex-girlfriend, backed up pieces of his testimony to which they were witnesses.

And if Hickey wasn't telling the truth, he had missed his calling as a screenwriter. Of his three full days of testimony, the most impressive stretch of dialogue came when he described the meeting, late in the conspiracy, in Spota's office in which he said he was threatened by the DA, chief of police, and the top corruption prosecutor in one fell swoop. When asked how he could be so sure what was said, Hickey shot back without hesitation: "It's seared into my memory."

Hickey spoke in a sonorous Long Island accent. He sparred smugly with the defense attorneys during his cross-examination, calling them "counselor" in an overly formal manner that dripped with cop sarcasm. He exuded no real remorse, only self-preservation, as well as an arrogance that was completely at odds with how badly the guy had fucked up his own life for no good cause. Hickey wasn't likeable, by a long shot. But he was, as even trial judge Joan Azrack conceded, believable. The jury found Spota and McPartland guilty in December 2019. They were supposed to be sentenced the following April. Instead, their case entered a seemingly interminable COVID-induced period of limbo.

On August 10, 2021, the two men were back in Central Islip, navigating the long ocean of concrete separating the parking lot from the federal courthouse. Spota looked a little lost as he was accompanied in by his lawyers. McPartland lumbered out of a silver Ford Taurus with a bumper sticker providing a reminder—unsurprising but still somehow remarkable—as to how Jimmy, McPartland, and Spota saw themselves.

It read: "Stand with the PROTECTORS NOT the Protestors."

* * *

In the two years between their conviction and sentencing, there had been a so-called revolution in American policing, sparked by national protests following the killing of George Floyd by Minneapolis police officer Derek Chauvin.

The aftermath of Floyd's murder felt different from past unrest following incidences of police brutality, in that the protests, and their results, had a determined focus on dismantling the systemic causes of police and prosecutorial misconduct. Across the country, new scrutiny was paid to some of the same levers of unchecked power exposed by the saga of Jimmy Burke: the omnipotent police union bosses, the politicians in the cops' pockets, and the prosecutors who ignored their mandate to be a check on dishonest police work.

The state of New York in particular adopted what seemed to be one of the most profound reforms in the country in the wake of Floyd's murder. Governor Andrew Cuomo repealed 50-a, the law that for decades made police disciplinary records inaccessible. In Jimmy's rise to the top of one of the country's largest police departments, he had 50-a to thank even more than Tom Spota. The law had shielded his disqualifying IAB past from the eyes of citizens, journalists, and even a top elected official, if a deeply uncurious one, in Steve Bellone.

The Jimmy Burke story of police misconduct was exceptional in the way it ended, with something like accountability. Jimmy went to jail, and Spota and McPartland were, barring a judge's pity, about to join him. But Jimmy's case only proved the near impossibility of punishing a cop, particularly one who has a measure of power and political savvy. It took highly motivated feds three years and two distinct investigations to bring him down for a reckless crime witnessed by a squad room full of police. And in order to do so, the feds had to hand out free passes to cops who had previously stonewalled and lied to them about Jimmy's crime, or their role in it.

Hickey and Leto worked toward lessening their own punishment by testifying in pursuit of 5K letters, the prosecutorial report cards that could reduce their jail time to zero. Other central actors in the beating and its years-long cover-up faced no criminal punishment at all, thanks to immunity deals, which in at least one case, the feds came to regret.

Prosecutors had tried their hand at making an asset of Billy Madigan, the former chief of detectives, by giving him immunity in return for grand jury testimony. That turned out to be a raw deal for the feds. Madigan was, as described in the prosecutors' court filing, "a difficult witness who often failed to answer direct questions, was evasive, suffered from convenient memory lapses and generally refused to give definitive answers."

A slippery witness is a risky proposition at trial, and the feds abandoned plans to call Madigan to the stand, meaning that the high-ranking cop enmeshed in the conspiracy for years got a free pass in exchange for virtually nothing. Madigan is still a licensed attorney in New York, and on LinkedIn advertises his services as an "expert and advisor in police force management."

Bombace, who did more than Madigan to earn his own immunity deal, runs a private security company, boasting of clients that included prominent presidential candidates. He noted with satisfaction recently that doing a few media spots—such as a video for *Insider* where he graded famous cinematic bodyguard scenes for their authenticity—had pushed all of his Google results concerning the Loeb beating to the third page. A bit more scrubbing of his image and who knows, maybe Congressman Kenny is still in play after all.

No charges have been publicly filed against Mike Malone. The belief among his co-conspirators is that he too testified in the grand jury in return for an immunity deal, though he was not ultimately used as a witness in Spota and McPartland's trial.

The detectives certainly don't see themselves as getting off easy. Bombace likes to point out that if he was caught hitting a prisoner under more typical circumstances, his punishment would be "the loss of fifteen vacation days, if that."

"Cops fucking smack people around every day," Leto said. "It doesn't turn into a federal fucking case."

* * *

Even in the case of cops convicted of crimes in the Loeb saga, including those who spent years of high-paying tenures immersed in a felony conspiracy, taxpayers will be compensating them for those services until they die. Just like Jim Hickey told Leto and Malone in encouraging them to continue lying: no matter what happened, they'd all still get their pensions. Each of the cops just mentioned, all of them considered by the feds to be Jimmy's co-conspirators, are paid an annual pension ranging from $110,000 to $121,000. Jimmy's own annual pension, which he collected even while he was in prison: $145,485. While New York police unions and their members rallied to decry the repeal of 50-a, they were likely secretly gratified that lawmakers hadn't mounted a credible effort against the real sacred cow: those direct deposits for life guaranteed in almost all cases, no matter how severe a cop's misconduct.

Many of the ambitious reforms promised in the aftermath of Floyd's murder met a sadly predictable fate once the national uproar had passed. The George Floyd Justice in Policing Act, an ambitious federal bill that once had bipartisan momentum, collapsed in late 2021. And in New York, the repeal of 50-a quickly began, in practice, to look like window dressing.

Departments and unions have continued to fight or even just ignore public records requests for police disciplinary files. In Suffolk, like other counties throughout the state, government lawyers have landed on a handy way to appear to be following the law while rendering it virtually toothless. I requested copies of the IAB files of Burke, Hickey, Bombace, Malone, and Leto in June 2020, a few days after 50-a had been repealed. More than seven months later, the police department responded with records. But in their interpretation of the law, as an IAB boss explained in a letter, all complaints that were not found to be substantiated were exempt because their disclosure would constitute an "unwarranted invasion of personal privacy."

Federal testimony had revealed that Jimmy had nineteen IAB complaints throughout his career. But only one—that involving Lowrita Rickenbacker—had been substantiated, and only on one count. As a result, the SCPD released only a heavily redacted copy of that single report. This was in order to protect the personal privacy of the former chief of department, who had been sent to federal prison, and whose Viagra prescription and proclivity for porn and sex toys, among many other extremely personal details, was disclosed in open court.

The department, and Suffolk County Attorney Dennis Cohen, who withheld its decision when I appealed, also found fit to protect the privacy of Burke's broken wing lieutenant Hickey. It's unknown how many IAB cases were opened concerning Hickey during his less-than-stellar career. The department again released documents involving only a single case, that of his alleged beating of Erroll Freeman, and because only a single obscure count was found to be substantiated, many of the pages were completely obliterated by black redacting ink. This was deemed necessary in order to protect the personal privacy of an admitted felon whose philandering and mental health issues were recounted in extreme detail in court filings and during grueling days of federal court testimony.

The Suffolk County policy suggested that a department's Internal Affairs Bureau was an infallible and independent judge of whether a complaint had any legitimacy. But for years, Burke and his cronies held sway, even if it was unofficial, over IAB. Tellingly, the SCPD released no documents concerning the years-long conspiracy that had forced each of the men into retirement, which meant that either no IAB probe had been opened on the Loeb matter, or the allegations had not been substantiated.

Then there was the matter of documents released concerning the career of retired Detective Tony Leto: there were none. Leto admitted to the feds during his proffer sessions that he had hit prisoners roughly half a dozen times before Loeb. Either the IAB had never opened any cases or these incidents of brutality had all been unsubstantiated. According to the SCPD's public disclosures, even following vaunted police transparency reforms, Tony the Torture Expert was squeaky clean.

* * *

As a prosecutor, Chris McPartland always looked impatient when he argued a case in front of a jury, as if he was frustrated that either the defendant was too dumb to take a plea or it was the rare case in which his work in the wire room, or poring over transcripts and witness statements, just wasn't thorough enough. Before he manned the register ringing up Jameson bottles in East Northport, his professional happy place was spending long hours poring over documents, hunting in the weeds to investigate every nook and cranny in an ongoing case.

During his own trial, McPartland appeared to betray that same preference, namely of digging into the details of a conspiracy over elements of courtroom ceremony. While his codefendant, Spota, had fiddled absently—chewing his eyeglasses or picking his ear and flicking the detritus—McPartland had written busily in his notepad during the trial's most pivotal testimony, as if not trusting his hired attorneys to catch contradictions and weak points.

But when it came time to argue for his life, during sentencing, the impetuous scowl was back; McPartland, fifty-five, just went through the motions. "I wanted to take this time to ensure you that I very, very much appreciate the seriousness of this entire matter," McPartland told trial judge Joan Azrack, the absence of any emotion in his voice indicating the precise opposite. "I would just respectfully ask that you consider the very severe punishment that myself and my family have already endured. I'll just say that it's been a very difficult five years, and I've already lost an awful, awful lot."

If it had left McPartland intact, the case appeared to have broken Tom Spota. The former DA had throughout his career been an incessant braggart, and a mosquito in arguments whose go-to trick was to drown his opponent in obfuscation. But by the time he pleaded for leniency from Azrack, those tendencies appeared to be gone. Replacing that blustery figure was a plain-spoken seventy-nine-year-old man who angled for something of which he had never previously had much use: sympathy.

Spota acknowledged his "shattered legacy" and said: "My family will be forever burdened with my disgrace." He said that "what the jury found had taken place"—not what he had done—"was a violation of the trust" in his office. Like McPartland, he made no apologies.

Spota, almost eighty years old and in failing health, mentioned that he had previously expected his career would end with a big retirement party. Instead he begged for his freedom. "I hope not to leave

Mary Ellen alone, which is something that I vowed I would never do," Spota said, referring to his wife. "I hope not to die in prison alone."

But there's a fair chance he will. When sentencing them, Azrack quoted from an essay by US Supreme Court Justice Robert Jackson, who wrote that a prosecutor's "discretion is tremendous. He can have citizens investigated and, if he is that kind of person, he can have this done to the tune of public statements and veiled or unveiled intimations. . . . While the prosecutor at his best is one of the most beneficent forces in our society, when he acts from malice or other base motives, he is one of the worst."

She then sentenced Spota and McPartland to five years each. It was longer than even that given to their buddy Jimmy.

* * *

During the five long years he spent watching justice get meted out to his cronies—with his help—Tony Leto grew a beard. He turned back to old hobbies he had before he was a cop. He began playing the acoustic guitar again, picked up smoking a little marijuana for his anxiety, and got back into art.

Leto augmented his $10,000-a-month pension by painting storefront and restaurant windows: A grinning polar bear on a sled, emblazoned with the words: "Slide in for hot chocolate." Gnomes in a pumpkin patch. And of course, Olaf. Once a henchman cop renowned for his brutality, Leto now painted, over and over, the snowman from *Frozen*.

The interminable limbo weighed on Leto. He initially expected to be sentenced after Jimmy Burke took his plea, in early 2016. But they never called, and two years later, when Spota and McPartland were indicted, he realized why: they wanted him on the hook for testimony in that trial. Leto was delivering packages for FedEx at the time, but his supervisors didn't respond well when he said he had to go on leave in order to testify about his role in a major corruption conspiracy.

The delays left plenty of time for harsh introspection. Leto's arrest back in late 2015 was an unusual proceeding for its secrecy and formality. He sat in a sterile room in the Central Islip courthouse, signed a document pleading to federal witness tampering, and was then taken for fingerprinting and a mugshot. His arraignment occurred in a judge's chambers, where he felt demeaned as he spoke to the judge as lawyers watched while waiting for their own business.

Leto used to harshly judge his dad, the wiseguy-adjacent thief who almost choked his mom to death. As a young cop, Leto refused to write a letter to a judge on his dad's behalf in order to lessen his prison time for some crime or another, and he remained standoffish toward him until he died. Now he looked at his dad's disaster of an existence differently. "I never thought this would be how my life ended up," Leto said. "The same way as my father, being a felon and I fucked up my whole family."

During his court testimony, Leto said he regretted his actions, and if he had the power to go back and change them he would. In conversation, he readily volunteers some of those biggest regrets: not leaving Criminal Intelligence when he realized it was a bullshit political bureau; going back into Loeb's interview room with Burke; not going to the feds earlier; not telling Mike Malone to shut the fuck up about pissing in the coffee cup.

The one thing he doesn't mention: smacking Christopher Loeb. The closest he comes to expressing concern for Loeb isn't exactly an apology. "You know, the kid was an asshole," Leto said. "Hopefully he changed his life."

And in the fall of 2021, Leto's fortunes began to brighten. For one, his favored DA candidate managed an unlikely victory. Ray Tierney, Kenny Bombace's brother-in-law, had campaigned for that office despite incumbent Sini owning the police union endorsements. Leto, whose ire against Sini stemmed partly from him confiscating his police shields upon retirement, joined Bombace and Cliff Lent, who made pro-Tierney signs and helped manage the campaign's social media. It was among the oddest remnants of the Burke scandal: Tierney the straitlaced former fed, cheered on by a troupe of disgraced palace guards as he trounced the union candidate and, on November 2, won control of Spota's old office.

Leto was on a nice run. The previous week, in secret proceedings sealed from the media and public, he received his punishment: three years probation. A few months later, his former boss faced an even lighter reckoning. For acting as middleman in the cover-up, Azrack sentenced James Hickey to one year probation. The sentence reflected the government's gratitude for Hickey's cooperation that he had plotted even while in the midst of the conspiracy, when he marked his calendar with notations he knew would later make for useful evidence.

In a letter to Azrack before he was sentenced, Hickey lamented the brutal police code he had helped to enforce. "There is still very much a blue wall of silence," Hickey wrote. "I have lost every friend I ever had in the police department over the years, including neighbors who I have known for thirty years. I still fear retaliation from the powerful people involved and the friends they still have out there."

* * *

Back in July 2017, more than a year and a half after Burke had been forced out, the SCPD felt it was finally putting some distance between itself and the scandals of its former leader. It was a professional police department again, ready to crack its knuckles and tend to those nagging bodies on Gilgo Beach and the murderous Salvadoran gang that had been allowed to metastasize in Hispanic neighborhoods for years.

What better sign of legitimacy for a police department than to host the president of the United States? And for Donald J. Trump, Suffolk County was as inviting as a flame to a moth, with its MS-13 problem giving life to his favored imagery: brown, foreign gangsters leaving bodies in woods surrounded by largely white suburbs. Trump arrived at an auditorium in the Suffolk County Community College that was packed, on the stage behind him and in seats in front of him, with county cops in full uniform. He was there to convey to the nation that the only thing standing in the way of murderous immigrants was himself, and his alignment with the proud cops like those in the crowd.

But it wouldn't be a Trump speech without a little improv. "When you see these thugs being thrown into the back of the paddy wagon," Trump told the cops, "You seen them, thrown in, rough. I said, 'Please don't be too nice.'"

The president then brought home the riff. "When you guys put somebody in the car and you're protecting their head, you know, the way you put their hand over like, don't hit their head," Trump said to the cops in the audience, his hand movements making clear that he was talking about an officer using their hand to make sure a prisoner doesn't hit their head on the door frame. "And they've just killed somebody, 'Don't hit their head?' I said, you can take the hand away, okay?"

As the president advocated being rough on prisoners in front of Jimmy Burke's old department, the cops behind him laughed and clapped their white gloves, while the rank-in-file facing him roared their approval.

BOOGEYMAN

In December 2016, while Jimmy Burke sat in lockup awaiting transfer to the low-security Pennsylvania prison where he expected to spend the next few years, reporters lugged cameras into a quaint house nestled among brambles on Long Island's North Shore.

Among incongruously cheery Christmas decorations in the converted law office, a woman described Burke paying her for sex years earlier at cocaine-fueled parties in a home on Oak Beach. That was by now a notorious location, the same gated community where Shannan Gilbert had in 2010 run off into the night screaming, leading to the discovery of ten slain bodies, mostly other women who had been sex workers, and ultimately to Gilbert's own skeleton finally being pulled from the marsh.

The press conference was put on by John Ray, longtime lawyer for Gilbert's family. Ray was a relentless agitator whose stated efforts to investigate the case sometimes bordered on stunt, such as when he and his legal team donned full army fatigues to wade into the marsh.

But with no news and barely even signs of life from the officials tasked with investigating the murders near Gilgo Beach, Ray—demanding attention in his dandy uniform of garish suits and fedoras—was also for years the only public figure piercing the apparent apathy surrounding the case.

Now the woman in his office, a self-described escort named Leanne, described seeing Burke at two Oak Beach parties in 2011.

She said Burke had grabbed a woman by her hair and dragged her to the ground. He later received oral sex from Leanne, which due to his aggressiveness was more like "choking," and then threw money at her while deeming her "not a good whore." Ray declared that her story put Burke "right at the center of the pool of suspects" in the murders.

Leanne's story was sensational and uncorroborated. By the given date of the alleged parties, ten bodies had already been found. That meant that if Leanne's story was true, Burke—at the time, Spota's top investigator in the DA's office—would have been partaking in just the sort of scene he knew was relevant to the open serial killer case.

For Burke, the press conference marked a surely unpleasant turning point. There had already been speculation about Burke being involved in the sex worker killings, theories fueled by his relationship with Lowrita Rickenbacker, his proclivity for violence, and the fact that he and Spota had blocked the FBI from assisting in the investigation of the murders.

But previously, such speculation had been mostly fodder for internet forums or, in one case, the back of a truck. A photograph circulated on Long Island of a box truck spray painted with the phrase, "Burke killed the Gilgo girls."

Post-Leanne, however, depictions of Burke as suspect firmly entered the mainstream. The possibility was debated in a feature in *Rolling Stone* and a segment on *48 Hours*. Burke was given the villain treatment in a fictionalized movie on Lifetime, which strongly suggested he had a hand in the killings.

By the time Burke was released from custody in 2019, a growing cottage industry of media had sprouted up suggesting that he was either directly involved in the killings or covering them up to protect a powerful Suffolk County cabal. Multiple popular podcasts trafficked in rumor and dubious accounts to that effect. One of them included interviews with Chris Loeb, who now claimed the porn he found in Burke's duffel bag was a "snuff film" of a "guy with a mask on, torturing a prostitute"—which Loeb had not mentioned before, including when he spoke with the FBI or testified in court.

There was an undeniable appeal to Burke as suspect. The Loeb saga had proven that betting against a major criminal conspiracy among the powerful of Suffolk County wasn't smart money. And the Gilgo Beach case appeared so poorly investigated, starting with Shannan Gilbert's disappearance, that to some it felt like deliberate sabotage.

Burke and the others who oversaw the case couldn't have messed it up that badly by accident, right?

* * *

One Thursday evening in July 2023, a burly, slightly slumped man with a crown of messy, dark hair walked with a New Yorker's casual haste down a sidewalk on Fifth Avenue in Manhattan. Wearing a short sleeve polo shirt tucked into khaki slacks, briefcase dangling from his left shoulder, he was just another Midtown commuter, one of hundreds of thousands, heading home from the office.

Then a man in a dark suit and tie stepped in front of his path, his hand subtly raised. Another figure appeared beside him, and more behind. In about a second, the empty span of sidewalk on which the commuter had been walking was replaced by an impenetrable circumference of quietly forceful men in identical suits. Passing pedestrians, true to local reputation, didn't offer a second glance at the *Matrix*-esque scene unfolding beside them. The men in suits shunted their captive off to a car.

The planned arrest had been a matter of top secret for weeks, which in Suffolk County meant everybody with the right cop buddy knew. Forty miles east, a brigade of police vehicles arrived at the normally quiet street in front of a dilapidated red house in Massapequa Park, near the South Shore of Long Island. Journalists started showing up too, and by the next morning the street was filled with gawkers who had heard gossip about the goings-on.

DA Ray Tierney planned an afternoon press conference, with no politicians invited. That didn't appeal to County Executive Steve Bellone, who preempted him by showing up at the growing carnival scene that morning with his own lectern. Flanked by SCPD Commissioner Rodney Harrison, Bellone publicly confirmed the rumors: a suspect in the Gilgo Beach serial killing case had been caught.

"The message to the public is that we have never stopped working on this case," said Bellone, presenting cool control.

A picture emerged of a suspected killer who for decades had been hidden in plain sight. Rex Heuermann, fifty-nine at the time of his arrest, lived in the same Massapequa Park house since he was a boy. He was married twice, with children, and commuted daily to Manhattan, where he owned an architecture firm.

Heuermann was charged with killing three of the women known as the Gilgo Four—Melissa Barthelemy, Megan Waterman, and Amber Costello—and would later also be charged with the murder of the fourth, Maureen Brainard-Barnes. His lawyer has insisted that he is innocent.

Suffolk County authorities had a few fleeting hours to bask in having caught a serial killer suspect—before the rest of the world began to piece together that the authorities could have solved the case, with the same evidence, over a decade earlier.

* * *

In late 2015, when Tim Sini was named police commissioner amid the smoking wreckage of Burke's ouster from the department, cops looked upon their new millennial leader with suspicion.

They regarded Sini as the least subtle FBI mole in history, as he filled his first days on the job interviewing high-ranking cops about their potential roles in a criminal conspiracy that was still unraveling.

Their suspicions were confirmed when Sini's former colleagues in the federal government indicted Tom Spota two years later. Sini was then elected to replace him as DA.

It was in this environment of mutual distrust that Sini attempted to introduce modern policing to the matter of the bones on Gilgo Beach.

Sini was appalled to find the neglectful state in which Burke's men had left the serial killer case. It wasn't just that Burke and Spota had barred an FBI analyst from accessing evidence in order to produce a suspect profile. But they also appeared to have considered evidence with any trace of a federal scent to be tainted and useless—even if it was among the best leads they had.

The killer had used burner phones to connect with his victims. And in 2011, before Burke took office, an FBI specialist used cell tower data from those burner lines to complete a report suggesting that the killer lived in Massapequa Park and commuted to Midtown Manhattan. It was an extremely strong start—which Burke and his men did nothing to advance.

They also rejected other obvious next steps, such as scouring cell towers for signals during periods when the killer's burner phones were active. Theoretically, it could've caught the killer toting his real cell phone alongside a burner—but Spota and Burke never tried. Sini considered those formative four years for the case under Burke to be essentially a lost period for the investigation.

Sini resolved to make his tenure overseeing the case a negative image of Burke's, as defined by the acceptance of federal assistance and the use of high-tech toys. He spent hundreds of thousands of dollars on a DNA vacuum and tools designed to pinpoint cell phone signals, such as a device investigators drove around with to simulate a cell phone user's precise location for each cell tower signal. Sini put Howard Master, a Yale-educated former federal prosecutor, in charge of the Gilgo investigation.

By 2021, Sini said, they had whittled the pool of homes where the killer may have lived from around 1,250 to 200. Basic vetting of those residents produced what Sini called a "large sheet" of possible suspects. Sini believed that now all they had to do was background each of those remaining residents until they honed in on the right guy.

Unfortunately for Sini, that was a job for the Suffolk County homicide squad.

The nerve center for the investigation was the "Gilgo room," an office at Police HQ stacked with filing cabinets and boxes full of evidence. The longtime master of this lair was a gruff detective with a bald, thick pate and a dark goatee accentuating a bulldog-like appearance.

Patrick Portela was a Burke appointee to the Gilgo case. His fellow detectives spoke with reverence about how Portela knew where to find any piece of paper or evidence spanning the investigation's many stops and starts. His memory of the case was encyclopedic—and his judgment absolute, as Sini would soon find out.

Sini's methods led the DA's office to focus on one man, a retired New York City cop living on a tree-lined street in Massapequa Park, just a couple of blocks from Rex Heuermann's house. The man had moved away years earlier, but had lived in the area highlighted by the cell tower data at the time of the killings. Sini's investigators pulled his NYPD file, and learned of a local reputation for patronizing sex workers.

The most exciting part was the man's initials. The killer had used belts to bind one of the victims. Detectives had long considered one of the belts to be a tantalizing clue, as it was stamped with the letters "WH" or "HM." True to the elusive nature of the case, it could be either depending on which way you held the belt.

Hold it the right way, and it matched the initials of the old ex-cop from Massapequa Park.

But when Sini and Master directed the homicide detectives to hone in on this new prime suspect, the cops mutinied. Portela said he had already ruled the man out, and his guys weren't going to waste their time pursuing a dead end.

Sini believed that the cops' predisposition against him—and the Ivy League product Master, who they viewed with even more disdain—was partly personal. Master oversaw Sini's newly created Conviction Integrity Bureau, which reexamined old convictions secured by the DA's office. In 2019, the bureau exonerated Keith Bush, who was convicted of killing a fourteen-year-old girl when he was seventeen, a 1975 case that had strikingly similar flaws to those in the John Pius murder investigation.

It was another case of a rights-violating teenage confession, with Bush later saying that detectives beat him over the head with a phone book and kicked him in the genitals until he told them he murdered the girl. A far more likely suspect then emerged: a man with a violent rap sheet who said he tripped over the girl's body, and even left his comb at the scene. The cops and trial prosecutor, Spota's former law partner, Gerald Sullivan, hid all traces of that suspect from Bush's attorneys—and Spota then spent most of his tenure as DA fighting Bush's attempts to have his case reexamined.

A difference between the Bush prosecution and the Pius case was that in the Bush matter, all of the subjects were Black. "That fucking n— did it," the retired lead detective, Augie Stahl, told Sini's investigators when they asked him about the case, before wondering aloud:

"Why is this being opened again? I thought Tommy Spota took care of this."

As the Pius and Marty Tankleff cases showed, Suffolk prosecutors and cops had a history of scrapping ferociously to defend even the most dubious homicide convictions. Sini voluntarily giving up a conviction—and embarrassing a ninety-year-old ex-homicide bull, Stahl, by including his racist quotes in a legal motion—drew battle lines.

The potential aftershocks for the Gilgo Beach investigation spelled the same story as ever in Suffolk County: tribalism and grudges derailing a case, this time one with at least ten murder victims hanging in the balance.

For the detectives' part, they felt that Sini's guys were misunderstanding their role, which was to prosecute the case the police brought them. They perceived Sini as desperate to get a win in the election year of 2021—and going about it all wrong. "They were doing a parallel Gilgo investigation," complained a Portela defender, referring to the DA's office. "They were buying their own computer program, doing their own investigation, and giving us errands to run down for them."

In response to such directives, the detectives alternately bickered with the prosecutors, ignored them, or did the bare minimum. When Master attempted to digitize the hundreds of thousands of pages of evidence in the Gilgo room, the detectives refused. "We don't want a second file floating around," one said.

Sini attempted to remove Portela from the task force, but faced what he called "fierce resistance" from within the police department. He said that after the FBI insisted they would pull out of the case if Portela stayed on, the detective was finally taken off the case—but only after his own police supervisor was threatened with demotion.

The investigation stalled out, doomed by twin cases of tunnel vision. Sini believed the only way to the Gilgo Beach killer was through his high-tech tools and his narrowing cell tower box. The detectives had little use for it, believing their judgment was worth far more than some $120,000 device sending up cell phone pings from a police van.

Both were wrong. While the two sides obstinately warred over high tech versus low tech, debating whether to pursue the old ex-cop in Massapequa Park who turned out to be a red herring, a few pieces of paper apparently sat forgotten in one of those Gilgo room filing cabinets Portela was said to know every inch of.

Those documents—witness reports neglected for a decade—proved the key to the case.

* * *

After Tierney ousted Sini in a surprise electoral victory and took office on January 1, 2022, he created his own Gilgo Beach task force alongside the new police commissioner Harrison, federal agents, and New York state troopers.

Their first step was digitizing the records—a step the detectives had previously refused to allow—and then sifting through the decade-old evidence and reports.

It was a female state trooper who first found them, reports nearly as old as the case itself.

A couple of men in Amber Costello's orbit were known for sometimes trying a ruse to rip off her johns, in which they would pretend to be her outraged boyfriend and chase away the client before any sex act could be performed, leaving them with the money.

According to the reports turned up by the trooper, witnesses told police that the day before Costello disappeared, she was meeting with a john at her home in West Babylon. One of the guys pulled the boyfriend ruse. The client, protesting that he was "just her friend," left.

A witness later gave the police a detailed description of the disappointed client: tall—between six-foot-four and six-foot-six—with "dark bushy hair," "big oval style 1970s-type eyeglasses," and the appearance of an "ogre." The witness also saw his vehicle: a first-generation Chevy Avalanche, a distinctive model of truck.

Later that night, Costello received a text message from somebody apparently feeling ripped off: "That was not nice so do i [sic] credit for next time."

The next night, Costello made apparent plans to meet the same man again, but this time, a witness explained to the police, "He didn't want to come back to the house because of her boyfriend."

Costello walked out her front door to meet the client, and a witness then saw a dark truck drive away. She was never seen alive again.

Even a rookie investigator could see the potential significance of witness statements giving a detailed description of Costello's last john—and his vehicle. Detectives would later be at a loss to explain how such important materials had gone overlooked for years. Given that the statements were gathered before Burke became chief, his vindictive transfer of power upon taking office—in which he hastily canned Chief of Detectives Dominick Varrone and the investigators overseeing the Gilgo Beach case without even arranging for a debrief on their findings in the case—suddenly took on a new significance. Was that break in communication responsible for the statements being forgotten?

Either way, now those statements were used as a Rosetta stone for rapidly cracking the case. Investigators searched for Chevy Avalanches that were owned in the Massapequa Park area where they suspected the killer lived. By March 14, 2022, less than a month after the new task force was announced, the investigators had honed in on Rex Heuermann—a giant, bespectacled man with bushy hair who loomed, undeniably, like an ogre.

The pieces of evidence that had led the new task force to Heuermann—the witness reports and the FBI analysis showing the killer likely lived in Massapequa Park—had been available to the case's investigators since, at the latest, 2012. The final, third major piece, that in the minds of investigators sealed their case against Heuermann, had also always been there.

Investigators had found a number of hairs on the women's bodies, including one stuck to a piece of tape inside the burlap wrapping of one of the victims. Using mitochondrial DNA analysis—a technology that long predates this case—investigators matched two of the hairs to the DNA of Heuermann's wife, using discarded bottles outside their house. And, after digging Heuermann's uneaten pizza crusts out of a garbage can on Fifth Avenue in Manhattan, investigators matched another hair to him directly.

After finding Heuermann, investigators spent much of the next sixteen months following a digital trail that, despite his avid use of burner phones, he ultimately did a poor job of hiding. That included old data—of the sort Spota and Burke chose not to pursue—showing that Heuermann's everyday phone was alongside burner phones tied to the murders.

And calls in which the apparent killer taunted the family members of a victim were placed by a burner phone in the general location of Heuermann's then-office near Penn Station, conjuring up the depraved image of the architect breathing vile threats into a burner phone during the workday in his office.

For twelve years, the Gilgo Beach killer had proven so elusive that the public imagined him to be a Keyser Söze–like mastermind. Theories were hatched to explain how he got away with it, including that he was a powerful top cop in a sex cult that controlled the county.

But the evidence against Rex Heuermann suggested a very different picture, one in which a sloppy psychopath controlled by his own hubris and rage allegedly left DNA on his victims, allowed himself and his car to be observed by victims, and turned burner phones into a detection tool against him.

A more credible explanation of why the Gilgo Beach killer got away with it for so long was because he operated in a county where cops for decades eschewed forensics in favor of scraped knuckles in an interrogation room, where the police chief and DA were for years too distracted by their own quest to stay out of jail to bother to file subpoenas for those cell tower dumps, and where, even now—with Rex Heuermann preparing for trial and at least six of the murders still officially unsolved—officials are consumed by infighting and jockeying for credit.

When cops and prosecutors botched this case, they were simply following local tradition. Just ask Marty Tankleff. Or Keith Bush. Or the four Pius defendants, three of whom remain convicted killers thanks to a prosecutor and a key witness who are now both federal felons.

If Rex Heuermann is indeed the killer, the only truly smart thing he did was dump most of his bodies in Suffolk County.

ACKNOWLEDGMENTS

I owe a debt of gratitude to dozens of people who helped with this book over more than four years of reporting and writing. There are four people—besides the subjects of the story—without whom it would not exist as it does today. Blame them:

My agent David Patterson (Stuart Krichevsky Literary Agency, Inc.) encouraged me since 2015 or earlier—before many of the events in this book took place—to pitch a project on cop culture in eastern Long Island. For years, we referred to this project as "Copland," before we wisely decided to get off Sylvester Stallone's turf. This book was, simply put, David's brainchild, and he expertly maneuvered it into reality.

Benjamin Adams, my editor at PublicAffairs, gleaned from my imperfect proposal the book's narrative, setting, and theme with incredible prescience. He understood the book not only better than editors at other houses, but even better than I did. Ben then trusted me to bring that vision home and tolerated with grace a deadline extension, or several, even as life outside the book took whacks at us both.

This is the second time that Matthew Doig, who has been my immediate editor at three different newspapers—*Newsday, Los Angeles Times,* and *USA TODAY*—expressed nothing but genuine support for me writing a book that required a balance with my day job. When Matt first hired me from an alt-weekly in Florida for the investigative team at *Newsday,* I knew nothing about anything, and I particularly knew nothing about Suffolk County. That I would have never written this book is one of many ways my life would be completely different if it weren't for Matt.

My wife, Jennifer, has always been a supporter of my career, but this book brought with it a personally unprecedented gauntlet of challenges: our first child, a new coast, a pandemic that shuttered our day care, lengthy reporting trips to New York, and a husband and co-parent who had to burn too many precious evenings and weekends writing about Suffolk County from our Los Angeles garage, all while tending to her own professional responsibilities. But Jenny proved apocalypse-proof, her stamina for curveballs prodigious. She was our family's most unyielding protector, as well as my best friend and the same, as well as a terrific mentor, to our amazing kid, Frankie. This book is as much yours as mine, Jenny.

Thank you to the editors who helped Ben bring this book over the finish line: Pete Beatty and Anupama Roy-Chaudhury. Pete's pinch-hitting line edits were extraordinary, filling this book with quips and turns of phrase I'm only too happy to take credit for. Copyeditor Mike van Mantgem flat out made this book better through his diligent and wise tweaks, lawyer John Pelosi patiently bulletproofed it, and production editor Kaitlin Carruthers-Busser kept the trains running on time. Researcher Christal Roberts helped me piece together vital parts of this book.

Legendary civil rights and criminal defense lawyer Ron Kuby filed a motion in federal court on my behalf, resulting in the unsealing of hundreds of pages of previously confidential documents related to Spota, McPartland, and Burke that informed the book in major ways and let loose a litany of government secrets Suffolk County residents and taxpayers deserved to know.

Certain subjects who were part of or adjacent to the story were incredibly generous with their time and resources, often for no apparent reason other than wanting the verifiable truth on the record. Among them: Paul Gianelli, Tania Lopez, Leslie Anderson, Jesse Kornbluth, Christine DeVallee, Suzanne Spina, Frank Bress, Andrew Polin, James Cohen, Susan Onorato, Peter Fiorillo, and many, many others. There are some who asked not to be identified in this book but whose insight and information nonetheless greatly shaped it, in some cases through lengthy conversations at obscene hours.

Other journalists and writers helped me immensely. Here I must lead with Pete Kotz, legendary alt-weekly editor, who for no discernible gain to himself helped hone my manuscript as I churned it out. Pairing Kotz's insight with Beatty's edits resulted in an embarrassment of riches stemming from Cleveland-area Petes. Doig and journalism/ acting wunderkind Brett Murphy also read chunks of the manuscript and offered great insight and encouragement. Robert Kolker was generous and unterritorial with his expertise as the author of *Lost Girls: An Unsolved American Mystery*. Jesse Kornbluth was one of the book's most important facilitators, and I retained his nuggets of wisdom on this story—shared over dinner and a subway ride—throughout the reporting and writing process. Author Peter Blauner helped me see the big picture. Tania Lopez trusted me to tell a story that was by all rights more hers than mine, given her role in breaking so much of the news at its crux, and the battle scars she got as a result. Joe Tone, who subsequently became my editor at the *Washington Post*, helped bring this thing into the world by reading and fine-tuning my proposal.

My big sister Chloe Garcia-Roberts, an incredible writer and poet, offered insight on my proposal and during the writing process, and has been a mentor throughout my life. Other family members I thank for their love and patience: my mother, Joan; father, Jose; in-laws, Connie and David; the aunt and uncle brigade led by Tia Paz; sister, Valentina; brother, Uriel; brothers-in-law, Jason and Jack; and sisters-in-law, Xaviela and Colleen; among many others. New York friends were absurdly accommodating to sometimes-lengthy invasions from a nomad LA family, helping to make my reporting trips possible. On that front, thank you Luke and Gary Schwartz; Gaspar and Sixto Caro and LuzElena Wood; Christy Claxton and Leon McAllister; Monica Baker; and Kristen Lyndaker.

Evan Wright, Vince Grzegorek, Caleb Hannan, Farah Stockman, and many others in journalism helped in ways as simple as sage advice and camaraderie. Much of my reporting in this book had roots in my tenure at *Newsday*, so I thank my former colleagues on that investigative team for those valuable early collaborations: Matthew Doig,

Sandra Peddie, Will Van Sant, Adam Playford, Keith Herbert, and Matt Clark.

Justin Meyers of the Suffolk County DA's office, Dawn Schob of the SCPD, and Kevin O'Reilly of the Suffolk County Sheriff's Office facilitated various freedom of information requests, some of them voluminous or unique in their method of production.

And lastly, a big, big, big hug and kiss for Frankie, whose smile greeting me after even the longest days working on this book never failed to remind me of the *two nine ten* ways in which I am absurdly lucky.

NOTES

Chief among the records I used for this book were transcripts and records produced in connection with the seminal events of Jimmy Burke's life: his testimony in the John Pius murder case and, decades later, his central role in the Christopher Loeb beating and cover-up investigation.

I obtained transcripts of the Pius cases from the Suffolk County Clerk of Court, the records on file at the DA's office, and the defendants themselves or their former lawyers. The Pius cases spanned eight trials or partial trials, and I wound up with transcripts for most of them.

The Pius cases reviewed, all of which represent multiple trials spanning from 1981 through 2003, and their Suffolk County indictment numbers are:

People v. Michael Quartararo, Peter Quartararo and Michael Brensic, 2678-79 (5 trials or partial trials)
People v. Thomas Ryan, 2470-81 (3 trials or partial trials)

The Loeb cases:

USA v. Burke, 2015-cr-00627, New York Eastern District Court
USA v. McPartland et al., 2017-cr-00587, New York Eastern District Court

Particularly in the latter third of the book, I relied on testimony in the McPartland and Spota trial to re-create scenes and dialogue. The federal case against the two men relied on more than two dozen witnesses, whose testimony largely corroborated each other, and evidence including cell phone records and cell tower data. In particular, the chief witness, James Hickey, spent three days recalling specific dialogue by the many characters in this book, including Burke, Spota, and McPartland. Spota and McPartland were convicted, and Burke previously pleaded guilty. Their attorneys challenged Hickey's version of events on several points following their conviction, but Judge Joan Azrack, who oversaw the trial, said that she found Hickey's testimony to be "credible and reliable."

Burke and McPartland each declined through their attorneys to be interviewed for this book, and Spota and his attorney did not respond to my request for an interview. They each also either did not respond or declined to comment on detailed findings I shared with them before publication.

Spota and McPartland's lawyers have denied the federal charges of which they were convicted, and are pursuing appeals.

PROLOGUE. SMITHTOWN

The account of Chris Loeb and Gabe Miguelez's activities on December 14, 2012, and other capers before then, are drawn from Loeb and police testimony and statements, SCPD reports, crime scene photos, and FBI 302s (the bureau's confidential reports), as well as interviews with Loeb and Miguelez. Jane Loeb's Town of Smithtown personnel file was also helpful.

There remain unanswered questions, if mostly obscure ones, about what was stolen from Chief Burke. This information was gleaned from police testimony, FBI 302s, police reports, and the interviews with Loeb and Miguelez. For example, there are conflicting reports on how many duffel bags were stolen from Burke and whether the gun belt was in one of those bags or if it was loose. Since these parties were either thieves under the influence of heroin or police actively attempting to whitewash the contents of Burke's items, there's no authoritative reliable account. I attempted to parse the most consistent and, in my estimation, truthful version.

The account of the minibike theft was drawn from interviews with Mike and Pete Quartararo, Rob Brensic, and Tom Ryan, as well as court testimony and police statements in the later Pius murder prosecution. The description of Peter Quartararo's interrogation relies largely on his and Detective Tony Palumbo's court testimony and the resulting confession tape, as well as interviews with Peter.

The account of the Loeb beating was pulled mostly from federal court testimony by Kenneth Bombace and Anthony Leto, though Loeb's own recollections in court and to federal agents were also used. There are again inconsistencies in their recollections of exactly what occurred. For example, Loeb recalled that Burke entered the interrogation room while the other detectives were already there, and he ordered them to leave. The detectives recall entering the room with Burke and being there for his beating. Given Loeb's state at the time and the rationale that the detectives had no reason to lie on this count once they had decided to cooperate with federal authorities, I relied on their version on this count. Photos of the precinct, filed as exhibits in federal court, were also used.

Burke's pre-beating jaunt to Turks and Caicos was revealed via roaming charges on phone records filed in court.

CHAPTER 1. HE WAS GONE

The Pius family's pre-Smithtown car accident was referenced in multiple news articles and in an interview with Tony Cannone, but the best primary source was a 1965 *Daily News* article: "Car Fleeing at 100 Per Crashes; 1 Dies, 4 Hurt." Other elements of the Pius background, including information about young Johnny Pius before he was killed either came from news coverage following John Pius's murder, my interviews with Cannone, or court testimony. Particularly useful articles: Jesse Kornbluth, "Trouble Boys," *New York*, August 30, 1982, and September 6, 1982; Leo Seligsohn, "A Suburban Tragedy," *Newsday*, August 9, 1981.

References useful in capturing historic racism in Long Island suburbs include Robert Caro, *The Power Broker: Robert Moses and the Fall of New York*, New York: Knopf, 1974 (which mentioned the KKK's history there); Bruce Lambert, "At 50, Levittown Contends With Its Legacy of Bias," *New York Times*, December 28, 1997; and various articles concerning Yaphank's German-American Settlement League, which settled a discrimination lawsuit by allowing non-Germans to live in the community in, yes, 2017.

The account of the elder John Pius finding his son's body comes from court testimony from himself and Joe Sabina. The detail of him punching the wall comes from Kornbluth's "Trouble Boys." Descriptions of his body and autopsy are from crime scene and autopsy photos, and from court testimony from Ira Dubey and an assistant coroner. Background on Detective Thomas Gill comes from court testimony and his personnel file in the Broward County Sheriff's Office, where he worked following retirement from Suffolk. The background information regarding Ira DuBey was pulled from his court testimony, a New York State Commission of Investigation (SIC) report on the Suffolk DA's office and police department, and Thomas Maier, "Records Show Expert Misstated Credentials," *Newsday*, December 10, 1986. Gill and DuBey both did not respond to multiple interview requests.

The discrepancies concerning Gill's investigation and the elder Pius's statements come from court testimony. My description of the WCBS-TV news interview of Pius came from a video of the segment. The account of the Lyde Kitchner case was pulled from various contemporaneous *Newsday* articles. The description of the woodsy site of Pius's death was pulled from aerial police photos reports and court testimony.

Adam Gromacki was referenced in a missing persons report in the Pius case, and I interviewed him in February 2020.

CHAPTER 2. PRIME SUSPECTS

This chapter is based largely on court testimony and police reports in the Pius homicide investigation. Some elements stated as fact here—such as trapping Tom Ryan in the boiler room and picking up the boys without flashing identification—were disputed by police detectives. However, the detectives' version of events stretches credulity.

As stated in the chapter, for example, they claimed they were focused on Mike O'Neill as a suspect even though they were parked with a view of Tom Ryan and Rob Brensic's homes, a rationale meant to justify them interrogating the boys without their parents. Other tactics of theirs that day are beyond denial, including lying to the boys' parents and a fellow cop about their whereabouts. The boys' versions of events, on the other hand, are largely in line with known practices of the Suffolk homicide squad at the time.

Some details of Eddie Pembroke's friendship with John Pius and his thoughts on the murder investigation were based on a transcript of Kornbluth's interview with Pembroke that was filed in court.

CHAPTER 3. AMITYVILLE

Much of the detail concerning Tom Spota's role in the DeFeo case comes from Gerald Sullivan and Harvey Aronson, *High Hopes*, New York: Coward, McCann & Geoghegan, 1981. Spota's personal history was largely pulled from federal court filings before his sentencing, his childhood yearbooks, family records on Ancestry (ancestry.com), and his and Sullivan's personnel files, which were obtained from the Suffolk DA's office via public records request.

The most comprehensive work of journalism on Long Island's volunteer fire departments is Elizabeth Moore, "Fire Alarm," *Newsday*, November 2005, which is an eight-day series. The passages describing the ways that the homicide detectives are "princes of the county" are based largely on the aforementioned SIC report, as well as: Thomas Maier and Rex Smith, "The Confession Takers," *Newsday*, December 1986, a seminal series on the problems inherent in Suffolk homicide cases. Interviews with multiple sources informed the ways in which Spota had a symbiotic relationship with homicide detectives.

The details on the Henry O'Brien–Eugene Kelley feud, as well as the outcome of the sheriff investigation in which Spota was involved, are pulled from various *Newsday* articles, as well as an interview with Pete Fiorillo about the phone call he received.

The account of Patrick Henry was also drawn from *Newsday* coverage, particularly: Rex Smith, "Suffolk DA a Veteran of Rough Seas," *Newsday*, October 28, 1985. The police inspector lambasting Smithtown parents for their "complaints, not cooperation," was according to Susan Giller, "Cop Says Probe of Boy's Murder Needs Neighbors," *Newsday*, May 2, 1979. The account of Spota's initial involvement in the case is largely from Spota's own court testimony during the Pius trials. The account of the DA's office and police department sniping at each other over the lagging investigation comes from court testimony.

CHAPTER 4. PIT PEOPLE

Much of the biographical background on James Burke comes from his highly detailed SCPD personnel file, as well as interviews with family friend John Ragano, Queens classmates Karyn Follar and Joseph Addabbo, Smithtown classmates including Christine De Vallee, Mike Quartararo, and Rob Brensic, and teachers Suzanne Spina and Jack Breen, as well as Pius-related court testimony, including his own. Spina recalled the scene where he stood out as a Catholic school product upon his introduction to a Smithtown classroom.

The biographical information on Robert Burke and details of his involvement in the Pius investigation came from records in that case—including a report prepared by investigator Herman Race that was filed in court—and his own various criminal proceedings, as well as interviews with his brother, Jose Echeverri, and close friend Tony Cannone. Spota's statement that Burke was largely ignored because there were "never any other suspects" came from an interview with Kornbluth, as quoted in "Trouble Boys."

The account of Burke's high school anthropological research was drawn from an interview with Spina and the various news coverage mentioned in the chapter, particularly: Robin Young Roe, "Youths Study 'Hanging Out,'" *New York Times*, January 6, 1980, and "Teens Looking at Themselves," the CBS *30 Minutes* interview, a transcript of which I obtained from the Pickler Memorial Library at Truman State University in Missouri.

The information on Jimmy Burke's Smithtown crew—in particular George Heiselmann, Danny Culotta, and Chip Brensic—is pulled from transcripts and police reports in both the Pius murder case and their own criminal matters. Chip Brensic has died; Heiselmann and Culotta did not respond to multiple attempts to interview them.

The threats against the Quartararos were documented in transcripts of the Pius murder trials. The account of Cannone's alleged attack on Mike Quartararo was based on a description of the incident in "Trouble Boys," and also Quartararo's written allegations concerning the incident at the time, which were in the DA's case file I reviewed via public records request. Though Cannone in an interview denied the attack, he freely admitted it to Kornbluth, according to "Trouble Boys."

The account of the communal outrage over the Pius case is from news coverage and court testimony. The description of the favorable plea deals offered the Pius defendants comes from court testimony and interviews with their lawyers. The article referenced is Rafael Abramovitz, "When Suspects Are Abused: Allegations of Beatings, Forced Confessions in a N.Y. Suburb Are Widespread," *National Law Journal*, June 11, 1979.

CHAPTER 5. TRAPPERS

The description of Spota's interviews with the teenage witnesses comes from video, which I obtained via a public records request from the DA's office. The account of the Piuses threatening the boys in court is drawn from: John McDonald, "Slain Boy's Parents Rage at Suspects," *Newsday*, June 5, 1980. The background on Nicholas Castellano is drawn from the Pius transcripts and news accounts, in particular an obituary. The most colorful source on William O'Leary's unimpressive lawyering, outside of the transcripts of the Quartararo trial and federal appeal hearings, was: Steve Wick, "In Defense of His Reputation . . . ," *Newsday*, February 16, 1988.

The account of the meeting in chambers in which O'Leary was appointed was drawn from the federal appeal transcript. Robert Doyle and Spota both denied that there were any racial slurs used during the meeting. Castellano swore to it under oath.

The information on the walkie-talkie heist was drawn from court and legal records obtained from the DA's office via public records request.

The account of Gwen Fox's testimony and recantation was via court testimony. In an interview decades later, Fox maintained that her testimony incriminating Mike Quartararo was coerced, as she stated in her recantation.

David O'Brien's apparent confessions about lying come from a document in a Florida law enforcement investigative file. O'Brien, a deputy who reached the top ranks of the Flagler County Sheriff's Office before being fired, was in 2017 accused of rape by his then wife. The document was among records in the investigative file maintained by the 7th Judicial Circuit of the Florida State Attorney's Office, which investigated the allegations. O'Brien's ex-wife told me that he created the document in therapy and provided an email chain which appeared to show that he sent her the same document in 2014. No charges were ultimately filed against O'Brien in the rape investigation. O'Brien did not respond to multiple requests for comment or an interview.

The inconsistencies in the witness testimony in the Pius case, including the issue with the bike being leaned against the tree, were drawn from court testimony and written and videotaped statements. O'Leary's statement about how his strategy was to "lay back" was from a federal appellate transcript, and the Castellano anecdote about lighting his client's house on fire was from the aforementioned obituary. The statistic on the rarity of an acquittal in a Suffolk murder case came from "Trouble Boys," which along with *Newsday* reported on Spota popping champagne with the Piuses following the Quartararo convictions. The details concerning Spota's goodbye party were drawn from a flyer in his personnel file.

Much of the factual background on Spota's career, including his rates of pay while in the DA's office, also came from his personnel file, and the SIC report. The passages on his nascent private law career are informed by the SIC report, the referenced news article—James Barron, "Law Firm's Growth Reflects the Times," *New York Times*, October 10, 1982—and an interview with lawyer Anthony Curto, who provided the $800,000 figure he said Spota and Sullivan were each paid for their work on the Harry Chapin case.

Spota and Sullivan's alleged shared pecuniary interest in his criminal prosecutions, in particular the Pius and Maddox cases, were examined at length before Robert Brensic's trial. The accounts here are drawn from court testimony and filings on that issue.

The Brett Locke saga was drawn from court testimony, and Miller's history of being the homicide squad's point man with dubious snitches came from, among other sources, the SIC report.

The details of Rob Brensic's criminal possession of stolen property charge was drawn from a news article—John McDonald, "Pius Case Suspect Held in Burglary," *Newsday*, March 5, 1981—a court file, references in probation documents, and interviews with Brensic and Tom Ryan.

Ryan's employment backstory, such as his boss discovering him crying upon learning news of his friends' convictions, came from probation documents. The description of Trappers was from a Ryan interview.

The details depicting Trappers as an enemy camp to Ryan and the other Pius murder defendants, as well as other information attributed to Herman Race, was drawn from a report prepared for the defense by the investigator. The report was then filed in court during Ryan's trial. In his personnel file, Jimmy Burke referred to Trappers as his most frequented bar at around this time.

CHAPTER 6. FIXED

The account of young Jimmy Burke's interactions with the police are from reports in his SCPD personnel file. His educational details are from grade transcripts in the file, and an interview with Jack Breen. The account of his drunk-driving arrest, and his early career stops and starts, are also from the personnel file. Homicide commander Richard Jensen wrote a character reference for Jimmy in his police application, and Bill Mahoney told me in an interview about the odd presence of young Jimmy in the homicide offices. Anthony D'Orazio's recollection of Jimmy deciding he wanted to leave behind the air-conditioning business to follow the family tradition of policing is from a letter D'Orazio filed in federal court pleading for leniency at Jimmy's sentencing.

The background on Leon Stern's murder is from news reports. The information about Andrew Polin's inheritance of the case, verbose legal writing, and negotiation of an ultimately rejected plea deal comes from filings in the case and an interview with Polin.

Billy Keahon's flamboyance and the background and descriptions of Judge Stuart Namm are pulled largely from two books: Richard Firstman and Jay Salpeter, *A Criminal Injustice: A True Crime, a False Confession, and the Fight to Free Marty Tankleff*, New York: Ballantine Books, 2008; and Stuart Namm, *A Whistleblower's Lament: The Perverted Pursuit of Justice in the State of New York*, Ashland, OR: Hellgate Press, 2014. The accounts of the Rob Brensic and Tom Ryan trials are from transcripts, news accounts, and Namm's memoir.

The resolution of Jimmy Burke's drunk-driving case and his musings on buzzed driving are from his personnel file. The allegation of Jimmy boasting that the case was "fixed," and the DA's denial of any involvement, are from filings in Brensic's trial. D'Orazio's letter to the judge included the detail about Jimmy's stepdad giving him the blessing to pursue policing. Keahon's letter that helped launch Jimmy's career was part of Jimmy's personnel file. Keahon, who is now a prominent defense attorney in Suffolk County, refused to discuss the letter when I asked him about its apparent inconsistencies.

CHAPTER 7. K-A-K-A

The passages on Stuart Namm, the trials that caused him to become a whistleblower, and the genesis of the SIC probe are largely drawn from either Namm's memoir or the SIC report. Namm declined to be interviewed. The description of the SIC hearings under protest is from transcripts of the proceedings and news coverage including Rex Smith, "To Picketing Cops, a Day at the 'Circus,'" *Newsday*, January 30, 1987, and Joshua Quittner, "Bitter Hearing on Suffolk Cops," *Newsday*, January 30, 1987.

The description of the tangle of investigations concerning Suffolk County law enforcement comes from the SIC report and the proceedings of the Suffolk County Legislature. The prosecutor testified in the latter proceedings as to his "asshole" comment, according to a transcript.

For an example of *Newsday* being a bullhorn for cops and prosecutors dur-ing troubled cases, see the aforementioned "A Suburban Tragedy," in which a journalist accepted flimsy suppositions pushed by the prosecution—such as Mike Quartararo having routinely bullied Pius before the murder—and turned to junk psychology to explain the kid-on-kid killing, including that it may be "one more example of civilization on the decline."

The account of the potential kickback scheme involving Spota's law firm is drawn from transcripts of the SIC and Legislature hearings, an inter-view with James J. O'Rourke, and news accounts, including Sandra Peddie, Adam Playford, and Will Van Sant, "DA contenders Spota and Perini: Ties to '80s probes of Suffolk law enforcement," *Newsday*, September 7, 2013, in which Spota and Woycik denied the allegations.

CHAPTER 8. FORTRESS MENTALITY

The account of Jimmy Burke's time as a police cadet came from his person-nel file. Henry's meeting with David Trager is drawn from the SIC report. The descriptions of the contents of the SIC report and the appellate deci-sions overturning the Pius convictions are from those respective documents.

Rob Brensic's decision to plead guilty, and the rationale of his attorney Frank Bress, are drawn from interviews with them. The information on the potential retrial is from filings and transcripts, and the judge's warning to the prosecutor in chambers is according to Bress's recollection. Other details of the court and parole proceedings are from transcripts of Brensic's plea, news articles, and the SIC report.

The information on the fallout, or lack of it, from the SIC probe is from the commission's report and news articles. The passages on the ensuing DA election is from news reports, including the following profile: Joshua Quit-tner, "Catterson, the 'Insider,'" *Newsday*, October 15, 1989.

The passages concerning Detective James McCready, his personal history, including salary, and the alleged assault come from the SIC report, *Newsday* reports, and McCready's deposition in a later lawsuit Marty Tankleff, a man wrongfully convicted of killing his parents as a teenager, filed against Suffolk County. McCready was the lead detective in the Tankleff case.

CHAPTER 9. ENTER RATMAN

The description of North Amityville, complete with corner boys yelling "Jumbo dimes!" was informed by D. J. Hill, "Fighting Fear at the Corner," *Newsday*, June 1, 1987.

The informal policy by the SCPD to assign its worst cops to the poorest and highest-crime neighborhoods with the most Black and brown residents was detailed in the "Suffolk County Bar Association Report on Police Brutality" (1980).

Burke's history as a young cop is based largely on his personnel file, which includes his commendations, as well as articles such as: Ele Olejede, "Crowd Protests Drug Arrest," *Newsday*, June 8, 1988. Tim Gozaloff shared his "Whiff of Gas" observations in an interview.

The account of James Hickey and Michael Crowley's arrest of Erroll Freeman is pulled from Internal Affairs Bureau (IAB) records, some of which were filed in Spota and Chris McPartland's later trial and others, which were obtained from the SCPD via public records request, as well as: Carolyn Colwell and Monte Young, "Judge Sets a Suspect Free," *Newsday*, April 25, 1992. That article included the quote from DA Patrick Henry.

The officers have denied the accusations of police brutality and perjury, but as is reflected in this chapter, Judge Namm reached a finding of "adverse credibility" against the officers, and the IAB also suspected their stories were contrived.

Hickey testified in the 2019 trial of Spota and McPartland as to the manner in which the Freeman case was his "broken wing."

The account of Namm's twilight years as a judge and his eventual ouster is drawn from "Judge Who Made Allegations Is Not Nominated for a 2d Term," *New York Times*, September 6, 1992, as well as *A Whistleblower's Lament*. Those passages were also informed by an interview with Arthur Pitts, who replaced Namm as judge.

The account of Ryan's retrial is drawn from news accounts and interviews with Ryan and his wife, Jodi. The account of Mike Quartararo's retrial is drawn from interviews with him, probationary and parole records with biographical information, transcripts of the proceedings, and the 1998 appellate decision in *Quartararo v. Hanslmaier* by United States District Judge Joanna Seybert.

The details of Gill's new employment at the Broward County Sheriff's Office stem from his personnel file there and Bob Norman, "The Wrong Keith," *Broward-Palm Beach New Times*, April 25, 2002. Norman's article detailed the conviction of a low-IQ fourteen-year-old who spent ten years in prison for murder before a judge found that he was "factually innocent." In shades of Robert Burke, Gill had determined, based on little more than his gut, that another suspect was innocent, before that suspect then allegedly told friends that he committed the murder.

The descriptions of Mike Quartararo's retrial come from court transcripts and news footage. Culotta's drug use was detailed in a probationary document, as well as various other police reports. The VCR theft was drawn from Broward County court documents. O'Brien's drug problems and infidelity were again drawn from the document provided by the Florida State Attorney's Office.

Details of Robert Michael Sexton's civil claims were drawn from a complaint in his 1994 federal lawsuit. It was settled confidentially, and Sexton didn't respond to multiple attempts to reach him.

The SCPD policy of not opening IAB investigations into allegations in which there was a civil case was a finding detailed in the SIC report. IAB records were not made public in New York until June 2020, following the national upheaval following the murder of George Floyd. The account of Burke's tenure as a street-savvy young supervisor comes from records in his personnel file.

CHAPTER 10. DEAR BOB

The story of Lowrita Rickenbacker's romance with Burke comes from the related IAB file and an interview with Rickenbacker. The appraisals of Burke by George Mullins and Kathleen Dominy are from letters they sent to a federal judge in 2016 pleading for leniency for Burke following his federal conviction. The account of Burke's relationship with Robert Grettler is according to interviews with Grettler.

Rickenbacker's personal biography is from an interview. Her rap sheet is pulled from various court records and transcripts.

The details of the Rickenbacker IAB probe are drawn from a resulting report and interviews with Rickenbacker, Vincent Posillico, and Thomas Spreer, as well as Posillico and Patrick Cuff's federal court testimony on the subject in 2019. Spota and Robert Kearon's relationship is drawn from their respective personnel files from the DA's office, news reports, and the SIC report.

The physical resemblance—subjective as it is—between Rickenbacker's daughter and Jimmy Burke was confirmed by photos shared by the mom.

CHAPTER 11. BROKEN WING THEORY

The details concerning Burke's personal life and his transfer to the Fourth Precinct are from records in his personnel file. The Suffolk cop who was briefly a suspect in the murder of two prostitutes was Michael Murphy. See: Andrew Smith, "Suffolk Police Sgt. Was Suspect in Double-Murder, Witness Says," *Newsday*, June 21, 2017. Posillico's run-ins with Burke were drawn from an interview with the former IAB cop.

The saga of Doug, Michelle, and Jimmy Burke was drawn from an IAB report, interviews with Doug and IAB chief Phil Robilotto, a transcript of Burke's deposition in their divorce, and private investigators, reports and other assorted notes. Michelle did not respond to several attempts to contact her. The description of Jimmy surprising an IAB tail was based on multiple sources who knew of it. The details of Burke's employment by Nissequogue PD was provided by the village, and his proclivity for "cooping" overnight was shared by a former colleague in the Fourth Precinct.

Robilotto's attempt to have Burke investigated criminally was drawn from a memo and an interview with Robilotto. Dennis Sullivan testified as to Burke's lasting hatred of Pat Cuff in the 2019 trial of Spota and McPartland.

The comparison of Burke and Hickey's career trajectories is from SCPD documents detailing their assignments and salaries. That they had vague enmity for each other was supplied by a person who knew them both. Hickey, during his 2019 testimony, described both Burke's "broken wing theory" and Spota's perspective that having tussled with Namm was a "badge of honor."

CHAPTER 12. DEAR BOB, PT. 2

The "snuff film" story is from interviews with Robert Trotta. Trotta's personal and career background is also drawn from interviews with him, John Rodriguez, Tim Gozaloff, and US District Court Judge Denis Hurley's October 3, 2007, decision in *United States v. Morrison* (515 F. Supp. 2d 340).

The account of the police exam cheating scandal is drawn from news coverage, including John Rather, "55 Suffolk Officers Avert Dismissals Over Tests," *New York Times*, October 4, 1998, and "Suffolk Police Test Ill-Conceived, Unsuccessful," *Newsday*, March 25, 1999. Sergeant Brian Bugge pleaded to misdemeanors and the indictment against Spota's partner, Thomas Spreer, was ultimately dismissed. In an interview, Spreer said that Catterson charged him in an effort to keep Spota from running for DA. Spota's quote about Catterson was from his interview on "Breaking It Down with Frank MacKay," which is available on Vimeo. That a disagreement over credit for the Katie Beers case contributed to a feud between Catterson and Sheriff Patrick Mahoney was according to interviews with several people, including Vincent DeMarco, whose own tenure as sheriff followed that of Mahoney. The details of Catterson's prosecution of Mahoney is drawn from news coverage. See: Andrew Metz, "Mahoney Lawyers Go on the Attack," *Newsday*, March 21, 2001. Richard Schaffer's background and description is drawn from court testimony and news coverage. See: T. J. Collins, "Movers: A Young Man Who Is Planning for His First Hurrah," *Newsday*, May 6, 1980. Schaffer's reputation for enemy crushing is widespread, and it is evident in his dealings with Spota and Catterson. He did not respond to multiple interview requests.

For the Independence Party's growth-by-confusion ethos, see: "Independence Party's Confusing Name Has Tricked Thousands of New Yorkers," *New York Daily News*, December 11, 2012. For Frank MacKay's Gracie Mansion Meet with Rudy Giuliani, see: Elizabeth Moore, "The Battle over Independence: Rudy Seeks Party Line; Hillary Not Sure," *Newsday*, April 26, 2000. MacKay's poor opinion of Burke, and his perception of Spota's faltering confidence in him, is from an interview with MacKay. MacKay described his recruitment of Richard Neil Thompson in interviews. Thompson's history as a sports agent was drawn from Darren Heitner, "New York Court Finds It Premature to Rule on Sports Agent Case," Sports Agent Blog (sportsagentblog.com), July 9, 2009. Thompson would not make himself available for an interview, and did not respond to a detailed email seeking comment. The description of Spota glad-handing at Waldbaum's is drawn from: Michael Rothfeld, "Sharp Exchange in Suffolk: Catterson, Spota, Trade Final Blows," *Newsday*, November 4, 2001. The account of Spota and Burke's celebratory mood following his DA victory is drawn from interviews with MacKay.

The description of Commissioner John Gallagher's unpopularity among the rank-and-file comes from interviews with several Suffolk cops. That Gallagher attended church with Spota, and the description of his handling of the request to put Burke in the DA's office, comes from Gallagher's testimony in Spota and McPartland's federal trial in 2019.

For details on Spota's swearing-in as DA, see: Andrew Smith, "Spota Moves Toward Cooperation," *Newsday*, January 4, 2002. The various letters and memos making clear Burke's insulation were filed as exhibits in Spota and McPartland's federal trial.

The account of Chris McPartland's past is primarily from a sentencing document filed by his lawyers. When shown the document, Terence McPartland, Chris's brother, disputed Chris's story of finding him and trying to extricate him from an ashram. "The document you shared depicts a yearslong mysterious absence, rather than a short-term educational experience," Terence wrote in an email.

That McPartland applied for a job outside the DA's office when Spota won was provided by a colleague who worked alongside him. The ad for Ron McPartland's truck showroom was in a 1976 issue of *Newsday*.

Catterson's acerbic management style, from thinking of his employees as barnacles to the "Follow Me" shields, was drawn from interviews with those who had worked for him and news reports. See: Carolyn Colwell, "Justice Speeds Up in DA's First Year," *Newsday*, January 2, 1991. The account of McPartland's career under Catterson comes from records, including evaluations, in his personnel file, as well as news reports. McPartland's prowess with wiretaps and white-collar cases was well known, and a major theme of testimony in his federal trial in 2019.

Office records documented McPartland's injurious run-in with his boss, Marty Thompson, who did not respond to messages seeking an interview. The description of McPartland's job-saving conversation with Spota is from the aforementioned colleague. John B. Collins discussed his favorite passage from *Bonfire of the Vanities* in an interview.

McPartland's proclivity for crying during trouble is drawn from 2019 court testimony, specifically Burke friend Anthony D'Orazio's recollection that he cried when asking for a financial loan to pay his attorney when the feds closed in on him. Spota's Italian background is from census documents and biographical records his lawyers filed on his behalf before his federal sentencing.

The account of Trotta encountering a drunken Spota was from an interview with Trotta. Spota's rumination on the corrosive effect of an obsession with power is from the aforementioned radio interview with MacKay.

CHAPTER 13. GLAZED DONUT

The story of Cuff's son's criminal trouble was told similarly by both Cuff and Hickey at the 2019 federal trial. Hickey's description of Burke telling him he should "get into the game" is from a memorandum of an interview Hickey did with federal authorities on April 17, 2018.

John Rodriguez's background is drawn from interviews with Rodriguez. He denies using force on suspects during interrogations. He told the story on the record about punching out the prosecutor, but then pointed at my notebook where I had jotted it down and said: "Yeah, I'll never admit to that."

As indicated in the passage about the failed bukkake sting, Rodriguez partly corroborated the version of events that was told to me by multiple sources, including a federal official, in that he acknowledged stripping naked during the operation, but denied that he masturbated.

The account of the takedown of the cop-laden drug ring was from news reports and files from the DA's office, obtained via public records request, and an interview with Larry Doyle. Grettler begging for forgiveness was from an investigator's notes in the files. The information on Marlowe Robert Walker III's film ambitions and criminal trouble was pulled from news reports, US Securities and Exchange Commission records, and federal filings in the criminal case against Walker. The police losing their investments is from multiple people with direct knowledge.

The account of Bruce Barket's attendance at a hockey game with Spota is from an interview with Barket. The lawyer's meeting with Spota about the early evidence exonerating Marty Tankleff is drawn from Richard First-man and Jay Salpeter, *A Criminal Injustice*, New York: Ballantine Books, 2008. Spota's Brookhaven takedown was drawn from news accounts and interviews with cops who worked on it. See: Sandra Peddie and J. Jioni Palmer, "SUFFOLK CORRUPTION PROBE; Pulling No Punches; District Attorney Thomas Spota Is Using Several Tactics in Year-Old Investigation That Has Ensnared Many," *Newsday*, May 16, 2004.

The account of the beginning of the SCPD Muslim-monitoring operation is from interviews with Rodriguez and Jim Rooney. The account of Burke's unusual ascent up the Suffolk ranks is from court testimony in Spota and McPartland's 2019 trial, particularly that of former Commissioner Gallagher and records in Burke's personnel file.

Rooney's "rocketing" from Criminal Intelligence is drawn from interviews with Rodriguez, Rooney, and others, as well as federal court testimony. Cuff's realization that Hickey was being rewarded for snitching about his lowest moment was from his 2019 testimony. Hickey described the counterterrorism conference, one of his first details atop Criminal Intelligence, during an April 17, 2018, interview with federal authorities, according to a memorandum. Burke's relationship with the widow of the man who chaired the group behind that conference was drawn from several sources, including references during the federal trial of Spota and McPartland. The description of the aborted mosque mission is from an interview with Rodriguez, as well as photos he provided.

Mike Quartararo's work release and parole saga were drawn from news accounts, transcripts of parole hearings, and interviews with Quartararo. The November 1998 decision in which Judge Seybert temporarily freed him was *Quartararo v. Hanslmaier*, 94-CV-5564.

The decision freeing Ryan, in the US Court of Appeals Second Circuit, was *Ryan v. Miller*, 01-2122. Ryan's manslaughter plea, and the decision-making that led up to it, was drawn from interviews with Ryan, his wife, Jodi, and news coverage of the court proceeding. The account of the Ryans burning the court transcripts is from interviews with them.

The account of Burke's grand plans, at the steakhouse and in the car with Madigan and Hickey, are from Hickey's 2019 testimony and other documents filed in the federal case. Madigan's background was drawn from personnel documents, including his official department photo.

CHAPTER 14. THE ADMINISTRATION

The account of Phil Alvarez's sting and how it led to a focus on Wayne Prospect, Dominic Baranello, and Steve Levy is from news accounts and interviews with investigators, including Alvarez. The account of Levy grabbing Schaffer in the Smithtown Sheraton following Spota's electoral victory and announcing he wanted to run is from Rick Brand, "Levy's Reform Message, Hard Work Pay Off," *Newsday*, November 5, 2003.

The details on the investigation, including utterances on wiretaps, concerning Prospect, Baranello, and Levy is from news reports—see: Rick Brand, "Stung by Recordings in Bribe Case," *Newsday*, April 24, 2006—and interviews with those involved, including Alvarez. The squabble over whether to release the wiretap tapes is from Tom Robbins, "Steve 'Budget Crusher' Levy and the Crew from Crookhaven," *The Village Voice*, April 6, 2010.

The account of Gerald and Tony Jacino's invention is from records filed in a federal lawsuit between them. I obtained the DA's lease of their "Blue Star" building space via public records request. The account of what corporate neighbors might witness, and Gerald's agreement to never enter the building without warning, was from investigators who worked in the offsite location. The allegation of abuse in the basement is from an affidavit of Larry Demetrius, a drug-dealing and money-laundering suspect.

Spota's disclosure of the Blue Star building was during his aforementioned radio interview with Frank MacKay. The details of the car rental deal were provided by an investigator. The details of Palumbo's employment were from his personnel file with the DA's office. The Thomas Pendick case was drawn from the Internal Affairs file provided by public records request from the Suffolk County Sheriff's Office, which showed that in July 2006, the deputy admitted to the administrative charge of trespassing on his ex's property. He was suspended for thirty days without pay, ordered to undergo an alcohol and narcotic treatment program, submit to random drug testing, and was barred from possessing a gun. But Pendick continued to enjoy a long career, uninterrupted even when he allegedly spat on the face of another deputy sheriff. Former prosecutor Susan Onorato also spoke about the case in an interview, calling its resolution a "sweetheart deal" made without her input. Palumbo's comment about "that rapist Pendick" is drawn from confidential Internal Affairs records related to the later Ed Walsh federal trial. Pendick did not respond to my attempts to reach him.

The background information on Bob Macedonio is drawn from his Instagram account, materials stemming from the wiretap of his phone, and a bar grievance hearing in which Suffolk County Judge Stephen Braslow referred to "50 Cents and 25 Cents." For more on Carmine Macedonio's contentious history with the SCPD, see: Gus Garcia-Roberts, Devan Patel, and Elizabeth Murray, "'I've Been Dying for 25 Years': How a Cop Has Stalled His Child Sex Abuse Trial for Decades," *USA TODAY*, November 20, 2019.

The information on the Macedonio investigation, and John Scott Prudenti's boat charters, are drawn from interviews including with officials who had direct knowledge of the Macedonio probe, including then-Det. John Gang, search warrant affidavits, wiretap logs, legal transcripts, and other records related to the investigation, and court filings. See: Gus Garcia-Roberts and Will Van Sant, "The Curious Case of Robert Macedonio," *Newsday*, February 7, 2016; Gus Garcia-Roberts and Will Van Sant, "DA Thomas Spota's Wiretap of Robert Macedonio: New Details of Probe," *Newsday*, May 12, 2016; Gus Garcia-Roberts and Will Van Sant, "Prosecutor's Party Boat: Spota Deputy Got Thousands for Use of Vessel," *Newsday*, April 25, 2016. Prudenti, now a defense attorney, did not respond to an interview request. Emily Constant's various observations concerning the Macedonio investigation are from a 302 report memorializing her March 28, 2017, FBI interview. The 302 was among exhibits unsealed in Spota and McPartland's trial. Constant declined my request for an interview.

McPartland and Burke's burgeoning relationship, including their profane greeting for each other, was pulled largely from testimony in Spota and McPartland's 2019 trial, including that of fellow prosecutor Spiros Moustakas. The details on McPartland's staid family life are from letters filed in his support during sentencing in that trial. His impression of Eddie Murphy is from a longtime colleague in the DA's office. The account of McPartland playing detectives was from an interview with Rodriguez.

The description of Butterfields is from myself dining at the bar there, and also the establishment's website. Owner Michael Shalley wrote a letter on Burke's behalf at his federal sentencing. His description of the DA's office as "the cabal" is from Shalley's interview with federal authorities.

The descriptions of the developments in the Tankleff case are from news accounts, *A Criminal Injustice*, and filings in Tankleff's civil suit against Suffolk County. The accounts of Jay Salpeter's marriage being harpooned by ransom letters and Bruce Barket being arrested were from interviews with Salpeter and Barket, the discovery filings showing that the DA's office was spying on Salpeter and his family, as well as a draft a notice of a complaint prepared by Barket.

CHAPTER 15. POWERPOINT JIMMY

Kenneth Bombace's background is pulled from interviews with Bombace and others who know him, his testimony in federal court, as well as his high school yearbook. His son's gun incident was drawn from interviews with

Bombace and the related Internal Affairs file, received via public records request.

Tony Leto shared his account of his troubled childhood and police career over several interviews. Some of the details concerning his father's criminal activity were pulled from appellate decisions, which are available online.

Hickey's management style of Haves and Have Nots was drawn from interviews with Bombace and his partner, Cliff Lent, and from the court testimony of Bombace and Tony Leto. Troy Gibson's allegations of racism are according to a federal lawsuit he filed. The story of Ray Tierney's aborted career in the DA's office is from interviews with multiple people with knowledge of it, including Tierney.

The Administration's yearslong plotting against Steve Levy is drawn from court testimony and filings in Spota and McPartland's later federal trial, particularly accounts stemming from Hickey. Levy's clash with cops and his race-baiting is drawn largely from news accounts.

The account of Burke sharing tidbits of the Levy investigation is drawn from filings in the federal trial. Lawyer Anthony LaPinta spoke to me on behalf of his client, Levy's former aide. Levy's exit from politics, and the glimpses of scandal surrounding his finances, are drawn from news accounts and an interview with Ethan Ellner. Levy declined to be interviewed, and he has sued to prevent the release of documents concerning the investigation and his agreement with the DA's office.

The manner in which The Administration used wiretaps to extort their targets was drawn from multiple people with knowledge of their tactics, on the sides of both the targets and the investigators.

Bombace and Lent creating Burke's PowerPoint was from interviews with them. Steve Bellone's meeting with the *Newsday* editorial board was drawn from an interview with writer Bob Keeler. See: "On Gilgo Case, Spat Can't Help," *Newsday*, December 19, 2011, in which the editorial board opined that Bellone "appears to have overstepped" in choosing a chief of department before a commissioner. Bellone declined to be interviewed for this book, or respond to a detailed request for comment on various findings and questions.

The account of Tim Gozaloff and Rob Trotta writing their warning letter about Burke was from interviews with the two retired cops, and a copy of the letter itself. Gozaloff's father is referred to in news reports concerning the Amityville slaying. The information on lawsuits against Trotta was pulled from court filings and Sandra Peddie, "Case Studies: Long Island Police Misconduct Cases," *Newsday*, December 18, 2013.

CHAPTER 16. SAMMY TO THE RESCUE

Bill Madigan's mockery of the chiefs was drawn from the 2019 federal trial testimony of Pat Cuff. The account of the chiefs learning their fate was based on an interview with former Chief of Detectives Dominick Varrone, who also said he learned later that Burke had told union officials the chiefs were all getting "whacked."

The account of Shannan Gilbert's disappearance and the discovery of bodies near Oak Beach is drawn from news reports; interviews with those involved, including Varrone; and the definitive work of journalism on the case: Robert Kolker, *Lost Girls: An Unsolved American Mystery*, New York: Harper Perennial, 2014. Varrone's insensitive remark to the Public Safety Committee of the Suffolk County Legislature was drawn from a transcript of the May 5, 2011, meeting.

The feud between Spota and Richard Dormer is drawn from news accounts. Geraldine Hart opined on how neither law enforcement head actually knew what they were talking about during an interview with this author.

The information on Pat Cuff's demotion was from testimony by Cuff and Hickey during the federal trial.

The account of the anonymous letter is based on a copy of the letter itself, interviews with its authors—Gozaloff, with an assist by Trotta—and court testimony including by Hickey, who described The Administration's reaction to its receipt. Spota's response is drawn from the letter he wrote and records concerning the burglary, which he used to confuse the matter.

That McPartland had requested Burke's IAB files, perhaps to conceal them, was mentioned at his federal trial and in Tania Lopez, "Chris McPartland, Spota Deputy, Sought Internal Affairs Files on James Burke, Sources Say," *Newsday*, January 9, 2016. Bellone saying that the letter seemed "crazy" to him is from *Unraveled*, the Discovery+ podcast by Billy Jensen and Alexis Linkletter, 2020–2021.

The account of McPartland and Burke's accident on the eve of him becoming chief of department is from filings by federal prosecutors in McPartland and Spota's trial. Burke's bragging of hog-tying a female colleague is according to a federal memo of Hickey's interview with federal authorities (marked Ex. 3500-JH-9 in McPartland and Spota's trial), and that he used the n-word is from multiple sources, including an interview with Bombace and a memo of a Bombace interview with federal authorities (Ex. 3500-KB-2).

Madigan and Sullivan's appointments under Burke are drawn from personnel documents and court testimony. That Burke used his field information officers as spies was from multiple sources including Bombace, who had that designation, and that he bragged of an affair with a woman who worked in the commissioner's office is from a source with whom he shared that boast.

CHAPTER 17. A TERRIBLE FOREBODING FEELING

The description of Burke's presentation to the legislators is from a transcript of that meeting of the Public Safety Committee, on February 2, 2012.

Tania Lopez's coverage of the machete murder was drawn from interviews with Lopez and the resulting story: Tania Lopez, "A Mother's Killing; Brownsville Woman Stabbed as Daughter Runs for Help," *Newsday*, July 2, 2001. Lopez's financial problems are drawn from interviews with Lopez and public records.

Burke's big introduction to *Newsday* as chief of department was Paul LaRocco, "James Burke: From Beat Cop to Suffolk's Top Cop," *Newsday*, February 18, 2012. In an interview, LaRocco acknowledged the article's failings but defended it as a symptom of a busy beat reporter operating in a vacuum of official information. He said he had read the online gossip about Burke but thanks to New York law, which sealed police personnel records, there was no way to research Burke's past while on deadline. Though the story didn't age well, Lopez was not critical of the article and said she's glad LaRocco wrote it, as it "shows how much Burke tried to bullshit us."

The account of Lopez's initial meeting with Burke, and the conversation that led her to build sources of information on him, are from interviews with her as well as one of those sources, John Oliva.

Oliva's interrogation with the gangster known as Unico, and the musings on chasing MS-13, were drawn from interviews with Oliva and others who worked with him. The account of Oliva's fraught history pursuing the gang was drawn partly from Shelley Feuer Domash, "Detectives Live Under Gang's Death Threat," *New York Times*, March 18, 2001. The accounts of Oliva, Willy Maldonado, Trotta, and other cops being removed from task forces is from interviews with Oliva, Trotta, others, and federal court testimony. Rodriguez's explanation as to Burke's decision was from an interview.

Hickey explained Burke's true motive as he saw it—removing Trotta—during his federal court testimony in 2019. He also described in that testimony the meeting with the feds where they tried in vain to reinstate the task forces, and spoke generally about Burke and The Administration's hatred of the feds. John Rodriguez shared what he saw as Burke's disdain for Oliva and other "federalized" cops in an interview. Current SCPD Chief of Department Stuart Cameron testified that Burke did not attain top secret clearance unlike other chiefs of department, and that he doubted he would have been able to given his background.

A memo prepared by Suffolk detectives that described the FBI being shut out of the Gilgo case in 2012 was reported in David M. Schwartz and William Murphy, "Steve Bellone: Thomas Spota Running a 'Criminal Enterprise,'" *Newsday*, May 12, 2016.

That Burke drove while intoxicated was mentioned in filings and testimony in federal court by witnesses including Hickey and Sammy Panchal. The description of the events Burke attended as chief of department, and his email referencing Charlie Daniels, are from emails from his SCPD account obtained via public records request.

Panchal testified during the 2019 trial that the night before the fateful break-in, they had returned from a function but he didn't remember which function. Federal prosecutor Lara Gatz mentioned during her argument for Spota and McPartland's sentencing that he spent the night drinking at a Hauppauge bar, and also that the party bag was for use in his trip to Florida the next day. Panchal suggested that Burke was drunk, as he had to ask the next day what they had done that night. Burke's phone records, later filed in federal court, revealed his Turks and Caicos vacation via roaming charges. Panchal also described the cigars he gave his boss as a gift. Lowrita Rickenbacker said in an interview that Burke often carried a party bag containing sex toys.

CHAPTER 18. PEE-PEE TOUCHER

The account of the night resulting in Frank Loeb's arrest was from a 302 report memorializing an FBI interview with Chris Loeb, and it is corroborated by other criminal documents and testimony. The background of Chris and Gabe Miguelez's relationship is drawn from interviews with both men and FBI and police documents. The account of the convoluted law enforcement scheduling, and how it resulted in Chris Loeb being free to alter the course of Suffolk County governance, is from police records and testimony, in particular the court testimony of probation officer Francine Ruggiero.

The account of the all-hands-on-deck effort to investigate the Burke break-in is from interviews with Bombace and Lent, and the state and federal court testimony of Bombace, Leto, and Hickey. The story of Brian Draiss's role in the Loeb investigation is drawn from his state and federal testimony, and a probation document reflecting his opinion of Loeb. The account of the scene at Loeb's home upon Burke's arrival is drawn from police reports and court testimony, including that of Draiss and Kenneth Regensburg.

That *I'm Here for the Gang Bang #2* was initially among Burke's stolen property is not in credible dispute, though Draiss has maintained that he found it on Loeb's nightstand. Federal witnesses including Hickey and Dennis Sullivan testified that Burke mentioned his duffel bag had contained at least one porn DVD.

Christopher Nealis's musings are drawn mostly from a 302 memorializing his interview with the FBI. The description of the squad room is from photos filed as exhibits in Spota and McPartland's trial. The description of the detectives' beating of Loeb is from the court testimony of Bombace and Leto, and interviews with both. Leto first mentioned in his testimony that he had struck five or six prisoners previously in his career. Loeb's background of violence and addiction is from interviews with him and 302s of his interviews with the FBI. He had accused his father of abuse in various court records, but there is no public indication that his father has ever been arrested for such. His father didn't respond to attempts to reach him.

The account of Burke heading into Interview Room Number 3 was from the federal court testimony of Bombace and Leto, and interviews with both. The account of Burke beating Loeb is drawn from the most credible and corroborated versions of the episode provided in court testimony by Bombace, Leto, and Loeb. Loeb said during an FBI interview he yelled "pee-pee toucher." He told me, and has said at various other times, that he yelled "pedophile." He has insinuated that federal authorities have preferred he testify that he yelled "pervert" in order to avoid the disputed—and in the determination of federal authorities, debunked—claim that Burke had child porn in his bag.

The account of Burke's interactions with Fourth Precinct cops post-beating is from FBI memorandum, including a 302 of Nealis's interview with the feds, Loeb's FBI interviews, and Kelly's testimony in the 2019 federal trial. The Intel detectives having coffee after the beating, and meeting with Burke for his statement, is from federal testimony by Bombace and Leto, interviews with Bombace, and Burke's statement. Hickey testified to Burke calling with congratulations for his guys' participation in the beating, and that Burke was on his way to West Palm Beach. Malone bragging about urinating in Loeb's coffee cup is drawn largely from the testimony and interviews of Leto. Malone declined to be interviewed for this book.

Moustakas's early involvement in the Loeb case is from his testimony in the federal trial, and the memos he filed. Through an intermediary, he declined to be interviewed. The account of Burke heading directly to Oheka Castle from West Palm Beach is from Hickey's testimony.

The description of Gary Melius is drawn from a project in which I took part: Gus Garcia-Roberts, Keith Herbert, Sandra Peddie, and Will Van Sant, "Pathway to Power: Gary Melius' Rise Through Long Island's

Cozy Political System," *Newsday*, February 22–25, 2018. In response to an email seeking comment, Melius—who declined an interview—took issue with some of my characterizations, including an alleged past affiliation with organized crime. "I am not associated with a 'MOB' and I find such a reference disparaging and an attack on my ethnicity," Melius wrote.

That Bombace wasn't billed for his charity events at Oheka is from a Bombace interview. The description of the discretion-free chatter at Oheka was drawn from the testimony of Leto and Hickey. Panchal and Sullivan testified about Burke's acknowledgment to them that he had laid hands on Loeb.

CHAPTER 19. ABSOLUTE PANIC

The account of the ousted task force members being in contact with federal authorities about the Loeb beating nearly as soon as it happened is from interviews with Trotta and Oliva and a federal close-out memo that appeared to refer to them without using their names.

The account of The Administration's fretful response to Trotta's visit to the Fourth, and the decision to promote Frank Catalina, is from Hickey's testimony.

Lopez was scooped by Shelly Feuer Domash, Timothy Bolger, and Christopher Twarowski, "Turf War: Is SCPD Brass Playing Politics by Backing Out of the FBI's LI Gang Task Force?" *Long Island Press*, October 11, 2012. Lopez's story is: Tania Lopez, "Anti-Gang Cops Transferred Off the Case," *Newsday*, January 29, 2013. Lopez's frustration with her editor on the story is from an interview with her. Hickey testified at trial as to Burke's longtime relationship as a source to top *Newsday* writers.

Oliva's meeting with union official Billy Plant, and Oliva's suspicion that Plant then gave him up to Burke, is from an interview with Oliva.

The descriptions of Moustakas's discussion with Loeb's attorney, Toni Marie Angeli, and the ensuing meeting with The Administration is from Moustakas's court testimony and Angeli's bill of particulars, a legal document. Angeli's nude photo dustup was widely reported at the time, and that the Loebs appreciated her rebellious resolve in the case is from Jeremy Tanner and James Ford, "Lawyer Who Dropped Defendant in Police Chief Beating Case Has Interesting History with the Authorities," PIX11, July 1, 2013.

That the police had printed out negative comments on articles about Burke was shown via documents in the case file of the eventual prosecution of John Oliva, provided to me via public records request. Spota's dislike of Nassau County DA Kathleen Rice was made clear via federal court testimony of Hickey and Richard Schaffer, and a sarcastic email referring to her which was filed as an exhibit in the federal trial. Hickey referred to the new mood as "absolute panic" during his trial testimony.

The descriptions of Bombace and Leto being served with subpoenas are from their court testimony and interviews. The account of Burke attempting to get his story straight with McPartland's help, and them handing off the case to the friendly Queens DA's office, is from Hickey's testimony. Michael Miller testified at McPartland and Spota's trial that he was unaware of the Burke brutality allegations mixed up in the Loeb matter, and an email filed in court showed that Peter Crusco and McPartland had discussed the law limiting the scope of a special prosecutor. Crusco, now a defense attorney, asked for specific questions in writing when I requested an interview. After I detailed some of my areas of interest, Crusco then never responded.

The stories of Kelly, Draiss, Leto, and Bombace having their own stories straightened are from their federal court testimony, and that of Hickey.

Burke's aborted fishing trip leading to Spota calling for an impromptu meeting at his house was drawn from court testimony, including that of Joe Sawicki, Jim Hickey, and Emily Constant.

The account of the hasty meeting at Hickey's house is drawn mostly from the court testimony of Hickey, Bombace, and Leto. Spota doing his own yard work was from character reference letters filed before his sentencing. Constant described the content of the meeting during her court testimony. Burke's angry phone call with Hickey is according to Hickey's court testimony.

The detectives' frustration with their union representation, and Ray Tierney connecting his brother-in-law with a lawyer, is from the court testimony of Bombace and Leto, and interviews with Bombace and Tierney. Joe Conway's involvement in choosing attorneys for the other cops, and then sharing information with them, was from Conway's federal court testimony. Leto testified about having his lawyer drive him down to Conway's office, and the fear he felt, particularly for his sons. He also described himself and the other two detectives buying burner phones to communicate.

CHAPTER 20. HICKEY'S BACKYARD THERAPY

The account of Loeb's FBI interviews is drawn from the resulting 302s, the court testimony of FBI agents Ryan Carey and Jeremy Bell, and the memo closing the investigation. In that memo, the details of the "cooperating witnesses" match the accounts given by Trotta and Oliva. The details of this first, failed phase of the investigation—often referred to as Loeb I—are drawn from Carey and Bell's testimony and the same memo. The account of Catalina speaking to the FBI agents is from a resulting 302.

Hickey's extramarital affairs were disclosed in detail in filings and Hickey's testimony during Spota and McPartland's trial. Hickey mentioned during testimony both his skill at multitasking and his wife's inability to remember where her cell phone is. His calendars, with his coded messages, were entered into evidence. Hickey's backyard therapy was described in testimony by Hickey and Bombace, and Hickey described Burke's attempt to put detective-spies in the federal court building. Hickey claimed he did not pass on that instruction to the detectives, so there's no evidence that the detectives, Brian Keegan and Marcus Rivera, actually did any spying. The Brady Park meeting with Burke, and Hickey's descent into binge drinking, are from Hickey's testimony. The doctor's notes were filed in evidence in the federal trial. That Hickey's father was a drill instructor was disclosed in an obituary, and his father's death from causes related to alcohol was gleaned from notes in Hickey's medical record. Through an intermediary, Hickey declined to be interviewed for this book. His attorney then did not respond to a more formal request.

The account of Hickey's detectives buying him a tea set is drawn from the court testimony of Leto and Bombace.

McPartland's role in a high school production of *Charley's Aunt* was revealed by his Walt Whitman High School yearbook. The description of McPartland prepping Burke for perjury was from Hickey's testimony. Hickey and Leto testified about Leto being informed he had been picked for the perjury. Leto's description of his suicidal ideation was from interviews. In court testimony, Leto described encountering Burke as he headed in for his meeting with the special prosecutor.

Lopez described her pursuit of Burke in interviews. The letter to *Newsday*, and the edits by Burke, were filed as evidence in the federal trial. Lopez's meeting with Vincent Posillico, in which he leaked Burke's IAB file to her, was described in interviews with both of them and during Posillico's testimony.

The Rickenbacker story is from Tania Lopez, "Suffolk Police Report: As Sergeant, Chief James Burke Twice Lost Gun," *Newsday*, October 19, 2013. Rodriguez's reaction to the Rickenbacker story was via an interview. Hickey testified as to Spota's outraged response, and that The Administration assigned Madigan to sleuth out who leaked the IAB report.

That Crusco allegedly left the 302s out for others to see was drawn from Leto's testimony. Hickey also later testified that Burke discussed how Crusco had left the 302s out for union boss McCormack. The description of Leto's testimony was from a transcript of the proceedings and my in-person impression of his demeanor during his testimony in the later Spota and McPartland trial.

The account of the testimony and ruling in the suppression hearing was from a transcript and Judge Martin Efman's decision. Draiss later testified in McPartland and Spota's trial about Hickey and Madigan being on his interview panel. Draiss's condemnation of Loeb was from a probation document. The celebratory emails between Spota and the Queens DA's office were later filed as evidence in Spota and McPartland's federal trial.

Nealis, Cottingham, Regensburg, and Keith Sinclair's statements to federal authorities were drawn from 302s and grand jury testimony. The end of Shattered Shield was reflected in Bell and Carey's close-out memo.

April Brooks's decision to inform Burke that the investigation was closed was a befuddling one. There is some speculation that it was a ploy. Most federal sources I spoke to weren't so charitable. Brooks, who is no longer with the FBI, declined to speak to me. But if in fact the strategy was to get Burke to feel confident enough to do something stupid, it worked. Burke's announcement that it was time to fuck John Oliva was from Hickey's testimony.

CHAPTER 21. LEAKS

Spiros Moustakas described the placement and logistics of the wire room during the operation against Oliva. Trotta's entry into politics despite having "zero" political ambition was from an interview. The content of the wire was drawn from the DA's file on the Oliva prosecution, as obtained via public records request. Moustakas testified as to "an incident where there was discussion of an affair that James Burke had with someone, and that a complaint was raised with the District Attorney's office," which matched Lopez's discussions with Oliva concerning the saga of Doug and Michelle.

Lopez provided a copy of the letter Rickenbacker wrote her from prison, and her planning the visit is drawn from an interview. Moustakas testified as to the alarm when the DA's office learned of her plans.

Hickey described the rest of the smaller meeting in which the finer points of fucking John Oliva were discussed. Multiple people testified as to the content of the larger meeting on the same subject, including Constant, who recalled her question about the Pentagon Papers.

The legal requirements of wiretap affidavits were discussed during Spota and McPartland's trial. The article used as a cover story was Tania Lopez, "Sources: Suffolk Robber May Have Used Body Shop Vehicles to Flee Holdups," *Newsday*, January 14, 2014. The account of the union press conference was from a news report, and a video of Spota's press conference was filed as an exhibit in his and McPartland's later federal trial.

Some of the information on the DA's office seeking permission to wiretap Oliva's phone, including the quote from their affidavit about the robbery suspect changing his pattern and the detective-investigator saying he did not fact-check McPartland on that claim, came from the DA's office's Affirmation in Support of Motion to Vacate Conviction, filed December 2, 2021, resulting in Oliva's misdemeanor plea being tossed.

McPartland's orders for his wire monitors to pay special attention to the calls involving Burke's enemies was according to Moustakas's testimony. Hickey testified about Madigan's request that he "put more red ink" on crime pattern documents to entice Oliva. The logistics of Oliva leaking documents to Lopez was from the case file, including Oliva's confession—which he refused to sign and some of which is in dispute—and interviews with Oliva and Lopez.

The account of the Juan Garcia leak was from wiretap logs concerning Lopez's conversation with Oliva, as obtained from the case file. The reasoning behind the DA's office wanting to pass the Oliva case on to the feds is informed by interviews with multiple people on both the Suffolk County and federal side of the equation. Hickey testified as to Madigan's eagerness to indict Oliva, and frustration when the deadline passed to screw him out of a pension.

The account of the Suffolk DA's office attempting to get the feds to indict Oliva, and setting up the doomed meeting with that goal, is from filings by prosecutors and the defense in McPartland and Spota's trial, as well as records in the DA's case file. Trotta's warning to Oliva soon afterward not to trust the phone was drawn from filings in the trial, though in an interview Trotta said that utterance was a running joke because in Suffolk County, phones should never be trusted.

The contents of the "dildo call" are drawn from interviews with Rickenbacker, Oliva, and Lopez, as well as the notation on the call log, which was obtained via public records request.

Lopez's perhaps-justified paranoia is from a wiretap log, interviews with her, and photos she posted to Twitter of her destroyed car tires. The document showing editor Steve Wick's phone tag with Spota, and voicemail updating him on her reporting, was obtained via public records request. I interviewed Wick about that document in July 2021. Rick Brand confirmed his near-weekly tennis matches with Spota in a December 2021 interview, maintaining: "I don't think it's an issue."

The details of surveillance on Oliva are from Vigilant Solutions printouts and investigator notes, all of which were in the DA's file. The account of Oliva's arrest and aftermath is drawn from police records, interviews with Oliva, and Tania Lopez, "Suffolk Detectives Questioned by DA's Office over Leaks to Press, Say Sources," *Newsday*, July 22, 2014.

Attorney Stephen Scaring's background is drawn from past news coverage. Oliva's decision, with Scaring's support, to plead guilty was drawn from interviews with Oliva. Documents concerning Oliva's plea negotiations, including the unsigned confession, were included in the DA's case file. I obtained a copy of federal prosecutor John Durham's plea for Oliva to keep his guns.

Multiple cops, including Bombace, testified during Spota and McPartland's trial as to the chilling effect of the Oliva case.

The renewed federal interest in Suffolk County law enforcement following the Oliva wire operation, including chief prosecutor Nicole Boeckmann subpoenaing materials from that investigation, was drawn from filings in the Spota and McPartland's trial. Hickey described learning about the ejection of the federal courthouse spy detectives, and the carpool parking lot conference with Burke and McPartland that followed.

CHAPTER 22. BAD PEOPLE

The description of the award ceremony is from a video that was filed as evidence in Spota and McPartland's trial. The account of Bombace's boat trip and being grilled about it was from interviews with Bombace. He testified at trial about his attempt to transfer to the Suffolk County Sheriff's Office, and he and Vincent DeMarco described their cagey meeting in interviews. The account of Hickey and The Administration having various paranoid conversations about the conspiracy is drawn from Hickey's testimony, and from emails and calendar items providing information on the various events.

Burke's texts with his friends were provided to the feds by Hickey and filed as evidence in the Spota and McPartland trial. Burke mentioned in the texts that he was on a road trip to CigarFest with Panchal, and photos of the event that year informed my description.

The account of Bombace's lawyer telling him about the update from the prosecutor at the portrait unveiling was drawn from Bombace's court testimony, and an invitation to the unveiling filed as evidence in federal court. The description of the Long Island division of the Eastern District, and the interrogation style of Bill Hessle, was from interviews with current and former colleagues. The account of the indictment against Edward Walsh, and Tierney and Spota's involvement, is from filings in the Walsh case.

That Tierney didn't talk shop with Bombace is from interviews with both men, and in an interview Tierney denied interceding with his fellow feds on Bombace's behalf. Bombace's soccer field meeting with Hickey is from the court testimony of Bombace and Hickey, and interviews with

Bombace. Hickey described the church parking lot meeting in testimony. That Burke also had a creeping suspicion that Hickey could be snitching was drawn from federal court testimony. Burke's then-girlfriend's description of his frenzied mood following the meeting with Hickey was drawn from her court testimony, and from phone records filed in evidence.

Hickey's meeting with Burke, Spota, and McPartland was drawn from Hickey's court testimony, and was bolstered in court with corroboration such as Conway testifying that he received the voicemail Hickey mentioned.

CHAPTER 23. PLAYING CARDS WITH MOBSTERS

Hickey testified that Burke instructed him to switch out cars and take different routes in case he was being tailed. The account of Hickey's busy day is from his testimony and text messages from Burke, which were filed in evidence. Others, including Dennis Sullivan, testified as to seeing Burke and McPartland at Golden Dynasty for Burke's mother's birthday party.

Bombace described his dinner with Russ McCormack, and his post-dinner stroll with Hickey, during testimony and in interviews. Hickey also testified as to his discussion with Bombace. Bombace described Commissioner Ed Webber's call to him in an interview. Bombace described his meeting with Bellone, and his run-up to testifying in the grand jury, during his testimony and in interviews. Leto also testified about his meeting with Bombace in which Bombace informed him he planned to tell the truth. The account of Leto's affair and divorce is from interviews. He described his decision to cooperate with the feds, and the details of those initial meetings, in both court testimony and interviews. His proffer agreement and cooperation agreement were both unsealed as exhibits in the McPartland and Spota trial.

Hickey's breakdown is drawn from the testimony of Hickey and Dr. Vinu Kurian, the Huntington Hospital doctor who treated Hickey, and medical records filed in court. The description of Stuart Cameron is from Cameron's own court testimony and the accounts of those who know him, and his meeting with Hickey is drawn from Hickey's testimony.

The account of Burke's timeline is from the testimony of his lawyer Joe Conway, Hickey, and others. The account of him quitting is drawn from Hickey's testimony as to how Burke later described it. Cuff described the spy at his retirement party during his court testimony. Sullivan described Burke's retirement party at Golden Dynasty.

The accounts of Hickey's trip to Florida—including how many times he messaged his mistresses—heading to the union offices after receiving the subpoena, and his menacing surprise meeting with Burke are all from his court testimony.

The description of Burke's arrest is drawn from news reports, photos, and interviews with those who are directly familiar with the events of that day, including Geraldine Hart. The story of the cash loan/gift to McPartland is drawn from the federal court testimony of John Toal and Anthony D'Orazio, as well as bank and federal prison records (corroborating Burke's jail meeting), which prosecutors filed in evidence. The account of Tim Sini and Stuart Cameron interviewing all high-ranking cops in the department, and giving Cuff his retirement shield, was from Cameron's court testimony. Joe Sawicki testified as to his golf conversation with Spota.

EPILOGUE 1. RATMAN'S REVENGE

The description of Burke's sentencing was from news reports and case documents. I asked Barket about the settlement amount during an interview.

Spota's resignation letter was obtained via his DA's office personnel file. Their mug shots were filed in federal court. McPartland's attorneys disclosed that he was clerking at a liquor store during their pleas for leniency before sentencing.

The shopping spree with Loeb was from first-hand observation. Loeb's arrest was drawn from news reports.

The description of Spota and McPartland's trial was from my own observations, transcripts, and exhibits. Judge Azrack's decision finding disputed portions of Hickey's testimony to be "credible and reliable" was also from that August 2021 decision.

The account of the events and reforms of the George Floyd protests are from various news reports.

Though it has not officially been publicly disclosed that Billy Madigan got immunity for his federal grand jury testimony in which he ultimately frustrated prosecutors, it was made obvious by several partly redacted filings in the Spota and McPartland trial. Additionally, in a decision by Judge Azrack dated August 4, 2021, she referred to information he disclosed at the grand jury, including that Burke told him he was behind the harsh handling of Cuff's son's case. When I reached him by phone, Madigan declined to tell me whether he had been granted immunity, or to be interviewed for this book.

The information on Madigan's post-SCPD career was from LinkedIn. Bombace's post-SCPD career information was drawn from sources including LinkedIn and interviews with Bombace. The 2020 pay information for the law enforcement officers involved in the conspiracy who kept their jobs was from *Newsday*'s database of Suffolk County employee salaries. The SCPD and Suffolk County Probation Department did not respond to multiple emails seeking information on their employment and requesting interviews with them.

During interviews, Leto and Hickey downplayed how the Loeb beating would normally be handled. The pension information was from See-ThroughNY (seethroughny.net). The information on the IAB records was from my own correspondence with SCPD.

The account of McPartland and Spota's sentencing was from news accounts and an audio recording of the proceeding. Leto described his life during sentencing limbo in interviews. Hickey's letter seeking leniency from the judge was filed in court.

The account of then President Donald Trump's speech in front of the SCPD crowd was drawn from news reports and video footage.

EPILOGUE II. BOOGEYMAN

The account of Leanne's story as told in attorney John Ray's office was drawn from a video of the press conference. The graffiti on the truck was referenced in "New Clues in the Hunt for the Long Island Serial Killer," *48 Hours*, CBS, December 13, 2020.

The article touching on Burke as suspect was: Ellen Killoran, "Why Hasn't the Long Island Serial Killer Case Been Solved?" *Rolling Stone*, December 15, 2016. The aforementioned *48 Hours* episode discussed the suspicion concerning Burke. Loeb told his snuff film story in the aforementioned podcast, *Unraveled*.

The description of Heuermann's arrest is from video. The details of the serial killer investigation, including the dysfunction and infighting that plagued it, is drawn from interviews with more than twenty legal, law enforcement and political insiders familiar with the case, and much of it was previously reported in the following article I wrote with a colleague: Alexandra Heal and Gus Garcia-Roberts, "Gilgo Beach Killer Hunt Slowed by Infighting Between Prosecutors, Police," *Washington Post*, August 1, 2023.

The details of the Keith Bush case were drawn from the motion by the Suffolk County DA's office to vacate his conviction (*New York v. Keith Bush*, 182-75), as well as the following articles: Thomas Maier, "An Innocent Man?" *Newsday*, May 20, 2019, and Gus Garcia-Roberts, "He Spent 33 Years in Prison for a Murder Conviction Based on a Coerced Confession, Concealed Evidence and Biased Detective," *USA TODAY*, May 22, 2019.

The detailed description of the evidence against Heuermann is drawn from a bail application document filed in court by prosecutors.

GUS GARCIA-ROBERTS is an investigative reporter in the sports department at *The Washington Post.* He previously worked on investigative teams for *Newsday,* the *Los Angeles Times,* and *USA TODAY.* He was a member of the *Newsday* team that was a finalist for the 2014 Pulitzer Prize for Public Service for its series on hidden police misconduct on Long Island. He is the coauthor of *Blood Sport: Alex Rodriguez, Biogenesis, and the Quest to End Baseball's Steroid Era.* He lives in Los Angeles.

PublicAffairs is a publishing house founded in 1997. It is a tribute to the standards, values, and flair of three persons who have served as mentors to countless reporters, writers, editors, and book people of all kinds, including me.

I. F. STONE, proprietor of *I. F. Stone's Weekly*, combined a commitment to the First Amendment with entrepreneurial zeal and reporting skill and became one of the great independent journalists in American history. At the age of eighty, Izzy published *The Trial of Socrates*, which was a national bestseller. He wrote the book after he taught himself ancient Greek.

BENJAMIN C. BRADLEE was for nearly thirty years the charismatic editorial leader of *The Washington Post*. It was Ben who gave the *Post* the range and courage to pursue such historic issues as Watergate. He supported his reporters with a tenacity that made them fearless and it is no accident that so many became authors of influential, best-selling books.

ROBERT L. BERNSTEIN, the chief executive of Random House for more than a quarter century, guided one of the nation's premier publishing houses. Bob was personally responsible for many books of political dissent and argument that challenged tyranny around the globe. He is also the founder and longtime chair of Human Rights Watch, one of the most respected human rights organizations in the world.

. . .

For fifty years, the banner of Public Affairs Press was carried by its owner Morris B. Schnapper, who published Gandhi, Nasser, Toynbee, Truman, and about 1,500 other authors. In 1983, Schnapper was described by *The Washington Post* as "a redoubtable gadfly." His legacy will endure in the books to come.

Peter Osnos, *Founder*